AN ART OF OUR OWN

AN ART OF OUR OWN

The Spiritual in Twentieth-Century Art

ROGER LIPSEY

SHAMBHALA
Boston & Shaftesbury
1989

Shambhala Publications, Inc.
Horticultural Hall
300 Massachusetts Avenue
Boston, Massachusetts 02115

Shambhala Publications, Inc.
The Old School House
The Courtyard, Bell Street
Shaftesbury, Dorset SP7 8BP

9   8   7   6   5   4   3   2   1

First Paperback Edition

Printed in the United States of America

Distributed in the United States by Random House
and in Canada by Random House of Canada Ltd.
Distributed in the United Kingdom by Element Books Ltd.

The Library of Congress catalogues the hardcover edition of this book as follows:

Lipsey, Roger, 1942–   An art of our own.
   Bibliography: p.
   Includes index.
   1. Spirituality in art.   2. Art, Modern—20th century.   I. Title.
N8248.S77L56   1988   701'.08   88-18206
ISBN 0-87773-362-7
ISBN 0-87773-496-8 (pbk.)

For Susan
ἁρμονίη ἀφανής

CONTENTS

ILLUSTRATIONS

Diligent efforts were made in every case to obtain rights from public and private collections, artists, and artists' estates to illustrate the works in this book. In a few instances, the efforts were unsuccessful. The author and publisher are grateful for the use of those illustrations in this publication.

PREFACE AND ACKNOWLEDGMENTS

When this book was first conceived more than ten years ago, its theme was more contrary than it is today, although the groundwork for study of the spiritual in twentieth-century art had already been laid. Among art historians, Sixten Ringbom and others had begun to explore the work of artists for whom art and spirituality were linked concerns. The historian of religions, Mircea Eliade, had published essays on twentieth-century art which, brief as they were, brought new understanding and a breath of fresh air. My debts to Ringbom and Eliade are large: the one showed a method, the other dared to think freely. Diane Apostolos-Cappadona has done every reader a service by collecting Eliade's essays in *Symbolism, the Sacred, and the Arts* (1986).

Other gifted scholars have been at work. Robert Rosenblum's *Modern Painting and the Northern Romantic Tradition* (1975) shows a knowing sensitivity to religious and philosophical issues. Like Ringbom, he demonstrated that interest in the spiritual in art need not reduce scholarship to muddle. Jose Argüelles' *The Transformative Vision* (1975) was a thoughtful and ambitious reconsideration of the history of art. More recently, Suzi Gablik's inquiry, *Has Modernism Failed?* (1984) is a compelling work with a perspective that complements the present book.

The theme of the spiritual in art was brought to public attention by a major exhibition originating at the Los Angeles County Museum of Art in 1986–87, traveling later to Chicago and The Hague. It occasioned an important publication bearing the exhibition's name: *The Spiritual in Art: Abstract Painting 1890–1985* (Los Angeles, 1986). Edited principally by Maurice Tuchman, the publication includes essays by fourteen scholars. I have learned from them all, and particularly wish to acknowledge the work of John E. Bowlt, Charlotte Douglas, Linda Dalrymple Henderson, Donald B. Kuspit, Rose-Carol Washton Long, and Robert P. Welsh. The catalogue to which they contributed is a landmark. Clearly, the contrary theme of ten years ago has now enjoyed fifteen minutes of fame, to paraphrase Andy Warhol. Its actual fate remains undecided.

The scholars mentioned above surely share in their own ways what William Morris long ago called "hopes and fears for art." My fear today is that we are moving toward an art dominated by commerce, stripped of great ideas and aesthetic subtlety. My hope is for art and architecture with deep roots in the nature of things—a wise art in touch with Nature and the depths of human nature, gratefully aware of tradition yet vertiginously free to invent. For this, we have much to learn from twentieth-century artists for whom the spiritual in art was an open or hidden agenda of compelling importance.

Among other things, this book conveys the collective voice, previously scattered in published statements and writings, of several generations of artists. I trust that its value, if nothing more, is to make that collective voice audible and to show that the spiritual has concerned not only artists known for their occult interests but also long-admired artists little concerned with the byways of thought. The spiritual is not necessarily the occult, although the occult may participate fully in the spiritual.

Readers of my biography of Ananda K. Coomaraswamy and my edition of his later essays (1977) may wonder why I have strayed from my mentor's concern for traditional religious art and thought into twentieth-century art, which he by and large detested. I believe that the study of traditional culture can enrich our lives without darkly judging what we are. A sound future will surely build in part on modernity, in part on ancient values and knowledge. Modern conditions are our specific challenge, our Sinai, and I suspect that if we continue walking, we will find the mountain. Twentieth-century artists have not worked all these years and strived for some realization of the spiritual in art only to be told that the enterprise was doomed from the outset and leads nowhere. On the contrary, it can lead far—particularly when the clarifying insights of tradition are brought to bear with affection, even complicity.

I hope that Coomaraswamy's admirers will find in this book an extension of his insights into a difficult world, where they are needed. Equally I hope that people interested in twentieth-century art will find clear statements of ideas they may have long sensed beneath the surface. I confess to sympathy both for the austerities of traditional religious philosophy and for our own pluralistic, religiously uncertain culture.

I have not intended a work of exhaustive scholarship, but something more in the nature of an informed conversation. I have, however, used the tools of scholarship, and this book cannot evade evaluation on those grounds. Errors of judgment and fact are very much my own.

I wish to thank Samuel Bercholz, director of Shambhala Publications, for his initial encouragement and subsequent patience. Emily Hilburn Sell and Kendra Crossen of Shambhala have been friends to this project. Among artists, Isamu Noguchi responded generously with his time, and many of the artists whose work is discussed in chapter 21 shared their thoughts. Years before publication, Harry Holtzman was kind enough to pass on a manuscript copy of Mondrian's collected writings, now available in a handsome edition. Among scholars I wish to record my gratitude to Colin Eisler and Margaret Betz, both of whom read the manuscript at an early stage and encouraged its completion. Günter Kopcke, Sidney Geist, and William Shannon all helped in various ways. I doubt that I would have dared to explore Romanian sources on Brancusi without Professor Geist's initial push and Diana Isveanu's later assistance with the translations. Mr. and Mrs. Alexandre Istrati, Brancusi's heirs and the coauthors of an important new monograph on the artist, were helpful guides to Brancusi's sayings. Brian Urquhart, author of the finest biography of Dag Hammarskjöld, was kind enough to share some of his knowledge with me. I benefited as well from the guidance of Marc Latrique at the United Nations Archive.

The André Emmerich Gallery, Pace Gallery, Schoelkopf Gallery, and Mrs. John Lefebre kindly made press files, publications, and photographs available; their help was important.

Carolyn Lahr Maxwell of the Institute of Fine Arts mounted the unexpectedly demanding campaign to collect illustrations worldwide. By making my project her own, she taught me. Miin-ling Yu of New York University faithfully assisted on bibliographic problems. Discussions with Mrs. Carla Binder concerning Julius Bissier's German stand out as bright moments along the way.

Throughout the writing of this book, I was employed as a senior writer for Arthur Young & Company, the accounting, tax, and management consulting firm. This was my "university," and a demanding one. I am grateful to Arthur Young colleagues in New York and across the country for their friendship.

Finally, I wish to thank my wife, Susan, to whom this book is dedicated.

Roger Lipsey

The historian was thus reduced to his last resources. Clearly if he was bound to reduce all these forces to a common value, this common value could have no measure but that of their attraction on his own mind. He must treat them as they had been felt. . . .

—The Education of Henry Adams

1 INTRODUCTION

Some seventy-five years ago, the Russian artist Wassily Kandinsky published a small but influential book in Munich, where he had studied art and stayed on to become a leading member of its congenial arts community. His book was called *On the Spiritual in Art.*[1] It was his credo, full of his concern for a new art that could reflect the deepest longings and insights of men and women. More than a personal credo, it was a call to other artists. Like so many who feel that times are changing, Kandinsky (1866–1944) did more than his share to change them. The new art that he needed, and that he knew to be evolving in Paris, Munich, and elsewhere, would no longer be a relatively realistic art of portrait, landscape, and still life, of mythologic and religious themes, of genre images reflecting the poignancy of daily life, of nudes transforming desire into beauty. It would bear little obvious relation to the art of the past.

Kandinsky thought that this new art could be based on an absolutely fresh sensitivity to line and color in themselves, to form as such rather than as description, and to space as such rather than as a setting for events. Further, to these raw materials of image-making he believed it possible to bring a new wisdom born of the artist's awareness of his or her own depths and of the resonant universe. He intuited two universes in one—the visible universe of matter, space, and time, and an invisible universe of spiritual energies. He understood that an awareness capable of encompassing such dimension cannot be bought cheaply, and he suspected that Asiatic disciplines of meditation, of which he knew little at the time, might provide a methodology through which artists could widen and reinforce it. But he intended his book primarily to wish away the old in art and culture and to sketch lightly, with conviction, what the new could and should be. His book was imperfect, but more than strong enough to launch its theme into the century.

The subtitle of the present work, *The Spiritual in Twentieth-Century Art*, pays homage to Kandinsky. His book was an intellectual salvo.

He succeeded in stating the hope of many artists in his time clearly and passionately enough to be widely heard. Since then many years have passed, many artists have worked, and many different concepts of art have had their moments in the sun. The century is now nearly complete, and there is an odd feeling of exhaustion in the visual arts. While there is no lack of gifted artists, astute critics, and well-endowed art institutions, the culture of the visual arts is nonetheless sad, as if we continue to produce art and think about it in the absence of some crucial inspiration or sense of direction that would make the venture more worthwhile. The speed and flash of the art market hardly disguise the malaise.

We speak of Postmodernism now, as if we have drained Modernism, the predominant art movement of the twentieth century, of its possibilities and find ourselves moving into bleak terrain, comforted largely by moods of educated irony or cheerful laissez-faire. There was, however, a hidden side of Modernism, and this means of course a hidden side of modern artists. It may be that we have not only failed to "drain" this resource but have nearly overlooked its existence. Many of the universally respected artists whose works are altogether familiar and whom we feel we understand have in fact escaped understanding because we haven't yet penetrated the spiritual history of modern art. These were men and women who cared for "the things of the spirit." Their art is in part dedicated to that concern and expressive of it. They shared Kandinsky's preoccupation with the spiritual, thought and often wrote of it in their own terms, worked for it to enter their creations not as a passing presence but as a central reality. Religious and philosophical matters preoccupied not only verbally gifted artists who were at ease discussing such things, but also a number of important artists who either chose silence or were shy.

There is a mixed record for this hidden side of our art. It is in part a literary record of artists' writings, interviews, and table talk, in part the mute but impressive record of the works of art themselves. Some of us already know a little of this record—have heard a few of Brancusi's aphorisms, read a little in Mondrian's essays, gained a general sense that the Bauhaus was not just a school of design but also a community of seekers. Similarly, many of us have looked at Malevich canvases, or the more recent works of Mark Rothko and Morris Louis, and acknowledged their transcendental theme. But our knowledge hardly constitutes a critical mass; it is vague and, like all knowledge largely unused, tends to dissipate.

The note first cleanly struck by Kandinsky was struck again and again by twentieth-century artists—of course, not by everyone and almost always in highly individual ways. Some sounded it subtly and tentatively, others loudly and even bombastically. Others simply did what they had to do, knew what they were doing, and tried in occasional writings or interviews to clarify the relation of artistic form to spiritual meaning as they experienced it. There is no orthodox spirituality in this century, and the culture at large has been amazingly unreceptive to the spiritual aspect of the artists' thought and work. Nonetheless, twentieth-century art set out to be an art of spiritual content, and succeeded to some real degree. The century has been dominated by science and material progress, distorted by world wars and totalitarian regimes, and unsure of its metaphysics—so much so that most professional philosophers, let alone most literate people, have discarded the very word "metaphysics." Yet many of the artists understood their art to be an avenue of search, not just for "form" or originality but for deep meaning and penetrating vision.

Kandinsky sought an art endowed with what he called an "inner sound," and the work of his middle years culminated in poetic images of a universe sacred or almost sacred, alive with gorgeous color and stately motion. Brancusi sought to embody an elusive "essence" in works of stunning simplicity and formal sophistication. Mondrian intuited "the universal that towers above us" and wished to bring it into our world without denaturing it; he too sought to release the essential from the world of accidental appearances. Henri Matisse sought the image of a stable and luminous equilibrium beneath changing appearances. Morris Louis never committed to words what he sought, but the evidence is there in a glowing icon that combines many things into one—sacred mountain, rainbow covenant, veil—and yet remains a thing apart, a new vision.

In some of our classic artists, we will discover artist-metaphysicians. We can hope to do so without violating their art and intentions or making them into something other than what they were. On the contrary, we may see them in a truer light. However, the enterprise of this book is not to prolong or restore Modernism as such or to "set the record straight," as if those were truly compelling goals. It is in part a retrospective study, an interpretation of history, but its purpose is more to gather working materials for the future than to praise and analyze the work of artists already much praised and analyzed.

We have unfinished work. The artists studied in this book began but were unable to complete a voyage toward a new art, an art of our own that would be entirely contemporary and spiritually alive. "Much,

much later, the *pure* art," said Kandinsky,[2] speaking not just from modesty but from the conviction that the new art had only begun to find its way. The first step in the resumption of that voyage is to understand better the changing, often incomplete, but nonetheless touching spirituality of twentieth-century art from its origins in the intensely creative years before World War I to the present time. Because there was so thin a common universe of discourse among artists, critics, and the interested public on philosophical and religious matters, we will do best for the most part to approach each artist individually. We will need to look at their works carefully and to distill from their thought its essential concerns.

In the process, we have an opportunity to learn to see twentieth-century art with new eyes and minds, more sensitive to its spiritual and psychological content, better able to relate the visual language and ideas of one artist to another. We will also need to assemble our own conception of the spiritual in art. The history of twentieth-century art is too diverse, and this theme too well hidden in it, to admit of an easy critical excursion. No single artist encompassed the entire theme. In reaching for an understanding of the whole, we will need to fit existing parts together and often add something from our own stock—ideas, recognitions, a sense of pattern that can make the elements reasonably coherent.

Inevitably, we will pay more attention to what seem to be the more fruitful lines of thought and works of art; not just inevitably but joyfully, for the time has come to make distinctions. We will make errors, and neglect excellent artists of true spiritual temperament—particularly in the chapter dealing with recent art. No one has faultless judgment, and few can be aware of everything currently taking place in the arts. Further, we will hardly explore certain well-established artists and celebrated movements in this book, which has no ambition to be a comprehensive history. The epigraph from *The Education of Henry Adams* is not just a grace note; it defines a working method. What has not "attracted my mind" over the years and imposed itself will not be brought before the reader as if I could write of it either with love or with authority. I have assembled the materials of twentieth-century art in terms of the importance I feel them to have and their impact on me as a concerned individual. The purpose will have been served if author and reader alike leave this book with the certainty that twentieth-century art wished to be a spiritual art, and that it achieved enough in this respect to provide current and future generations with a fertile beginning.

Henry Adams' despair arose from the overwhelming diversity of forces at work in human affairs; the Virgin and the Dynamo somehow had to be encompassed in a unified vision. The uneasiness that helped bring this book about bears on the gap between twentieth-century art and authentic spirituality. What spirituality there is in our art has been poorly understood, or for the most part paid lip service; it hasn't mattered. Further, that spirituality when summed is only a beginning. We are not yet ready as a culture to build a house of worship or meditation hall—most of us don't know what or whom to worship, not really, and have only vague notions of what might go on in a meditation hall if we were to build one. Contemporary people engaged on a spiritual way or a personal quest for self-knowledge are often indifferent or unfriendly to twentieth-century art; preferring traditional religious art and architecture, they tend to regard modern art as spiritually blind. Conversely, contemporary artists and critics often have scant relation with the stream of spiritual and well-informed psychological teachings that existed not only in the past but also in this century. We need to bridge the gaps and deepen the shallows in our culture.

There are "two cultures" little connected to each other. C. P. Snow's classic essay of the 1950s described a gap between science and the humanities; the gap that I have in mind, more parochial but no less real, separates the culture of the visual arts from a second culture that hardly has a name. This second culture is not centered on psychology, although the thought of C. G. Jung and others is important to it. It is not centered on religion, although D. T. Suzuki, Mircea Eliade, and other teachers are important to it. To describe it primarily as a "new gnosis," with some observers, is to use an unfamiliar word and to imply that this second culture is biased toward intellect, which it is not. To describe it in terms of a new approach to the life of the body is to limit it, although re-understanding the human body is one of its tasks and achievements. To speak of an "alternative culture" or the "new age" emphasizes sociopolitical and pop-cultural aspects, but they are only parts of the whole, and the terms are too public in tone to reflect the discretion of the second culture at its best. In any case, those are recent terms, and the second culture has been evolving since the turn of the century. Whatever we call it, the name matters less than the recognition that it exists.

But this topic is best reserved for later pages, where it has imposed itself as a recurrent theme. Twentieth-century art embodied a stronger and wiser spirituality than we have fully acknowledged. At century's end, we ourselves have greater spiritual resources in our culture than we generally acknowledge. In this book, we will start with history. It is immensely interesting to explore the ideas and works of major twentieth-century artists whose careers are now complete. But in the end we will return to ourselves in this time and place, enriched by whatever the artists have been able to convey, better prepared to examine our own situation. If art matters at all, it will shed light on something more than itself.

A word might be appropriate about the title, *An Art of Our Own*. It is a direct quotation from Constantin Brancusi, who told an interviewer when he first came to the United States in 1926 that he felt it was time we had an art of our own. Brancusi added that he hoped the sculpture he had come to exhibit in New York would be recognized as of and for our time, an art of our own.[3] His phrase resonates far beyond its immediate context. It raises enriching questions, perhaps obvious and bare when stated, but nonetheless living questions: Who are we? What do we wish to be ours? Is there any distinction at all between what we think we are from day to day and what we are essentially? Is there some distinction between essence and accident in our lives, not just in books of philosophy? Do we have an art that speaks to essence and arises from it? Is the very idea of "we" presumptuous? Are we a collection of isolated individuals, or do enough of us have enough in common to be able to answer together on some matters? The phrase "an art of our own" raises the question of identity, as art should. An art of our own must be one that belongs to real selves, selves that have been sought and won, matured and looked after. Such an art would help us look after ourselves.

We will explore these questions and many others in later chapters. But we should think two questions through before we begin to listen to the artists and try to approach their work with new eyes: What is the spiritual, and what is the spiritual in art?

WHAT IS THE SPIRITUAL?

Spiritual is an old-fashioned word, recalling eras in which people were more sure of themselves and of the order of things divine and human. For many of us in the closing decades of the twentieth century, the order of things divine and human is not so clear. The meaning of *material* is obvious enough: it is our bodies and minds and everything around us, the universe at large, however many light-years it may extend and however great the physical forces at work in it. Most sectors of twentieth-century culture—the arts, the empirical and social sciences, technology, history—can carry on without any particular reference to the spiritual. Only in the spheres of religion and the history of religions is the term current, although it has no specific meaning in academic analysis. It is a word for sermons; parishioners know at once that it distinguishes between a religiously concerned attitude and egotistical materialism. It is, of course, a recurrent word in ancient religious texts, still very much read. We sometimes use it to describe a special person, one who knows or senses that "something else" is at work among and through us, and who seems closer than others to that "something else"—serving it, however informally, with more sincerity and wisdom than commonly encountered.

All of this duly noted, *spiritual* remains an old-fashioned word of vague meaning. Yet it is this word that Kandinsky seeded into twentieth-century art, and apart from any individual, it still speaks. It requires a positive response from us.

When is it that people begin to look beyond or within themselves for a strength to face life or a wisdom to understand it that surpasses their ordinary capacity? The beginning of the spiritual must be this "looking beyond" or looking more deeply within. For some it is an inheritance, received from parents or a religious community in a form alive enough to enter without much quarrel. They are raised *knowing of* this world and another, Heaven and Earth, "inner man" and "outer," time and eternity, sacred and mundane, holy day and day to day. It hardly matters what words or images, Greek or English, Buddhist or Biblical, convey this perception to the young person, provided that they create a sense of the visible and the invisible—both real, both wondrous—to be found in the world at large and in the inner world of the individual. *To know of* is not to know, but it can be a beginning.

There are tales of saints and sages, probably in all traditions and even in our century, who simply knew of the spiritual at an early age; they not only looked beyond spontaneously but could already see. Such exceptional people quickly begin their pilgrimage. Most of us lack that inspiration, and in modern society many do not inherit a living religious or spiritual tradition. On the contrary, to the extent that such traditions survive, they often seem dogmatic and ceremonial, hardly invitations to a larger life. Many people never look beyond, at least not long or frequently enough to be marked by what they see; it is just not in their natures to do so, and there are few cues for it in strictly modern culture.

Most of us, in fact, only begin to look beyond at times of extremity when we experience a great deal of ugliness or beauty, a great deal of fear or love, a great deal of loneliness or intimacy. At these moments it is more possible to feel in one's marrow that "this can't be all" or to be struck by an obscure sense of promise. Again, it is not the words but the consequence that matters: we begin to look beyond.

Beyond, there may be a void: whole sections of modern literature address the perception of a profoundly unwelcoming void. The generation of which I am a part explored the void at the earliest possible age, under the influence of Existentialist literature. We sat on park benches trying to validate Sartre's compelling description of metaphysical nausea; we rode buses, with gloomy eyes seeing death all around us or at least trying. We pondered Gide's "gratuitous act" and Camus's apathetic hero in *The Stranger*. It was clear to my generation that metaphysical events were mysteriously confined to the European continent and for the most part could be expected to occur on trains and in cafés. We were only sixteen or seventeen years old, and all of this activity was our best bet at the time to make contact with truth. Our "void" was inspired by literature, and we imitated—but it wasn't only literature and adolescent experimentation that pushed us on: we had suffered, and we were beginning to respond to that suffering.

It may be just a stroke of luck or timely intervention from a wiser person that brings one who has begun looking beyond to see not only the void but the possibility of plenitude—of life fulfilled in wider and deeper terms. Here biographies split off in many directions, but they have in common the moment when a message is delivered, and the messages are not all that different from each other. Even those who receive strong messages in their youths from family or traditional sources need to make them their own.

The essential message is that we live in ignorance and pain, but great and healing knowledge exists; that we sleep and could awaken; that we experience ourselves as isolated but could discover that we are participants in a large and grandly meaningful whole. The message suggests that suffering and death are included and eventually transcended within the greater whole which preserves us and—however impersonally—wishes us well.

The message is a revelation. It describes in vividly new terms both the individual and his or her "world," that is, the world beyond self that once seemed coldly alien. The interdependence and even secret identity of the inner and outer worlds are revealed at least in a rudimentary way. St. Francis speaks of Brother Sun and Sister Moon; the Buddha nature is within you and also within all creatures; the philosophers speak of man as a microcosm mirroring the macrocosm in all respects. Whatever the formulation in image or word, it carries the message that human beings, deeply mingled with the world, are addressed by all things and in turn can learn to address all things, provided that we grasp the language. Whatever its nature, the message conveys shaky but real confidence that our lives may not be just empty exercises soon concluded. It offers direction. Taking that direction can initiate a lifetime of work.

The spiritual makes itself known slowly in the course of that work. It needn't even be called "the spiritual," but words of some kind will be found to describe an intelligence, a vitality, a sense of deliverance from pettiness and arrival at dignity that always seem a gift. It includes a perception of grandeur in the world at large, which cannot help but strike one as sacred, quite beyond oneself and yet there to be witnessed and even shared in. How everything fits together—one's own small life with the cosmos, one's own brief illuminations with whatever enduring light there may be—may never be altogether resolved on the level of experience. Metaphysical and theological maps, profound psychologies and spiritual teachings may indicate the pattern of the whole quite convincingly, but what one really knows is what one has experienced. Experience may tell one only that one is somewhere on the map.

The spiritual will always remain largely unknown; this is a part of its greatness. Heraclitus, forerunner of Socrates, expressed this life-giving truth unforgettably:

> You could not discover the limits of soul, even if you traveled by
> every path in order to do so; such is the depth of its meaning.[4]

Traveling those paths with difficulty, the traveler, now a pilgrim, is changed. The spiritual is not an abstract knowledge of cosmos or human nature; it is a renewed discovery, a beginning again and again. The pilgrim gains new eyes, a new feeling for things, a new sense of life, and this newness within cannot help but brighten the world at large and reveal its exquisite order. Then the new way of being fades or abruptly vanishes, together with all that it naturally reveals. The pilgrim is left wondering. However grand all that was, it lasted only a short while and cost a great deal. Is there any reason to go on? Who but a fool would collect *moments* of vision and coherent being, when one obviously needs permanence?

These are doubts, only a small sampling of the doubts that come to mind. Some pilgrims stop; it is the sensible thing to do. Others only imagine they continue. Looking beyond and responding to a message, beginning a voyage of discovery—originally such natural and life-giving acts—have not led very far. They have led for the most part to new unrest and to a haunting, almost inaccessible vision. The unrest is worse than before because now the pilgrim knows that unrest is not all that exists; he or she has experienced something else, however intermittently. Pilgrims who continue accept the discomfort of having virtually two minds, two distinct ranges of experience. It is a part of pilgrimage, not a detour, to explore the relations between these two. The metaphysical maps indicate that duality is a long episode in the pilgrim's journey, but not its destination.

A pilgrim way of life includes undeniable moments of peace and beauty but also suffering, because most of us are marginally suited to the enterprise. Pilgrims often experience themselves as burdened, resistant creatures, poorly made for a life of spiritual travel, donkeys on a path meant for a more gifted sort of creature. That is an image, another form of doubt. In spite of everything, some pilgrims continue—artists among them.

What is the spiritual? It is an incursion from above or deep within to which the ordinary human being in each of us can only surrender. It is the *daimon* to which Socrates listened, to which he could not but listen when it spoke within him. In this sense the spiritual is a dramatic shift in experience and an undoing of what we take to be ourselves. No understanding of the spiritual can altogether exclude this dramatic dimension.

On the other hand, lives dedicated to spiritual search are not incessantly lived "on edge" or subject to internal devastation at a moment's notice. If the spiritual were only that, it would remain at the margin of our lives, like Krishna drawing the village girls into the forest at night by the charm of his fluting. We obviously cannot all join Krishna in the forest—at least, not often—although the legend is a reminder that He is waiting.

The spiritual can also be a reasonably stable presence in individual lives, an internal capacity that slowly grows in strength and understanding. It is the wiser thought that appears when the chatter dies down, the clearer vision achieved by looking again, the greater kindness reached by recognizing selfishness in time.

We cannot evade incursions and surrenders. As the Old Testament authors never tired of stating, we are a "hard-necked people" little moved by gentle reminders. On the other hand, the incursions leave cumulative traces—and from these a new understanding draws together and moves to the center of a life. There it is not just a passive block of memory, but a force that can be sensed almost physically in those who have it.

WHAT IS THE SPIRITUAL IN ART?

We have been speaking of the spiritual largely in terms of individual experience, but of course that focus has omitted a great deal. Over millennia, individuals have lived within and been nourished by great traditions rooted in the commanding insights of religious teachers and uncommonly penetrating philosophers. Some of these insights have been called divine revelations, others such as the Platonic and the original Taoism of Lao Tze have retained a human face although they move far beyond the human, all too human. Our emphasis on the individual makes sense in terms of the enterprise ahead, because twentieth-century artists have for the most part worked individually and without formal adherence to religious or spiritual traditions. But it is difficult to approach the spiritual in twentieth-century art without understanding the spiritual in traditional cultures where art served religion willingly, and religion allowed art to be itself—that is, to explore the visible no less than the invisible, to report the beauty and finesse that it discovered, and to be inventive.[5]

In such cultures—ancient Greek or Hindu, Buddhist or Muslim, medieval Christian or Plains Indian—complete sets of inherited teachings, myths, symbols, images, and patterns were the common responsibility of leaders and ordinary citizens, institutional priests and unaffiliated sages, artists and craftsmen. Society was organized by a certain body of knowledge, moral lives were conducted in light of it, and spiritual lives were undertaken in keeping with the accumulated counsel of generations of forerunners. This diverse yet consistent knowledge was preserved and experienced, enlarged and transmitted not only by spoken or written words but by forms and images also, ranging from grandiose architecture to temporary dwellings, from works of art on sacred themes to utilitarian objects of daily life. Works of art and architecture created an environment, silent yet eloquent, which reminded people of those things held to be self-evident: the shape of the lofty cathedral or ground-hugging kiva, the altar painting or sand painting, spoke as clearly as a word. Traditional religious cultures were not utopias; they had their share of social injustice, war, child mortality, and so on. But the religious understanding reflected in their art will richly address any modern person who takes the time to explore them.

The tasks of art in such cultures were multiple and surely of consuming interest to artists charged with them. A twelfth-century Christian sculptor in Western Europe, for example, would have apprenticed with mature artists for many years—learning to handle the classic materials and tools of the trade, perhaps carving routine brackets while his betters carved figured capitals, lintels, and cult statuary. He would watch, absorbing a repertory of sacred images, symbols, and decorative devices inherited from earlier Christian centuries and Classical antiquity, and by various routes from much more ancient times. He would also learn the politics of cooperation with masons, stained-glass workers, metalsmiths, and other artisans and artists who brought their skills to complex projects. He would perhaps witness tense parleys between the head of his shop and the religious or secular patrons guiding and financing the project. In time, he might rise to become the head of his own shop, and rise from there to become an innovator—not merely a competent transmitter of traditional forms and methods, but a critical contributor to the further development of his tradition. Slow as these traditions often were to move on, they did move on; even pharaonic Egypt, slowest among historical traditions to change artistic norms, went through periodic spells of self-criticism and evolutionary change.

The twelfth-century sculptor had no doubts about his role: it was to provide artistically vivid and symbolically correct embodiments of the sacred persons and narratives that defined his tradition; to give palpable, physical form to religious truths and ideals; and to mirror the moments of epiphany in the joint history of God and man. And because Nature reflects the glory of God, he was also free to praise Nature through the richness or simple beauty of his decorative carving.

Art accepted a special mission in virtually every preindustrial culture: to depict the sacred. The sacred is the realm of the larger truths surrounding and conditioning our lives or dwelling within; it is the realm of the hidden, and therefore of revelation. In the great theologically based cultures, art almost entirely overcame the hiddenness of the sacred. Art gave form, color, and material presence to the gods and saints, to the participants in sacred narratives, to the mythic mountains, forests, caves, and long since crumbled towns and cities to which the narratives refer. Art depicted other worlds, heavens and hells; other states of being, both more refined and more devilish than ours;

facts other than those with which men live from day to day. Art also learned to represent ideas of the orderly kind which we would call doctrines—a word whose Latin root refers to teaching. These teachings were among the great themes of traditional art.

Artists in traditional religious cultures were far from being only metaphysicians. They served the religious institutions of their time and at their best interpreted religious meanings with extraordinary sensitivity, but they were also acutely aware of the world around them. Art has rarely ignored daily life. Even in ancient Egypt, which developed an elaborate imagery of the gods and of man's traffic with the gods, there was a tender, observant art depicting the round of daily life: craftsmen at work, musicians performing, workmen shouldering burdens. Thanks to art, we know how to saddle a horse in the manner of fifteenth-century Siena, how to set table in the way that pleased seventeenth-century Dutch burghers, how to arm for medieval battles, how to crouch into a discus throw on ancient playing fields. Even in the ascetic culture of the strictest medieval monasteries, art insisted on its warm relation with the everyday, and so in the margins and decorative lettering of sacred texts we find monks chopping wood, ringing tower bells, stooping over scriptorium desks—none of the images quite necessary, all of them in keeping with the artists' regard for life around them. Hsieh Ho gave this thought definitive form some thirteen hundred years ago:

> The solitudes and silences of a thousand years may be seen as in a mirror by merely opening a scroll.[6]

The bond between sacred art and the commonplace survived in Western art into sophisticated eras that we regard as virtually modern. For example, a painting by the eighteenth-century artist Jean-Baptiste-Siméon Chardin depicts a young man at a window, blowing soap bubbles from a pipe (Fig. 1). A so-called genre scene, a subject from everyday life, it is lovely in itself and yet larger than a mere report. The scene directs the receptive viewer to a broader vision, in which he or she can experience the evanescence of life and happiness without bitterness, as simple fact.

Chardin's gentle masterpiece is akin to many Chinese and Japanese paintings that transfigure the commonplace. The flash of insight requires no temple, no dogma to sanctify it. A cock strutting across a scroll is oneself strutting, too; the viewer can feel such affinity with the creature, grand like ourselves and just as fragile.

1. Jean-Baptiste-Siméon Chardin (1699–1779). *Blowing Bubbles.* Oil on canvas. 24″ × 24⅞″. The Metropolitan Museum of Art.

The spiritual in art confronts us with what we have forgotten. Humorously, solemnly, gently, heroically, mockingly, resplendently, it confronts us. A Zen master with a frisk of hair and a vast belly is napping with two companions, his arm idly thrown over a napping tiger.[8] The image has infinite charm, contagious gaiety. The old monk has so thoroughly befriended his passionate energies, externalized as the tiger, that he and they are now boon companions, bonelessly relaxed together.

The examples are endless. A fragment of fresco from a twelfth-century Coptic church in the Sudanese desert depicts the Archangel Michael, the fierce warrior of heaven (Fig. 2). Generally clothed as a soldier with sword and armor, in this fragment he is given a pale oval face with deeply sad eyes, from which he looks out with great inner

2. *The Archangel Michael* (detail), 12th century. Fresco detached from the interior of the basilica at Faras, in the Sudan. 76″ × 53″. Warsaw, The National Museum.

distance. This is an objective face, not given to useless sentiment and yet filled with feeling. Details of color and pattern soften its severity— the plaid shawl around his shoulders, a touch of green accenting the eyes. This, too, is the spiritual in art: a commanding image that recalls the need for rigor in the conduct of life. The Archangel Michael is both a mythic figure and oneself—oneself as one might be, not literally but inwardly; not always, but when required.

Oneself as one might be. The reminder of what one has forgotten is a call to action. The spiritual in art offers a transient experience of intensity, of a larger world and larger self. One begins to care again, reawakened to old longings, to remorse, perhaps to new thoughts and feelings, almost always to a clarified sense of direction. This blend of hope and remorse is a sign that one has encountered the spiritual in art. Familiar or unfamiliar, such experiences are new at the moment, and they fade. Sometimes gradually, sometimes with a sudden sense of loss, the *artificial* impact of even the highest art is effaced by familiar thoughts and feelings. Refined impressions from works of art fall under the same law as other refined impressions that on occasion reassure pilgrims: they come and they go. However, their influence joins other influences in a life and becomes part of what the individual knows to be true. The spiritual in art makes its contribution to the pilgrim's halting progress. It is a resource for those who look beyond, understand that there is work to do, and undertake it.

EYES FOR ART

Eyes for art. The phrase came to mind while reading a letter by Thomas Merton, the Trappist monk and author, in a recent selection from his correspondence. Speculating on a topic all too obvious in its answer, Merton asked Ananda K. Coomaraswamy's widow:

> What would you say AKC would have thought of abstract expressionism in art? It has much to be said in its favor, but as a fashion it is a bit obnoxious. What did he think and say about people like Picasso, who is undoubtedly a great genius . . . but perhaps that is the trouble.[9]

Merton's simple comments reveal keen eyes for art and a monk's knowledge of tainting.

The phrase owes a debt to Henri Corbin, a most unusual student of

Islamic religious history, who once called attention to a Sufi text that contrasts "eyes of flesh" and "eyes of fire." [10] Eyes of flesh perceive the world and mankind as densely material; in such eyes life is a losing struggle for permanence, although sometimes full of beauty. Eyes of flesh acutely perceive details of time, place, person, action, and idea, but in relation to one another rather than to anything beyond them.

Eyes of fire perceive each thing as the outer sign of an inner fact, or the local sign of a distant power. For such eyes nothing is lonely matter, all things are caught up in a mysterious, ultimately divine whole that challenges understanding over a lifetime. Eyes of flesh focus on the thing itself, eyes of fire on facts but still more intently on their participation in a larger meaning by which they are raised.

Merton's brief reflections evoke the idea that *eyes for art* strike a balance between these sensibilities. They are at one and the same time eyes of flesh and eyes of fire. They are surely eyes of flesh because artists and those who love art are willing conspirators in the world of matter. Such people are entranced by things as they are and as they might become, in their frail beauty and unrepentant materiality. Moreover, they are fond of technique, cherish a craftsman's fascination with the right way of doing things. Technical concerns ranging from the correct way to render the curvature of a rose petal to the correct positioning of dynamite charges in an architectural excavation are not matters for apology among them. On the contrary, such things are in their life's blood.

But there is sometimes more. Developed eyes for art measure not only the distance between two points but, so to speak, their common distance from God. They see the form, and then its power as a symbol for some part of life or for the whole. A tower is not only an impressive pile of brick or stone, it is a vertical avenue between the lower and the higher. The question is how effectively and with what new insight it expresses its larger function. A sculpture is not just a technical accomplishment and a lovely or intriguing object; it is also a message conveyed by the sculptor to himself and all selves about the nature of things.

Encompassing these poles, eyes for art can never really rest. There can never be enough knowledge of matter, and never enough of spirit; never enough, then, of their relation in life as in art. One of the great and rather sad secrets of art is that ordinary reality goes largely unobserved. The artist who truly sees a flower, a dingy street, a face, or a hillside is already reaching beyond most of us. He or she is turned in the direction of epiphany. Moses standing within sight of the Burning

3. Georges Braque. *The Beach at Dieppe*, 1929. Oil on canvas. 9½″ × 13¾″. Moderna Museet, Stockholm. Photo: Statens Konstmuseer. Copyright ARS NY/ADAGP 1987.

Bush realized that he stood on sacred ground and removed his sandals. This is the realization of every artist who possesses in some degree both eyes of fire and eyes of flesh.

All of this was evident to Merton. In the modest passage that kindled these reflections, we can sense him reaching for a clear perception of the physical, paint-and-brush reality of art, and reaching no less actively for insight into its underlying seriousness, its place in the scheme of things.

This reaching is just as evident in a little-known canvas (Fig. 3) with which we might begin our exploration of twentieth-century art. Frequenting the fishing villages of Normandy over the years, Georges Braque (1882–1963) painted a series of beach scenes full of the poetry of place but also larger than place and moment. Under a moody Norman sky, overshadowed by cliffs, fishing boats are pulled up on the beach, their sails furled, their hulls sprawled on the sand. However much the boats may toss on the ocean at other times or the beach teem with men, this image is all silence, solitude, and stillness.

It becomes a contemplation. The artist leads us to sense our own stillness between activities, and beyond that an abiding stillness. The viewer may feel called by that stillness, as if fine thought or emotion could spring from there. With Braque's guidance, contemplation becomes a natural movement. Yet this remains a modest work; it is not a religious icon, self-assured, dogmatic. It allows itself to be understood as a vignette of ordinary life, without a trace of insistence on greater meaning. The viewer is free to follow the artist into a broader, more feeling vision or to remain with the image as a report on time and place. Braque's canvas recalls a dimension of experience that cannot help but get lost and always remains to be rediscovered. It is art that is a friend to man.

His friend and early comrade-at-arms, Pablo Picasso (1881–1973), understood the camouflaged presence of that dimension of experience in the art of our time. "Something sacred, that's it," Picasso once said.

We ought to be able to say that word, or something like it, but people would take it the wrong way, and give it a meaning it hasn't got. We ought to be able to say that such and such a painting is as it is, with its capacity for power, because it is "touched by God." But people would put a wrong interpretation on it. And yet it's the nearest we can get to the truth.[11]

2 ABSTRACTION: A RELIGIOUS ART— SOMETIMES

Figurative artists from Matisse and Braque to Henry Moore and some of our own contemporaries have contributed as much to the spiritual in art as artists known primarily for their work in abstract idioms. Abstraction has nonetheless been a dominant vehicle for spiritually concerned artists. For Kandinsky, Malevich, Brancusi, and many others, it proved to be an endlessly fertile study. For this reason, we would do well to collect our thoughts about this visual language and the kinds of meaning it conveys.

Abstract art remains new and at root little understood, although we can now look back over more than seventy years of its development. Most of us still approach it warily, knowing that it is "received" and therefore to be respected, but we are uncertain of its meaning and value. By and large, we don't expect abstract art to *mean* in the way, for example, that Renaissance art means. It is generally accepted or rejected on the basis of the beauty or fascination of its physical character. We welcome the sensitive feelings sometimes kindled by its handling of color, space, and form; we ponder the personal psychology of the artist somehow reflected in what we see. But this art is generally excused in advance from the responsibilities of making sense, of speaking a known language, of demonstrating an awareness of the human condition that can nourish our own awareness. In short, we don't expect abstract art to have intellectual content or to reflect the life of feeling except in a general, nonspecific way. Less is demanded of it than of music, that other abstract art, which reflects and even shapes emotions with stunning precision.

Yet abstract art has proved to be one of the enduring passions of the century. Born in the years just prior to World War I, sustained in the 1920s and 1930s at the Bauhaus and elsewhere, it became the dominant visual art after World War II. Since then it has withstood fluctuations in taste to remain a constant presence in galleries and museums around the world, at times overshadowed by other styles but never rendered obsolete. This degree of acceptance, if not understanding, was made possible by the formal vigor of the abstract tradition. However incomplete our grasp of the underlying content of abstraction, critics and the public have learned to appreciate its expressive play of forms, and an elaborate critical literature has evolved largely on the basis of this appreciation alone. It is generally acknowledged that abstract art has another aspect, an elusive spirituality or transcendental aspiration, but until recently there has been little interest in exploring it, and for good reason. The formal qualities of abstraction provide sufficient topics for observation and thought; artists, if they speak at all of underlying content, tend to do so in broad, evocative terms that hardly lend themselves to a solid *Kunstwissenschaft,* a criticism beyond criticism. Mondrian, a notable exception, spoke in such dense philosophical terms that he often defeated understanding rather than furthering it. The subjective individuality of abstraction seems to condemn in advance any attempt to achieve a general understanding. One feels threatened, as Coomaraswamy once wrote, by the possibility of needing as many theories as there are artists.

While we can and should assume that what the early twentieth-century artists had to say is best said in their work, their writings, at the very origin of the abstract tradition, can help us understand why this art evolved at all. The early evidence is overwhelmingly clear. Abstract art was born a religious and metaphysical art, and only later came to seem a bodily thing when its spiritual aspiration was ignored or misunderstood. It was first, and has secretly remained, a means of exploring several interwoven realities: the psyche with its movements of joy and suffering, clarity and confusion; Nature and its laws; and beyond these, their common origin in a greater reality. Mondrian calls this greater reality "the universal"; Klee calls it the *Urgrund* or ground of being. In Mondrian's notebooks of 1912–14, there is a terse entry: *"Stof minder, kracht meer,"*[1] less matter, more force. Provided that we understand the full burden of meaning carried by his words, this statement can be taken as the theme of all art that follows in the philosophical, speculative tradition of abstraction that he and others founded.

This view of abstraction, current among its founders and crucially important to them, never persuaded or much interested professional art critics and the general public. The spiritual revolution awaited by the more speculative artists never took shape. What took shape instead was new and deadlier forms of war, a massive dislocating world depression, and more war. It was not generally a world that needed, or could even see, the nascent spirituality of the new art. Described by Kandinsky as a prophetic art, abstraction remains to this day prophetic, an art whose time comes and then goes. Abstraction has survived and occasionally flourished over the years because, as previously suggested, it is often beautiful and interesting as design and as a psychological self-revelation of the artist. Its original aspiration to transcend personal psychology and explore a transpersonal world of meaning and energies—to make images that can be shared by us all from the stuff of such a world—was largely forgotten, even denied.

Professional critics and the concerned public are much better able now than in previous decades to acknowledge the full intention of abstract art.[2] Similarly, artists working today can face more squarely the question of spirituality raised by the founding artists. On this point, Kandinsky and Mondrian separately reached the same conclusion: while too much deliberation can destroy the spontaneous creativity of the artist, the master-artist is able both to do well and to think well. In 1913, responding to criticism of his recently published *On the Spiritual in Art*, Kandinsky wrote:

> Nothing was farther from my mind than an appeal to the intellect, to the brain. This task would still have been premature today and will lie before artists as the next, important, and unavoidable aim (= step) in the further evolution of art. Nothing can and will be dangerous any longer to the spirit once it is established and deeply rooted, not even therefore the much-to-be-feared brainwork in art.[3]

In the same years, Mondrian made this point—as always more abstractly—when he observed that the "path of learning" generally leads to the "corruption of art" in today's world, but that art and learning complement each other at a higher stage of evolution.[4]

If artists and concerned people prove better able today to do brainwork about abstract art and to understand its religious undercurrent, the reason for this change lies outside the field of art itself, in the general culture. Certain aspects of the spirituality from which the founding abstract artists drew—Hinduism, Buddhism, and Western occultism, which they encountered in various forms, notably in Theosophy—are no longer fringe elements in Western culture. An early harbinger of East–West contact, Theosophy has long since been surpassed as a medium of East–West exchange by living representatives of Asian traditions active in the West, and by a thorough doctrinal, textual, and historical scholarship that has bound Asia and the West together. Jungian thought and humanistic psychology have created and legitimized quite new perspectives relying hardly at all on Asian thought, although they point in much the same direction. The Western religions, in part revitalized by the challenge from the East and from humanistic psychology, have entered a period of questioning and renewal. Thomas Merton, for example, demonstrated in his writings an understanding of the spiritual content of abstract art and practiced abstract calligraphy himself.

These movements in our culture point toward a new future for abstract art, in which its two aspects, form and meaning, can advance together. No other art seems better able to catch and reflect the values animating the new cultural matrix. This strength of abstract art can be affirmed without denying the perennial role and power of figurative art. The figurative sculpture of Henry Moore, for example, incorporates many abstract elements (see chapter 16); its eloquence often derives from the tension between natural and abstract form. Were there a religion of our time, or a series of kindred religious philosophies old or new that required an art, abstract art would do.

The difficulty is to understand abstract art simply, to be able without too much fuss to grasp its meaning and import just as we grasp the meaning and import of more familiar phenomena. For this to be possible, we need a few helpful keys—not so many that we lose them, not so few that we fail to understand. The keys must be simple and generous, not strongly ideological or dogmatic. They will have to fit many different doors, providing access to the individuality of different artists rather than reducing them all to a single model.

The most useful key at our disposal is the idea of *analogy*. This alone can open abstract art to understanding. It will probably never be stated with greater clarity and depth than by A. K. Coomaraswamy, but Coomaraswamy's field of interest was traditional religious art, in which analogy is a dominant organizing principle; he took little interest in the possibility that analogy operates securely in the abstract tradition.[5] Analogy means that one thing can be like another, not in all respects but in sufficient number and in a sufficiently interesting way to establish a significant relation. Material analogies can be created from the stuff of art that are close enough to immaterial things—ideas, feelings, the things of the inner life—to shed light on them and open them to our awareness in a new way. Such visible analogies for invisible things can even be felt to proceed from the invisible source as true and inevitable picturings of the source (the Orthodox Christian theology of the icon is the classic development of this reasoning). When such images are examined without regard to their analogical purpose or in ignorance of it, they may seem to be simply designs—at best dynamic structures of form, color, and space with a life of their own. But serious abstract art—the art that claims Kandinsky, Mondrian, Klee, and others as parent and guide—is made up of analogies.

We need to recognize two kinds of analogy: allegory and symbol. Allegories are external to their sources; they are patterns analogous to the source-pattern, but they do not necessarily participate either in its more instinctive, feeling aspects or in what might be termed its higher intellectuality. They can be devised mentally—this "stands for" that— and fully appreciated mentally. Symbols, on the other hand, are more than allegories: thought alone cannot devise them. They appear or they are inherited. They participate in and even shape the instinctive and feeling life of human beings. They retain a quality of mystery, and they can convey metaphysical thought of tremendous scope in the form of a pattern or image. They lend themselves to acute intellectual inquiry, but since they encompass more of human life than intellect alone we need more than thoughtfulness to assimilate them fully and appreciate them at their worth.

We can now revise an earlier statement as follows: serious abstract art is made up of symbols. In its new form, this statement is likely to make artists and critics wary, for excellent reasons. To contemporary ears, the word *symbol* implies ideology, be it religious, psychiatric, political, or literary, and ideology in turn implies the servitude that artists escaped in the nineteenth century and have no wish to resume. Symbol seems associated with an unacceptable loss of the freedom to create spontaneously from personal insight and impulse.

There is a second difficult connotation in the word *symbol*. Ever since early Impressionism rediscovered the expressiveness of *paint* quite apart from its ability to create transparent windows on pictorial worlds, artists have nurtured a genuine reverence for the physical materials of art. They explain, through such concepts as "truth to materials," that the raw materials themselves are a reality worthy of exploration and capable of guiding them to stronger creations than they could achieve without this attitude of cooperation. There is an integrity in paint that is often lacking in men's minds, a closeness to the *materia prima*. When visiting an artist's studio, one refrains instinctively from touching the brushes, paints, and other materials; they are charged with a separate life, best known to the artist. In the name of this separate life, artists are inclined to fear the implications of the word "symbol," which seems to emphasize intellectual content and premeditation at the expense of physical effort, physical perception, and physical joy.

Nonetheless, serious abstract art is made up of symbols. Some artists, such as Mondrian, could bear to look the symbol in the face and call it by its name; others, no less true artists, never did so, and yet their work is richly symbolic. To ask that viewers look at the painted surface or sculpted form itself without poring through their minds for its meaning ("What you see is what you see," as Frank Stella once put it) is, from my point of view, a legitimate request for simplicity. But that simplicity allows the viewer to appreciate more directly the physical presence of an image and its implicit symbolic statement. The meaning exists in the image, thus the image must be seen and received.

The idea of analogy, balanced by appreciation of the eloquent physical presence of works of art, is the most useful key to understanding abstraction. But in order to make it as useful as possible we should consider the two "poles" related by the force of analogy: the inner life of the human being and the outward language of art, its peculiar vocabulary and grammar. The inner life reflected outwardly in art is as deep and diverse as the artist. For that reason, a complete guide to this element in the pattern of analogy is impossible; it would have to be a psychology, a biography, a spirituality, and more. Yet something should be said.

Many ancient and modern descriptions of man divide our being into three parts, or relatively distinct vitalities: in Christian philosophy, body, soul, and spirit; in Tibetan Buddhism, body, speech, and mind. A modern version especially germane to modern art is the Jungian formula: consciousness, subjective unconscious, and collective unconscious. Some structure of this kind is required to collect the diversity of inner life.

Abstract art is capable of reflecting the three levels of being, however they are described: a superficial level, a second and deeper level of personal hopes and fears, and the deepest level at which we often know not what we say, nor what we say through works of art. Manifestations from the deepest level often surprise the artist no less than the viewer; he or she knows that the beauty or insight that entered the work of art did so thanks to receptiveness rather than to a fully calculated program of action.

The first two levels roughly correspond to "style." If an artist is predominantly a sensualist, the style will be luscious and ripe; if, on the contrary, he or she is closely attuned to fine feelings and atmospheres, the style will be refined. An austere person will make austere work, a playful person playful work. Style—the way in which the artist presents forms and colors—will also respond to the deeper subjectivity of the artist. Hidden hopes and fears, the underlying emotional condition, be it glad or dismal, will speak through abstract forms. These two levels are often all that speak and all that are incontestably present; the third level can never be assumed. It is the level of intuition, perception, sheer inspired guesses, blessed certainties regarding essential things: how the world is put together, the laws around us and within us, the relationships that connect us to others and to the world and the pressures that tear us away. For the deeper spirits that practice abstract art, this is their field of predilection. Whether sensual or austere, playful or refined, their work is also an image of underlying realities—personal realities in the sense that they are matters of experience, but also transpersonal realities in the sense that they are felt to be greater than one's own life and to characterize some sizable portion of the world at large.

For this to be so does not require explicit or formal acknowledgment by the artist. As Setsuya Kotani once wrote of his studio practice, "In the end, immediate problems are of a plastic nature"—that is, they are workshop problems, not problems of verbal philosophy (see chapter 23). Images can have intelligence and understanding, and their meaning can be quite faithfully translated into words, but they need not start from philosophical or religious concepts and rarely do so in our time. Universal meaning finds its way into art with or without discursive intellectual effort, but it requires a certain receptivity from the artist who turns toward that level of meaning, that aspect of his or her inner life. Mondrian and others articulated philosophies that parallel their visual creations, but wisdom can speak through the work itself no less clearly and often more movingly. The third level of meaning, flowing from the truly inner part of our inner lives, is not reliably under conscious control. But the most moving abstract work resonates—in Kandinsky's terms, reveals an "inner sound"—in such a way that it exposes the viewer to an unexpectedly large world of meaning and intelligent feeling.

The remaining pole in the pattern of analogy is the *language* of abstract art, its repertory of forms, colors, and renderings of space. This language is not wholly separable from the meanings which it expresses. Form and content in abstract art are partly interdependent: we are not speaking of a horse and its rider, but of a horse-and-rider capable of action far surpassing the range of the separate elements composing it.

The reason for this interdependence lies in the suggestive power of form: as the artist works, the forms taking shape speak and suggest new gestures, new details. As Herb Jackson, a gifted contemporary American painter, has written: "It is often unclear where I stop and the painting begins. We are as one in the effort to make this new presence manifest."

A dictionary of the language of abstract art could be written, although it would have to be looseleaf to allow for new entries. Kandinsky in effect offered such a dictionary with his Bauhaus publication *Point and Line to Plane* (1926). Contrary to the general impression that the forms of abstract art constitute a universe of singularities, each artist's work radically unlike any other's, there is in fact a common reservoir of forms from which all derive their own preferred forms and develop new ones. This reservoir consists of forms that express *energy* and *structure* through the age-old means of art (point, line, plane, space, mass, texture, color, and so on), with liberal borrowings from nature, science, and thought of every order. The canvas, stone, or bronze in which the artist arranges these energies and structures corresponds, in its broadest reference, to two realities: human being and the universe, microcosm and macrocosm. The work of art is a "world"—full of events which are invariably in the image of the artist, and at times also in the image of the world at large.

The premise of abstract art is that its signs of energy and structure can truly describe our lives and the life of the world, which also consist of energies and structures. Abstract art is never anecdotal, but it is fully capable of mirroring life and the world in essence. It has no means and no inclination to depict anger through the angry face and threatening stance of a man, but it may flash a fiery invasive sign through a quieter pictorial zone to express the essence of anger. It cannot address the theme of meditation through the image of the seated Buddha, but it may present refined colors within a geometry or flow in order to suggest differently, but effectively, something of the same. It does not photographically depict the galaxies and nebulae of modern cosmology, but it readily expresses intuitions of world-order. These examples are too obvious; the genius of abstract art lies in its ability to evoke human being and the world in full complexity, or full simplicity. The abstract image is a riddle which viewers may gradually understand and so come in touch with things new or forgotten, or familiar but now seen freshly. A quiet look at the energies and structures in a serious work shows them to be decidedly *about* something: to be about ourselves and our world.

We now have in hand the four keys that make abstract art sensible: the idea of analogy or symbol, an acknowledgment of the primary force of the image itself (not to be tampered with or chatted away), a concept of the inner life in terms of multiple levels of being and expression, and a preliminary grasp of the language of abstract art. We also need to remember that not all abstract art is deep or great. It is no accident that, over the years, hundreds of *New Yorker* cartoons have poked fun at abstract art, abstract artists, and abstracted viewers who can't make head or tail of what they see. Like walking, abstract image-making can be accomplished by saints, fools, and sinners.

3   EARLY GUIDES

St. Bernard of Clairvaux, the twelfth-century preacher and mystic, was surprised when a visitor remarked on the beauty of the decor in the cell where he had long been meditating; he hadn't noticed. Yet the architecture of the many Cistercian monasteries that he founded remains to this day one of the great exercises in pure unornamented design, starkness worked into beauty. Bernard was one of the guides of his era, a man indifferent to art whose vision nonetheless inspired those who were far from indifferent to it.

To speak of guides in the modern world and in relation to twentieth-century art requires a shift in perspective. We will not meet many St. Bernards, teachers who influenced the arts simply by who they were and what they said. On the other hand, there have been guides, often described by other names, who offered some elements of a luminous, difficult vision and implicitly challenged artists to make images touched by its light. There have also been artists who, as they aged, acquired something of the prestige and force of a spiritual teacher. Just as often, young artists searching for insight have had recourse only to their own minds and hearts—and to the history of art, which became something of an archaeological dig explored by artists until they discovered eras that intimately addressed them.

The spiritual in twentieth-century art, announced with such force by Kandinsky, drew from many different sources. It owed its most immediate debts to an austere painter, a flamboyant seer, and a late nineteenth-century movement—Symbolism—which was as lively in theater and literature as in the visual arts. The painter was Paul Cézanne (1839–1906), and the seer Helena Petrovna Blavatsky (1831–1891), co-founder of The Theosophical Society. Both Cézanne and HPB, as she was called, need brief investigations on our part. Symbolism, on the other hand, entered so deeply into Kandinsky's thought that we can rely on him to convey its essential concerns in the following chapter on his early art and writings.

PAUL CÉZANNE: THE MASTER OF US ALL

It was Henri Matisse who called Cézanne "the master of us all."[1] Cézanne was a guiding parent to the generation of artists in France that came into its own at about the time of his death in 1906. He incarnated the image and virtue of the artist for the young Matisse, for Picasso, and many of their companions. Both Cézanne's art and his later correspondence make dramatically clear why this could be so. His life as an artist was one of uncompromising struggle to *see,* to penetrate to the essence of Nature. Late in life, he wrote to his son:

> I must tell you that as a painter I am becoming more clear-sighted before Nature, but that with me the realization of my sensations is always painful. I cannot attain the intensity that is unfolded before my senses. I have not the magnificent richness of coloring that animates Nature.[2]

The ascetic intensity communicated even by these few words resonates in all of his major works. *The Bather* (Fig. 4), for example, a familiar work from the years 1885–87, transforms a potentially carefree, sensual subject into a complex counterpoint: the figure strong and yet clumsy, the setting pleasant and yet ignored by the pensive bather, his stance a deliberate pose but also a fleeting moment as he walks forward. Paint itself participates in this counterpoint by driving toward illusion and yet resisting it: the visibility and patchiness of the brushwork do not allow us to believe in the figure and landscape as "real." Throughout the painting we sense the brooding presence of the artist as mind, eye, questioner. The art of painting has become a visible dialogue between the artist and his sensation of reality, rather than a finished report from which the artist absents himself. Cézanne taught the primacy of questioning and seeking over polished results. "I proceed very slowly," he wrote to a younger painter,

> Nature offering itself to me with great complexity, and the need for progress incessant. One has to see the model and sense very rightly; and beyond that to express oneself with distinctiveness and force.[3]

There was a metaphysic implicit in Cézanne, a peering from oneself—anxious, temporary, yet part of the communion of all things—toward the stability and grandeur of Nature. He discovered the experience of consciousness in the world as a question and as the inexhaustible basis for a quest. The man himself was a marvel of complexity—assertive and self-deprecating, never satisfied yet sometimes

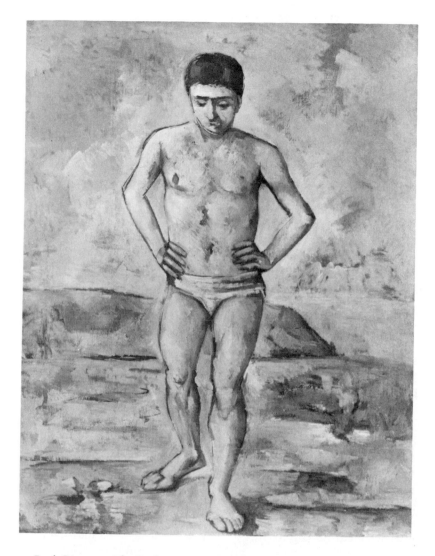

4. Paul Cézanne. *The Bather,* ca. 1885. Oil on canvas. 50″ × 38⅛″. Collection, The Museum of Modern Art, New York. Lillie P. Bliss Bequest.

anxious to please, grandly irascible in conversation yet lucid and cool-minded in his art, isolated in the Provençal town of Aix yet sought out in later years by cultural pilgrims who had already recognized his uniqueness.

His legacy passed down: light and color to Matisse and others, structure and complexity to Picasso and the Cubists, and from these first recipients to twentieth-century artists of every generation.

He was a systematic painter, not a systematic thinker. It was left to other guides in this formative period to construct entire world-views that inscribed the human being in a larger universe, set forth the task of being human, and inspired artists by the sheer scope of their vision.

THE FIRST ALTERNATIVE CULTURE: THEOSOPHY AND ANTHROPOSOPHY

Helena Petrovna Blavatsky

Chronologically first among these visionaries was a woman who even today retains a gamy reputation, a prolific and now little-read author, an adventuress with a deeply serious side to her nature: Madame Helena Petrovna Blavatsky.[4] Cofounder of the Theosophical Society in New York in 1875 and its guiding spirit, she glares from her best-known photograph with the intensity of a seer, the appetite of one who has long since abandoned fastidiousness, and unfeigned weariness. She was, among other accomplishments, the author of two enormous books: *Isis Unveiled: A Master-Key to the Mysteries of Ancient and Modern Science and Theology* (New York, 1877) and *The Secret Doctrine: The Synthesis of Science, Religion, and Philosophy* (London, 1888). Genuine "riverruns," to borrow a word from James Joyce, these thousands of pages of cosmology, philosophy, comparative religion, science, history, magic, occult studies, and spiritualism, punctuated with defiant growls against the stuffy nineteenth century, may not have been read cover to cover by artists, but their influence reached the arts community and contributed mightily to the transformation of painting.

For apart from the occult dramas which she infused into Theosophy in its early days—the telepathic Mahatmas who instructed her, the apparitions and *apports* in darkened salons—this titanic woman grasped the poverty of Western culture in her time no less acutely than Nietzsche and found remarkable resources for its renewal. These resources were, broadly speaking, the "wisdom of the East" and Western thought not just in its familiar highways but in its occult and heretical byways. "When, years ago, we first traveled over the East," she wrote,

> exploring the penetralia of its deserted sanctuaries, two saddening and ever-recurring questions oppressed our thoughts: *Where,* WHO, WHAT *is* GOD? *Who ever saw the* IMMORTAL SPIRIT *of man, so as to be able to assure himself of man's immortality?* It was while most anxious to solve these perplexing problems that we came into contact with certain men, endowed with such mysterious powers and such profound knowledge that we may truly designate them as the sages of the Orient.

Later in the passage, she summarized:

> Centuries of subjection have not quite congealed the life-blood of men into crystals around the nucleus of blind faith. . . . Our work, then, is a plea for the recognition of the Hermetic philosophy, the anciently-universal Wisdom-Religion, as the only possible key to the Absolute in science and theology.[5]

This intellectual program of Theosophy was not altogether unfamiliar. Emerson, Thoreau, and their circle of Transcendentalists in mid nineteenth-century America explored the newly translated sacred books of India and China with great sensitivity and recreated their wisdom in a well-bred, gentle version that remains an unfaded strength of American literature. HPB wasn't gentle and, although originally well bred, had successfully resisted. Drawing together everything she had ever heard or read in this area, she offered it to the world with little art but overwhelming conviction. And to the intellectual program she added something more, rooted in her since childhood: a pragmatic will to experience the reality of spirit directly, in action. Her pragmatism took two divergent forms: a willingness to investigate the practical meditational disciplines of the East, and an urge "to experiment practically in the occult powers of Nature," as she wrote—that is, to conduct seances and to seek direct communication from spirits on the other side.

As Theosophy moved into the twentieth century, aided by gifted newcomers such as Annie Besant, sifted for wheat and chaff, spreading vigorously from country to country, it became for a time the dominant alternative culture. It was the "school" toward which artists and seekers could look for a radically *other* description of the world and man. Its pragmatic impulse to open to spiritual reality and to *prove* spirit bodily underwent refinement and elaboration.

Wassily Kandinsky was one of the artists to whom Theosophy brought new hope. That hope is still audible in *On the Spiritual in Art,* first published in Munich in 1912 and soon after in Russia and England. "The number of people who set no store by the methods of materialistic science," he wrote,

> in matters concerning the "nonmaterial," or matter that is not perceptible to our senses, is at last increasing. And just as art seeks help from the primitives, these people turn for help to half-forgotten times, with their half-forgotten methods. . . . Mrs. H. P. Blavatsky was perhaps the first person who, after years spent in India, established a firm link between these "savages" and our own civilization. This was the starting point of one of the greatest spiritual movements, which today unites a large number of people. . . . This [Theosophical Society] consists of brotherhoods of those who attempt to approach more closely the problems of the spirit by the path of inner consciousness. Their methods . . . are the complete opposite of those of the positivists. . . . Even if some observers are skeptical of the theosophists' tendency to theorize and their somewhat premature delight in putting an answer in place of the great eternal question mark, nonetheless the great, yea spiritual, movement remains. It is a powerful agent in the spiritual climate, striking, even in this form, a note of salvation that reaches the desperate hearts of many who are enveloped in darkness. . . .[6]

However mixed the stew of ideas served up by Theosophy, it was *food* in a time of famine. Many promising men and women across Europe and America, who as they matured into prominence would speak little of it, were to be found in these years in the Lodges of the Theosophical Society, hearing for the first time about "the path of inner consciousness" and the wisdom of the East.

Unexpectedly, almost by the way, Theosophy generated a visual language that entered into the mainstream of twentieth-century art. The history of this transfer has been richly studied and narrated by Sixten Ringbom and later scholars.[7] Publications were the key vehicles through which Kandinsky, a Russian settled in Munich and its region just after the turn of the century, would become aware of the speculations and experiments of the second-generation English Theosophists C. W. Leadbeater and Annie Besant. The books in question are *Man*

Visible and Invisible and *Thought-Forms,* both translated from original English editions and published in Leipzig in 1908.[8]

Through the exercise of psychic clairvoyance, which he acknowledged to be disreputable in the West, Leadbeater perceived—and in effect "dictated" to a team of artists—the appearance of the human aura in various conditions. To this, Leadbeater in collaboration with Besant added a parallel exploration of the "etheric" forms of a great variety of emotions, ranging from the gambler's avidity to anger, compassion, joy, and so on. Shifting their focus from the physical world to the next world up, where they perceived aura and emotions to have form and color, they created what can only now seem to our eyes to be a new abstract visual language. The two books report their research through color plates and texts, much as any art book would.

Intense Anger, for example, is represented in the oval aura by stormy cloud-forms against which tense brown spirals and orange-red lightning-forms swirl and crackle. Nearly invisible behind this turmoil is the outline of the angered man whose aura this is. The aura of a victim of sudden fright, on the contrary, resembles an unaccountably cheerful Easter egg, with zigzag patterns and bands of varied color. The aura of the man of developed mental capacity is a soft field of color, the region of the head bathed in solar light. All of these color phenomena, far from being regarded as random occurrences, are ranged in a color chart at the beginning of *Man Visible and Invisible,* where they seed the idea that knowledge of the emotional content of color could be attained and conveyed into art—an idea to which Kandinsky would respond.

The imagery in *Thought-Forms* is no less fascinating, and would prove to be just as fruitful for twentieth-century art when Kandinsky filtered its lessons through his critical mind. *Thought-Forms* disregards the oval aura, and depicts each thought-form with the unique shape and other characteristics uncovered by clairvoyance. *Vague Pure Affection,* for example, is a rose-colored blob with fuzzy edges, suspended in mid-air, while *Vague Selfish Affection* shows the blob with a dark stained core. *Definite Affection* is a splendid form, blobby at left but stretched tautly toward the object of affection, unseen at right. *At a Shipwreck* (Fig. 5) is an entire scenario of thought-forms psychically photographed by the authors, which captures the varied emotions of participants—fearful, prayerful, intent on rescue—in images that may strike us now as funny, but also as touching and imaginative.

The impact of Theosophy on art was selective but enduring. Its multilevel universe, its promise that human consciousness can evolve,

5. Annie Besant and Charles W. Leadbeater. *At a Shipwreck,* reproduced from *Thought-Forms,* London, 1901, fig. 30. Reproduced by permission of The Theosophical Publishing House, Madras.

its assurance that human beings belong to an unseen world of grace and power no less than to the daily grind, its rudimentary abstract imagery and color symbolism—all of these would enter into the work of a handful of pioneering modern artists in forms now familiar to many of us. The beautiful early work of František Kupka (see chapter 7) remains little known to all but scholars and critics; but who among us hasn't seen and enjoyed the works of Piet Mondrian, an adherent of Theosophy throughout his life? Kandinsky, long a "painter's painter" and an acquired taste, come into his own in recent years through comprehensive exhibitions and studies. Never a proper Theosophist and diverse in his interests, he was a lifetime seeker of truth who seems to have derived his basic understanding of what "truth" means from the scope and audacity of the Theosophical world-view. In his marvelous study, *The Sounding Cosmos,* Sixten Ringbom has demonstrated the many ways in which Kandinsky's language of forms is indebted to Theosophical thought-forms.

Without Cézanne and Theosophy, no modern art. This affirmation, which falls short like all generalizations on complex matters, serves to underscore the importance of a person and ideas, seemingly larger than life, that shook up the world and gave it its work. Painstakingly gathered over a lifetime, Cézanne's knowledge of art had the power and compactness to motivate an entire generation of artists who were determined to be the originals of a new artistic culture. Similarly, the knowledge of the Theosophists, culled from books and temples and audacious dreaming, was powerful enough to point artists toward a new inwardness and the possibility of translating that inwardness into visible form. Beyond that, it taught a few to take the cosmos into account—to depict the world at large as a majestic play of energies and forms visible to "eyes of fire." Imagery generated by scientific means, whether of wheeling galaxies or twirling subatomic particles, can never record how we feel about these things nor what they prompt us to think. An informed poetry of the cosmos is needed no less than an informed science, and Theosophy gave some the courage to seek it.

Rudolf Steiner

Founder in 1913 of a movement known as Anthroposophy, Rudolf Steiner (1861–1925) will be familiar to some today as the originator of the Waldorf schools, which still flourish in a number of major cities and have gained widespread acceptance as educational institutions. Students of religious philosophy and esoteric thought may have read his many books on such topics as *Christianity as Mystical Fact and the Mysteries of Antiquity* (1902) and *Knowledge of the Higher Worlds and its Attainment* (serialized in 1904). He will be known to others, oddly enough, as the inspiration for a series of remedies and cosmetics derived from herbs and minerals, much in evidence in American health stores today. Organic farmers may recall that he and his circle developed the principles of composting with the use of bacterial additives. Historians of art acknowledge his contribution to German Expressionist architecture; his second institutional center, the Goetheanum completed in 1928–29, was a powerfully innovative creation. His followers and admirers today around the world continue to build on the wealth that he originated,[9] perhaps most significantly in recent years in the Camp Hill communities for the mentally retarded and developmentally handicapped. It is the very nature of alternative cultures, Steinerian and other, to drive toward the comprehensiveness found in standard culture—as if everything *can* be reconsidered from the new perspective, and *must* be reconsidered.

Difficult to recognize in this recitation of unbelievably diverse achievements is that it was all new in the early 1900s, much of it still remaining to be accomplished, none of it fixed. Rudolf Steiner, like the

Sp + human nature ✓

Theosophists with whom he was associated until 1913, incarnated the new spirit of research in the realms of spirituality, cosmology, and the redefinition of human nature—research from which artists could draw nourishment even if they hesitated to become "believers." In photographs from his mature years, Steiner seems somewhat wrought, the eyes invariably dark and intense, the face Germanically handsome, the mouth a little tense, as if reflecting the challenges he faced and their human cost. Many who met him in his prime were deeply impressed:

> I had indeed expected a man who might have the same goal as myself. However, I was rather indifferent when Rudolf Steiner came to meet me. Then—as he stood in the doorway and looked at me with eyes which revealed an understanding of infinite heights and depths of development, expressing and instilling kindness and boundless confidence—he made a tremendous impression upon me. . . . I was certain that an initiate stood before me. For a long while I had lived in spirit with initiates of the past. . . . Here at last, one stood before me. . . .[10]

The speaker is Edouard Schuré, author of *The Great Initiates* (Paris, 1889), a "secret history of religions," as the subtitle reads, which Piet Mondrian would recall many years later when he made a brief and strikingly modest assessment of his achievements (see chapter 6).

Based in Berlin and lecturing far and wide, Steiner found in the artist community of Munich before World War I a particularly attentive audience. Kandinsky was there, and his émigré friend Alexei von Jawlensky (1864–1941) among others; his publications in translation reached Mondrian. Hilla Rebay (1890–1967) as a young art student was captivated by Steiner and Theosophy. In later years, when she created the Museum of Non-Objective Painting in New York, forerunner of the Guggenheim Museum, she remained ardently mystical, incomparably more so than Kandinsky, of whose work she built the first great collection.[11] Unexpectedly, then, one of the leading art institutions of our time owes its debt to Steiner.

Until 1912 or 1913, Steiner's teaching was perceived as part of the Theosophical movement, from which he withdrew at that time. Like his Theosophical allies of the first decade, Steiner spoke and wrote of the evolution of consciousness, the higher levels of understanding to which seekers could attain, and the secret history of mankind—which was no secular history of spent creatures but a spiritual adventure, a transmigration of souls.

Artists received from Steiner powerful assurance of the reality of a larger world reaching past Munich to the cosmos, and a confirmation of their own imaginative powers. They felt invited to the initiation, empowered to dream their dreams, to imagine a new art and make it real. It was again Kandinsky who absorbed this influence most thoroughly and poured it, transformed, into his art and writings. Missionary recognizes missionary. Never formally an Anthroposophist and alert to many other cultural currents, Kandinsky nonetheless drew from Steiner's work intellectually and imaginatively—finding in it, for example, the theme of Apocalypse which preoccupied him for years, as well as support for his faith in the coming "epoch of the great spiritual." [12] Kandinsky knew how to take such ideas, gathered in the lecture halls of free-thinking Munich, and cast them into the mainstream of twentieth-century art.

4 WASSILY KANDINSKY IN THE YEARS OF ON THE SPIRITUAL IN ART

More deliberately than any artist of our time, Kandinsky explored the spiritual in art through his work as a painter and through writings—articulate, generous, impassioned—which circulated the idea of the spiritual more widely than his paintings ever did. It was his central idea, and he regarded it as the central idea of the art emerging all around him in 1912 when his small masterpiece, *On the Spiritual in Art,* was first published. In his eyes the spiritual was also the emerging task of the twentieth century, which he thought destined to correct the materialism of nineteenth-century culture. His prewar work as a painter and printmaker may not fully demonstrate for all viewers the vision captured in his writings, but he was prompt to recognize that art had only begun to find its way along a new path. His early writings need to be sifted for ideas that have stood the test of time and even gained in substance. But Kandinsky does not disappoint at the conclusion of this process. Some of his art is very beautiful, and much of his thinking.[1]

Born in Moscow in 1866 in comfortable circumstances, schooled in Odessa and at the University of Moscow, Kandinsky abandoned a promising career in law at age thirty to study painting in Munich, to which he moved in 1896. In a graceful autobiographical essay, *Reminiscences,* he evoked a childhood and adolescence filled with precursor experiences that marked him as a born artist.

> When I was thirteen or fourteen I bought a paintbox with oil paints from money slowly saved up. The feeling I had at the time—or better: the experience of the color coming out of the tube—is with me to this day. A pressure of the fingers and jubilant, joyous, thoughtful, dreamy, self-absorbed, with deep seriousness, with bub-

bling roguishness, with the sigh of liberation, with the profound resonance of sorrow, with defiant power and resistance, with yielding softness and devotion, with stubborn self-control, with sensitive unstableness of balance came one after another these unique beings we call colors. . . .[2]

It is a splendid passage—and notification to us here in the cynical residue of the century that we are attending to a Romantic from its flower-fresh debut.

Reminiscences chronicles Kandinsky's groping evolution from a richly decorative pictorial world, in which knights and their ladies were at home, to a fully abstract visual language such as the world had never seen. Arguably the father of abstraction, which was to become a dominant visual language of our time, he was an observer and born teacher; hence the extraordinary record he kept and the ease with which he assumed leadership in the world of art. In his journey from depicting known objects to the discovery of pure abstraction, perhaps most important for him was the realization that painting need not attempt to imitate the grandeur of Nature. It can conjure up a world of its own, prompted only by the artist's sense of "inner necessity." In a striking passage in *Reminiscences,* he related this discovery to his conviction that humanity had reached the threshold of a new age.

> For many . . . years . . . , I was like a monkey in a net: the organic laws of construction tangled me in my desires, and only with great pain, effort, and struggle did I break through these "walls around art." Thus did I finally enter the realm of art, which like that of nature, science, political forms, etc., is a realm unto itself, is governed by its own laws proper to it alone, and which together with the other realms ultimately forms the great realm which we can only dimly divine.
>
> Today is the great day of one of the revelations of this world. The interrelationships of these individual realms were illumined as by a flash of lightning; they burst unexpected, frightening, and joyous out of the darkness. Never were they so strongly tied together and never so sharply divided. This lightning is the child of the darkening of the spiritual heaven which hung over us, black, suffocating, and dead. Here begins the epoch of the spiritual, the revelation of the spirit. Father—Son—Holy Spirit.[3]

How did Kandinsky understand the spiritual in art, in these years before World War I when he made his greatest contributions as a thinker? The answer to this question lies for the most part in the pages of *On the Spiritual in Art*. He shows there that he had no doubt about the crucial role of the guide ("a man like the rest of us in every way, but who conceals within himself the secret, inborn power of 'vision'").[4] He had personally responded to the guiding influence of Theosophy and Steiner and became in turn a guiding influence in the world of art. He shucked off the paralyzing notion that he himself might be a "great initiate" by reasoning that some artists stand in a special relation to inspiring guides, better able to hear them, more quick to respond. The voice of Moses, he wrote, inaudible to the crowd dancing around the Golden Calf, "is heard first by the artist. At first unconsciously, without knowing it, he follows the call."[5]

Apart from the inspiration of a Moses, a teacher, Kandinsky found value in contemplative watchfulness, guided from within by what he insistently called "inner necessity." This watchfulness, not a physical listening but similarly receptive, led in his experience to awareness of the "inner sound" of each thing, be it a color on the palette, a composition on canvas, or an object in the world. "Inner necessity" within the human being and the "inner sound" of all things are the complementary realities that showed him the way to abstract art.

> . . . It must become possible to hear the whole world as it is without representational interpretation. . . . Abstract forms (lines, planes, dots, etc.) are not important in themselves, but only their inner sound, their life. . . .
>
> *The world sounds. It is a cosmos of spiritually active beings. Even dead matter is living spirit.*[6]

The concluding sentence, more than any passage in his writings, is his credo—Romantic, to be sure, but clean in its affirmation and never betrayed in his art.

The ideas of inner necessity and the inner sound, expressed by Kandinsky in what may seem old-fashioned terms, deserve a restorer's attention. They are in fact powerful ideas, more ancient by far than the early twentieth century and important to creative people in any era. The idea of inner necessity was cast into Western tradition by Socrates, who spoke of the guiding *daimon* within that arrested him at the edge of a misstep and plunged him into thought while others moved on. "I am subject to a divine or supernatural experience . . . a sort of voice which comes to me."[7] He could only obey. This was internal necessity at work. "Internal necessity," wrote Kandinsky, "which might be called honesty"[8]—of the most demanding kind, obliging the artist to search, to wait, to pay close attention.

> [The artist's] eyes should be always directed to his own inner life, and his ears turned to the voice of internal necessity. Then he will seize upon all permitted means and just as easily upon all forbidden means. This is the only way of giving expression to mystical necessity.[9]

He speaks here of a discipline, and speaks with the freshness of rediscovery. Kandinsky rediscovered art as a way austere in method yet potentially ecstatic and liberating in its results. In his experience, attention to the inner life promises to free the artist from superficial self-centeredness:

> . . . The artist works not to earn praise and admiration, or to avoid blame and hatred, but rather obeys that categorically imperative voice, which is the voice of the Lord, before whom he must humble himself and whose servant he is.[10]

The concept of the inner sound of all things is found among the earliest recorded instructions to artists in Chinese tradition. The first of the Six Canons of Hsieh Ho reads "Spirit Resonance, which means vitality," in the Bush-Shih translation of *ch'i-yün-sheng-tung*.[11] Gnomic words translated in various ways over the years, they clearly call on artists to attend to *ch'i-yün*, "spirit resonance," and it isn't stretching matters to recognize in this phrase Kandinsky's "inner sound." The eye defines, searching and poking among things, while the ear tends toward greater breadth and more constant openness. Hearing is less "material," telling us not how things appear but what vibration they emit. The ear reports on the invisible. This difference between eye and ear confers metaphorical power on hearing. To perceive the "inner sound" is to make use of eyes as if they were ears. Kandinsky's rather mystical expression in fact summons artists to a practical discipline of perception which does not ignore details but cannot rest until it apprehends the fine intrinsic signature of each phenomenon.

On the Spiritual in Art remains the largest fragment of the still incomplete whole of twentieth-century thought on the theme. Establishing Kandinsky as a central figure in the world of the avant-garde, it attempted to gather up many aspects of his own experience and that of artists around him. Liberal in praise of others, it speaks sincerely to the general condition without boosting its author's merit before a general public that still hardly knew or valued his art. Its essential achievement was to identify the new art as a legitimate language of the spirit and to lay groundwork for a way of thinking, particularly about abstract art, that made sense.

The key element in Kandinsky's reading of the historical moment was his conviction that a spiritual awakening had begun and would make its way in spite of dramatic clashes within individuals and the culture at large. Shared with other artists of his generation, Piet Mondrian and Franz Marc among them, his intuition of a general change in the quality of life and persons would be betrayed by later events many times over, but its force of sincerity at the time cannot be overestimated. The damnable nineteenth century was giving way. "Only just now awakening after years of materialism," wrote Kandinsky,

> our soul is infected with the despair born of unbelief, of lack of purpose and aim. The nightmare of materialism, which turned life into an evil, senseless game, is not yet passed; it still darkens the awakening soul. Only a feeble light glimmers, a tiny point in the immense circle of darkness. This light is but a presentiment; and the mind, seeing it, trembles in doubt over whether the light is a dream and the surrounding darkness indeed reality. . . . Our soul rings cracked when we sound it, like a precious vase, dug out of the earth, which has a flaw. . . . The soul is emerging, refined by struggle and suffering. Cruder emotions like fear, joy, and grief, which belonged to this time of trial, will no longer attract the artist. He will attempt to arouse more refined emotions, as yet unnamed. Just as he will live a complicated and subtle life, so his work will give to those observers capable of feeling them emotions subtle beyond words.[12]

No doubt, many readers will be put off by the excesses of this passage—its tendency to confuse autobiography with history, hope with necessity. On the other hand, passion of this kind is essential in human affairs; it is the passion of a good man dreaming. Creative people often call out the names of things loudly, like Adam, to confirm their existence. Kandinsky is doing magic in this passage, not scholarship, incantation rather than cogitation, and he keeps his dignity as he does so. His concluding reference to "refined emotions, as yet unnamed . . . subtle beyond words" within lives subtle and complicated, is quintessential Kandinsky; he could be a prophet of the inner life because he had an inner life, pressing on him.

He had a scholar's temperament as well. In *On the Spiritual in Art* and other publications, he regularly took note of other artists' work, provided pocket analyses, and allied the best in them to his presentiment of emerging spiritual vision. Of Cézanne, for example, whom he described as "a great seeker after a new sense of form," Kandinsky wrote that "he was endowed with the gift of divining the internal life in everything." Wary of Matisse's charm, Kandinsky nonetheless perceived enormous value in his work:

> He paints "pictures," and in these "pictures" endeavors to render the divine. To attain this end he requires nothing but the subject to be painted . . . and means that belong to painting alone. . . .[13]

In this brief appraisal, Kandinsky implies the aversion to organized religion and conventional sacred imagery true of most twentieth-century artists who cared for the spiritual at all. Some would try "to attain this end"; few would rely on tradition. Artists were asking the materials of art itself, approached with few certainties apart from "inner necessity" and the answering "inner sound," to reveal what religion no longer revealed.

It is worth remembering that many of the opinions Kandinsky offered in his book were extraordinarily prescient. The year was 1912, much of the book was written in 1910, and yet he already knew much:

> Matisse—color. Picasso—form. Two great signposts pointing toward a great end.[14]

He labored patiently in *On the Spiritual in Art*—sometimes wisely, sometimes with what now seems a wobbly, subjective method—to develop a new art theory that would allow reasoning about abstract and near-abstract form. His ideas about composition were prescient: in one swoop he recognized how to think about forms in art that modify or depart altogether from forms in Nature.

> The flexibility of each form, its internal, organic variation, its direction (motion) in the picture, the relative weight of concrete or of abstract forms and their combination; further, the discord or concord of the various elements of a pictorial structure, the handling of groups, the combination of the hidden and the stripped bare, the use of rhythmical or unrhythmical, of geometrical or non-geometrical forms, their contiguity or separation—all these things are the elements of structure in drawing.[15]

Thinking of this kind moved on to the Bauhaus and later schools and evolved into a reasonably standard approach to compositional analysis not only in the fine arts but also in commercial design.

Color, about which Kandinsky cared so much, was more resistant to hard-headed analysis. Not that he didn't try. He was conversant with classical nineteenth-century color theory as well as fringe experiments ranging from medical chromotherapy to the Theosophists' clairvoyant studies. The challenge was to account for his own extreme sensitivity to color and to find a way of reasoning about color as an element of the spiritual in art. As always, he drew from the notion of the evolution of consciousness, relayed to him from Hindu and Buddhist sources largely by Theosophy. He did not expect much of the "average man"—and did expect much of the developed man.

> Only with higher development does the circle of experience of different beings and objects grow wider. Only in the highest development do they acquire an internal meaning and an inner resonance. It is the same with color. . . .[16]

Building on established color theory but rapidly departing from it, Kandinsky found himself expressing the impact of color in poetic and metaphorical terms. For example, "The unbounded warmth of *red* has not the irresponsible appeal of yellow, but rings inwardly with a determined and powerful intensity."[17] Such observations do not add up to a science, but they bear witness to brave effort, providing a rudimentary grammar of color in itself apart from forms in Nature. At the conclusion of the exercise he himself was not fully persuaded, but his general sense of direction hadn't failed him. Toward the end of *On the Spiritual in Art,* he could return to fundamentals with great simplicity:

> Construction on a purely spiritual basis is a slow business, and at first seemingly blind and unmethodical. The artist must train not only his eye but also his soul, so that it can weigh colors in its own scale and thus become a determinant in artistic creation.[18]

The other great literary effort of this period in his life, *The Blaue Reiter Almanac* (Munich, 1912) represented a further attempt to explain and celebrate the new orientation of art, not only in painting and sculpture but also in music and theater. It was the first "textbook" on twentieth-century art. Serving as an author and as coeditor with his friend Franz Marc (1880–1916), Kandinsky anthologized the works and ideas of many of the founders of the new art, together with illustrations from the ancient, tribal, and folk arts from which they drew inspiration. The message of *The Blaue Reiter Almanac,* parts of it delivered most attractively by Franz Marc, was consistent with that of *On the Spiritual in Art:* humanity was entering upon a new spiritual adventure to which artists had much to contribute. The new art, far from capitulating to the forces of materialism and academic convention, would renew the spiritual in grand, partially unforeseeable ways. Already, wrote Marc about certain artists featured in the anthology,

> their thinking has a different aim: to create out of their work symbols for their own time, symbols that belong on the altars of a future spiritual religion. . . .[19]

He enlarged on this striking thought in his introduction to the second edition of *The Blaue Reiter Almanac,* published in 1914, two years before he lost his life in the war:

> We know that everything could be destroyed if the beginnings of a spiritual discipline are not protected from the greed and dishonesty of the masses. We are struggling for pure ideas, for a world in which pure ideas can be thought and proclaimed without becoming impure. Only then will we or others who are more talented be able to show the other face of the Janus head, which today is still hidden and turns its gaze away from the times.
>   We admire the disciples of early Christianity who found the strength for inner stillness amid the roaring noise of their time. For this stillness we pray and strive every hour.[20]

"The other face of the Janus head" remains a powerful image, implying a reserve of love, sensibility, and artistry. Franz Marc himself embodied his feeling for life in visionary paintings of horses and other creatures that stand apart from human violence. He was, one might say, a Nature mystic—in any case a man of great sweetness and intellectual capacity who recognized in animals an innocence something like his own.

Kandinsky's art in the years of *On the Spiritual in Art* has been studied in detail by gifted, persevering art historians.[21] I will not attempt to summarize the research of Ringbom, Washton Long, Peg Weiss, H. K. Roethel, and others. It may seem something of an indecency that an artist of our own time has required such extensive interpretation; common sense whispers that a near-contemporary should be more transparent. On the other hand, in creating his first partially (and soon fully) abstract works, Kandinsky moved into an ambiguous imagina-

6. Wassily Kandinsky. *Black Lines,* 1913. Oil on canvas. 51″ × 51¼″. Solomon R. Guggenheim Museum, New York. Photo: Robert E. Mates. Copyright ARS NY/ADAGP 1987.

tive world. Not quite willing to abandon all reference to real objects and familiar ideas, he often dissolved objects in his paintings so that, as he once put it, they could not be immediately recognized.[22] Scholars have naturally been drawn to provide interpretive keys, and their work has been both necessary and effective.

The fully abstract works of these years, such as the especially beautiful *Black Lines* of 1913 (Fig. 6), can be approached without fear of misperceiving hidden imagery. Such works swirl. Seemingly suspended in turbulent liquid, broad color patches and a nervous linear network stream freely across the canvas—colliding, blending, moving on. The viewer looks in vain for the classical elements of composition, finds instead a passionate clash of color and abstract form, a dominant mood, and in time a theme that can be more or less clearly stated. *Black Lines* resolves into a combat between the positive, joyful energies of color and the scratchy, threatening overlay of lines. The painting surely conveys Kandinsky's experience of positive energies rising and dark energies subverting their expansion in a struggle between joy and constraint.

Is this the height of the spiritual in art? The inspiration, the sense of impending greatness, the untiring insistence on spirit in Kandinsky's Munich writings are not quite matched by the art of those years. Kandinsky's passion to break free and soar seemed unable to tolerate a more deliberate order in the world of his paintings. In these earlier years, he had broken down the old order of pictorial signs but had not yet evolved a new order. Obeying his sense of inner necessity, he brought brilliant color and dynamic interactions to the canvas—in a somewhat melted, unstructured visual language. In time this would change. In the art of his Bauhaus years, the 1920s and early 1930s, we will encounter more fully realized work in which Kandinsky's love of color and movement is contained but not constrained by geometric forms.

Yet in the years before World War I Kandinsky discovered and explored much of the pictorial vocabulary that would reappear in the late 1940s as Abstract Expressionism. The Munich works were intensely original, while the Bauhaus works were derivative of the art of Russian colleagues whom Kandinsky came to know in the early years of the Revolution. The Bauhaus works nonetheless represent his artistic maturity, if maturity means a mobile balance between passion and reason, impulse and restraint. Kandinsky, author and thinker, matured earlier than Kandinsky, painter, although the passionate turmoil in his early paintings exerted a great influence on the future.

"In the final analysis," he wrote in 1912,

> every serious work is tranquil. . . . Every serious work resembles in poise the quiet phrase, "I am here." Like or dislike for the work evaporates; but the sound of that phrase is eternal.[23]

Here again is the voice of his early writings, which in their great passages have lost none of their appeal. In those writings, Kandinsky conveyed many of the ideas that inevitably govern and nourish the spiritual in art—ideas about human consciousness and the inner life, about the obvious and subtle in Nature, about the artist's discipline as seer and technician. To all of this he gave a new voice, sometimes Romantic and of its age, sometimes echoing the timeless affirmation, "I am here."

5   CUBISM

The influence of Cubism, often transformed beyond easy recognition, is felt everywhere today. Cities are Cubist, furnishings and objects are often Cubist—many of us live in Cubist worlds. Yet Cubism, particularly in its earlier phases (1907–12), remains puzzling for many people, who would rather look at something else and not bother with its willful complexity. Complexity, however, is a keynote of our culture. By addressing it, by offering that part of twentieth-century sensibility a visual language both profound and witty, Cubism earns its place in the modern spiritual. It is an art with two faces: on one side, destructive of previous values and conventions, joyous in its power to undo; on the other side, an authentic and surprisingly traditional meditation on form, fertile enough to inspire decades of serious work.

In Cubism, art itself and words only secondarily provided a firm guiding spirit in the opening years of twentieth-century art. The Cubism of 1907–12 began with painstaking analysis of the geometry of natural form; evolved into a fiercely energetic poetry that tied the rationality of geometry to *felt* purposes; then developed from the lessons learned into a new Cubism, quieter than the one that preceded it and destined to influence the course of art through the remainder of the century. Cubism pretends to be analytical, and so it is, but it is also full of fantasy. It pretends to be austere, but it also delights in the sheer presence of form and the endless antiphonies of light and shadow. It is a visual language that can only be learned—and ultimately savored—by a persevering observation that takes note of its various elements and labors, at least initially, to perceive how they merge into a whole. The effort is repaid. What may begin as a dutiful effort can issue out into recognition of a poetry.

The history of Cubism will be familiar to many readers, although its details remain subject to controversy among scholars. Pablo Picasso originated the style in the famous *Demoiselles d'Avignon* of 1907, and Georges Braque joined him in discovering and elaborating its resources. The early, spare phase of Cubism is beautifully represented by Braque's 1909 painting, *Château at La Roche-Guyon* (Fig. 7). It is a dramatic work: a rush of bare, angular geometry and dense foliage moves toward the top of the canvas beneath a strong summer light that dematerializes objects and conveys a quality of dream or vision. Braque's meticulous attention to the cubic geometry of the buildings and his rendering of their abstract presence under the sun are at once impressive. The contrasting foliage seems to stream among the stable buildings, perhaps driven by the natural wind but no less, one senses, by an idea in the mind of the artist.

Braque's characteristically Cubist handling of space also conveys this impression of ideas at work. In naturalistic terms, we are looking down from a certain height toward a village which climbs a steep hillside across from our vantage point. Yet there is something more, an unnatural compression as if the entire scene has been condensed within a narrow box of space, causing its elements to blend with each other and to read quite strongly as pattern on the surface of the canvas. The treatment of the lower right-hand corner reinforces the impression of surface pattern, where Braque abandons illusionism and offers a smudged blending of foliage and stucco. Like Cézanne before him, he is not just mirroring Nature but engaging in a threefold exploration of human perception, things seen, and the artifice of picture-making. The vitality of his work springs from this breadth of exploration.

The viewer's eye assembles further details into the whole: the multiple diagonals of rooftops, the overall pyramidal composition with stabilizing verticals running through it. But having asked how this painting looks, we must be ready to ask what it is about. A key question where the spiritual in art is concerned, it will not yield interesting answers if we assume that images translate words. There *is* thought in Braque's painting—however, not necessarily thought first cast in words and only later translated into an image. Images, like words, are vehicles of consciousness; they allow us to think silently. They can be regarded as silent words, and words as speaking images. We are not as distant from hieroglyphics as we are likely to believe when looking at ancient inscriptions; our minds are filled with hieroglyphics. We call them, more simply, images. When an artist of Braque's ability develops an image such as this one, he is engaged in a kind of thinking. He may not have fully verbalized his ideas, either while creating the image or later. He may simply have followed feeling, instinct, and an artisan's thought about how best to develop the image. And yet, twenty-seven years old at the time, he succeeded in making an image rich in thought.

7. Georges Braque. *Château at La Roche-Guyon*, 1909. Oil on canvas. 31½″ × 23½″. Moderna Museet, Stockholm. Photo: Statens Konstmuseer. Copyright ARS NY/ADAGP 1987.

"I like the rule that corrects the emotion," Braque wrote in 1917,[1] in one of his characteristic aphorisms. This alone is enough to send us back to the painting, ready to recognize it as an image of two complementary energies coexisting, confronting each other, blending. The angular pattern of buildings reads as the Cartesian reality of order and logic, while the foliage streaming in and around it reads as a complementary energy, freer, less predictable, dynamic. We might say that Braque has explored here the relations between intellect and the combined powers of body and feeling. Landscape becomes portrait while remaining landscape, a portrait not of face and shoulders but of an intuition of self. The painting is a meditation on Nature and human nature.

This interpretation is, I suppose, unusual. Critics have brilliantly explored Cubism and twentieth-century art in terms of formal dynamics and many other factors, but they have not been much concerned to relate what they see on canvas to philosophical, religious, and psychological ideas. Kandinsky knew better. "Consciously or unconsciously," he wrote in *On the Spiritual in Art*,

> [artists] are obeying Socrates' advice: "Know thyself." Consciously or unconsciously, artists are studying and investigating their material, weighing the spiritual value of those elements with which it is their privilege to work.[2]

His words capture the thoughtfulness of Braque's canvas—its acute attention to landscape, to the possibilities of Cubism, and to something more, best described as the self of "Know thyself." Cubism was a powerful coming together of a new notation for visual reality and a new interest in the nature of human consciousness.

Picasso's drawing, the *Nude* of 1910 (Fig. 8), is a splendid example of Cubism in its next and more developed phase. Angular, odd, at first difficult to read, there is nonetheless a languid grace in the overall pose of the figure that recalls Classical sculpture—for example, a figure of Athena in the Louvre Museum, familiar to generations of Parisian artists and schoolchildren. This reminiscence of Classical art is not accidental. In earlier years, Picasso had mastered academic style, with its stress on accurate rendering of the human figure and a learned repertory of traditionally sanctioned poses. The transformation of divine Athena—smooth, harmonious, ideal—into converging planes and scaffolded lines, with shadows trailing across her like strands of fog, is a very modern and contrary enterprise.

Homage to the Classical ideal is there, but so transformed as to be

8. Pablo Picasso. *Nude*, 1910. Charcoal. 19$\frac{1}{16}$″ × 12$\frac{5}{16}$″. The Metropolitan Museum of Art, The Alfred Stieglitz Collection, 1949 (49.70.34). Copyright ARS NY/SPADEM 1987.

almost unrecognizable; homage much like good-by. Within the limits of art history, this apparent disfiguration of the Classical ideal was Picasso's way of distancing himself from the past. Like Kandinsky, he needed to start anew, to be the originator of a new culture rather than a gifted latecomer to an outworn one. Decades later, in 1956, Picasso reminisced about his motives at the time:

> I saw that everything had been done. One had to break to make one's revolution and start at zero. I made myself go towards the new movement.[3]

Within the larger context of twentieth-century art, we will find a number of major artists who could neither accept the Classical ideal unchanged nor dismiss it. The great calm, the collectedness in action, the sheer physical beauty of Classical sculpture and painting recurrently haunted these artists and prompted them to seek their own rendering of those values (see Chapter 16). Picasso's drawing is our first encounter with this powerful nostalgia. As the historian of religions, Mircea Eliade, has lucidly explained,[4] nostalgia for values that many of us can neither abandon nor embrace outright plays no small part in the spirituality of our time. We are bad Greeks, but we are Greeks nonetheless. Their era was the childhood of Western society, and it is difficult not to look back longingly to that childhood and measure our distance from ourselves by our distance from it.

Cubism was unbelievably audacious. Its early critical champions liked to describe it as scientific, as if its planar structure reveals the mathematical core of reality and its multiple views of a single object deliver a greater truth. But they protested too much to defend the new art, which is poetry not science. Picasso's *Nude* is as much a fantasy as it is an analysis of figure geometry. The main contours of legs, torso, shoulders, neck, and head are faithfully translated into line and plane, but they are caught in a network of freely conceived geometric notation and an unpredictable play of light and shadow which all but overwhelm them. As in Braque's landscape, the figure exists to a degree in three dimensions, yet it is also a surface design; surface and depth are entangled with deliberate ambiguity. The joy of studying Cubist works from these years is to experience their complexities, to get lost and found again in their little labyrinths, to witness carefully rendered planes vanish irrationally—and to experience all of this in relation to the elusive whole image of which these enigmas are a part.

Cubism in this period is a series of brilliant variations on the age-old theme of "the whole and its parts," and never in the history of art has there been such a high regard for parts. They have a vitality of their own, and only the most summary respect for the whole of which they are supposed to be dutiful members. Even minutely detailed designs in high Islamic art—for example, *Koran* frontispieces—draw the viewer toward perceiving a magnificent overall harmony. The geometries of Islam are complex, but they obey a secret order which the eye can uncover and the mind delight in as a reflection of surpassing Reality.

The geometries of Cubism, our art, play with disorder and do not aspire to regularity or lucidity. Early Cubism skewed the ancient norm of the whole and its tributary parts. In so doing, it expressed the psychic complexity of our times and broke through to a new kind of order—tentative, ambiguous, but visibly marked with intelligence. There is a quality of serious play in earlier Cubism, as when a child builds a high, complicated tower with blocks and can't wait for the delicious moment when it topples. There is, as well, a quality of unmitigated seriousness, for Cubism evolved new and important imaginative freedoms—to structure things as one feels and thinks them, to take any bold step that one wishes, to create new realities obeying new laws with a freedom that had not been experienced in Western art since the early Renaissance explored optical perspective. One of the signs of this deliberate seriousness is the characteristic palette of the first years of Cubism—somber earth colors borrowed from sculptor's stone and bronze rather than from the painter's rainbow of possibilities. The charcoal drawing that we have been looking at shares this austere coloration, which attracts the observer's mind to the structural bones of the work.

Picasso's *Ma Jolie* of 1911–12 (Fig. 9) is a remarkable canvas that can show us more about the structure and reflective mood of early Cubism. Permanently exhibited in the Museum of Modern Art and widely reproduced in basic art texts, it has become the touchstone for students attempting to grasp the dynamics of the style. Like many works of the period, it appears at first to be an excessively complex patchwork of planes and lines. Perseverance reveals the trapezoidal shape of the zither's sounding box, its strings, and the arm of a highly enigmatic lady, bent at the elbow while her fingers strum the instrument. Face, shoulders, and torso come into view, followed by a generalized background not fully distinguished from the central figure. As so often in Cubist works of these years, the image thins and disappears as it approaches the edge of the canvas, thus insisting on itself as a vision, an artifact of imagination.

But detective work is not the heart of developed Cubism, it can even

9. Pablo Picasso. *"Ma Jolie" (Woman with a Zither or Woman with a Guitar)*. Oil on canvas. 39⅜″ × 25¾″. Collection, The Museum of Modern Art, New York. Acquired through the Lillie P. Bliss Bequest. Copyright ARS NY/SPADEM 1987.

be an irritant. The heart of Cubism is the poetry of structure, space, and light that we found in simpler form in the 1910 drawing. *Ma Jolie* is more baroque by far, with a stridently complex structure of interpenetrating planes and spatial ambiguities such that we cannot, and we clearly are not intended to, rationalize what we see. Cubism was the first great aesthetic "deconstruction" of the twentieth century, the archetype of others to come. Its structural complexity is compensated by the warmth and sobriety of its bronze surface and orderly brushwork: short, for the most part horizontal brush strokes—visible and shimmering—send a warm pulse through the entire canvas. The image as a whole seems fragmented and excessive, but there is an underlying poetry of a positive nature, full of lessons that would only be drawn out as the century progressed.

Picasso and Braque were laconic in the early years of Cubism; they did not feel obligated to explain. In 1908 or 1909, Braque spoke briefly with an American journalist:

> I couldn't portray a woman in all her natural loveliness . . . I haven't the skill. No one has. I must, therefore, create a new sort of beauty, the beauty that appears to me in terms of volume, of line, of mass, of weight, and through that beauty interpret my subjective impression. . . . I want to expose the Absolute, and not merely the factitious woman.[5]

From time to time as the years passed, Picasso would make revelatory comments, but almost always casually. Throughout his life he affirmed the primacy of image-making over any possible commentary. In the early 1950s, for example, speaking of a new project he had in mind, he acknowledged the nucleus from which Cubism had emerged:

> . . . One couldn't do it all by oneself, one had to be with others, as in the past with Cubism, it needs the work of a team.[6]

Critics and artist-friends around Picasso and Braque in those years, members of the team, reasoned at length about the new art and tried to warm its public reception. One of the clearest-minded among them was Guillaume Apollinaire (1880–1918), poet, critic, journalist, author of the pioneering study *Les peintres cubistes* (1913), and a man of great charm—one of many who did not survive the war. "Wishing to attain the proportions of the ideal," he wrote in 1912,

> to be no longer limited to the human, the young painters offer us works which are more cerebral than sensual. They discard more and

more the old art of optical illusion and local proportion, in order to express the grandeur of metaphysical forms. This is why contemporary art, even if it does not directly stem from specific religious beliefs, nonetheless possesses some of the characteristics of great, that is to say, religious art. . . . [This] is the art of painting new structures out of elements borrowed not from the reality of sight, but from the reality of insight. All men have a sense of this interior reality. . . . The geometrical aspect, which made such an impression on those who saw the first canvases of the . . . cubists, came from the fact that the essential reality was rendered with great purity, while visual accidents and anecdotes had been eliminated. . . .[7]

The passage is prophetic, describing not only the Cubism of its day but its development in years to come, when Robert Delaunay, Piet Mondrian, Paul Klee, and Ben Nicholson among others would draw out the inherent metaphysic of the new visual language.

Apollinaire uses a word that would recur throughout the next decades: purity. Whatever else can be said about the art of our time, however much it was constricted by political and economic events and fell short of its own ideals, it respected the idea of purity and sought to embody it again and again in works of art. The idea first became powerful in the Cubist circle. Jean Metzinger, a talented painter among them, was already using the word in 1910:

Picasso unveils to us the very face of painting. Rejecting every ornamental, anecdotal or symbolic intention, he achieves a painterly purity hitherto unknown.[8]

Maurice Raynal, critic and champion of Cubism in the early years, was no less certain that "this very strange and pure principle of painting things as one thinks them" represented a great new beginning.[9]

Like so much else in our time, Cubism evolved rapidly. The art of ancient Egypt evolved over millennia; the art of ancient Greece evolved over centuries; our art has evolved over years and at most decades, plunging through full cycles of birth, maturation, and death, changing its identity again and again. Cubism opened out in 1912 into a less complex, more "livable" art which became one of the steadier, more enduring currents of modern art. Artists even today make explicit use of its language, while others borrow one or another element from it to suit their purposes. This new Cubism, termed "synthetic" or late Cubism, came about when Picasso and Braque began to experiment with collage, pasting paper and other materials onto canvas and creating more placid compositions with fewer fragmented parts. The freedom of Cubism remained—its bold inventions, its new sense of space, its quasi abstraction—but the fierce energy that broke up the standard images of Western art into crowded planes had done its work and begun to mellow.

A still life (Fig. 10) by Juan Gris (1887–1927), an extraordinarily gifted painter in the Cubist circle, points toward this less feverish art, although it is not itself a collage. In this work, a raking light traverses and transforms simple objects on a tabletop, creating an impression of stability and movement in delicate balance. An austere palette of earth colors and off-whites contributes to a sense of weight and calm. The characteristic fracturing of Cubism has been gentled: some objects appear as if seen through a prism, their forms mildly distorted, while others remain intact or nearly so. The surface of liquid in the bottles, oddly detached, makes an independent statement. The composition as a whole is two-dimensional and yet as three-dimensional as low-relief sculpture—a further enigma that delights the eye as it picks out objects against the background, and then sees them as part of the background as well.

The painting may well strike one as an utterly serious work, sober and measured, lyrical yet quiet. But this perception again raises the question of meaning. To be about bottles, a knife, and light is hardly enough to arouse such a strong intuition of seriousness; there must be something more. This something more finally makes itself known: we are looking at ordinary things—objects from any dining table—undergoing a transfiguration as light streams across them. The ordinary is caught up in a larger movement of change, its plainness converted.

A folded newspaper toward the center of the painting shows not the complete word JOURNAL but only the letters OUI, yes—the curved strokes of the R are missing. It is difficult not to interpret this as the artist's joy in his vision and as an invitation to join him. Verbal description is often clumsy, always different from the visual art it hopes to describe, but here, recognizably, is a work of worship—spirit made matter and matter made spirit.

The new Cubism to which Gris' canvas points is beautifully represented in a 1913 collage by Georges Braque, *Clarinet* (Fig. 11). The perennial European interest in aesthetic harmony reasserts itself in this work, which makes use of the Cubist language but speaks more softly by far than the complex work of the preceding years. This is a new kind of composition, one of such enduring fascination and expressiveness that artists ever since have explored its variations and poten-

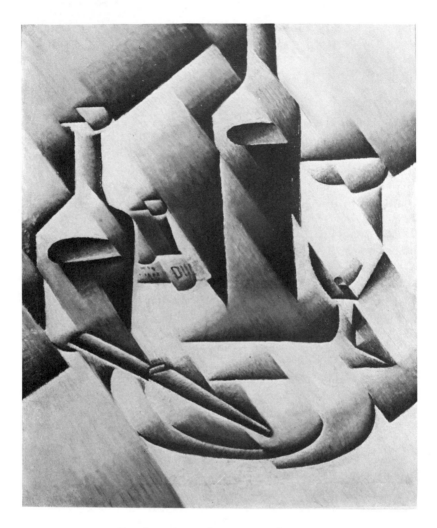

10. Juan Gris. *Still Life with Bottles*, 1912. Oil on canvas. 21½″ × 18″.
Rijksmuseum Kröller-Müller, Otterlo. Copyright ARS NY/SPADEM 1987.

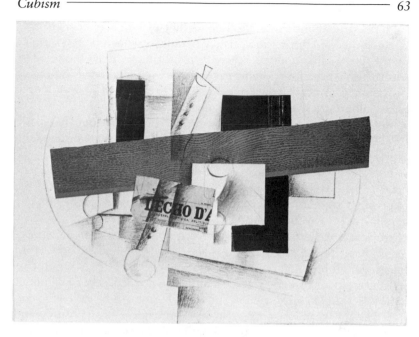

11. Georges Braque. *Clarinet*, 1913. Pasted papers, charcoal, chalk, and oil on canvas. 37½″ × 47⅜″. Collection, The Museum of Modern Art, New York. Nelson A. Rockefeller Bequest. Copyright ARS NY/ADAGP 1987.

tial. Regular, but with telling departures from the expected, this is a "small" work that grows in impact as the viewer becomes increasingly aware of its play of forms. Objects and textures borrowed from ordinary reality—a clarinet, a fragment of newspaper, a wine glass, a tabletop, the texture of oak—are reassembled in a world purely of the imagination, where they seem to have floated into a calm yet varied pattern. There are dominant horizontals and verticals, but the order of the composition is free, not strict. The sketchy oval surrounding the main composition, the true vertical at the lower center (perhaps a table corner), and the rectangular band framing the image are enough to convey a stability that complements the easygoing quality of the composition as a whole.

Braque has established two degrees of materiality: the solid assertiveness of the pasted paper, roughly occupying the center, and the airy sketched periphery. Between them he introduces a kind of play—the clarinet, for example, passing from sketched lightness through the denser central region and reemerging as an airy sketch. Viewers may feel a delight defying rationalization as they experience these changes in materiality and the curious pliancy of objects, which do not seem to mind being slightly undone, released from routine. Even the smallest detail sings—a shadow clinging to the table edge, slight dislocations of form in the clarinet. The instrument seems drawn by a wise child free of the dull propriety that requires things to look strictly like themselves or suffer the consequences. The viewer's eyes move from the gentle grey "world" of the sketched portions to the denser world of the pasted papers and back again, fully and unexpectedly at home.

In its stormy debut, Cubism undid an outworn world of forms; now it has learned to make a new world. The rules of this new world are surprisingly traditional, much in keeping with the hard-earned understanding of composition evolved by European art since Classical times. There is balance but not strict symmetry, regularity but also surprise, center and periphery, object and space, light and shadow—these old values and more, caught up in a new aesthetic.

Cubism, at this stage of its development, opened new possibilities for the spiritual in art through what quickly came to be called the collage. The collage at best applies timeless principles of composition and harmonization to disparate, occasionally random odds and ends. The fundamental act of ordering raises the odds and ends—ennobles them, one might say—at the same time that it challenges the artist to deepen his or her insight into order. There is a more authentic alchemy here than in some prominent twentieth-century works for which critics (if not artists) have claimed its occult prestige. As Braque practiced it, the ordering process is gentle: objects are perceived lightly, not grabbed. They are placed with a fine hand, blended with one another yet not denatured. This ordering has something of the spirit in it. Braque approached this little world as one could wish to approach the larger one.

In the art of the following decades, artists have returned to the sonnet-like world of the Cubist collage to find out new things about it. The fundamental act of ordering, undistracted by the demands of realism, has retained its appeal. Such works return both artist and viewer to a contemplative simplicity in which all that matters is consciousness: the artist's receptive and shaping consciousness, the viewer's ability to grasp the order created by the artist and delight in it. Collage at best tunes one's awareness.

By looking carefully at five works from the Cubism of 1907−13, we have been able to share the perception that Cubism was not just a passing style, a bravura way of undoing the world and doing it up again strangely. From the beginning, its creators and friends thought of it as a new vision that moves toward the essential, an instrument for exploring the real nature of things. From the perspective of this book, I would say that Cubism represented a fulcrum, the uneasy middle between sheer aesthetics and spiritual research—moving in one direction or the other at different times and in different hands. It could, and often did, explore visual reality and complexities of imagination for their own sake. It was also on occasion carried to a higher power, so to speak, becoming a language beautifully adapted to exploring not only Nature but also our own natures, the order and disorder of consciousness, and the complexity of modern times.

Twentieth-century art has been agitated, but it has nonetheless had steady undercurrents. Cubism has become integral to so much of the art of later decades that it is scarcely noticed. Offering compositional possibilities ranging from the simplicity of a grid to the complexity of a maze, it has been both a philosopher's language and a "dumb" language. It has attracted Platonists and esotericists for whom geometry evokes the universal order, but also ironists who have used geometry to create deliberately sterile form. Cubist art can spring from spirit and address spirit; it can also be nothing more than a way of organizing form. Its fullness or poverty depends, as always, on the fullness or poverty of the artist.

6   PIET MONDRIAN: THE UNIVERSAL TOWERS ABOVE US

MONDRIAN'S IDEAS

We have "a nostalgia for the universal," wrote Mondrian. "This nostalgia must bring forth a completely new art."[1] Such ideals are to be encountered in the central lineage of twentieth-century art, but they are likely now to seem alien, neither of our language nor of our time. Hence the need to reconsider Piet Mondrian (1872–1944)—not according to the academic values that have correctly but narrowly assigned him prominence in the history of abstract art and architectural aesthetics, but according to values more in keeping with his own. They reveal him distinctly as one of the artist-metaphysicians of our time.

Among the artists who match this description, Mondrian is unarguably the most difficult to approach. Reading the many pages of his writings from the notebooks of 1912–14, the formal writings of his middle years, and the concluding notes of his last years in New York, even willing readers cannot help but feel that they have blundered into a marathon. Schooled in the nineteenth century and deeply attracted to formal philosophical discourse in a neo-Hegelian mode, Mondrian more often than not wrote his apologia for the new art of our century in the forbiddingly abstract rhetoric of German Idealism. To approach his writings requires sifting through dry rhetoric for passages that have immediacy for our ears and minds, and requires a willingness to translate faithfully when the original expression is intriguing but opaque. He was a simple, modest man personally, and his art sprang from intuitive processes unhampered by the creaking machinery of highly formal thought; but when he turned to the task of making himself clear in words, he became intensely formal, high-minded, and cautious.

His correspondence and occasional articles were otherwise. In a letter of 1932, for example, he wrote:

> People do not see why a painter should concern himself with the laws of life; they do not understand that the laws of life realize themselves perhaps most clearly in art.[2]

It is difficult to recognize that this clear and rather touching statement has much the same content as a passage in his formal writings where he evokes the idea of "unity in a single outwardness."[3] I am not suggesting that we must learn to speak Mondrian's difficult language; a reading knowledge will do. I believe that he countered public suspicion that his art lacked meaning by invoking the most formal rhetoric of meaning that the world has known. Since there is no longer any need to defend his art, we can afford to do without his most chilling weapon.

Mondrian did not have the kind of mind that easily coins aphorisms, although the paintings for which he is remembered have the nature of aphorisms, condensed statements of far-reaching consequence. A few of the aphorisms in his writings can, however, lead us toward the complexities that we will eventually want to explore at greater length. "The surface of things gives delight, their inwardness gives life"[4]— from the notebooks of 1912–14, this already breathes the spirit of his mature writings. "The universal—although its germ is already in us— towers far above us; and just as far above us is that art which directly expresses the universal."[5] Or again, "Through our intuition, the universal in us can become so active . . . that . . . it pushes aside our individuality. Then art can reveal itself."[6] Further, he thought, "art advances where religion once led,"[7] and ". . . we are still far from knowing inwardness."[8] This last is haunting; it echoes the doubt and hope of Kandinsky at nearly the same moment.

Mondrian's thinking represents a deeply felt recurrence of Neoplatonism in the heartland of twentieth-century art: the intuition of two worlds, the near one of surface appearance and individual ignorance, the far or high one of the universal to which we may gain access through inwardness. Mondrian also shares the Neoplatonic view of the purpose of art. "Art," he wrote, "although an end in itself, like religion, is the means through which we can know the universal and contemplate it in plastic form."[9] Despite his deep connection with Neoplatonism, Mondrian made a strong claim for the novelty of his thought, and coupled that claim with a fierce rejection of the past that he only occasionally softened or reversed. Mondrian and his contemporaries wrestled free from the past and continued long after the initial act of self-liberation to sound the alarm against tradition. Beneath their rhetoric of denial can be heard from time to time acknowledgments of debt and communion, but the louder voice is the defiant one. "Let us not forget," he wrote in 1920, "that we are at the turning point of culture, *at the end of everything ancient: the separation of the two is absolute and definitive.*" [10] And in 1927, he wrote: "For some time yet, unfortunately, the tolling of bells and many other signs will remind us of the old culture." [11] His thought was little different in 1940:

> For modern man, the great art of antiquity reveals itself more or less as *darkness*. . . . In general, all particularities of the past are as oppressive as darkness. The past has a *tyrannic influence* which is difficult to escape. The worst is that there is always something of the past *within us*. We have memories, dreams—we hear the old carillons. . . ." [12]

The references to church bells at an interval of thirteen years from each other undoubtedly reveal the ineradicable trace of Mondrian's childhood in a strict Calvinist household.

Mondrian was of two minds with respect to the art and thought of the past. As avant-garde artist and philosopher of art, he maintained a negative stance, but from time to time he changed. In his most important writing of the 1930s, *The New Art—The New Life,* he could state:

> Just as traditional aesthetic truths reappear in the new art but are expressed differently, so the new life reveals traditional philosophic ideas and concepts, but practiced differently. [13]

Mondrian did feel that he had been preceded in the recent past by cultural innovations and deepenings upon which his art and point of view were expressly based. In the sphere of visual art, the chief precedent was Cubism, which he discovered on arriving in Paris from his Dutch homeland in 1911. In the sphere of ideas, he evokes the chief precedent in a mysterious passage from his first major published writing, *The New Plastic in Painting* (1917). There he cautioned readers "to see in today's awful turmoil a storm that will bring our outer life into harmony with our inner life, whose *rebirth* began quietly long ago. . . ." [14]

Mondrian must be referring to the cultural innovations of Theosophy, which represented for him a rebirth of spirituality. A member of the Theosophical Society from 1909, he owed much also to the Dutch philosopher M. H. Schoenmaekers, whose language and cosmology he borrowed in his writings on the universal and its expression in art. From sources ranging in time from Plato to Schoenmaekers, he absorbed Western Idealism, while from Theosophy he absorbed a current of thought that might be called Eastern Idealism. Around 1920, he could comfortably cast a new exposition of his ideas in the form of a Platonic dialogue. No other major artist of our century, to my knowledge, has written a Platonic dialogue or would even care to have done so.

We have scanned Mondrian's sources, neglecting only to mention that Christian ideals found their way into his writings, unidentified as such but essential to his world-view. We have also looked briefly at his uneasy relation with the past, characterized by strong inner reliance crusted over with a rhetoric of denial. Mondrian and a number of his associates represent a first attempt to fit perennial spiritual ideas into the context of twentieth-century art—a first attempt to devise a visible form for these ideas, accompanied by explanatory texts which tried to tell the public what was taking place.

What were these ideas, and how did they shape his art? The opening words of his first formal publication (autumn, 1917) retain the power of a manifesto:

> The life of modern cultured man is gradually turning away from the natural: life is becoming more and more *abstract*.
>
> As the natural (the external) becomes more and more "automatic," we see life's interest fixed more and more on the inward. The life of *truly modern* man is directed neither toward the material for its own sake nor toward the predominantly emotional: rather, it takes the form of the autonomous life of the human spirit becoming conscious. . . . Art . . . as the product of a new duality in man, is increasingly expressed as the product of cultivated outwardness and of a deeper, more conscious inwardness. . . . The truly modern artist *consciously* perceives the abstractness of the emotion of beauty: he *consciously* recognizes aesthetic emotion as cosmic, universal. This conscious recognition results in an abstract plastic—limits him to the purely universal. . . . The new art is *the determinate plastic expression of aesthetic relationships.*[15]

Even before exploring the grammar of ideas in this passage, we can note their rich vocabulary: the abstract, inwardness, the human spirit, consciousness, the cosmic, the universal, beauty—as well as the rather clumsy word "plastic" (Dutch *beelding*). Courageously, perhaps blindly, Mondrian held the conviction that the twentieth century represented a new occasion for the appearance of inwardness and beauty in the general culture—and he began to write on this topic while troops were still in the trenches. Artists' responses to the carnage of World War I ranged from the nihilistic high jinks of Dada to the sober spirituality of Mondrian who, with his comrades in the De Stijl movement, was already preparing what they called "the new consciousness: individual-universal equilibrium." [16]

The American poet Wallace Stevens wrote that "for Mondrian the abstract was the abstract" [17]—a satisfyingly circular thought that captures the irreducible essence on behalf of which Mondrian worked as an artist. Mondrian did associate a series of terms with the abstract, but they help only a little to grasp his meaning: the universal, the absolute, the immutable, the beautiful, the true. An admittedly difficult passage from 1921 may move us closer:

> The "abstract" in art . . . is established by *the most profound interiorization of the outward and by the purest (most determinate) exteriorization of the inward*. . . . Neither in music nor in painting does it negate reality. [18]

This formulation, itself quite abstract and expressed in his most characteristic language, describes the abstract as a midpoint between the innermost life of man and the outermost manifestations of Nature. The artist observing Nature according to Mondrian's discipline comes gradually to see and to represent the universal dwelling in it. At the same time, the artist is moved from within by an intuition of the universal which, in gradual stages, finds its way to expression in the work of art. These two expressions of the universal within and the universal without become increasingly one and the same as the artist's consciousness evolves—a "unity in a single outwardness." The single outwardness is the work of art, necessarily abstract to encompass so broad a scale.

We should look into the meaning of one of Mondrian's most characteristic words, *determinate*. He wrote: "The abstract is *the inward that has become determinate, or the most deeply interiorized externality*." [19] He enlarged on this idea as follows:

> . . . Most people can recognize the universal only in and through the vague, because of the vagueness in themselves. They cannot recognize the universal in its *pure* plastic manifestation because the uni-

versal has not become *conscious* in them. However, as soon as we have formed a *determinate image* of the universal in ourselves, we can recognize it in a determinate plastic expression. . . .[20]

What, then, does *determinate* mean? Antonym of *vague*, it refers to a fully formed, precise, philosophical notion or vision of the universal that leads the artist to definite outer expressions, more in keeping with mathematical sensibility than any other. Mondrian in fact speculated about the importance of mathematics to the new art of our century. In 1918, he wrote:

> Through painting itself, the artist became conscious that the appearance of the *universal-as-the-mathematical* is the essence of all feelings of beauty . . .

Later in the essay he spoke with uncustomary warmth of "the *mathematical artistic temperament* of the future."[21]

Mondrian's word *determinate,* then, carries the burden of his moral determination to achieve an art exactly ordered by universal law and free of the vague subjectivity to which art is characteristically vulnerable. It was this element in his sensibility that caused even some close comrades to fear his dogmatism, his tendency toward overdetermination. Mondrian tempered his insistence on precision and objectivity in several ways. He never presumed to have achieved full understanding of "the universal" and always regarded himself as a seeker. "The task of art," he once wrote, "is pure expression of that incomprehensible force that is universally active, and that we can therefore call *the universal.*"[22] Many years later, he was still somewhat tentative before the unknown. He also recognized that the artist is inevitably subjective to some degree, however much he or she seeks an impersonal art that pays homage to the universal.

> It is to be understood that one would need a subject to expound something named "Spiritual riches, human sentiments and thoughts." Obviously, all this is individual and needs particular forms. But at the root of these sentiments and thoughts there is one thought and one sentiment: these do not easily define themselves. . . .[23]

Mondrian even insisted on the primacy of intuition in the artist's work; he conceived the intelligence that directs a more or less conscious artist as a blend of intuition and pure thought. "Those who do not understand this intelligence," he wrote, "regard nonfigurative art as a purely intellectual product."[24] In a touching anecdote from the last years of his life, when he was living in New York, Mondrian is recalled all but skipping down the hall of his apartment toward a visiting friend with the announcement, "I dreamed a beautiful new composition last night!"[25] This, too, was Mondrian. That he was driven toward the determinate in his art and thought cannot be doubted, and the historian Peter Gay is surely correct to have attempted a psychological portrait of the artist as an anxious man to whom exactitude was soothing.[26] However, the call for precision that Mondrian, beyond all others, introduced in the art of our time cannot be written off as merely an unconscious survival strategy. As William Blake put it in 1809,

> The great and golden rule of art, as well as of life, is this: That the more distinct, sharp, and wiry the bounding line, the more perfect the work of art. . . . Great inventors, in all ages, knew this.[27]

Mondrian once defined the work of art as a "subjectivization of the universal." This passage is one of his most memorable:

> The subjectivization of the universal in art brings the universal downward on the one hand, while on the other it helps raise the individual toward the universal.
>
> Subjectivization of the universal . . . can express the consciousness of an age either in its relationship *to the universal,* or in its relationship to *daily life,* to the *individual.* In the first case, art is *truly religious,* in the second, *profane.*[28]

The entirety of Mondrian's mature art represents an effort to "bring the universal downward," and by his own definition must be thought of as "truly religious." It is becoming evident, as we assemble his ideas, that we need to view his art not only as a major aesthetic innovation but also as a religious art struggling toward a pure expression of truth. This is nowhere more apparent than in Mondrian's various assessments of the nature and summoning power of the universal, "the core of all things."[29]

> If the universal is the essential, then it is the basis of all life and art. Recognizing and uniting with the universal therefore gives us the greatest aesthetic satisfaction, the greatest emotion of beauty. The more determinately (consciously) this recognition is experienced, the more intense our happiness. The more determinately (consciously) this union with the universal is felt, the more individual subjectivity declines.[30]

For Mondrian, the concepts of relativity and evolution accompany the thought of the universal. Although the universal in us is "the most deeply inward,"[31] and although a universal order shines forth in Nature, both the one and the other are "veiled" to "unpracticed eyes."[32] He put all this succinctly in the course of his first major writing:

> All art is *more or less* direct aesthetic expression of the universal. This *more or less* implies *degrees.* . . . The subjectivization of the universal is *relative.* . . . a great heightening of subjectivity is taking place in man (evolution)—in other words a *growing, expanding consciousness.* Subjectivity remains subjective, but it diminishes in the measure that objectivity (the universal) grows in the individual. Subjectivity ceases to exist only when the mutation-like *leap* is made from subjectivity to objectivity, from individual existence to universal existence.[33]

This passage is astonishing on more than one count. Mondrian considered the quality of humanity around him confirmation of his "firm belief in the spirit's rising development,"[34] and he considered this belief a necessity if one wishes to "see life and art purely."[35] In terms of the history of ideas, his conviction is theosophical Darwinism, a spiritualized version of the ascent of species which maintains, as Mondrian put it, that "the physical has reached its apogee, but we 'men' will attain our apogee only in the distant future."[36]

The great obstacle to the "struggle toward clear vision of the universal"[37] is the human trait that Mondrian variously calls "individuality," "personality," "particularity," "the domination of the ego." He had enough insight into the apparent willfulness of his own performance as an avant-garde artist at odds with his time to remark that "while the mentality seeking the universal (by freeing itself from the domination of the individual) is found everywhere, it is still *most unusual* and thus it appears rather as a *personal* expression."[38] He conceived the artist's task as requiring self-liberation from egotistical subjectivity. The call to an ascetic way of life rings unmistakably throughout his writings— qualified by his recognition of the relativity of a person's state and the ever-present possibility of further evolution. "The new culture," he wrote,

> will be that of the *mature individual;* once matured, the individual will be open to the universal and will tend more and more to unite *with* it.[39]

He held out assurance that as the artist learns to express universality "more and more consciously," it will appear "spontaneously and intuitively," "effortlessly unfolding" without struggle.[40] In his early note-book not intended for publication, Mondrian favorably contrasted the spiritual possibilities of the artist with those of the disciple on a formal spiritual path:

> There are two paths leading to the Spiritual, the path of learning, of direct exercises (meditation, etc.), and the slow certain path of evolution. One may observe in art the slow growth toward the Spiritual, while those who produce it remain unaware of this. The Path of learning in art usually leads to the corruption of art. Should these two paths coincide, that is to say, that the creator has reached the stage of evolution where conscious, spiritual, direct activity is *possible*, then one has attained the ideal art.[41]

Written in a period when Mondrian, like Kandinsky, seems to have been experimenting with the spiritual exercises proposed by Theosophy and by Steiner, this passage reflects his growing confidence in the inherent spiritual tendency of art to transform the artist.

Believing that art naturally conducts the mind inward to an increasingly intuitive knowledge of the universal, Mondrian also liked to insist on what he quite beautifully called "the way of art, an outward way."[42] He maintained that

> advanced evolution of the spiritual cannot be truly pure for a man in whom the natural has not matured correspondingly. That is why so many relapse into a superficial spirituality.[43]

Criticizing those who "lack a feeling for the 'real',"[44] he frequently restated his conviction that concentrating solely "on culture of the inward comes to negate the evolution of art," and amounts to nothing more than a life "half-lived."[45] The art that he wished for is a "*reconciliation* of the matter-mind duality,"[46] by no means merely a bodiless spirituality. These observations correct the widespread misunderstanding of Mondrian as an unqualified ascetic. On the contrary, as an artist he took his stand on behalf of an integration of the universal with the material world. He coined the clumsy term "abstract-real" for his art and the art of his colleagues to reflect that integration.

Despite the humanity that Mondrian brought to his understanding of the struggle between consciousness and egotism, he plainly conceived of art as an initiatic way that exacts its price for its joys. Writing to a friend in 1934, he said,

> it is in my work that I am something, but compared to the Great Initiates, I am nothing.[47]

His words throw us back into the religious and philosophical context for which, ultimately, Mondrian cared as much as he cared for the frontier of new art and design.

There is a powerful recurrence in Mondrian of a theme from St. Paul. In *Ephesians* 4:23–24, Paul says, "Be renewed in the spirit of your minds, and put on the new man." Mondrian's Modernist restatement phrases the thought as follows:

> The "new man" must indeed be completely different from the old . . . Earlier, *man himself* was a machine, but now he *makes use of* the machine, whether his own body or the machine that he has created. He uses the machine, so far as possible, to perform the rough work so that he can concentrate his *self* on the inward. Ultimately, his soul also becomes a "machine" for him: his *self* becomes *conscious mind.*[48]

> In the new man, the life force can be called *a conscious radiation of the universal.* Generally it is expressed as wisdom rather than joyfulness, but it is actually both in one.[49]

> *In the vital reality of the abstract,* the new man has transcended the feelings of nostalgia, joy, delight, sorrow, horror, etc.; in the *"constant" emotion of beauty* these feelings are purified and deepened. . . .[50]

Mondrian might dislike the association of his thought with St. Paul's, since his concept of the new man pointed the way toward a new human and social reality beyond reach of the "old carillons" of Christendom. Nonetheless, Mondrian's new man seems to be Christian man, redeemed.

"Behold, I make all things new," says the figure on the throne in the *Book of Revelation.* "God himself . . . will wipe away every tear. . . , neither shall there be mourning nor crying nor pain any more. . . ." (Rev. 21:3–5). The list of sorrows eased is not unlike Mondrian's list of feelings transcended by his more impassive new man. Mondrian, no less than traditional Christian authors, looked toward a conquest of time and flux:

> . . . The new spirit . . . , as it becomes more conscious, is increasingly capable of transforming the *moments* of contemplation into one moment, into a *permanent vision.*[51]

> Things are beautiful or ugly only in *time and space.* The new man's vision being liberated from these two factors, all is unified in one *unique beauty.*[52]

With texts such as these before us, it is difficult to underestimate the centrality and passion of Mondrian's search for a degree of consciousness far transcending the ordinary. His version of the artist as metaphysician and spiritual seeker, however dry, is one of the foundations of the spiritual in twentieth-century art.

Mondrian gave an idiosyncratic but fascinating value to the word *tragic*. He used it as Buddhism uses the term *dukkha*, pain or suffering, to refer both to the obviously painful things in life and to all transient experience, however joyful. Nature and man's life insofar as they are untouched by the universal are tragic. "As long as the duality of inward and outward is manifested," he wrote,

> whether as nature and spirit, man against man, male and female . . . as long as this duality has not achieved complete equilibrium and recovered its unity, it remains *tragic*. . . . The artist must be able to abolish tragic expression.[53]

In speaking of the tragic, Mondrian used a warrior's vocabulary: it would eventually have to be "abolished," "annihilated," "suppressed," "destroyed." While admitting that "total destruction of the tragic *in us* will be achieved only in the very distant future,"[54] he conceived his art to be a premonition of the decline of tragedy and the appearance of a way of life and art that transcends it. The passion of his comments on the tragic prompt us to ask why. The cool surface of his writings ruptures here—we witness a profound aversion to the push and pull of life. "The sensitivity of artistic temperament," he wrote in his 1917 essay,

> is necessary in order to perceive the plastic expression of the tragic; one must be an artist to express it. *The artist sees the tragic to such a degree that he is compelled to express the non-tragic.* In this way he finally found a resolution. . . .[55]

This should be read as autobiography, and the odd shift in voice from the present tense to the past tense rather confirms this view. Mondrian's painful sensitivity is beyond question, and to it can be attributed his compulsion to express the non-tragic. When he wrote that "one can escape tragic emotion only if one has learned to transform the individual into the universal,"[56] Mondrian was reporting his own necessity.

Individuals, in Mondrian's view, are better able to strive beyond the tragic than society at large. Nonetheless, he was deeply committed to a social philosophy and often said that his art represented the abstract of the new society for which he hoped: it pointed the way, foreshadowed, inspired a new and compassionate social order—at least for those who understood his art. "Painting achieved . . . what the new mentality has yet to realize in outward life,"[57] he wrote while the Great War still raged on. In 1930, he continued to propose his art as a paradigm, as in this description of promising features in contemporary life, which is really a description of his art:

> Today's mentality is . . . moving toward a life that is optimistic yet serious, manifesting in everything clarity, certainty, precision, equity, straightness, speed associated with stability, and above all, truth.[58]

"The day will come," he wrote in the years when the Depression was undermining Europe, "when the individual will be capable of governing himself. The new art demonstrates all this."[59] Wonderfully cavalier, this last assertion—but it notifies us that throughout his later years Mondrian adhered to a concept of the moral function of art which was deeply Platonic in character. It was similarly censorious. The forbidden musical modes of Plato's *Republic*—those that tend to damage the moral growth of the individual—are comparable to Mondrian's "morphoplastic art" and "pathetic lyricism," pejorative terms with which he described most contemporary art.

A corollary follows from Mondrian's view that the new art presages a new social order: if the new art teaches society what to be and what order to establish, then the new art will gradually cease to be distinct from the new society that evolves under its influence. Art, in other words, will come to an end—easel painting and sculpture will be absorbed into an environment modeled after them. "Art will merge into real life."[60] He generally wrote of this merging and disappearance as a prospect for the remote future, but in a letter to Laszlo Moholy-Nagy in 1939, when Moholy was gathering faculty for the New Bauhaus in Chicago, Mondrian offered his services as "an artist but an artist *free from 'art,'*" saying that "pictures, sculptures, decoration are of no use in the new life and are an obstacle to realizing it now in the present."[61] Apparently, the end of art was a distant event for humanity as a whole, but might already be approaching on the scale of the individual and select institutions.

Mondrian's "end of art" reflects both his philosophical concern for unity and a sound recognition that his own art had much to contribute to architecture. Beyond this, however, the theme reflects a myth-making tendency. Perhaps it should be viewed as an artist's version of the Marxian myth of the withering of the state. Curiously, this odd passage in his thought had a vigorous afterlife in the polemical writings of the American painter Ad Reinhardt, and it affected the development of Minimal Art—an art that also saw itself as a termination.

MONDRIAN'S ART

Were I allowed just two exhibits in a court of law where the worth of twentieth-century art was on trial, I would choose Matisse's bronze relief *Backs* (see chapter 15) and Mondrian's sequence of trees from his formative years 1909 to 1913, when his great and narrow formula had not yet been achieved. They demonstrate with astonishing precision the forced march from a somewhat realistic vision based on nineteenth-century art to a new abstract vision that is truly the work of artist-metaphysicians. The words "forced march" reflect the pressure of internal necessity, as Kandinsky would say, obliging these artists and the generation to which they belonged to move on from the familiar into a new territory of imagination, thought, and feeling. At its best, as in these series by Matisse and Mondrian, the art of our time bears comparison with the art of any time.

But the case needs to be argued fairly from the evidence. Mondrian's *Red Tree* of 1909–10 (Fig. 12) can begin the series. Reminiscent of Van Gogh in its brushwork and expansive tension (as if the tree's wiry branches push against the air), *The Red Tree* also draws from the nearly contemporaneous color conceptions of Matisse and his Fauve companions. These historical references plot the shared starting point of a development that quickly moved toward individual research. *The Red Tree* has great appeal, although one has to know the works that follow from it to interpret the early signs of Mondrian's developed vision. The entanglement of Nature is secretly beginning to respond to a force of simplification which draws the branches out horizontally and vertically, just as the infinite variety of natural color has been reduced to a dramatic contrast between heavenly cool blue and earthy fire-red. One has, too, the impression that differences—land, tree, sky—are melting into one another; the branches at the upper right, for example, acquire a billowing, cloud-like form as they continue up and out of the picture. The tree divides, curiously, between a more natural rendering on the left and a visionary rendering on the right, where clustered

12. Piet Mondrian. *The Red Tree,* 1909–10. Oil on canvas. 27⁹/₁₆″ × 39″. Gemeentemuseum, The Hague.

branches rise toward a faintly suggested sun while others dip toward the earth. There is a passage from left to right, from mere Nature to more than Nature. Within the painting, visually delightful in itself, hide Mondrian's questions and his search for the transcendental pattern into which all life falls. *The Red Tree* is an eloquent example of art that investigates Nature and self, physical fact and metaphysical pattern simultaneously.

Dating to 1910–11, an image on the same theme (Fig. 13) charts Mondrian's further meditations on the arcing rise and fall of vital energy and the power of a central axis to support its passage. In this image, the central trunk is firmly rooted in the earth. Some of the tree's branches stray into the upper region of the picture and move on out, but the composition as a whole sets aside the "question" of the hidden sun toward which the branches in *The Red Tree* found their way. This is a strong composition, symbolizing the cycle of human life and our rootedness in the earth. A comparable drawing from the same years introduced the rational rectilinear grid of Cubism, against which the drama is played out. In time, this grid would supplant the natural im-

13. Piet Mondrian. *Tree,* 1910–11. Chalk on paper. 22¼″ × 33¼″. Gemeente-museum, The Hague.

14. Piet Mondrian. *Gray Tree,* 1912. Oil on canvas. 30¹⁵⁄₁₆″ × 42⅜″. Ge-meentemuseum, The Hague.

age altogether and become the sole object of Mondrian's pictorial meditations.

Gray Tree of 1912 (Fig. 14) is a magnificent work, cool in color but dramatic in design. Mondrian has adopted the Cubist reinterpretation of space, which acquires here the quality of flat scales or mosaic chips occupying the zones between branches. To the horizontal arc of the heaviest branches and the steady vertical axis of the trunk, he has added a new rendering of the sky presaged by *The Red Tree:* its energies billow down in wide arcs that seem both to weigh on the tree and to allow its uppermost branches to penetrate. We are witnessing a dramatic encounter between earth energies and another energy descending from the heights. *Gray Tree* is a Tree of Life, an archetype to which virtually all cultures since ancient times have paid homage. It is the axis of encounter and merging between higher and lower, and its fruitfulness is the sign of the riches that derive from this encounter.

A later work of 1912, *Flowering Apple Tree* (Fig. 15), continues Mondrian's adaptation of the Cubist language and brings to fruition the metaphysical poetry of *Gray Tree*. Mondrian's language is now an extraordinarily gentle restatement of Cubism, here yielding one of the masterworks of the spiritual in twentieth-century art. From above, an insistent but almost immaterial down-draft enters the world of the picture along its central axis. From below, the tree—transformed into a pattern of tinted light—lifts itself toward the sky along the same central axis. In the zone of encounter between higher and lower, billowing arcs and a few light horizontals create an impression of movement and mutual absorption. Half-effaced behind the image, and in some areas integrated into the image itself, a Cubist grid provides a stable, measured context for the play of universal forces.

"As above, so below," wrote Hermes Trismegistus, the Egyptian author (or authors) of antiquity whose works were familiar to the Theosophists of Mondrian's era. Mondrian was surely not attempting to "illustrate" Hermetic doctrine, but he created an icon that makes the doctrine live before one's eyes. The spiritual in art is no more than this, and no less: an idea of vast scope conveyed through an image, not a word, complete in itself, not an illustration but an illumination.

Flowering Apple Tree and a handful of related works from 1912 completed and fulfilled Mondrian's study of the metaphysical expressiveness of natural form. He quested beyond the discoveries of that year. Had I been *Ministre de Culture* at the time, I would have asked him to consider exploring this icon for a year or two more. He moved

15. Piet Mondrian. *Flowering Apple Tree,* 1912. Oil on canvas. 30¾" × 41¾". Gemeentemuseum, The Hague.

instead toward a new, more abstract language. *Oval Composition (Trees)* of 1913 (Fig. 16) literally melts the previous harmony of forms, colors, and recognitions to achieve . . . at that moment, he surely didn't know quite what.

This painting becomes visible when viewed as a mobile, vibrating field rather than as a stationary image. It depicts a tree, yet not a tree; autumnal leaves filled with ricocheting light, yet not leaves at all. The image resists being perceived as natural form, asks instead to be seen as an abstract depiction of forces. A vibrant central axis extending from the bottom to the top of the oval becomes less material as it moves upward and merges with the stepped linear pattern that seems to float slowly downward. Darting brushwork breaks up the already loosely patterned network, so that the eye tends to keep moving inside the image, resting nowhere for long. Following the lead of Picasso and Braque, Mondrian has set his rectilinear composition within a complementary oval frame, the image thinning as it approaches the edge as if

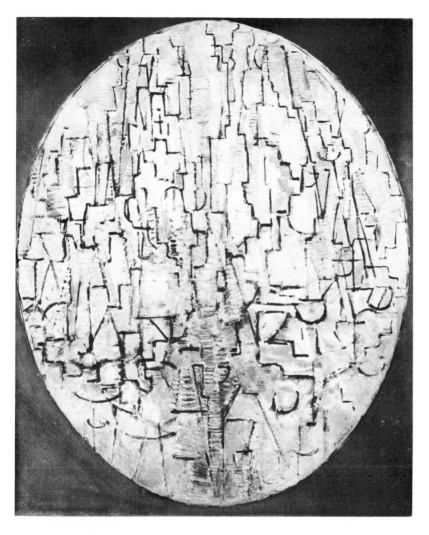

16. Piet Mondrian. *Oval Composition (Trees)*, 1913. Oil on canvas. 36⅝″ × 30¾″. Stedelijk Museum, Amsterdam.

the intense drama at the center dissipates energy centrifugally.

This work brings to mind Mondrian's idea of the tragic. "There is no escaping the *tragic*," he wrote, "so long as our *vision of nature is naturalistic*. That is why a deeper vision is essential." [62]

> Because it is part of the whole, the new spirit cannot free itself entirely from the tragic. The *New Plastic,* expressing the vital *reality of the abstract,* has not entirely freed itself from the tragic but it has ceased to be dominated by it. [63]

Even its title, *Oval Composition (Trees),* reflects Mondrian's movement of escape from the tragedy of Nature to the liberating spirit of abstraction. A new art is emerging, undoing the old.

In this chapter we cannot chart the many stages of Mondrian's art between 1913 and 1921, the year in which he crystallized the spare and beautiful pictorial formula which was to preoccupy him to the end of his life. One of those stages, the "pier and ocean" studies of the years around 1914, produced a series of austere masterpieces which are fully part of the spiritual in twentieth-century art. We should look, however, at the developed formula, the classic Mondrian painting which in the artist's lifetime was little prized by the world but now enjoys such prestige that it has become a commonplace—and difficult to see with fresh eyes. How hard it is to see the painting and not the "Mondrian," although he was among the most impersonal of artists of our time, single-mindedly interested in "bringing the universal downward" and effacing the person who serves as its vehicle.

One such painting is illustrated in Fig. 17. The elements with which Mondrian worked in these years were red, yellow, blue, black, white, gray, and rectilinear bands of differing thicknesses, always positioned differently from one composition to the next. No more, and at times much less because he often worked with fewer colors. As many observers have pointed out, these canvases appear to have a machine-like precision when reproduced on the printed page; in reality, the paintings are softened by the artist's visible brushwork and occasional *pentimenti* (changes that remain visible in the underpainting of a canvas). On the other hand, Mondrian has written that the artist

> is constantly obliged to weary himself with technique and execution; and this effort more or less dilutes the universal with his individuality. . . . *Exact* plastic demands *exact* means. What could be

17. Piet Mondrian. *Composition 2, 1922.* Oil on canvas. 21⅞″ × 21⅛″. Solomon R. Guggenheim Museum, New York. Photo: Robert E. Mates.

more exact than mechanically produced materials? The new art needs adept technicians.[64]

Obviously, Mondrian did not derive the satisfaction from his handwork that later generations would.

A work such as the one illustrated defies commentary when one stands before it. The viewer is struck by the asymmetrical balance of the composition; one may find oneself reading the balance with the eyes and almost physically testing its "rightness" against what the body knows of balance. One absorbs the placement and weight of colors,

one measures subtle differences in hue between one white panel and
another, one gray and another. The icon is simple, and it simplifies the
willing viewer. At best it is magical, an excerpt from another world or
its essential pattern.

And yet it is fixed, enormously fixed. Personally, I miss the "tragic,"
the challenge of Nature and the turbulent or gentle exchange of energies that appeared in his earlier work. Was his art at that earlier stage
more whole—moved both by the universal and by the particular, the
splendor of Nature and the intuition of a simple order that transcends
it? I feel so—without presuming to "judge" Mondrian's later work,
which had enormous impact on design and architecture, and which
deserves acknowledgment in itself.

Human wholeness is a perpetual challenge. Something approaching
wholeness can be achieved by draining one's personal reality of its
wilder energies and its vulnerability to disorder, but it is a diminished
wholeness. Mondrian's classic canvases have something in common
with shields: they are bright, rather hard surfaces. In his very last
years, the New York years, Mondrian himself began to break up the
pattern of his classic formula in the celebrated *Broadway Boogie
Woogie* of 1942−43 and other canvases. A fearless energy entered his
work; new ideas were stirring.

Mondrian's writings on the meaning of his classic paintings stand at a
considerable distance from the works themselves. It is difficult to
imagine that any viewer could reconstruct his ideas purely from acquaintance with the paintings. Mondrian himself often insisted that
his art evolved in part "unconsciously," by which he meant that in the
studio over many years he intuitively discovered the formula which his
writings were intended to clarify.

> . . . The layman is justified in asking for an immediate explanation
> of the new art, and it is logical for the artist, *after creating* the new
> art, to try to become *conscious* of it.[65]

The primary terms in his writings that directly describe his art are
dynamic equilibrium, equivalence, opposition, and *the new plastic.*
Mondrian believed that in individual history, as in world history, there
is an unfolding toward unity and balance, driven by the very nature of
man. This unity, under the conditions of daily life, is neither static nor
symmetrical. On the contrary, the dualities with which life is filled will
at best come together in a state that Mondrian called dynamic equi-

librium, a precise balance of disparate and even opposed elements. He believed that Nature is constantly demonstrating this essential law of equipoise, but in a veiled manner that the visionary artist translates into a determinate, precise notation in form and color. Similarly, the maturing inner life of a human being demonstrates the law of "constant contrast" and constant recovery of balance. For this, too, the visionary artist seeks a suitable notation, discovering as he does so that it can be identical to the notation for the essential law prevailing in Nature. A true expression of the inner and outer law will be simple enough to encompass both, and it will derive great beauty from the beauty of the universal, now perceived without the vagueness and veiling characteristic of the natural order. "The man of the past," wrote Mondrian, is an "unbalanced whole." Continually maturing and growing, man achieves understanding of the *"equilibrated whole"* and becomes capable of revealing the new spirit.[66]

> The desire for freedom and equilibrium (harmony) is inherent in man (due to the universal in him). Man has an inherent urge to regain the original unity of his duality. . . .[67]

As a notation for all active, masculine forces, Mondrian evolved the vertical line; as a notation for all receptive, feminine forces, he evolved the horizontal line. He could then abstractly represent all oppositions without exception—the entire fabric of life—by perpendicular meetings of vertical and horizontal lines. Curved lines and diagonals were subsumed by the vertical and horizontal, which Mondrian took to imply them and thus render them unnecessary. Designing with perpendiculars alone need never become dry and schematic, he thought, because the artist's subjectivity constantly varies the scheme in accord with personal intuition. "Bringing the universal downward," the artist uses a linear notation corresponding to objective, universal law, but in a manner that is his or her own.

Through studio practice and subsequent reflections, Mondrian subjected the pictorial elements of color and space to a similar analysis. Just as an equivalent for all oppositions without exception is to be found in perpendicular design, so too the essence of all colors and the essential drama of their interactions is to be found in the primary colors red, yellow, and blue. These colors contain all others by implication, and their presence in the new art is taken as a revelation of the nature of color rather than as a limiting austerity. Similarly, Mondrian noted that the simple series white, gray, black communicates the essential impression of space. To this he joined the perception, long before formalized in color theory, that planes of red, yellow, and blue give differing impressions of recession in space: a blue plane will appear to be deeper and more distant, yellow more shallow and closer to the viewer.

Through these limited means, Mondrian believed that he could express the fullness and infinite variety of dynamic equilibrium, the harmonious coming together of oppositions into unity. His mature work is not a picture of Nature, but of the nature of Nature both in ourselves and in all things.

The foregoing summary of the ideas closest to Mondrian's art can be capped by a passage from one of his last writings:

> It has become progressively clearer that the plastic expression of true reality is attained through dynamic movement in equilibrium. Plastic art affirms that equilibrium can only be established through the balance of unequal but equivalent oppositions. The clarification of equilibrium through plastic art is of great importance for humanity. It reveals that although human life in time is doomed to disequilibrium, notwithstanding this, it is based on equilibrium. It demonstrates that equilibrium can become more and more living in us.
>
> Reality only appears to us tragical because of the disequilibrium and confusion of its appearances. It is our subjective vision and determined position which make us suffer. . . . But we can escape the tragical oppression through a clear vision of true reality, which exists, but which is veiled. If we cannot free *ourselves,* we can free our *vision.*[68]

The last sentence is touching in its witness to the artist's and every seeker's dilemma: the disparity between what is known at the height of consciousness and what imposes itself in daily life. "The man of complete daylight will conquer night,"[69] Mondrian once wrote, but he knew that freedom is expensive. Even to free his vision cost him a lifetime of work.

> All individual thought is dissolved in universal thought, as all form is dissolved in the universal plastic means of Abstract-Real painting.[70]

This is the sound of Mondrian's mantra, words addressed to himself, but also beyond himself to the Order that he seized lightly in his art and massively in his writings.

The poetry of Mondrian is unique, both on canvas and on paper. It reaches for the heights of understanding, but cautiously; it gives us a bright and simple icon for the law of things, but surrounds it with excessive philosophizing. He tells us, both in his writings and in his art, a very great deal about what the artist-metaphysician of our time must be. To evade his example, difficult as it is in some respects, is to evade the possibility. His simple, profoundly optimistic art and the writings that demonstrate its intentions form a major part of the spiritual charter of twentieth-century art. "Let us now perform the work of daylight."[71]

7 ORPHISM: GIVING ALL TO THE SUN

Orphism was declared to exist virtually by fiat, without consulting the artists in question, by Apollinaire in the fall of 1912.[1] Pablo Picasso, Robert Delaunay, Fernand Léger, Francis Picabia, and Marcel Duchamp were the beneficiaries of this critical insight, while František Kupka—as much "Orphist" as any—went strangely unmentioned in Apollinaire's published account of the new trend. Most of the artists shrugged off the title; Duchamp, for example, was an Orphist for one month. A trial rubric, improvised to confer order on the ever-changing avant-garde, Orphism has in fact survived as a designation for the work of a number of artists in the years just before the world war. What Apollinaire perceived, accurately, was a new art that had learned from Cubism but was not Cubism, an art that dared to be fully abstract. Its raison d'être was different for different artists—Delaunay's almost ecstatic perceptions of light and color moved toward an art less austere and fussy than Cubism, while Kupka's search (like Kandinsky's) led away from Nature toward expression of the "intimate events, the 'soul' of the artist-creator."[2] This chapter will focus on Delaunay and Kupka, each of whom has earned a place in the spiritual history of twentieth-century art. Their art *was* briefly magical, Orphic. Lines from Apollinaire's poetry capture something of their intensity and their darker side, which much affected their art as time went on:

> I have given all to the sun
> All but my shadow[3]

ROBERT DELAUNAY: LET US SEEK TO SEE

Robert Delaunay (1885–1941) is remembered for four series of paintings from the years before World War I, of which two possess enduring potency: the *Windows* and the *Sun and Moon* series. The serial work that preceded them—variations on a church interior and images of the Eiffel Tower—is energetic but a little ungainly; it prepared the way. For reasons unclear, Delaunay's art was strong, original, and touching only in the years between 1912 and 1914. He was still searching for his art before these years, and thereafter gradually lost not skill but vision. He might be compared to the type of desert plant that flowers once; but it remains a mystery why certain artists discover and convey a powerful vision and then subside, often without knowing of the change. Biography might well reveal the specific circumstances determining these extinguishments. In general, they seem to occur when gifted people become bored. Unable to move on to another or deeper insight, in some cases unwilling to repeat themselves, they capitulate. Delaunay continued working but never recaptured either the musical delicacy of his *Windows* or the vigor of cosmological imagination in the *Sun and Moon* series.

Delaunay went to school with the Neo-Impressionists for an understanding of color, and with the Cubists for an understanding of form. In 1912 he was able to synthesize what he had assimilated into an original and quietly powerful vision. The influence of Georges Seurat's brilliant Divisionist technique, aided and abetted by scientific color theory, led Delaunay to his lifelong concern with the "simultaneous contrast of colors." The concept was borrowed from the nineteenth-century color theorist Michel-Eugène Chevreul, who explained it in simple and approachable terms:

> If we look simultaneously upon two stripes of different tones of the same color, or upon two stripes of the same tone of different colors placed side by side . . . the eye perceives certain modifications which in the first place influence the intensity of color, and in the second, the optical composition of the two juxtaposed colors respectively.[4]

In Delaunay's art, his attention to simultaneous contrast is clear and expressive; in his writings, it is otherwise. "Simultaneity" became both slogan and mantra, indicating the power of color to convey a wealth of impressions through interactions, as well as a mélange of other values and meanings rarely sorted out. No matter. The word will recur and perhaps clarify as we examine his art and writings.

Close to the Cubists and an intimate friend of Apollinaire's, Delaunay absorbed the lessons of Cubist construction but never accepted the austere coloration of early Cubism. In the series of *Windows*, virtually abstract views of Paris painted in 1912–13, Delaunay retained the complex planar construction of early Cubism but freely introduced the full spectrum of colors. The black-and-white illustration (Fig. 18) included here conveys nothing of the warm oranges and reds, cool blues and violets, and light-saturated yellows that make this painting and others of its kind a discreetly glowing mosaic of color.

Still, its compositional genius is evident: a dynamic balance between a stable rectilinear grid and a series of prominent diagonals. At the upper center, a form reminiscent of the Eiffel Tower organizes the upward movement of many of the diagonals, while other diagonals move through the image like shafts of light, seemingly descending rather than ascending. At the lower center, a pair of small rectangles reads as windows seen from a distance, while diagonals evoke the eaves of gabled roofs. Like the suggestion of the Eiffel Tower (conveyed largely through its characteristic profile), these familiar yet nearly abstract elements offer a small anchor for the viewer's eyes and mind. We know where we are, but the scene has been transmuted by energies of light and color into a vision rather than a report.

One further element of Delaunay's visual poetry should be noted. The color planes are not dense and therefore do not come to the surface of the canvas as if it were a checkerboard. On the contrary, the color planes are airy, open, and suffused with light; they create a sense of space. The "materiality" of the image is highly refined—air and light, nothing heavier.

Few twentieth-century paintings suggest with such a gentle touch the interpenetration of this material world and another. This is Paris, but Paris bathed in quite another light, all traces of squalor or pride erased. The City of Light is rendered as such. Further, the planar design of the painting is simple enough to make each part easily perceptible but complex enough that the viewer never feels definitively oriented—one's eyes are always moving on. The balance between simple and complex, stability and movement, quiets the mind: the dual experience of movement and tranquility seems, enigmatically, to fulfill its needs. Similarly, color strikes a balance between brightness and muted reticence; there is life but no exaggeration, drama but also calm, vitality obedient to the internal order of the picture.

One of the tasks of the spiritual in art is to prove again and again that vision is possible: that this world, thick and convincing, is neither the only world nor the highest, and that our ordinary awareness is neither the only awareness nor the highest of which we are capable. Traditionally, this task falls under a stringent rule: the vision cannot be random and entirely subjective, but must be capable of touching a common chord in many men and women.

18. Robert Delaunay. *Window*, 1912. Gouache on cardboard-backed canvas. 17¾″ × 14½″. Musée de Grenoble. Copyright ARS NY/ADAGP 1987.

Like much twentieth-century art that reaches for impressions of another world or of this world transfigured—rendered as we feel it when we love it most and have greatest confidence—Delaunay's painting shows little trace of formal theology or spirituality. Like many seekers at the time, he was probably aware of the Hermetic formula, "As above, so below," which we found reflected in Mondrian's kindred studies of trees; but this is hardly the "text" of the painting. Delaunay's articles and correspondence in his best years were often written in an odd, additive language of juxtaposition, as if perceptions crowded richly in, taxing his ability to set them in order. They were not erudite, far from it. Something had opened him to Light (he occasionally capitalized the word in his writings to add to its dignity), and for the few years when the opening was fresh in him, his art moved well ahead of his thought, which stumbled behind trying to convey in faltering words what he knew to be so.

In 1912, he initiated a second series of works destined to develop magnificently. Delaunay may well have owed a debt to Kupka for the conception, but he brought to it a joyousness and clarity very much his own. *Simultaneous Contrasts: Sun and Moon* of 1912–13 (Fig. 19) is perhaps the strongest and most complex of the series, a provisional, somewhat improvised, and yet persuasive metaphysical poem. Delaunay's worlds in these years were the city of Paris and, it seems, the universe itself. ". . . Reality is endowed with *Vastness,*" he wrote in 1912,

> (we see as far as the stars). . . . Human vision is endowed with the greatest *Reality,* since it comes to us directly from the contemplation of the Universe.[5]

From a catchall of sources—astronomical imagery, homemade experiments with the *camera oscura,* fascination with new street lamps on the Boulevard Saint-Michel, the segmented wheels of color theory publications, the patchy, vibrant brushwork of Cubism—Delaunay created an exuberant vision of the cosmos, tumbling with light and energy yet orderly enough to be understood in terms of the familiar idea of the One and the Many.

"The goal of painting," he wrote in 1917, "is to represent the Universe."[6] In the universe of *Sun and Moon,* the sun at upper left must be the source of light, but like the crowd of wheeling, spiraling, shimmering colors in the right half of the painting, it is caught up in dynamic movement. Pressured by blue and green forms, ringed around by a

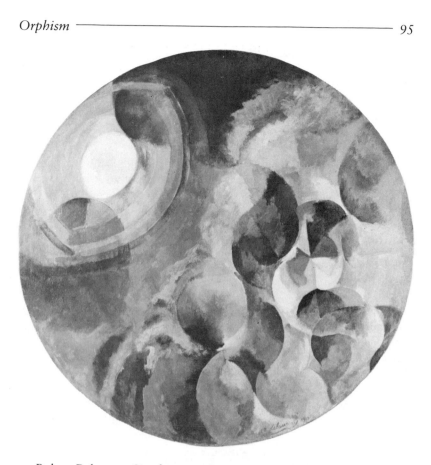

19. Robert Delaunay. *Simultaneous Contrasts: Sun and Moon,* 1913 (dated on painting 1912). Oil on canvas. 53″ diameter. Collection, The Museum of Modern Art, New York. Mrs. Simon Guggenheim Fund. Copyright ARS NY/ADAGP 1987.

partial rainbow as if seen through a refracting lens, this visionary sun is separated from its tumultuous progeny by a cool swath of blue that reads as space and atmosphere. The work as a whole is a hymn to light and color, but also to a simple order that can be jostled incessantly without losing its integrity.

Sun and Moon is an abstract work only in the sense that it relates the microphenomena of color, light, and refraction to the macrophenomena of world-order, skipping over the intervening world of objects, people, and landscape. The direction found by Delaunay in these naive metaphysical works would prove of enduring interest to twentieth-century artists. As suggested in chapter 2, abstraction became a means through which we can compellingly state—some artists would prefer the word *discover*—intuitions of order and disorder, insights into the design of self and world. Like mathematics, abstraction must be studied to be understood, and it permits general statements of far-reaching implication. Delaunay was among the first to discover these possibilities.

In medieval Europe and many traditional religious cultures, art included diagrams. Its task was not only (often not at all) to depict local realities, but to make vivid diagrams of larger realities and the divinities at work in them. Hence the great encyclopedic portals of medieval churches, the complex psychocosmic maps (mandalas) of Hindu and Buddhist art, and the diagrammatic sand paintings of American Indian art. In post-medieval Europe, the fine arts and the art of diagrams split off from one another: diagrams increasingly became vehicles of scientific communication, while the fine arts concentrated on rendering natural appearances in various accomplished styles, ranging from the meticulous realism of the early Flemish masters to the flickering poetry of light of the Impressionists. The fine arts cultivated techniques for creating the illusion of depth in painting, while scientific diagrams were generally two-dimensional renderings on a page. The fine arts pursued beauty; diagrams pursued accuracy and clarity, although many were beautiful because skilled artisans fashioned them.

The distinction between fine art and diagram does not imply that later European art was incapable of conveying religious and speculative content; it was, and with great power. But for centuries the unique ability of diagrams to plot the structure and internal relations of a "system" and to provide a sign rather than an illusion was absent from mainstream European art. It was largely confined to science and to certain byways of art such as heraldry, allegorical emblems, and the illustration of speculative works such as those of Robert Fludd, Jakob Boehme, and alchemists.

Delaunay, Kupka, and other pioneering artists (among them Marcel Duchamp) spontaneously reunited these two streams of representation. They were able to perceive in the color wheels of nineteenth-century scientific publications a new vocabulary for the exploration of color, light, and cosmos in the context of easel painting. Readmission of the diagram to the fine arts accompanied and supported the rebirth of a speculative, philosophical art. Artists, like scientists, could now take the measure of things in general and fashion signs of the unseen. If the goal of art is to represent the universe, as Delaunay believed, adequate means are required to do so; Delaunay was among those who provided them.

What he could not provide was a fully adequate way of thought to accompany the images. His best-known article, "Light," often makes difficult reading:

> Light in Nature creates color-movement. Movement is provided by relationships of *uneven measures,* of color contrasts among themselves that make up *Reality.* This reality . . . becomes *rhythmic simultaneity.* Simultaneity in light is the *harmony,* the *color rhythms* which give birth to *Man's sight. . . . Let us seek to see. . . . The synchromatic movement (simultaneity) of light,* which is *the only reality.*[7]

A passage from another version of the same article speaks more clearly:

> . . . When light expresses itself completely, all is color. Painting is in fact a luminous language.[8]

The following excerpt from a letter of 1912 to Franz Marc clarifies his preference for workshop discipline—the artisan's *métier*—over sophistication of thought.

> In Art I am the enemy of disorder. The word "art" means harmony for me. I never speak of *mathematics* and never bother with the Spirit. Everything I say is relevant to my craft and is consequently connected to results. . . . None of the finite sciences has anything to do with my passion for light. My only science is the choice of impressions that the light in the universe furnishes to my consciousness as an artisan, which I try, by imposing an Order, an Art, an appropriate representative life, to organize. . . . I have a purpose, an artistic belief that is unique and that cannot be classified without risking becoming ponderous. I love poetry because it is higher than psychology. But I love painting more because I love light and clarity and it calms me.[9]

Delaunay's insistence on craft served him and other speculative artists of our time as a means of remaining true to sensation and body, despite the appeal of what some called "literature"—talking too much. Paint and brushes and solvents are excellent tools—and a liberating focus—for a searching spirit that does not wish to be bound by its own capacity for explanation. Willing of course to speak and write at length about art, Delaunay nonetheless knew that his work evolved directly from visual sensation and from his painter's hands, from *métier* and not from thought. "I never bother with the Spirit" is both true and false—true because he did not value abstruse or mystical words about the spirit, false because his vision encompassed a larger world than the everyday and continues to invite us to see. "Let us seek to see," he wrote—simple words, a caption for the work of his clairvoyant years.

The later years were active, thoroughly committed to art, yet in hindsight disappointing. Collaborating with his gifted artist wife Sonia, he was interested in applying his aesthetic to "sculpture, furniture, architecture, books, posters, dresses, etc. etc." [10] He had wider ambitions than in years past but a stiffer style, a lifeless reflection of his early achievements. And style is the man, in art; it registers what one is. Somewhere here is the "shadow" that Delaunay refused to give the sun. On balance, it hardly matters; his work of 1912–14 is permanent.

FRANTIŠEK KUPKA: THE REALM
OF RHYTHMS AND SIGNS

František Kupka (1871–1957) is a difficult artist. For all the documentation and interpretation that has surrounded his work since his death, he remains difficult to know and rather difficult to appreciate. Virginia Spate, one of his recent critics, described his style, "with its coarse colors and its lingering debt to Art Nouveau," as "not a sympathetic one." [11]

> . . . one is uncertain how to approach Kupka's paintings, for he gave no information as to their possible esoteric meaning, and must therefore have believed that if one contemplated their curiously immaterial dynamism, one would intuitively become conscious of their internal meaning. . . . [12]

Her reservations are my own—yet he belongs here. Kupka was a pioneer in the development of abstract art and an authentic spiritual seeker. The difficulties of his art are exemplary in the old-fashioned sense that we can learn from them. The intensity of his quest and its premises are impressive, although his art, apart from some relatively early canvases, often seems tense and strangely dour.

The material on which an American reader can conveniently draw to understand Kupka's art is not quite in order. While some of his writings are available in French or English, his most important longer writing, published in Czech, has not yet been translated into any of the languages commonly used in international scholarship. Living in France in the years before World War I, Kupka drafted a substantial manuscript, *La création dans les arts plastiques,* which was translated and published in his native Czechoslovakia in 1923. While the manuscript underlying the book was apparently confiscated by the Gestapo in the next war and lost from sight, a number of earlier French drafts have survived and proved helpful to scholars. Unable to obtain copies of the French manuscripts or to read Czech, I have relied on the publications of scholars fortunate enough to have been able to study one or the other.

Born in the eastern Bohemian town of Opočno in 1871, his father a civil servant, Kupka was apprenticed at an early age to a saddlemaker. This artisan was also a "spiritist" who conducted séances to which the boy was invited, and in time Kupka began serving as a medium—an activity that he is known to have continued into early adulthood and is said to have continued throughout his life. These circumstances may seem strange to us, but according to the Czech scholar Ludmila Vachtová eastern Bohemia had a long sectarian history, and séances and such were not all that unusual. The intense interest in spiritism in Western Europe and the United States in those decades and thereafter was chronicled by the well-known *Président d'Honneur de la Fédération Spirite Internationale,* Arthur Conan Doyle, in his *History of Spiritualism* (London, 1926). We have come across the same interest in early Theosophy.

As a boy, Kupka was spontaneously drawing and painting. Some thoughtful parental surrogates—he was little related to his own family—sent him to a provincial school for crafts, from which he later went on to the Prague School of Fine Arts. On the strength of scholarships and earnings from drawing lessons, he remained four years and acquired strong studio skills while reading widely and catching up with his peers who had enjoyed a classical early education. Vachtová alludes to dark episodes owing to the strains of his mediumship— "nervous breakdowns." In any event, he successfully moved on to the School of Fine Arts in Vienna, where he found the curriculum dull but Viennese culture lively. He was reading Nietzsche, Schopenhauer, and Paracelsus, astrology, alchemy, and Theosophy, Plato and the Vedas. He was also educating himself in the natural sciences, including astronomy, which he pursued later in Paris and which found its way into his mature art. He spent time at the countercultural art colony of Karl Diefenbach, a figure mocked by some as the "Kohlrabi Apostle." It was here that Kupka adopted his lifelong practice of exercising unclothed in his private garden in any weather, with sunbaths when possible and a cold shower. An artist's exercise regimen is generally not worth mentioning, but in Kupka's case he apparently pursued it with a cultist's vigor.

By the time he settled in Paris in 1896, Kupka had collected much the same education and values as Kandinsky: sound technical training as a painter, a broad liberal education, and an affiliation with the alternative culture that united Asian thought, speculative currents of Western thought, and practical disciplines ranging from meditation to exercising in the sun. These ingredients, however blended in individual lives, figure among the raw materials from which the abstract vision emerged.

Kupka's early work to the year 1908 varies in character from Symbolist paintings, at times of Theosophical inspiration, to angry but fluent satirical drawings for anarchist and other publications. There were also serene works such as a 1905 portrait of Eugénie, who became his wife and lifelong companion. It was while painting a placid domestic motif—his skinny young stepdaughter naked in a sunny garden, with a ball in her outstretched hand—that Kupka seems to have first encountered the imperious internal demand for a new vision. He appears to have halted work on the painting, and in the course of the years 1908 to 1909 he pushed the image of *Girl with a Ball* through multiple permutations. In pencil drawings it became in turn a dynamic swirl of circular forms, rough indications of lines of force, smoky marks indicating atmosphere rather than substance. Kupka was searching.

A small painting of 1909, nostalgically titled *The First Step* (Fig. 20), marks a new stage in Kupka's development. It is a work of considerable charm, almost a talisman of the fundamental health, curiosity, and imaginative powers animating his search. Kupka's vision changed over the next few years and lost much of the naive simplicity and quiet cheerfulness that appeared in this image; something of the child in him is visible here. Virginia Spate has speculated that this cosmic image, like Kandinsky's early work, owes a debt to the Theosophical idea of thought-forms (the Besant/Leadbeater study was published in Paris in 1905).[13] No one to my knowledge has established a detailed interpretation of this painting. Against a black ground, Kupka imagines a solar system of mysterious disks and rings, each differing from its neighbor. Eccentric and yet altogether recognizable, it is Kupka's first image of macrocosmic order, a theme to which he would return often in later years.

Toward the end of his life, Kupka spoke to the critic, J. P. Hodin, in terms that shed surprising light on this painting:

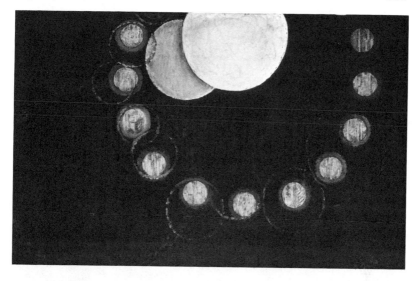

20. František Kupka. *The First Step,* 1910–13? (dated on painting 1909). Oil on canvas. 32¾″ × 51″. Collection, The Museum of Modern Art, New York. Hillman Periodicals Fund. Copyright ARS NY/ADAGP 1987.

> Painting is concrete—color, form, dynamics. What matters is invention. One must invent and then construct. . . . And you need no knowledge for it—physics or mathematics or geometry—no. The greatest artists were the most ignorant ones, but they had the spirit of believers: the Byzantine, the Romanesque artists, the masters of Chartres. . . .[14]

In some curious way, *The First Step* has "the spirit of a believer."

Denying late in life the relevance of learning, Kupka was nonetheless perennially studying in his strongest years. His knowledge of color theory underlies a series of works to which *The First Step* was prelude. Known under the general title *Disks of Newton,* they are well represented by the example from the Philadelphia Museum (Fig. 21). Kupka's transformation of color theory diagrams into a rotating, complex, genuinely spirited evocation of cosmos and light—the black-and-white illustration does not begin to do it justice—represents the high point of what might be called the naive phase of his work, a phase of mobile search without the hardening that often occurs when answers are attained or, on the contrary, doubt gains the upper hand. The image moves freely and glows, conveying sensations of ease and pleasure. It is, as much as any painting, an Orphic work of strong poetic

21. František Kupka. *Disks of Newton. Study for "Fugue in Two Colors,"* 1912. Oil on canvas. 39½" × 29". Philadelphia Museum of Art: Louise and Walter Arensberg Collection. Copyright ARS NY/ADAGP 1987.

appeal, sunny and confident, pitched to the scale of the cosmos and yet approachable.

Kupka intersects here and is generally thought to precede Delaunay. Their paintings projecting the humble color wheel out into the cosmos constitute, to my mind, an undeniable manifestation of the spiritual in art. Perhaps neither closely reasoned nor metaphysically elaborate, they are nonetheless a celebration of cosmos that can leave few untouched.

The abstract analysis of forms and forces embodied in Kupka's drawings on the theme of *Girl with a Ball,* fused with the cosmic imagery of *The First Step,* led on in these cardinal years of his search to *Amorpha, Fugue in Two Colors* (Fig. 22), first displayed at the Salon d'Automne in 1912. It may well have been this canvas that prompted Apollinaire to speak of an art of "new structures . . . created entirely by the artist himself." This painting, with the complementary *Vertical Planes III* [15] exhibited in the following year, stated Kupka's developed art and may well have sealed his fate in terms of an externally satisfying career. France, his adoptive home, was not ready for pure abstraction, and Kupka proved less agile than others—for example, Brancusi—in attracting foreign collectors and accepting that recognition would be slow in coming. His accomplishment paralleled that of Kandinsky in Germany and preceded both Malevich and Mondrian. It was a considerable and, needless to say, daring step to devise a fully abstract language and bring it before the public at a time when the quasi-abstraction of Cubism was still highly controversial. Alfred Barr, founding director of the Museum of Modern Art, seized the significance of Kupka's accomplishment in a 1936 catalogue. "Within a year's time," he wrote, "Kupka had painted what are probably the first geometrical curvilinear and the first rectilinear pure abstractions in modern art." [16]

Kupka himself spoke of "a realm of rhythms and signs" to shed light on his art:

> We have to try . . . to separate two incompatible elements, that is to say, the imitative work which today is superfluous, from art itself. This is a realm of rhythms and signs too abstract to be captured easily and which form the *leitmotif* of all compositions, the basic arabesque, a kind of framework which the painters . . . as of old fill with a vocabulary of forms taken from nature. If we sacrificed the intruding element we would of course have to face the danger of talking in an unusual language. Yet there is a kind of pictorial geometry of thought, the only possible one, which forces the painter to lie less. And that is what I am trying to achieve. [17]

22. František Kupka. *Amorpha, Fugue in Two Colors*, 1912. Oil on canvas. 83⅜″ × 86⅝″. Collection Národní Gallery, Prague. Copyright ARS NY/ADAGP 1987.

Some of this is arguable—surely there is more than one "geometry of thought"—but the gist is clear and helpful. *Amorpha, Fugue in Two Colors* remains nonetheless somewhat remote and opaque; it does not yield gracefully to interpretation as a symbolic statement encompassing both image and meaning. A complex red and blue band undulates across the canvas, against a simple ground of paired white disks and black areas implying cosmic space. The band, with its stretched cellular structure, evokes a dancing figure, as Washton Long has suggested, while the disks and surrounding darkness are tranquil. There is something here of a visual poem about the restless movement of life in a large and still cosmic setting. Yet it may not draw the viewer in. Unlike the *Disks of Newton,* with its whirling good cheer and confidence, there is a studied, chilly quality here. I find myself acknowledging the achievement without being touched by it.

Much the same can be said of *Vertical Planes III:* a pioneering work of abstraction bearing some relation to the Hermetic formula, "As above, so below," it is nonetheless chilly. We are in the realm of rhythms and signs—but somewhat adrift. Kupka's prescient exploration of abstraction is touched by some personal trait—some "shadow," in Apollinaire's terms—that rather saps it of joy and light.

In his highly creative years preceding World War I (in which he served with distinction), Kupka evolved a further image-type that laid the groundwork for later canvases. Bearing such titles as *Cosmic Spring* and *Creation,* these canvases depict highly colored, cloudlike forms, often arranged in numerous tiers on the model of the superstructure of a Hindu temple; one has the impression of looking into a mysterious cosmic space. This image-type relates back to certain Theosophical thought-form illustrations and shows some reliance on astronomical photography, but Kupka exaggerated little when he described these works as "created from scratch by the painter's poetic imagination." [18] He developed as well a series of complex geometric compositions which, roughly speaking, embody a complementary vocabulary.

Reclusive in his later years, subject to depression, and for the most part passed over by galleries and museums, Kupka nevertheless remained a productive artist. His wife lived to witness his belated recognition among critics and the public as a pioneer of abstract art and as an artist-metaphysician. "Yes, painting means clothing the processes of the human soul in plastic forms," he said in 1924, "[it means] to be a poet, a creator, to enrich life by new views." [19] And years earlier, in the French manuscript, he had written:

> It is by sounding the microcosm of our own being that we will find ways to extend the means of unveiling the most subtle states of the human soul: by "we" I mean the collective self. [20]

He was no less concerned to sound the macrocosm, the larger world beyond the human which he was convinced we mirror, as like to like. Kupka assembled the characteristic elements of the spiritual in abstract art: the personal inwardness, the "sense of the cosmos," the certainty of kinship between human nature and Great Nature, belief in the fruitfulness of an art based not on natural appearances but on something else, the "realm of rhythms and signs too abstract to be easily captured." He viewed the artist, at best, as "a priest of 'the other reality.'"[21] At his best, this he was.

8 MARCEL DUCHAMP: BURNING UP ALL AESTHETICS

Marcel Duchamp (1887–1968) was a legend in his own time, the adoptive father of many younger American artists after World War II. The second generation of the New York School (see chapter 17) and artists interested in Happenings, Conceptual Art, Process Art, and Pop Art drew much inspiration from Duchamp's revolutionary activities in the decade of 1913 to 1923, and from the living example of the man— quizzical, free spirited, iconoclastic without zeal. In the years since his death, critics have interpreted his work with impressive scholarship and insight.[1] An irresistible canonization has occurred which makes following Duchamp's own irreverent model all but impossible:

> The dead should not be permitted to be so much stronger than the living. We must learn to forget the past, to live our own lives in our own time.[2]

He, the great ironist, may hardly seem to belong in a book that deliberately avoids the sophistication of irony. Concepts of the spiritual in art may seem naive or dreamy in comparison with Duchamp's "burning up of all aesthetics."[3] Yet Duchamp had his own camouflaged naiveté. The purgative fire of a brilliant mind contended in him with the studied offhandedness of the perpetual *lycéen*, the precociously weary Parisian high school student. However he is taken, he cannot be dismissed. He was both a friend of the spiritual in art and a cool adversary.

Duchamp's denial of the conventions and pretensions of art, deeply intelligent and good-humored, has exerted a positive influence to this day. Yet his constructive gestures toward a new art strike me as incomplete, as great wit without great wisdom. His questioning is immensely attractive, remaining fresh and interesting to this day. But some of

his answers are dated—appropriate to their time, place, and his specific genius, but apt to encourage self-indulgent intellectuality in artists today.

Born in Normandy in 1887 and precocious beyond measure, he was
participating fully in the Parisian art world by the time he reached
twenty. His famous *Nude Descending a Staircase, No.* 2 became for
Americans the very symbol of Modernism when it was exhibited at the
New York Armory Show in 1913. That superbly energetic work, depicting a stiff man-machine paradoxically gliding down a staircase in
multiple images, demonstrates that Duchamp had already attained exceptional skills with paint and brush when he entered into a quite new
world of ideas and experiments.

Looking back many years later, he said:

> The basis of my . . . work during the years just before . . . 1915 was
> a desire to break up forms—to "decompose" them much along the
> lines the Cubists had done. But I wanted to go further—much fur-
> ther—in fact in quite another direction altogether.[4]

He was ready to "burn up all aesthetics," a powerful phrase from his
notes of the period. Some pervasive doubt, perhaps reinforced by the
precocious ease with which he had mastered the new language of art,
prompted him to ask in 1913: "Can one make works which are not
works of 'art'?"[5] A crisis of respect had come over him. Not just the
vulnerable academic art of the nineteenth century, which few bothered
any longer to defend, but also the aggressive, avant-garde arts of the
first years of the twentieth seemed wholly questionable to him. He
found himself responding to his doubts by experimenting with chance
as a creative agent. The first chance-governed work was a modest family affair: he jotted some musical notes on bits of paper, scrambled
them in a hat and, in whatever order they emerged, patched them into
a score which he and his sisters proceeded to sing. The operation of
chance offered a fascinating alternative to the convention-laden subjectivity of "art."

His second chance work entered the history of art as the *Three Standard Stoppages* of 1913–14 (Fig. 23). One peers at them respectfully
through a glass museum case—but what one is peering at makes no
sense without the story behind them. He recorded the concept in his
notes as follows:

3 Standard Stops =
    canned chance—

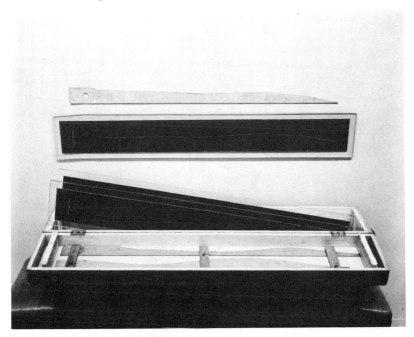

23. Marcel Duchamp. *Three Standard Stoppages,* 1913–14. Assemblage fitted into a wooden box measuring 11⅛″ × 50⅞″ × 9″. Collection, The Museum of Modern Art, New York. Katherine S. Dreier Bequest. Copyright ARS NY/ADAGP 1987.

The Idea of the Fabrication
—If a straight horizontal thread one meter long falls from a height of one meter straight on to a horizontal plane twisting *as it pleases* and creates a new image of the unit of length.—

—Regime of gravity—
Ministry of coincidences [6]

One is peering into a battered wooden box, resembling a musical instrument case, which contains a series of enigmatic items. The three lengths of string are there, glued just as they fell onto rectangles of canvas. The randomly curved profiles of the strings have been meticulously transferred to templates, thin wooden lathes that preserve the new measurements in more permanent form for future use (Duchamp would incorporate these shapes in later works). The box also houses a pair of true one-meter sticks, presumably for comparison with the eccentric measures he had generated.

Many years after performing this experiment with chance, Duchamp told an interviewer:

> That was really when I tapped the mainspring of my future. In itself it was not an important work of art, but for me it opened the way—the way to escape from those traditional methods of expression long associated with art. I didn't realize at the time exactly what I had stumbled on. . . . For me the *Three Stoppages* was a first gesture liberating me from the past.[7]

There is genius in the work, which consists not just of an "art object" suitable for exhibition, but of a concept, its execution, and a documentation. Duchamp's iconoclastic flair sent him right to one of the fundamentals of material culture, the measuring system, and prompted him to transfer his subversion of that system into the art "system" where it became another subversion—of the very idea of the aesthetic object. To the aesthetic and spiritual affirmations of the new art all around him, he opposed a wily negation that could only challenge and clarify. This act already binds him into the spiritual history of twentieth-century art as the devil's advocate, the Fool who is no fool.

Three Standard Stoppages is the root of innumerable Conceptual works in recent decades modeled on its eccentric concept, meticulous execution, and solemn documentation. Such works often enough have a touch of the idiot savant in them: they lavish enormous attention on trivia. Their psychology is complex. Conceptual artists seem to wish to be acutely aware of themselves working as artists. Duchamp-like, they also distrust the ideals and affirmations (of beauty, truth, inspired artistic personality) traditionally associated with art. The result is meticulously crafted works, documentation of the working process with an accountant's eye for detail, and deliberately trivial subject matter to which intricate intellectual operations have often been applied. It is a curious art, and sometimes saddening because it illustrates the failure of "the spiritual in art" to make a convincing case for itself among strong minds which quite rightly resist sentimental values. Conceptual artists prefer their own intricacies and solemn play to an unconvincing spirituality.

From 1913 forward, Duchamp continued his new line of questioning and art-making, from which emerged the Readymade. "I'm not at all sure," he said in later years, "that the concept of the Readymade isn't the most important single idea to come out of my work."[8] As many readers know, a Readymade is a found object which the artist works little (if at all) before declaring it to be a work of art. The first Readymade was a bicycle wheel on its stanchion, attached upside down to a four-legged stool. Another was a typical French bottle-dryer, a cone of progressively smaller metal hoops with multiple prongs. The Readymade from these early years that aroused the greatest notoriety was a urinal signed "R. Mutt 1917" and submitted to a New York exhibition of contemporary art under the title *Fountain*. A later work in the series that has imaginative appeal was his dust-breeding experiment: a pane of glass on which he had been working was allowed at length to gather dust, and was then photographed by Duchamp's friend, Man Ray. The resulting photograph, which documents this most ephemeral of Readymades, raises dust-balls to a larger place in the cosmic scheme of things. The concept of *breeding* dust implies a farmer's concern and a certain innocence; it is, of course, another reversal of values, witty and purgative.

Through these works and the interplay with the public which they aroused, Duchamp explored a series of ideas that he often explained in later years when questioned by younger critics and friends.

> In 1913 I had the happy idea to fasten a bicycle wheel to a kitchen stool and watch it turn.
>
> A few months later I bought a cheap reproduction of a winter evening landscape, which I called "Pharmacy" after adding two small dots, one red and one yellow, in the horizon.
>
> In New York in 1915 I bought at a hardware store a snow shovel on which I wrote "In Advance of the Broken Arm."
>
> It was around that time that the word "Readymade" came to mind to designate this form of manifestation.
>
> A point which I want very much to establish is that the choice of these "Readymades" was never dictated by aesthetic delectation.
>
> This choice was based on a reaction of visual indifference with at the same time a total absence of good or bad taste . . . in fact a complete anaesthesia. . . .[9]

Here is the real "burning up of all aesthetics" promised in his early notes. Anaesthesia replaces aesthetics, visual indifference replaces taste. "I force myself to contradict myself," he once said, "so as to avoid conforming to my own taste."[10] His crisis of respect led, with brilliance and sincerity, to the assertion of art's opposite—for example, to capping off the great tradition of ornate fountains in public squares by exhibiting a urinal. A pseudonymous article defending exhibition of the urinal, thought to have been written by Duchamp, adds another central thought:

> Whether Mr. Mutt with his own hands made the fountain or not has no importance, he CHOSE it. He took an ordinary article of life, placed it so that its useful significance disappeared under the new title and point of view—created a new thought for that object.[11]

On the liberatingly destructive side (the "vitriol of the possible," Duchamp wrote in his notes[12]), Readymades showed for the first time that one can slip altogether free of the bonds of tradition and received ideas about art. Duchamp revealed the invisible web of agreements governing the creation and exhibition of painting and sculpture to be a series of conventions, not beyond good-humored yet serious assault. A new and irreverent spirit entered twentieth-century art with Duchamp. No sacred cows were left standing and munching. "NON est mon nom / NON NON le nom" wrote the poet René Daumal in the mid-1930s, when he was exploring some of the same terrain[13] and reaching, like Duchamp, for something beyond it. "Whether you are 'anti' or 'for,'" Duchamp once said, "it's the two sides of the same thing."[14] On another occasion, he resorted to the old paradox of the Cretan who asserts that all Cretans lie:

> . . . Words such as truth, art, veracity, or anything are stupid in themselves. Of course it's difficult to formulate so I insist *every word I am telling you now is stupid and wrong.*[15]

What is there other than "anti" or "for"? What could Duchamp accept without jumbling it into a paradox? His richest response to these questions appears in a number of late talks from the years when he had become an elder statesman of twentieth-century art.

> I wanted to get away from the physical aspect of painting. I was much more interested in recreating ideas in painting. . . . I wanted to put painting once again at the service of the mind. And my painting was, of course, at once regarded as "intellectual," "literary" painting. It was true. . . . In fact until the last hundred years all painting had been literary or religious: it had all been at the service of the mind. This characteristic was lost little by little during the last century. The more sensual appeal a painting provided—the more animal it became—the more highly it was regarded.[16]

One further remark of Duchamp's might be remembered: "Painting should not be exclusively retinal or visual; it should have to do with the gray matter, with our urge for understanding." [17]

The Readymades pulled Duchamp free, opened to him the possibility of an art "at the service of the mind." True, their dry wit and prankishness differ from the maturity evident in the passages just quoted. But they were stations on the path toward his late attitudes and already implied them. In a daffy, unexpected way, they belong to the spiritual in art; they are a horse-laugh dispelling false reverence on the one hand and merely retinal art on the other. They had enough Zen in them to withdraw from conventional values and suggest a way of seeing without judging: an inspired flatness.

Duchamp's most elaborate work, produced in 1915 to 1923 and never quite completed, is *The Bride Stripped Bare by her Bachelors, Even* (Fig. 24), also known as *The Large Glass*. Now in the Philadelphia Museum of Art, it has been commented upon by many critics, not least by Duchamp himself, who published his notes about the work from its inception through many stages of thought and its actual manufacture. For a proper interpretation of this complex work, readers should turn to the scholars and writers who have labored over it. [18] In brief, it is a courtship-and-copulation machine in which the "bachelors," rendered as a fantastic machine for the delivery of sperm, wait in the lower panel for their opportunity to reach the "bride" in the upper panel, herself an intricate machine.

This work has become a sacred cow. It sometimes seems that the only proper response to it is to launch into an utterly complex, obscure interpretation. To do so is to follow in Duchamp's footsteps: his notes are lengthy and for the most part defy common sense. Here one is on "pataphysical" ground, as Alfred Jarry put it at the turn of the century—ground on which meanings shift and change, and the ruling spirit is an ironic wit and mock seriousness that doesn't drive toward truth so much as toward an obsessive intricacy.

The sheer difficulty of the notes and the abidingly enigmatic nature of *The Large Glass* itself betray an impulse toward the esoteric—toward hidden, difficult knowledge. The impulse seems to have settled on the sexual theme, the metaphor of man the machine, and some of the arcana of alchemy, with which Duchamp was acquainted. Duchamp then went on to elaborate an "esoteric" work of art, one that is endlessly puzzling, difficult to grasp in its entirety, always inviting new associations that expand the intellectual context in which it has to be considered.

24. Marcel Duchamp. *The Large Glass*, or *The Bride Stripped Bare by Her Bachelors, Even*, 1915–23. Oil and lead wire on glass. 109¼″ × 69⅛″. Philadelphia Museum of Art: Bequest of Katherine S. Dreier. Copyright ARS NY/ADAGP 1987.

Mircea Eliade has analyzed the "esoteric" and difficult in modern art as a disguised impulse toward initiation.[19] When the deep, perhaps innate desire to gain a saving knowledge by means of a challenging initiatic passage fails to find a suitable object in modern culture, it tends to invent the object; hence our difficult art, according to Eliade. He dwells on the example of *Finnegans Wake,* a supremely difficult work, curiously satisfying to delve into and half-understand.

Hence too, I believe, *The Large Glass* and its accompanying notes— together they are an arcanum, an "esoteric" experience that challenges understanding and presses one forward to the limit of one's intellectual range. I qualify the word "esoteric" here with quotation marks because authentic esotericism is simply expressed and difficult to carry out, while inauthentic esotericism is complex in expression and gives one nothing to carry out. Authentic esotericism—for example the Upanishads, which were not intended for young, unprepared people— almost always has devastating common sense and simplicity. The inspired aphorisms of the thirteenth-century Egyptian sage, Ibn 'Ata'illah, are simply expressed, although difficult to carry out or verify.[20] Demurrals from this generalization are of course needed; many esoteric teachers from Meister Eckhart to Jakob Boehme are intellectually demanding. But the gist holds true.

I believe that Duchamp's priceless ideal of an art "at the service of the mind" remains unfulfilled. In his own work, it ran afoul of personal passions that seem to have driven him into the long and ultimately unfinished sortie of *The Large Glass* (Arturo Schwarz, a leading Duchamp authority, has explored what those personal passions may have been).[21] It also ran afoul of our culture, which may make us witty and "brilliant" but does not readily ground us in self-knowledge. Duchamp's ideas are Zen without Enlightenment, a brilliant movement of negation and emptying that did not know how to continue. They are nonetheless homegrown Zen.

In one of his later interviews, Duchamp said:

> . . . As you know, I am interested in the intellectual side, although I don't like the world "intellect." For me "intellect" is too dry a word, too inexpressive. I like the word "belief." I think in general that when people say "I know," they don't know, they believe. I believe that art is the only form of activity in which man as man shows himself to be a true individual. Only in art is he capable of going beyond the animal state, because art is an outlet toward regions which are not ruled by time and space. . . .[22]

Duchamp left much to be accomplished before we near an art "at the service of the mind" that moves with some small understanding toward "regions not ruled by time and space." These words from his later years echo a passage in Mondrian's own late writings:

> The new art, and through it the future, can be seen and understood *exclusively* through pure and intuitive contemplation that is free of the limitations of time and space.[23]

The great rebel, French to the core and too clever to believe much, was in the end not so unlike the Dutch mystic.

9   CHANCE

The great twentieth-century commentators on traditional religious art—A. K. Coomaraswamy and others—have stressed the depth and clarity of *intention* governing sacred art. Through a deliberate work of meditative imagination, the artist internalizes the image and presence of the god before shaping the god in stone.[1] But some twentieth-century artists—poets, painters and sculptors, composers—have had another interest, an interest in chance. They have explored and celebrated the impersonal form-making power of coins tossed, strings and papers dropped, alphabets shuffled, computers programmed to rattle off permutations, truckloads of tar dumped down cliffsides. Far from succumbing to the criticism that chance operations bypass the responsibility to deliberate and choose, they have used some of the traditionalists' own weapons against them—quoting spiritual teachings, smiling: there is a world beyond our petty choices, our entanglements in convention, our heavy beliefs.

Reading these artists on chance and experiencing their work, one may well feel a movement of fellowship, an unexpected readiness to join them. "These works are Realities, pure and independent, with no meaning or cerebral intention,"[2] wrote Jean Arp, an early experimentalist with chance. The interest that perhaps many of us will take in his statement is sign enough, whatever the outcome, that we should look into chance. The venture may initially seem wayward, but I suspect that we will come upon a cleansed and strengthened understanding of intention by making the detour.

I am tempted to formulate the thesis in a few obscure words; the evidence will bear it out or not. Chance is creative, a random bubbling of possibilities in the absence of which intention becomes repetitive and servile. Chance is, however, uncreative when given a greater or different place than its nature justifies. Chance participates alongside intention in a larger movement which encompasses them both.

We know Duchamp, inventor of "canned chance" and the Readymade. Most historians regard him as a proto-Dadaist, precursor and in time partner in the Dada movement which originated in Zürich, early in 1916, and spread rapidly to the European capitals and New York.[3] A movement of revulsion against the carnage of World War I and the settled bourgeois cultures that gave rise to it, Dada refused all artistic conventions and rampaged with despairing humor, vulgarity, refinement, and spells of genius into new territory where the irrational and the odd became forms of protest and entertainment. In doing so, it swept up some of the experiments with the irrational and anti-conventional which were already under way, experiments with chance among them.

The sensitivity of artists to chance phenomena of color and form vastly predates the twentieth century and must in fact be innate, bound into their gift. "Do you see yonder cloud that's almost in shape of a camel?" asked Hamlet. Leonardo da Vinci counseled artists:

> If you look at stained or dirty walls . . . with the idea of imagining some scene, you will find analogies for landscapes with mountains, rivers, rocks, trees, plains, wide valleys and hills of all kinds. You will also see battles and figures with animated gestures and strange faces and costumes and an infinity of things.[4]

One of the shocks that impelled Kandinsky toward abstraction was the chance viewing of a canvas stored upside-down against a wall: its enigmatic beauty, when he entered his studio at sunset, startled him into a new line of thought. Similarly, he was entranced by the random pattern on his palette:

> In the middle of the palette is a curious world of the remnants of colors already used. . . . Here is a world which, derived from . . . pictures already painted, was . . . determined and created through accidents, through the puzzling play of forces alien to the artist. And I owe much to these accidents: they have taught me more than any teacher or master. Many an hour I have studied them with love and admiration.[5]

In practice, however, Kandinsky sought strict control over his canvases, even combatted the potential for vagueness in abstract imagery through his emphasis on the idea of internal necessity, the opposite of randomness, and his pedagogic interest in art theory. It fell to other artists to explore the role of chance in the work of art itself.

At much the same time that Duchamp was doing so in Paris, Jean Arp (1887–1966) and his wife-to-be, the artist Sophie Taeuber (1889–

1943), were exploring chance in their Zürich studio. Remembered primarily as a sculptor, Arp was a fluent poet and essayist in whose writings a patient reader can find gems. Like virtually all participants in Dada, Arp and Taeuber associated what they were doing with the Great War.

> In Zürich, in 1915, disgusted by the butchery of World War I, we devoted ourselves to the Fine Arts. Despite the remote booming of artillery, we sang, painted, pasted, and wrote poetry with all our might and main. We were seeking an elementary art to cure man of the frenzy of the times. . . . The Renaissance taught men to arrogantly exalt their reason. Modern times with their sciences and technologies have consecrated men to megalomania. The chaos of our era is the result of that overestimating of reason. We sought an anonymous and collective art. . . . In 1915, Sophie Taueber and I painted, embroidered, and did collages; all these works were drawn from the simplest forms. . . . These works are Realities, pure and independent, with no meaning or cerebral intention. We rejected all mimesis and description, giving free rein to the Elementary and the Spontaneous. Since the arrangement of planes and their proportions and colors seemed to hinge solely on chance, I declared that these works were arranged "according to the laws of chance," as in the order of nature, chance being for me simply a part of an inexplicable reason, of an inaccessible order.[6]

William Rubin is surely right in his view that Arp's works in this period, such as *Collage Arranged According to the Laws of Chance* (Fig. 25), are not the artistic equivalent of throwing examination blue books down a flight of stairs. Nonetheless, the shapes "chosen" by Arp and their disposition owe a great deal to a spontaneous, nondeliberative activity new to the history of art.

Arp's concluding references to "the order of nature," "an inexplicable reason," and "an inaccessible order" dramatize the uncertainty surrounding chance as we perceive it. Is chance mere chaos or an order that escapes our understanding? Arp evidently felt that by surrendering intention to a process of spontaneous form-making which he did not presume to control, he was opening to a greater intelligence rather than closing off his own intelligence—predisposing himself to a movement upward and inward rather than down and out. Duchamp, infinitely more ironic in spirit and tolerant of absurdity, seems to have perceived the movement toward chance as neither greater nor lesser but

25. Jean Arp. *Collage Arranged According to the Laws of Chance*, 1916–17. Torn and pasted papers. 19⅛″ × 13⅝″. Collection, The Museum of Modern Art, New York. Copyright ARS NY/ADAGP 1987.

simply more detached, freer of egotistical illusion: chance liberated his spirit of play. In later years, Duchamp tried for a time to crack the code of chance as manifested by the roulette wheels of Monte Carlo.

"I continued to develop the collage," wrote Arp,

> eliminating all volition and working automatically. . . . "The Law of chance," which comprises all other laws and surpasses our understanding (like the primal cause from which all life arises), can be experienced only in a total surrender to the unconscious. I claimed that whoever follows this law will create pure life.[7]

> Today, as in the days of the early Christians, the essential must become known. The artist must let his work create itself directly.[8]

We are encountering two versions of chance: a religious or spiritual version and a more ironic, playful version. Both reflect an aversion to "civilization"—to its great senseless war, its millions of random deaths. "Philosophies have less value for dada than an old abandoned toothbrush, and dada abandons them to the great world leaders."[9] Born both of despair and of hope, chance became a new spiritual idea among artists during the Great War, as well as a new and racy anti-aesthetic principle.

When chance enters in, art speeds up. On the one hand, artists have to outrun their habits, which pull them involuntarily toward conventional gestures; on the other hand, chance substitutes its unpremeditated "artistry" for the time-consuming techniques of traditional painting and sculpture. Literature reflects this speed more clearly than visual art, where a certain fixity and stillness are inherent to the medium. Witness Tristan Tzara's writings from the period, of which the following is a slower and more coherent example than many:

> Active simplicity
> The inability to discern degrees of brightness: licking the penumbra and floating in the great mouth full of honey and excrement. Measured by the scale of Eternity, all action is vain. . . . Let every man shout: there is a great destructive, negative work to be accomplished. Sweeping, cleaning. The cleanliness of the individual affirms itself after the state of madness, the aggressive, complete madness of a world left in the hands of bandits who vandalize and destroy centuries.[10]

In Zürich, Tzara and Hugo Ball explored chance poetry according to a recipe that recalls Duchamp's methods: "To make a dadaist poem, take a newspaper. Take a pair of scissors . . ." [11]—he is heading, of course, straight toward the magician's hat, and there *is* a kind of magic in chance operations.

The Dada experiment with chance was absorbed and continued by Surrealism, the movement formalized by André Breton in 1924 and announced in his well-known *Manifesto of Surrealism*. Responding to Freud's exploration of dreams and his study of psychic automatism (slips of the tongue, the uncovering of unconscious concerns through free association), Breton developed a new aesthetic based on "psychic automatism in its pure state . . . in the absence of any control exercised by reason." [12] "Reason's role," he wrote, is best "limited to taking note of, and appreciating, the luminous phenomenon" [13] of the deeper workings of the undeliberative mind. "Put your trust in the inexhaustible nature of the murmur," [14] he exhorted would-be Surrealists—advice still worth considering if one cracks through the metaphor to the experience.

Surrealism substituted for conventional logic the seeming illogic of dreams and of the intellect outrunning its habits through exercises such as automatic writing, in which one writes down whatever comes to mind, rapidly, without imposing literary or moral judgment. Surrealism was a sort of Cubism of the imagination, a fracturing of the traditional patterns of imagery and metaphor to find the next order, deeper down. Art governed by chance, for the Surrealists, was not a mindlessly random batching of one thing with another but rather the spontaneity of the unconscious mind revealed and recorded—and respected for the new kind of order it suggested.

The Surrealists spawned a new world of images in art and literature, some farfetched and irritating even when clever, others luminous. They entered the inner world of man with tremendous energy and, perhaps, too little knowledge: they were often trapped by sex and became at times pornographic artists who had wished to be more. They also often fell prey to the glamour of "difficulty," in Eliade's sense. Intriguing and vividly imaginative work came to seem enough.

The next elaborate exploration of the artistic power of chance drew both from the modern sources we have been discussing and from Zen teachings. John Cage (b. 1912), composer, essayist, and graphic designer, a fresh and irreverent thinker of great personal charm, has for decades introduced chance operations into the composition and performance of his music. "What I do," he has written, "I do not wish blamed on Zen, though without my engagement with Zen . . . I doubt whether I would have done what I have done." [15]

The powerful Buddhist idea of *tathatā*, suchness, seems to underlie much of Cage's aesthetic and his work with chance. *Tathatā* is the irreducible, indescribable nature of an object, a sound, a person. From the point of view of the perceiver, it is a recognition of the fullness and sufficiency of each thing in itself. Aesthetic and intellectual grammars break down under the impact of this perception; associations matter not at all, while direct wordless perception matters a great deal. One only has to come across one's dog or cat unexpectedly to have a small domestic experience of *tathatā*.

Because chance as a principle of artistic composition also breaks down standard grammars, it can be viewed as an avenue toward the completeness and self-sufficiency of *tathatā*. This similarity was not lost on Cage.

> One has a choice. . . . One may give up the desire to control sound, clear his mind of music, and set about discovering means to let sounds be themselves rather than vehicles for man-made theories or expressions of human sentiments. . . . New music: new listening. . . . Just an attention to the activity of sounds. Those involved with the composition of experimental music find ways and means to remove themselves from the activities of the sounds they make. Some employ chance operations, derived from sources as ancient as the Chinese *Book of Changes*, or as modern as the table of random numbers used also by physicists in research. Or, analogous to the Rorschach tests of psychology, the interpretation of imperfections in the paper upon which one is writing may provide a music free from one's memory and imagination. . . . It goes without saying that dissonances and noises are welcome in this new music. But so is the dominant seventh if it happens to put in an appearance.[16]

Like Duchamp and Arp (although decades later), Cage is drawn to an art that subverts and transcends the all too human; he seeks to release sound from bondage to conventional music theory and emotional expectation—in a word, from intention. Music will recover its original nature when the composer dares to assign a major compositional role to chance, which patterns sound in ways that a trained musician could not even conceive. A random lottery spin is preferable to the overdetermined, overeducated spin of the composer's mind. External automatism is preferable to the automatism of a composer who only imagines that he is creating freely without subjugation to rigid conventions that strip sound of its *tathatā*, its primordial impact.

"What is the purpose of writing music?" asks Cage.

One is of course not dealing with purposes but dealing with sounds. Or the answer must take the form of paradox: a purposeful purposelessness or a purposeless play. This play, however, is an affirmation of life . . . which is so excellent once one gets one's mind and one's desires out of its way and lets it act of its own accord.[17]

This is the language of Zen, not musicology, and it has great appeal. But what music does it foster? Difficult, often unlistenable. The beauty of Cage's thinking and its rich promise of a fundamental art cannot be fulfilled by work in which chance plays the central role. Conscripted to serve as the composer—to select notes, timbres, durations—chance behaves badly like the idiot it is. Cage's ideas are effective cultural criticism, forcing basic questions, and his music is effective as a full-dress working-out of his critical ideas. It cannot be denied that he has brought authentic spiritual ideas and a liberating attitude of play to the enterprise of Western art. But his art for the most part doesn't work. It represents the reduction to absurdity of the surrender of intention to chance, and like many such reductions it has pedagogic rather than ultimate value. Locating the operation of chance *outside of* the artist in an engine of chance such as the throw of three coins, Cage applied the idea of chance and expressed the Buddhist value of purposeless purpose more heavy-handedly than he might have.

There are further vivid episodes in the history of the idea of chance in twentieth-century art. It was harmoniously integrated into the image-making of American painters after World War II. Jackson Pollock's great loops of paint follow a generally purposeful design although they are random in detail; Morris Louis's poured *Veils* mix control and spontaneity to create a superb poetry of color (see chapter 17). Similarly, the mobiles of Alexander Calder respond to the breeze or nearby movements of people in ways that the artist designed into his work. Recently reflecting about his impressions in a stoneyard, Isamu Noguchi (see chapter 18) contrasted the dry purposiveness of industrial production with the unpredictable vitality of the waste it leaves behind:

> [We] can still save for art that which is discarded by machines. . . . A lot of art today . . . has to do with Nature and the quirks and accidents and what-not which are so extraordinarily beautiful and so contrary to industrial production. . . .[18]

He was in fact speaking more of his own art and sensibility than of the art around him.

In addition to these famed examples, revivals of the raw spirit of Dada in recent years have led to many experimental works in which chance plays a major role. There have been, as well, computer-based experiments yielding serial forms or unpredictable intricacies of line and space through the application of mathematical formulae. But enough detailed material has already been gathered to allow us to step back and question.

In my experience, chance is a part of the mind. Often unnoticed, it faithfully collaborates in the elaboration of virtually every work of art. To notice its contribution, we should no doubt start by exploring intention, which is its creative partner. At the beginning of the creative process, an artist's intention can be extraordinarily immaterial—nothing more than an odd pressure, a need that cannot define its object, a dim awareness of a gap that might be filled. Or, on the contrary, intention can spring fully formed into the mind, together with much or all of the materials needed to fulfill it. However clear or ghostly it may be initially, intention comes to outward expression through a blending of the artist's present awareness with varied materials from the past stored in his or her mind, feelings, and physical being. Literally embodying the intention, these materials are assembled from what the artist often experiences as an unlimited collection of memories and associations. However short and dreary one's life has been, artist and nonartist alike have accumulated enough memories to generate infinite patterns of recombination.

A little self-observation shows that memories are inscribed in a definite order in the composite human intelligence of thought, feeling, and body, all of which "remember." Memories form an intensely interactive internal encyclopedia based on a few simple principles of order, primarily chronology and similarity/contrast, and activated by a "search" function that allows us to test possible relationships among memories of all kinds and to create new patterns among them. A "truth" test allows us to evaluate new patterns in terms of their relation to established ones. This description, while not a masterpiece of cognitive psychology, indicates something of the remarkable order and wealth of material from which artists and all of us draw.

The process of gathering memories for artistic purposes is similar in some respects to the way in which a great whale sweeps through the ocean gathering the tiny plankton that are its primary food. Just what the artist scoops up is a matter of chance: whatever happens to be available will do, if it is generally appropriate. Similarly, whatever happens to "think itself" and "offer itself" to the artist from his or her wealth of associations will do, if it is generally appropriate to the intention. If it will not do, a later working session eventually reveals the inadequacy and forces further exploration for more suitable prey in the vast inland sea of associations. The analogy of a feeding whale fails, however, to reflect the experience of artistic intentions *attracting* appropriate associations, which willingly emerge from the mass and enter provisionally into the developing composition.

Associations are the realm of chance within the mind and total person. Memories may well be stored in a precise order, but they are overwhelmingly plentiful and curiously self-willed. We can acquire them deliberately and draw from them just as deliberately—memorize texts, repeat complex choreographic sequences, learn elaborate techniques. But just as often unwanted associations assault us, or we seek lost ones, or simply stand in a daze, waiting for a needed association to turn up. Artists may spend days, weeks, or more waiting for a solution to appear. One's relationship with associations is chancy—and apparently needs to be that way.

The loose relation between intention and memory is one of mankind's secrets, something of an embarrassment and yet a source of unanticipated mutation and evolutionary change kindly built into our natures. For every deliberate act of memory, there are a dozen involuntary rememberings. For every sharply intentional gesture that shapes a work of art, there are as many that arise initially as random offerings from the sea of associations, attracted to the surface by the artist's intention. Much of the sense of play and courtship in the creative process is this play and this courtship. Neurological research is said to have demonstrated that a small percentage of our brain cells are firing off randomly at any given moment, on occasion presumably generating unexpected thoughts and feelings. These, too, find their way into works of art; intention is uncannily quick to seize on useful materials that arrive without explanation from the past or from present awareness.

Artists have traditionally prayed to the Muses for help before setting to work, for they enter a world of very real uncertainty. They are gambling, not under the lights at Monte Carlo but in the intimacy of self and its enigmatic resources. The best trained and most relentlessly clear-minded artist can have a bad day, a bad week, a bad year. If a quiet sense of risk is altogether absent, the artist is probably imitating himself or someone else. Even in the realm of traditional religious art, in which many features of images are fixed by centuries of practice and intended for imitation, there is an acknowledged risk of imperfect attention and lax form.

We have been exploring the inner world of associations and our remarkable relation to it, governed partly by the magnetic pull of intention and partly by chance. This inner world is matched outwardly by a wealth of chance occurrences in the world at large and in our dealings with it. A brushstroke happens to fall on the canvas just so, unintended—but more expressive and appropriate than the gesture intended by the artist; it will be retained. An unanticipated rhythm happens to emerge; it will be gratefully retained. The artist, stumped and uninspired, decides to take a walk on the chance that it will refresh him. He hears a woodpecker at work, and its uniquely intent sound enters him as if the bird were hammering on his belly, awakening him. He returns to his studio with a new impulse owed, of all things, to a woodpecker.

The outer world and our movement through it are a second roulette wheel, ever turning. The task of intention, so to speak, is to negotiate the inner and outer worlds of chance without forgetting, but also without losing the ability to respond to promising material or events that happen along. We live in close proximity with chance. Because it dwells inside of us no less than our intentions, we *are* chance—chance and intention.

What is accident? In the terms we have been pursuing, accident within ourselves is chance that we neither draw into the pattern of an intention nor deliberately reject. It is chance lingering unseen, therefore able to throw things off. In the world at large, chance becomes accident when it reduces or destroys our well-being. In itself, chance is not inimical to intention; it is simply a resource designed into our natures and into the world. Accident, on the other hand, is the true enemy of intention.

But there is something more which many people instinctively recognize and respect. It has been called fate, destiny, providence. It is easy to deny its existence—it figures among the many things that cannot be proved and often seem immensely unlikely. Perhaps it is the opposite of accident. If so, it is born not of carelessness inside or violence outside but of an absolutely commanding intention that makes use of everything thrown in its way to achieve its purpose. It is the "inaccessible order" and "inexplicable reason" toward which artists from Jean Arp to John Cage have been drawn.

Because chance operations occur within us and all around us, we need no special manipulations to come to grips with it, only a somewhat knowing entry into oneself as one is and into the world as it is. Twentieth-century artists who have deliberately experimented with chance have performed a great service by dramatizing the need to see and experience the rules of art freshly. They have also reminded us of the need for an art that is not all ego, all "personal genius," although they did so by moving toward external "chance machines" rather than toward the vigorous internal play of chance and intention. Their work with chance has been a necessary step in freeing Western art from outworn inner conventions, just as Cubism and other revolutionary movements freed art from external conventions.

One of the conditions for great art is a delicate, mobile balance between chance and intention. Intention alone is cold and schematic; chance alone is irresponsible and vacuous. Together, under the eye of the working artist, they are an immense resource.

10 · THE RUSSIAN
AVANT-GARDE: IDEA
AND IDEOLOGY

Ideas open. Individual men and women conceive and exchange them, visibly bear them and stand ready, within limits, to alter or replace them. Ideas are units of thought that associate spontaneously with other units of thought to create new structures. Innocently promiscuous, they couple and uncouple until they find a satisfactory combination or a promising fertility from which in time a greater idea may be born. It is never definitively clear whether people choose their ideas or ideas choose their people; probably it is sometimes the one, sometimes the other. Hence the courtship, good-humored, imperious, going on for a lifetime, that helps to keep thinkers open to the unforeseen.

Ideologies close. They establish a perimeter within which certain ideas are acceptable, outside of which others are not. Within the perimeter, numerous ideas are tightly fastened to each other in such a way that they lose their inherent mobility. An ideology is never one idea, it is many, held with catechistic force in an approved pattern. Ideologies never apply to one person only; they always count in larger numbers. They subordinate individuals and encourage a heated allegiance that leaves little opportunity for the sometimes clumsy, sometimes delightful exercise through which ideas are refined and adapted to circumstance.

Idea is one of our most ancient words, *ideology* a recent inheritance. British philosophers coined *ideology* in the late eighteenth century, while in the course of the nineteenth it acquired its current reference to strongly advocated social, political, or religious doctrine.[1]

Ideas can migrate into the rigid circle of an ideology; the reverse seems rarely to be true. Few ideas, once locked into an ideology, reappear in the more tolerant zone of mere ideas. Few thinkers, once they have tasted the fervor of ideology, seem to have any further taste for the uncertainty of conceiving new ideas and the painfully diplomatic procedures associated with the exchange of ideas. Yet ideas are not weak. Certain ideas—principles—are very strong and will never be abandoned by some individuals, even under fierce attack. But even principles remain open to discussion: there may be a better formulation, a new adaptation to circumstance. Coomaraswamy once wrote that the difference between the religion of the Delaware Indians and Christianity was that Christians had armies; in all other respects, Delaware religion was no less suited to become a world religion. Ideologies are ideas with armies—and if not armies, then militant supporters for whom words are weapons.

In the years 1915 through the mid-1920s, Russia was shaken by the clash of ideas and ideologies to an unprecedented extent. The Revolution of October 1917 marks the turning point in the history of those years, but artists had not waited for the Revolution to engage in tumultuous battles of their own. The revolution in art was already well launched by October, so much so that Vladimir Tatlin (1885–1953), one of the leaders of the avant-garde, could write with some justice in 1920: "What happened from the social aspect in 1917 was realized in our work as pictorial artists in 1914. . . ."[2]

But to speak first of conflict and rivalry would be to fall victim to the romance of ideology. It is good theater when artists conceal their latest styles from one another until the very day of an exhibition, refuse to exhibit together, or issue broadsides condemning one another's views. All of this took place in the years just before and after October, but many of the ideas and works of art that occasioned bursts of melodrama were in fact serious.

We will find some of the deepest modern insights into the spiritual in art in the Russian avant-garde, embodied, as so often in our century, both in works of art and in strong-voiced writings. We will also find resolute, thoughtful opposition to a spirituality that sometimes seemed little more than fine words, a poor substitute for engaging vigorously with "materials, volume, and construction" (Tatlin). Two new arts of enduring importance, Suprematism and Constructivism, were shaped with great intentness in the years just prior to the Revolution. As they entered into the new world defined by the Revolution, they gradually changed; they made the Revolution their own and tried to serve it. In time, the revolutionary government rejected the one (Suprematism) and narrowed the scope of activity of the other (Constructivism) so much that it had no real future in Russia. Bitter internal politics in the art world also weakened the positions of separate movements and groups. Making an alliance with conservative artistic circles, the Communist party and the military encouraged a public art that served their purposes more directly and with less controversy than the avant-garde arts that had briefly dominated the institutes, exhibition halls, and streets of the new Russia.

In brief, this is the drama of ideas, artistic accomplishments, and embattled artists that we will follow. It is, up to a point, a classic dialectic: the powerful spiritual affirmation of the Suprematist circle was countered by the technological, rationalistic affirmation of the Constructivists. From their disputatious but essentially nonviolent encounter, a synthesis had begun to emerge when another force entered to impose its will, with vastly superior material resources and an attitude of coercion. The struggle was so bitter that all ideas tended to harden into ideology, the spiritual no less than the materialistic. But this was not so at the beginning.

KASIMIR MALEVICH: A SINGLE BARE AND FRAMELESS ICON OF OUR TIMES

"I search for God, I search within myself for myself. . . . I search for God, I search for my face, I have already drawn its outline and I strive to incarnate myself. . . ."[3] The words are from a poem, unpublished in the artist's lifetime. They shed an intimate light on one aspect of an artistic career that had its fair share of irritating bombast and plain misfortune but is nonetheless central to this book. Kasimir Malevich (1878–1935) created some of the masterworks of the spiritual in twentieth-century art. His strongest paintings explore with simplicity and visual elegance a new language of geometry, movement, color, and space that recasts the world as a dynamic, spiritualized, and joyful realm. Side by side with explorations of new imagery, his work includes touching recreations of old Russian religious motifs, camouflaged as stridently modern Suprematist works but at base meditations on the Cross and on the stately compositions of the Russian icon tradition.

Suprematism is the ungainly name given by Malevich to the new artistic vision. Originally drawn toward calling it "supranaturalism," he discovered a school of German philosophy that had already adopted the term, and in time he found his way to Suprematism. It retains to this day a polemical ring, not unintended. It may be the least appropriate movement name of our time: an oddly dry battle cry that evokes nothing of the gentle, often buoyant vision it is meant to designate.

More limited in imagery and native inventiveness than others who explored the spiritual in twentieth-century art, Malevich nonetheless drove toward the center and found much there. He and his closest followers established a visual language that recurred fruitfully in American art after World War II. The simple, large geometries and color fields of Kenneth Noland and others are more than foreshadowed in Suprematist art—they are sometimes present in full. Nothing was "plagiarized"; the language was effective and called for further use, for the insights that it conveyed were not parochial and temporary.

The other half of Malevich's achievement lies in his writings, where he explored the meaning of his experience as a painter and as a consciousness, and tried to assess in reasoned historical terms the forces converging on Russian art that led to Suprematism. On occasion, no one is more eloquent than Malevich. He had a genius for autobiography, not for the long narrative that takes in everything but for bursts of self-reflection, delivered with high drama, which can remain vivid in a reader's memory for years. His was a genius for evoking epiphany, the moment of breakthrough when a sense of direction makes itself massively felt; a genius also for evoking the ordeal that often precedes epiphany. In addition, like many Russian artists of his era, he was a vastly energetic polemicist. He loved to argue and went about it with tools ranging from subtle insight to sheer nastiness. Like his art, his writings are at their best when simplest. A comment by Anatoli Lunacharsky, an early ally of Lenin's who served with genuine distinction as People's Commissar for Enlightenment in 1917 through 1929, somewhat overstates Malevich's shortcomings, but does so with memorable verve:

> The trouble begins when Malevich stops painting and starts writing pamphlets. I have heard that this artist's writings have thrown even the Germans into a state of confusion. . . . Malevich has tried to link his aims and his ways by one means or another with both the Revolution and God, and he has got muddled.[4]

Yet the voice of Malevich is penetrating, far more penetrating than most. Selections from the writings of 1915 through 1927, set alongside his paintings and drawings, yield another strong charter document of the spiritual in twentieth-century art.

Kasimir Malevich was born in the Ukraine in 1878. His father worked at a beet sugar refinery, his mother looked after the family, and apart from the customary display of Orthodox icons at home, there was no art in his environment. "There was no mention of art," Malevich recalled, "and it took me quite a long time to find out that the word art exists. . . ."[5] But he had found his way to Moscow as an art student by 1904, he was exhibiting by 1907, and by 1912 he was painting works that richly deserve to be remembered.

The history of Russian art in these years is a complex weave of native and foreign influences. The most important sources for Malevich in his early years of search were French and Italian avant-garde art and Russian peasant traditions typified by the *lubok,* the simple narrative or symbolic woodcut. Malevich and his contemporaries were able to draw from their experience of the great private collections of French art brought to Moscow by the wealthy merchants, Sergei Shchukin and Ivan Morosov. In their sumptuous homes were masterworks of Monet, Gauguin, Cézanne, Matisse, and Picasso, offering in effect a complete education that was not lost on the artists of Malevich's generation who were generously invited to study them. Like Malevich, those who had not traveled to Paris and directly mixed with the new French artists made their acquaintance here. The ideas and visual language of the Italian Futurists were familiar at first through their vociferous manifestos and later through exhibitions and the 1914 Moscow visit of F. T. Marinetti, principal spokesman for the Futurists. New art in Germany was publicized in Russia through exhibitions and art-critical commentaries in Russian periodicals by Wassily Kandinsky and others. The visual resources and typical themes of Russian folk art were being explored and reinterpreted by the avant-garde artists Mikhail Larionov and Natalia Goncharova, with whom Malevich was associated. In the background of all of these trends and sources, avant-garde and neo-primitive, was a long history of skilled academic painting, which in Russia as elsewhere in Europe gave artists of the decade 1905–1914 a strong resistance against which to push and seek a new self-definition.

Malevich began to come into his own as an artist in 1912, with a series of paintings on peasant themes which possess a unique and very real poetry (Fig. 26). Blending an adaptation of Cubist drawing with the naiveté of a peasant woodcut, and endowing the images with warm prismatic colors, Malevich created icons of the peasant life—simple, curiously still, and felt. His woodcutter attacks the felled tree with the solemnity of an Orthodox St. George confronting the Dragon, the chips from his axe-blows bursting from the log like little abstract rainbows. Malevich's joy in simple geometries is everywhere evident in the composition, from the confusion of bright cylindrical logs in the background to the abstracted figure of the woodcutter himself and the almost rhetorical presentation of circle and cylinder in the lower right,

26. Kasimir Malevich. *The Woodcutter*, 1912. Oil on canvas. 37″ × 28⅛″. Stedelijk Museum, Amsterdam.

as if these were measures for the composition as a whole. It was impossible to predict at the time where Malevich would move from this accomplished art, which does not represent the spiritual in any deliberate or elaborate sense but nonetheless transfigures peasant life and offers it, bright and solemn, to the viewer. These works must have been his homage to his past.

Restless, and already a leader of the avant-garde by virtue of his artistic talent and strength of conviction, Malevich in effect worked his way through various avant-garde styles until 1915. Neo-Primitivism, Cubism, Cubo-Futurism (a Russian coinage), Alogism (Cubist in style, influenced by the exploration of nonlogical structures in the work of the Futurist poet Velimir Khlebnikov)—these terms mark the way-stations on Malevich's path toward an art truly his own. He moved quickly but was not superficial; his Cubist works, for example, exercise a fine understanding of the peculiar grammar and syntax of that visual language.

Suprematism was first made public at the end of 1915 in an exhibition that included so many works, with such a well-defined artist's statement to accompany them, that Malevich had clearly been working in privacy for some time. Like Kandinsky, who just a few years earlier had made his step into abstraction, Malevich was seized both by a new vision and by passionate disavowal of the past. The most innovative arts at this time did not drop easily into the world; they were painfully born. Malevich's poetry of 1915, which remained unpublished until the 1970s, reflects the tearing from the familiar, the contempt for established standards, and the prayerful longing that accompanied his passage toward a genuinely new vision. "Try not to repeat yourself either in an icon or in a picture or in words," he wrote. "If something in your action reminds you of . . . the past, the voice of new birth tells me: wipe it off, remain silent. . . ."[6] He had entered into a period of ceaseless activity, the privileged time in certain lives when a previously hidden and even unknown mission is recognized and for the first time forcefully expressed.

> . . . The sky, the angels, prayers—all this is a surrounding, for in fact the reincarnation of the world takes place here in tireless work and movement, casting off the world of the past.[7]

Despite the dynamism of his mood and resolute self-reliance, he retained a religious sense that would come and go in his art and writings over the next years. A receptive, contemplative attitude—altogether genuine—conflicted in him with a warrior's reformist impulses, no less genuine.

"We must prepare ourselves by prayer to embrace the sky," he wrote in the 1915 poetry.[8] The imagery that preoccupied him was of the desert and transformation, austerity and its inner reward, flight in the spirit (and, if it could be arranged, flight in an airplane—an innovation of great fascination at the time). A later American generation, appreciative of native Indian traditions, might recognize the potency of a "vision quest" at this moment in Malevich's growth as man and artist.

> In order to hear the breath of the new day in the desert, cleanse your hearing and wipe away the old days. . . .[9]

The emblem and in effect campaign banner of the art that occasioned so much inner and outer furor impresses one more by what is absent from it than by what it is: *Black Square* (visible in Fig. 27) was the vehicle of Malevich's breakthrough to a new vision, but it is incomparably less nourishing for viewers today than the works that followed it.[10] Historians of the period have pointed out that in the so-called 0.10 exhibition of 1915 in Petrograd, where he first showed Suprematist works, Malevich hung *Black Square* high across a corner in the place where one might expect to find the principal religious icon of an Orthodox home. In the first years of the Revolution, when avant-garde artists designed temporary decorations for public rallies, Malevich again offered a black square as an emblem of the new spirit. Even in the pinched Stalinist atmosphere of 1935, Malevich's friends saw to it that the artist's grave was marked by his beloved black square. However much greater the eloquence and sheer beauty of other works by Malevich, *Black Square* was his first-born.

Some years after its first exhibition, Malevich wrote:

> The black square on the white field was the first form in which nonobjective feeling came to be expressed. The square = feeling, the white field = the void beyond this feeling.[11]

But these simple words are not enough to orient us, and they probably contain a small treachery of translation: "feeling" translates German *Fühlung*, and this in turn may mistranslate the lost Russian original of one of Malevich's most impressive texts, *The World of Non-Objectivity*, first published by the Bauhaus in 1927. It wasn't feeling that drew Malevich's attention so imperiously, it was what he called sensation (Russian *oshchushchenie*). Paul Cézanne, whom Malevich revered, had based his working discipline on the clarification of sen-

27. Kasimir Malevich. *0.10 Exhibition Photograph, Petrograd, 1915.* Reproduced from Christina Lodder, *Russian Constructivism,* New Haven and London, 1983, by permission of Yale University Press.

sation: "To paint," he said, "is to record colored sensations. . . . It all can be summarized as follows: to have sensations and to read Nature."[12]

To understand *Black Square,* one of the simplest forms ever to be presented as a work of art, and to grasp the meaning of sensation in Malevich's experience, we need to look at three aspects of his creative formula: what *Black Square* is *not,* what it *is,* and how the artist experienced his passage toward it. Malevich vehemently expressed both the denial and the positive vision in a pamphlet written for 0.10. He also effectively conveyed his positive vision in his Bauhaus book, while his writings as a whole reflect his taut experience. The 0.10 text reads in part as follows:

> Only when the conscious habit of seeing nature's little nooks, Madonnas, and Venuses in pictures disappears *will we witness a purely painterly work of art.*

I have transformed myself *in the zero of form* and have fished myself out of the *rubbishy slough of academic art.*

I have destroyed the ring of the horizon and got out of the circle of objects, the horizon ring that has imprisoned the artist and the forms of nature. . . .

To produce favorite objects and little nooks of nature is just like a thief being enraptured by his shackled legs. . . .

Objects have vanished like smoke to attain the new artistic culture. . . .

The square is not a subconscious form. It is the creation of intuitive reason.

The face of the new art.

The square is a living, regal infant.

The first step of pure creation in art. Before it there were naive distortions and copies of nature.

Our world of art has become new, nonobjective, pure. . . .

A surface lives; it has been born.[13]

There is an unmistakable and moving tone of triumph in these words. Like Kandinsky and Mondrian, Malevich made a psychic sacrifice of objects and of the familiar world so long served by art. In exchange, he felt that he had gained a new and comprehensive vision that was pure, abstract, non-objective, contacted by intuition, and expressed through the "weight, speed, and direction of movement" of simple geometric forms in space (as he wrote elsewhere in the 0.10 pamphlet). In its mute stability, *Black Square* ill bears the burden of Malevich's intensity, but within the same vocabulary of forms his *Suprematist Composition: White on White* of 1918 (Fig. 28) justifies his conviction that something new and great had come to light.

The white square is subtle, gentle, wise; it affirms an orderly and definite presence, yet one that shares its environment to the point of suffusion, as if it were not different from its setting. The slight tilt creates movement and the promise of change, thus with a gesture lightening the inherent weight of the square. An image of "distinction without difference," to borrow a classic phrase from Meister Eckhart, of diversity and unity, and movement without tension, this is a philosopher's statement simple in means but far-reaching in scope. In essence, it reflects the liberating ambiguity of contemplative experience in which the observer and the observed, the knower and the known, no longer stand entirely apart.

28. Kasimir Malevich. *Suprematist Composition: White on White,* 1918? Oil on canvas. 31¼″ × 31¼″. Collection, The Museum of Modern Art, New York.

Something of what Malevich meant by sensation is evident in this work: a non-intellectual, *sensed* vitality or energy that takes form without being rigidly constrained by form. When Malevich spoke of sensation, he was speaking of fundamental consciousness and of his own most refined experience of being, experience far enough removed from the ordinary to require a new artistic vocabulary and to challenge the assumptions of critics and viewers who did not know the world as he, on occasion, must have known it.

In his quiet times, reflected in the poetry, Malevich explored with reverence the ample reality that he had sensed within and around him:

I imagine a world of inexhaustible, unseen forms.
From that which I do not see—an endless world arises. . . .
[Artists] open the hidden world and reincarnate it into the real.
The mystery remains—an open reality and each reality is endlessly
multifaceted and polyhedral.[14]

In starker times, when he faced adversaries in art and in the quest for
patronage, he was anything but gentle. He dryly dismissed those who
could not share his vision:

> [Suprematist] construction . . . is highly complex, it is built not for
> the sake of building, but in order to transmit the graph which is
> drawn according to the changes of my inner oscillations; thus it be-
> longs to me, and only those who are of my kind can say so.[15]

This sentence is revealing not only for its arrogance in the face of those
who opposed him but also for its concept, close to Kandinsky's "inner
necessity," of transmitting the changes of an inner oscillation. Both
Malevich and Kandinsky experienced image-making as an act of attention to oneself rather than to outer objects. They were deliberately
"blind." Malevich said as much:

> The philosophy of Suprematism . . . does not look at the world in
> detail, does not see it, only senses.[16]

The internal rigors of Malevich's movement toward pure abstraction and the external conflicts into which the new art threw him are
reflected in one of his finest passages, drawn from the Bauhaus publication which for many years was his only writing readily available in
the West.

> When, in the year 1913, in my desperate attempt to free art from the
> ballast of objectivity, I took refuge in the square form. . . the critics
> and, along with them, the public sighed, "Everything which we
> loved is lost. We are in a desert. . . . Before us is nothing but a black
> square on a white background!"
>
> "Withering" words were sought to drive off the symbol of the
> "desert" so that one might behold on the "dead square" the beloved
> likeness of "reality". . . . The square seemed incomprehensible and
> dangerous to the critics and the public . . . and this, of course, was
> to be expected.
>
> The ascent to the heights of non-objective art is arduous and pain-
> ful . . . but it is nonetheless rewarding. The familiar recedes ever fur-

ther and further into the background. . . . The contours of the objective world fade more and more and so it goes, step by step, until finally the world—"everything we loved and by which we have lived"—becomes lost to sight.

No more "likenesses of reality," no idealistic images—nothing but a desert!

But this desert is filled with the spirit of non-objective sensation which pervades everything.

Even I was gripped by a kind of timidity bordering on fear when it came to leaving "the world of will and idea," in which I had lived and worked and in the reality of which I had believed.

But a blissful sense of liberating non-objectivity drew me forth into the "desert," where nothing is real except feeling . . . and so feeling became the substance of my life.[17]

The text is classic. Dramatic, even melodramatic without offending, it expresses an authentic quest in the psychic realm.

However alone Malevich often felt in his desert passage, he also drew from a restless, experimental spirituality that had gifted champions in the complex cultures of Petrograd and Moscow.[18] He spoke virtually a common language with these men and women, although he expressed impatience with the tendency of some who went too far seeking "a new man [and] new paths":

They even go to India and Africa and delve among the catacombs, holding forty days and forty nights funeral fasts in the graveyards among the skeletons: they think they will find something. . . .[19]

Malevich had not gone to these extremes. On the other hand, he had certainly read and assimilated a pair of works by P. D. Ouspensky, *The Fourth Dimension* (1904) and *Tertium Organum: The Third Canon of Thought, A Key to the Enigmas of the World* (1911)—and Ouspensky was one of those travelers, although far more sensible than implied by Malevich's comment, which embraces Ouspensky in its gloom.

Pyotr Demianovich Ouspensky (1878–1947) has been so thoroughly adopted as an author in the English-speaking world that it requires an act of imagination to resituate him in pre-Revolutionary Russia.[20] There are two Ouspenskys. The first is the Russian author, journalist, and lecturer who restated for his generation the fundamental questions of mystical philosophy, bringing to the enterprise a logical and mathematically oriented mind that did not exclude a veiled exuberance. This Ouspensky belonged in the crosscurrents of pre-revolutionary Russian culture. Not deliberately avant-garde (a category for which he had little respect), he nonetheless attracted the interest of artists and writers who were. The second Ouspensky is the penetrating author of *In Search of the Miraculous: Fragments of an Unknown Teaching* (New York, 1949), first published in English after years of revision stretching from the 1920s through World War II. This book is an account of his apprenticeship with G. I. Gurdjieff (1877–1949), the Greek-Armenian teacher whom he met in Moscow in 1915. Unquestionably the fruition of Ouspensky's work in later years, when he lived in London and for a time near New York, *In Search of the Miraculous* represents in part a deepening and clarification of *Tertium Organum*. Well known to general readers today, *In Search of the Miraculous* has received little notice from the gifted scholars who have studied Ouspensky's contributions to the avant-garde. Scholarship sets useful limits, but in this case the majority of art historians have misconstrued Gurdjieff, taking him for one of many dubious fellows drifting among the intelligentsia in Russia's principal cities on the eve of revolution. The recently established Ouspensky archive at Yale University, with its informed introduction by Merrily E. Taylor,[21] may help to correct this misapprehension, which in broad terms reflects the mistrust of scholars for "seekers of truth"—a mistrust generously returned.

From the scholar's point of view, the world of the seeker of truth dematerializes uncomfortably in its upper reaches. Moreover, facts in the upper reaches are accessible only to individual awareness and thus lack historicity until expressed through literature or art. Even then scholarship cannot prove them, but can only examine them for internal consistency and compare them with similar expressions. In any case, scholars have other concerns, and find seekers of truth a little foolish unless they manage to accomplish something on the world stage that they can evaluate in the light of sound standards.

The world of the scholar is narrow from the point of view of the seeker of truth, and the scholar's methods sadly limited. The revelatory texts and contemplative practices of the seeker convince him that he is living at the bottom of a well, and he is likely to devote considerable time to mastering the skills of climbing. He finds it odd that the scholar does not feel confined by the well and learn to climb, which from his point of view is a most interesting thing to do and has its own little scholarship.

These two species have not always been unfriendly, nor are they always today. There *is* a kind of scholarship that seeks larger truth, and a kind of seeking that respects the mind.

Tertium Organum was, by all accounts, a dramatically eye-opening book when first published in Russia in 1911. Certain of its chapters provided an intellectual and spiritual framework for Malevich's art and ideas. Ouspensky vividly reimagined art as a privileged means of penetrating to the hidden noumenal reality underlying phenomena; his language derives partly from Kant but also from Asian religious texts and a keen perception of the need for initiation. Where there is mystery, there must be initiation. In two passages bearing on art, Ouspensky wrote:

> The phenomenal world is merely a means for the artist—just as colors are for the painter, and sounds for the musician—a means for the understanding of the noumenal and the expression of that understanding. At the present stage of our development we possess nothing so powerful, as an instrument of knowledge of the world of causes, as art. . . . In art it is necessary to study "occultism"—the hidden side of life. The artist must be a clairvoyant: he must see that which others do not see. . . .[22]

> There is in existence an idea which a man should always call to mind when too much subjugated by the illusions of the reality of the *unreal*, visible world in which everything has a beginning and an end. It is the idea of infinity, the fact of infinity. . . . Let us imagine for a moment that a man begins to feel infinity in everything: every thought, every idea leads him to the realization of infinity.
>
> This will inevitably happen to a man approaching an understanding of a higher order of reality.
>
> But what will he feel under such circumstances?
>
> He will sense a precipice, an abyss everywhere, no matter where he looks; and experience indeed an incredible horror, fear and sadness, until this fear and sadness shall transform themselves into the joy of the sensing of a new reality. . . .
>
> This sense of the infinite is the first and most terrible trial before initiation. Nothing exists! A little miserable soul feels itself suspended in an infinite void. Then even this void disappears! Nothing exists. There is only infinity. . . .[23]

Suprematism can be viewed in part as an artist's response to the world-view and implicit challenge of *Tertium Organum*. In this brief account of the book, its complex rendering of the idea of the fourth dimension need not be explored in depth. Malevich adopted this concept of a higher dimension that is both real and immaterial, and he included references to the fourth dimension in the titles of early Suprematist paintings. One source of his highly simplified geometric vocabulary is thought to be the illustrations of a related book on the fourth dimension, Claude Bragdon's *A Primer of Higher Space* (1913).[24] But there was something else in Ouspensky, an initiatic account of art, and this had immense appeal for Malevich. Everywhere evident in Malevich's writings and early Suprematist art is his adoption of Ouspensky's concepts of the artist as seer, the fearful initiatic approach to the abyss and nothingness, and beyond this the advent of a transformed and joyous sensation of a new reality.

These ideas will seem sheer religious fantasy unless we allow for an order of experience based, not on the report of the eye and the assessments of discursive thought, but on the intelligence of sensation. For Cézanne, as indicated earlier, sensation referred to the perception of external reality which challenged his art over decades. In 1904 the aging Cézanne wrote with a touch of amazement and gratitude, "I remain under the sway of sensations. . . ."[25] "Painting from Nature," he said, "does not mean copying the motif, it means realizing one's sensations"[26]—as if sensation is a mysterious middle ground between the outward object and the mind that forms concepts of it, a ground on which Nature inscribes itself fully and to which man can accede through acute attention. Malevich acknowledged this formulation but, more mystical in temperament than Cézanne, he carried it altogether into the internal realm. Among the papers that he left in Berlin in 1927 is the following passage:

> Our life is a radio station into which the waves of different sensations find their way and turn into various aspects of things. The switching on and off of these waves depends on the sensation controlling the radio station. . . .
>
> Are not all people artists, striving to represent various sensations in images? Is not a spiritual patriarch a robed artist, expressing his spiritual sensation, are not the general, the soldier, the bookkeeper, the bureaucrat, the office clerk, the fighter with the hammer, all roles in various plays which they enact, because they become ecstatic, as though such plays exist in the world in reality? Yet in this eternal world theater we never see the true face of man, for whoever you ask who he is, he will answer: I am an artist, acting in a particular theater of perceptions, I am a businessman, an accountant,

an officer. . . . We are a mystery, hiding the human image from ourselves. . . .[27]

Malevich had sensed a reality prior to the narrower realities that he lists with such exuberance in this passage. At its best his art is a series of notations for what he might have called the oscillations of that prior reality. Given to human beings at the core, it can be directly perceived only at moments of unusual inward intensity. A passage from Malevich's publication of 1922, *God Is Not Cast Down,* is far more touching as autobiography than as a persuasive general psychology:

> To value and concern oneself with the inner life is man's true plan and he strives to convey what is inner to life, struggling with the external and trying to make all external things inner. Stimulation, as a cosmic flame, wavers in the inner man without purpose, sense or logic—in action it is non-objective. . . .[28]

The reference to purposelessness arises from his bitter quarrel in the 1920s with the advocates of industrial design, who wished with typically Russian vigor to abandon fine art altogether in favor of industrially useful production. But it also reflects Malevich's irreducible discovery of a fact of his inner life and, by extension, a fact that he presumed to be true of all inner lives: the existence at the heart of human beings of a reality beyond words and pragmatic purpose. He described it as "nothing" in order to emphasize the extraordinary freedom with which valid artistic images appear:

> Creation by utilitarian reason has a specific purpose. But intuitive creation has no utilitarian purpose. Until now we have had no such manifestation of Intuition in art. . . . The intuitive form should emerge from nothing. . . .[29]

He also spoke of this realm as the realm of the absolute, inaccessible to ordinary consciousness but touched upon by another order of consciousness which he described, indecisively, as "sub" or "super"—in any event, not the workaday mind:

> Nothing but the expression of the pure feeling of the subconscious or superconscious (nothing, that is, other than artistic creation) can give tangible form to absolute values. Actual utility (in the higher sense of the term) could therefore be achieved only if the subconscious or superconscious were accorded the privilege of directing creation.[30]

The quality of Malevich's thought must now have begun to appear for the reader. There are imprecisions even in this selection of texts, chosen for their clarity and directness, a sense of direction but not always a map. This impression is stronger still for many readers of his collected writings, in which page after page resists stolid understanding. Like his bookkeepers and bureaucrats, Malevich was "enacting a role because he became ecstatic"—the phrase, enigmatic and very rich, captures something of the outpouring that came from this man in the years when he could work unhindered. Precision figured among his ideals ("The artist should know what, and why, things happen in his pictures"[31]), but he was no more able than most of us to adhere at all times to his ideals. There was finally something that he could not explain and for which he provided no methodology, only totally convincing signs that he had traveled in the psychic and spiritual lands he described.

Our excursion into Malevich's thought and experience has been framed thus far by the Black Square on the one hand and the White Square on the other. Now it is time to fill the gap between these works with examples of Suprematism at its best. Although the Suprematist vocabulary of forms is limited (Malevich regarded the quadrilateral and circle as its building blocks), it gave rise to extremely varied compositions and rich combinations of color. The illustrations that follow are largely chosen from original drawings first reproduced in Malevich's 1927 Bauhaus publication; they represent his art effectively, although certain paintings that rely in part on color for their impact are unforgettable.

Among those paintings, one that demands our attention is a watercolor of 1920, like many of his works entitled simply *Suprematism* (Fig. 29). A great black rectangle, bisecting three freely aligned orange-red bars, floats in quiet equilibrium above an orange-red form, not quite a regular square. There is nothing more, apart from the blank sheet of paper that reads as undifferentiated space. Design, one might say—a happy juxtaposition of form and color that creates visual drama by "floating" a heavy form in a spacious environment. The slight wobble of the beams contrasts nicely with the axial alignment of triangle and square and accentuates the floating sensation. And one is done; one has seen the work and is ready to move on.

But many viewers don't move on so quickly; the eye lingers, taking in some value, some magic more difficult to define than the visual order of the work. Memories awaken. The axial order with multiple

29. Kasimir Malevich. *Suprematism*, 1920. Watercolor and gouache on paper. 11½″ × 8½″. Los Angeles County Museum of Art. Purchased with funds provided by Day Sage Tanguy, Rosemary B. Baruch, and Mr. and Mrs. Charles Boyer.

bars passing obliquely through it brings to mind the Orthodox Cross; the vivid contrast of black and orange-red within simple geometric bounds recalls the patterning of the robes of patriarchs and saints in the old Russian icon tradition. The open, unmodulated space surrounding the geometry evokes the continuous golden "sky" or heavenly background in many icons. None of this appears to be quoted from icons or even deliberately evoked; perhaps it would be truer to say that one and the same tradition was working its way forward with uncalculated naturalness.

Malevich's search led to an unfamiliar domain, but while moving away from both academic painting and the complexities of Cubo-Futurism and such avant-garde matter, he brought with him a deeply Russian sensibility. He had no interest in explicit service to traditional religion or any other power or inheritance:

> Art no longer cares to serve the state and religion, it no longer wishes to illustrate the history of manners, it wants to have nothing further to do with the object, as such, and believes that it can exist, in and for itself, without "things." . . .[32]

But he was also the man who wrote at the very outset of his years of discovery, "We must prepare ourselves by prayer to embrace the sky." No less than Kandinsky and Mondrian, Malevich was instinctively attuned to Franz Marc's call for "symbols that belong on the altars of a future spiritual religion."[33]

A small selection of the drawings published in Germany in 1927 will allow us to explore further (Figs. 30–32). Malevich provided them with oddly thorough titles, as if he wanted no mistake regarding his meaning. The first, *Suprematist group (white) sensation of dissolution (non-existence)* (Fig. 30), declares again an awareness of sensation as a force that dissolves boundaries, uniting a separate entity with its environment. It is a bold yet enigmatic depiction of energy in movement, the tilted rectangle traversed by mobile arcs which seem in part to impede its upward motion and in part to endow its motion with impetus, as if the design as a whole depicts an otherworldly crossbow under tension. The viewer may recognize here a just image, may sense a knowing poetry of movement and direction, substance and rarification as the eye passes over the drawing. But what is in motion here, what dissolves, what is dense and stable? From where does this image arise? Toward what is it moving? Malevich would answer with other riddles:

Non-objectivity in art is an art of pure sensations, it is milk without the bottle. . . .

Suprematism is that end and beginning where sensations are uncovered, where art emerges "as such," faceless. . . .[34]

But we do not undermine Malevich's will to achieve art "as such" if we regard this image and others of its kind as notations for conditions of Self—graphs, in his terms, of the oscillations of being. Malevich has captured the rhythm of aspiration, an upward movement that passes through resistances and gathers strength from its encounter with them.

The second drawing, *Mixed Sensations* (Fig. 31), to which Malevich appended the note, "The year '13, two basic productive elements, the circle and the square," is not a masterpiece but it helpfully illustrates some of the compositional norms of Suprematism—and also its key difficulty. Floating compositions in which geometric elements interact loosely, as in this example, or more intensively as in many other examples, can easily lose precise suggestive power. They become a pattern that does not quite draw together into a meaning. The non-objective artist always walks a razor's edge between pattern and meaning. To drive only toward "meaning" can strip a work of its visual power; it becomes a diagram or demonstration. To drive only toward "pattern" can strip a work of its substance, its intelligent participation in the human condition. Between the two extremes lies fully endowed art, in a middle ground where Malevich was often at home. *Mixed Sensations* is a pedagogic piece, a demonstration of the Suprematist elements in play, but it lacks the religious resonance that gives such dignity to Malevich's finest work.

A third drawing from the Bauhaus series, *Suprematist sensation of a mystic wave of the universe* (Fig. 32), attaches a nineteenth-century, occultist title to a work of unquestionable power. Both a seam in the fabric of the universe and a revelation emerging from emptiness, this mystic wave is the Cross itself, which need not be named to be known. Unconventional as he was, Asian in his apprehension of the fruitful Void beyond all form, Malevich gave his century some of its most original and striking works of Christian inspiration. This simple image is "most collected," as the monk Thomas Merton would say many years later of Ad Reinhardt's work (see chapter 17). It is "milk without the bottle," Christianity without convention.

This is Malevich, an artist of our time. That his theology, or philosophy, was at times difficult to follow and even confused detracts not at

30. Kasimir Malevich. *Suprematist group (white) sensation of dissolution (non-existence)*, before 1927. Pencil on paper. 6½″ × 5″. Kupferstichkabinett Basel.

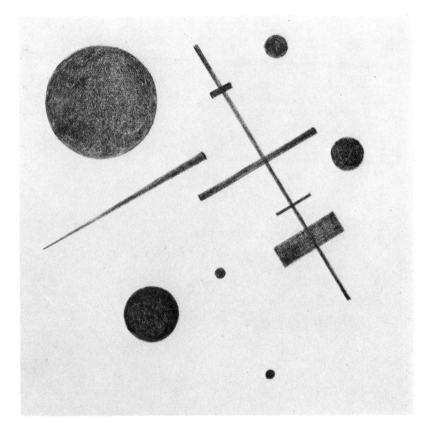

31. Kasimir Malevich. *Mixed Sensations,* before 1927. Pencil on paper. 5½″ × 5½″. Kupferstichkabinett Basel.

all from his achievement when we consider the strength of his religious *instincts* and image-making power, and the clarity of his keenest insights. Artists in earlier centuries, supported by well-ordered theologies and enlightened religious patronage, have often achieved far less. Malevich was an odd blend of modesty and defiance, succinct insight and pedantic length. Much of this makes itself known in a marvelous passage from a letter of 1916 to Alexander Benois, a renowned artist and critic of the old school who had ridiculed Suprematism:

> I have only a single bare and frameless icon of our times. . . and it is difficult to struggle.
> But my happiness in not being like you will give me the strength

32. Kasimir Malevich. *Suprematist sensation of a mystic wave of the universe,* before 1927. Pencil on paper. 5½″ × 3½″. Kupferstichkabinett Basel.

to go further and further into the empty wilderness. For it is only there that transformation can take place.[35]

CONSTRUCTIVISM: INTELLECTUAL- MATERIAL PRODUCTION

Looking back in 1924, Malevich wrote: "We have drawn two conclusions from Cubism, one is Suprematism, the other Constructivism. . . ."[36] Like Suprematism, Constructivism received its first formulation before the Revolution and first fully public showing in 1915. The founder of Constructivism, and for a time its focal point, was Vladimir Tatlin, a Ukrainian who entered the Moscow avant-garde by way of a thorough art school training, supplemented by a visit to Paris from 1913 to 1914. Tatlin met Picasso, saw at first hand the Cubist experiments in collage and three-dimensional construction, and returned to Russia keenly challenged to explore the new approach in his own terms.[37] From 1914 to the mid-1920s, Tatlin and his Constructivist allies created art and design that increasingly emphasized "materials, volume, and construction," an art that welcomed industrial materials and moved toward industrial design. With Constructivism, the artist became an engineer of form. Those of this circle who could not bring themselves to accept the transition from fine art to industrial art eventually found their way to the West or in time found ways to conform.

In the course of their work, the Constructivists attacked Malevich's art and philosophy, assailed the entire inherited notion of "fine art," and tried in their material productions and sharp-tongued writings to align their work with the needs of a revolutionary society. Deliberately materialistic, they were not fools, nor victims of inflexible Party ideology until the later 1920s; on the contrary, they enjoyed government support and their work, exhibited internationally, largely defined the Western European idea of Soviet art. The Constructivists' sometimes violent critique of the spiritual in art, Malevich's reply, and their common efforts toward an art that could belong to society at large constitute one of the richest documents in twentieth-century art. Here the spiritual was actively tested and challenged; at other times and in other places, it was merely forgotten or sentimentally assumed. The rigor of the Revolutionary era had much in its favor.

The Constructivists' work is intelligent rather than spiritual; it sees well what it sees, but no more. It reaches for rationality, social utility, and visual interest based on design and proportion rather than sensual appeal. It is stridently modern, a cooler-minded continuation of the Futurists' loud celebration of the Age of the Machine. It "knows not Joseph," acknowledges no perennial wisdom that might conceivably guide the human adventure, no transcendental context in which the adventure unfolds. Although comparable to Mondrian's work in its debt to Cubism and its development in the turbulent years from 1914 on, it differs entirely from Mondrian in its aggressively secular perspective. It cannot be ignored. The Constructivists' anger and disdain are enlightening; their affirmative aesthetic yielded fine work at home, and in time contributed centrally to Western European art. The austere humanism of industrial design at the Bauhaus, the International Style in architecture, and the broad movement in Western art that long flourished under the name Constructivism, and more recently as Minimalism, all owe debts to the original Russian Constructivists.

Malevich's admission that *we* have drawn two conclusions, Suprematism and Constructivism, implies an underlying solidarity in the avant-garde, however much it was tested and frayed. Nikolai Punin, an art historian and museum official (and husband of the celebrated poet Anna Akhmatova), recalled in his memoirs:

> [Malevich and Tatlin] shared a peculiar destiny. When it all began, I don't know, but as far as I remember they were always dividing the world between them: the earth, the heavens and interplanetary space, establishing their own sphere of influence at every point. Usually Tatlin would assign himself the earth and would try to shove Malevich off into the heavens because of his non-objectivity. Malevich, who did not reject the planets, would not surrender the earth since he considered it, justifiably, to be also a planet and could also be non-objective.[38]

The rivals' common point of departure is still visible in Tatlin's constructions of 1914 to 1915, most of which are known only through photographs of work now lost or destroyed. His *Painterly Relief. Collation of Materials* of 1914 (Fig. 33), assembled iron, plaster, glass, and asphalt with the often powerful aesthetic intelligence that emerged in Cubsim. This intelligence might be described as an impartial acceptance of varied materials and their arrangement into a pattern of unexpected harmony. Alternatively, it can be understood as an application of refined aesthetic perception to unrefined materials. The procedure often results in work that makes good sense to viewers, as if it at least symbolically redeems the random pile-up of industrial materials evident everywhere in the modern urban world. The very words "con-

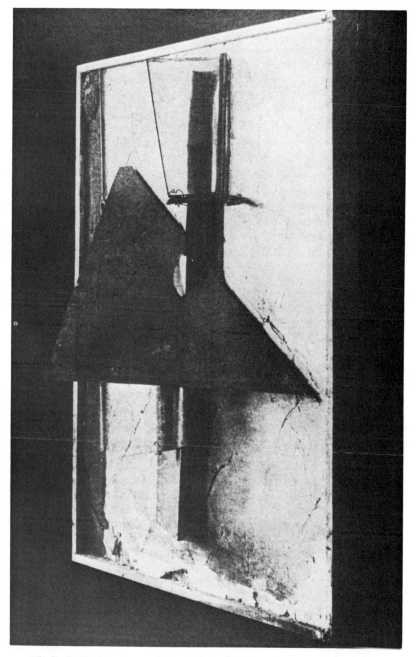

33. Vladimir Tatlin. *Painterly Relief. Collation of Materials,* 1914. Mixed media (iron, stucco, glass, asphalt). Reproduced from Christina Lodder, *Russian Constructivism,* New Haven and London, 1983, by permission of Yale University Press.

struction" and "constructive," which began to be heard among Russian artists and critics in these war years, reflect a positive spirit, an intended redemption through mind and calculation that could easily migrate from small studio projects to public commissions.

The vocabulary and order in Tatlin's *Painterly Relief* bear a family resemblance to Malevich's early Suprematist works. Much the same can be said of the earlier work of Alexander Rodchenko (1891–1956), who began exhibiting with Tatlin and Malevich in 1915–16 and became a leading member of the Constructivist group. Rodchenko's work in the years just after the Revolution is an eerie compendium of formal ideas and materials that would reappear decades later in American art to live again and at greater length, although not with more genius. A beautiful painting, now in the West (Fig. 34), only begins to evoke the restless creativity of his experiments with forms reminiscent of Malevich in their reliance on geometry in motion to evoke a sense of the cosmos. This painting hardly anticipates Rodchenko's sculptural constructions, in which he stacked what appear to be small cuttings of squared-off lumber to create assemblages of unexpectedly monumental character that anticipate the best Minimalist art of recent years. Nor do the constructions anticipate his delicate suspended mobiles of nested rings, calling to mind the orbiting of planets as well as purely technical-industrial concerns, as if he were prototyping a machine. Like many of the artists in this era, Rodchenko was torn between a traditionally Russian, speculative turn of mind and an immense desire to contribute practically to the Revolution.

The avant-garde artists of Moscow and Leningrad welcomed the October Revolution jubilantly. Their voices rose together with unbelievable fervor, praying toward the new, crying down the old. Malevich, an apocalyptic spirit well before this apocalypse occurred, wrote in 1918:

> Clean the squares of the remains of the past, for temples of our image are going to be erected.
> Clean yourselves of the accumulation of forms belonging to past ages.[39]

These words appeared in an anarchist periodical which would, in fact, be closed down by the Bolsheviks only a year or two later. In the same review in 1919, when the mood of demolition was still strong, Malevich continued, "The Book of Centuries is burnt, and the ashes thrown away."[40] Tatlin, always a cooler and more reasonable spirit, wrote some years later in a memoir:

34. Alexander Rodchenko. *Non-Objective Painting: Black on Black,* 1918. Oil on canvas. 32¼″ × 31¼″. Collection, The Museum of Modern Art, New York. Gift of the artist, through Jay Leyda.

To accept or not accept the October Revolution. There was no such question for me. I organically merged into active creative, social, and pedagogical life.[41]

In one of his rare public writings, dating to 1920, Tatlin uses in part abstract Marxist language, but through it shines the social idealism that animated the Constructivists in this era:

Our work of creating a new world . . . [calls] upon the producers to exercise control over the forms encountered in our new every-day life.[42]

Both circles, Malevich and his followers, Tatlin and his followers, sensed an unprecedented opportunity to relate the creative arts to mass culture and industrial production, including architecture. As Christina Lodder has pointed out, Marx and Engels had little to say about art, thereby leaving it to develop freely in the first Communist state. Influenced particularly by Anatoli Lunacharsky, Lenin's friend and culture minister, the government was hospitable to avant-garde art and the artists' rudimentary administrative skills. Many artists, not only those we have been discussing but also Kandinsky and others, became officials of new government units devoted to teaching, exhibiting, and encouraging the visual arts. Vera Pestel, an administrator in the Moscow arts board in those early years, reminisced long after:

> Apart from commissions, not one of these artists had ever worked until then in any organization. Now artists could decide their own fate completely independently. . . . We were full of hopes, and of the most fantastic projects.[43]

A longer memoir by the composer, Arthur Luria, reflects the situation in more detail:

> Like my friends—young avant-garde artists and poets—I believed in the October Revolution and immediately sided with it. Thanks to the support shown to us by the October Revolution, all of us, young artists—innovators and experimentalists—were taken seriously. At first boyish visionaries talked about being able to realize their dreams . . . but in general neither politics nor power really intruded into pure art. We were given complete freedom in our field to do everything that we wanted; it was the first time in history that there had been such an opportunity.[44]

Often at odds with each other in private and in the arena of published criticism, artists of different tendencies joined together to man the administrative and pedagogic ranks and launch a new art for a new world. Punin, an ally of Tatlin's, might well write:

> There is no way out of Suprematism. It is a closed concentric formation where all the roads of the world's painting have met in order to peter out.[45]

But in practice the various artists had roughly equal opportunities within government-sponsored institutions and participated in officially sanctioned exhibitions.

In 1920, Malevich joined the faculty of the art school at Vitebsk, where he worked fervently with loyal students to put Suprematism at the service of societal needs without forgetting its non-objective genius. He taught the principles of Suprematist design, adapted Suprematist geometry to architectural planning, relegated easel painting to the status of preparatory work, and even went so far as to design surface decorations for tableware—cups and saucers. For the State Pottery of Leningrad, he created a perfectly marvelous Suprematist teapot, abstract and impractical, the Idea of a Teapot from which all finite teapots could be derived.[46] He also continued his writings and found opportunities in the new Russia to publish them.

Like almost everyone else at the time, he occasionally lost his head. He wrote in 1920, for example:

> The painter . . . is no more than a prejudice of the past. . . . Long live the unified system of world architecture.[47]

But in so writing, he was only responding as best he could to forces within the arts community that were attempting to denigrate and undo his lifework. He was bent on showing the practical applications of his artistic vision—although he must have known in his heart of hearts that Suprematism was born of privileged moments of individual consciousness and could never be altogether subordinated to the needs of mass art and industrial design.

Like many Constructivists, Malevich developed a defensive version of the artist as scientist, virtually an administrative worker conscientiously fulfilling preestablished goals—a figure incomparably more sure of himself than the actual artist at work in his studio. In 1922, for example, he wrote:

> The modern artist is a scientist. . . . The artist-scientist develops his activity quite consciously and he orients his artistic effect in accordance with a definite plan; he reveals the innermost motives for a phenomenon and for its reflex action; he endeavors to move from one phenomenon to another consciously and according to plan. . . . So an artistic science now begins to take shape. . . .[48]

Kandinsky shared this dream and was surely better equipped to pursue it than the volatile Malevich. That Malevich had to dream it at all reflects the pressures on him of a society committed to organizing the future, uneasy in face of the inward and spontaneous.

Tatlin flourished more securely than Malevich in the new world of Russia; he received, in fact, the leading commission of the early post-revolutionary years. His *Monument to the Third International* of 1919–20 (Fig. 35), never carried beyond the stage of elaborate models, has been the focus of extensive recent scholarship and now stands more clearly revealed than ever.[49] This classic photograph of the monument shows it to be a work of engineering, a new Eiffel Tower, and leaves no doubt in our minds that Constructivism had entirely diverged from its original kinship with Suprematism. But the photograph does little to clarify the internal structure of the tower and its general intentions. Within the double spiral, three large glass-enclosed spaces—the lowest a cube, the next a pyramid, the topmost a cylinder—were to house various government and news media functions (in at least one version of the model, a fourth hemispherical chamber surmounted the others). The stacked chambers were to rotate slowly, each at its own speed, and great passenger elevators were to have tracked up and down the tilted spine of the structure. Intended to be taller than the Eiffel Tower and, Colossus-like, to span the River Neva in Petrograd with its great arches, it was a massively original and ambitious structure. Engineers studying its design today doubt that it could have been built, but Tatlin was confident that the technology to realize it would appear. In a brief and quite modest statement accompanying the first exhibition of the model, Tatlin wrote of the emergence in this work of "the possibility of uniting purely artistic forms with utilitarian aims."[50]

The Constructivist program, so stated, seems cool-minded and sensible. In a number of schools and institutes, most notably the Higher State Artistic and Technical Workshops, founded in 1920, this program was in fact pursued with remarkable results for a number of years. Rodchenko recalled with real pride—and a touch of revolutionary presumption:

> I was head of the metal workshop . . . and in charge of projects. Out of the same department which once made mounts for icons, lamps and other church plate, there began to emerge constructors producing electrical devices, metal objects of daily use and metal furniture.[51]

Rodchenko's complete ensemble of furnishings for a Workers' Club— tables, chairs, magazine and book racks—was displayed at a major showing of decorative art in Paris (1925), and clearly held its own. His geometrically conceived chairs, like many in the period, fall unin-

35. Vladimir Tatlin. *Model for the Monument to the Third International,*
1919–20. Photo: The Museum of Modern Art, New York.

vitingly between the naive comfort of Victorian seating and the calculated ergonomic comfort of seating today. But their similarity to the most advanced European work of the era indicates that in 1925 Russia was artistically still a part of Europe, its leading art school a small Bauhaus not to be ignored.

Rodchenko formulated the core view of the First Working Group of Constructivists, an influential artist grouping of which he was a member, in the following words:

> All new approaches to art arise from technology and engineering and move toward organization and construction. . . . The real construction is utilitarian necessity.[52]

Not evident in this rather extreme but thoughtful formulation is the vilification heaped during these years on every other tendency in art. Rodchenko was second to none in this regard.

Constructivism has been described by Stephen Bann, a leading historian of the movement, as a "delayed reaction to romanticism." Looking toward the New Man, the deliberate socialist worker, Constructivist writings evince a true revulsion, virtually organic disgust, toward what seemed the emotional excesses and imprecision of pre-Revolutionary culture. In such writings there is a half-truth worth investigating, but also hidden self-castigation, as if the authors protest not only the sins of others but also their own lurking imprecision and emotional needs. The "feminine," receptive sensibility of the fine artist was an insult to revolutionary machismo and threatened to disqualify the artist. *The New Man* (Fig. 36), a lithograph by El Lissitzky (1890–1947), who was close to both Malevich and the Constructivists, captures the heroic self-image of the era: a New Man more machine than man, cured of the tentative human condition. Its vigorous upward reach across the page and its thorough recasting of the human image are nonetheless oddly memorable.

In these years, art declared war on itself. It sought, half-knowingly, a new balance between the sober calculations of intellect and the more volatile contributions of feeling and instinct to the artist's work. It did so aggressively. There arose an extraordinary litany of complaint and contempt, for example in a text of 1919 by Boris Kushner, an author and critic who was among the first to formulate Constructivist ideas. "They used to think that art was beauty," wrote Kushner.

> They defined art as divination. Revelation, incarnation, transubstantiation. . . . [Art] was served by the trivial godlings of ecstasy,

36. El Lissitzky. *The New Man,* 1920–21. Plate 10 from the portfolio *Figurines,* Hannover, 1923. Lithograph. 12⅛″ × 12⅝″. Collection, The Museum of Modern Art, New York. Purchase Fund.

intuition, and inspiration. . . . To the socialist consciousness, a work of art is no more than an object, a thing.[53]

He was not alone in his contempt. A selection from Rodchenko's slogans, published in 1921, reflects both the austere affirmations of the Constructivist group and its boundless disregard for pre-Revolutionary culture, which it identified with self-deception and indulgence.

Construction is the arrangement of elements.
Like every science, art is a branch of mathematics.
Art that is useless for life should be kept in museums of antiquities.
The future is not going to build monasteries for priests, or for the prophets and clowns of art.
The art of our age is conscious, organized life, capable of seeing and creating.
Consciousness, experiment . . . function, construction, technology, mathematics—these are the brothers of the art of our age.[54]

These points are restated again and again in documents of the period, and something of the fervor of the age is conveyed by repetition. "The task of the Constructivist group," wrote Rodchenko and his companions in 1920,

is the communistic expression of materialistic constructive work. . . . The cognition of the experimental trials of the Soviets has led the group to transplant experimental activities from the abstract (transcendental) to the real. . . . Down with art. Long live technic. . . . Religion is a lie. Art is a lie. . . . Long live the Constructivist technician.[55]

Alexei Gan, artist and polemicist, echoed all of this in his book *Constructivism* (1922), in which he indirectly identified Malevich as the last bourgeois artist rather than an acceptable revolutionary:

. . . In our revolutionary age the "spiritual" culture of the past still stands firmly on the stilts of reactionary idealism. . . . Art is indissolubly linked with theology, metaphysics, and mysticism. . . . Death to art! It arose naturally, developed naturally, and disappeared naturally. . . . Constructivism is advancing—the slender child of an industrial culture. . . . A new chronology begins with October 25, 1917. . . .
Intellectual-material production establishes labor interrelations and a productional link with science and technology by arising in the place of art—art, which by its very nature cannot break with

religion and philosophy and which is powerless to leap from the exclusive circle of abstract, speculative activity.[56]

For all the polemical fanfare in these writings, they may strike an unexpected chord of sympathy in the reader. Certainly, the affirmative program of Constructivism has its appeal. The call for "consciousness, experiment, function, construction" hardly leaves one unmoved; it evokes a striving for clarity of mind and an earthy, workmanlike attitude. Further, Constructivism was driving toward what Europeans would soon be calling industrial design, a branch of art that has proved to be part of the genius of the century. We need apologize to no one, neither our ancestors nor our heirs, for works ranging from Mies van der Rohe's keenly designed Barcelona chair to the common American milk carton.

But most important, there is a measure of truth in the Constructivists' unease with both the aestheticism of nineteenth-century art for art's sake and the mysticism of Malevich. We can suppose that Malevich is the "prophet" cried down by Rodchenko, and he must be somewhere near the center of that "exclusive circle of abstract, speculative activity" rejected by Gan.

A mysticism that intends to survive and generate cultural forms of interest to numbers of people must be robust and inclusive. It cannot only be sensitive and inward; it cannot rely only on moments of great insight. Such moments will be rare, and this world churns on. It needs a thoroughly practical side, an ability to put people to work at occupations they understand, for reasons they understand. It cannot defy common sense every step of the way, although a proper mysticism defies common sense and ordinary preference at certain junctures. The new enters where the old cedes, and enters unaccountably. But surrounding this inscrutable event must be a stalwart culture big enough to include ordinary values. The issue is one of cultural levels and the healthy distinction between private and public—mysticism in its place, artisan work in *its* place.

Malevich did and did not understand this. From Vitebsk, where he worked with art students in 1920–21, he wrote:

Many young people have entered technical school in order to create their own animal, objective kingdom—to sew good leather, and make good houses, beds and mattresses, thinking that by this they are engaged in "the great creative work of production." Well, let them go, but someone should remain on the other path to create man's idea. We, the members of "Unovis" [acronym for his circle in

Vitebsk] are carrying out the work of Suprematism as man's new non-objective technical school. People are hostile to us because they do not understand this division of the world into two planes.

We know no aim, just as we know no practical considerations or other expediency, any more than any other being in the universe. . . . Of course, in developing a non-objective idea, we are attracting to ourselves a hail of stones; we will be called idealists, mystics, nihilists, utopians. . . .[57]

Would we ourselves throw a stone? Perhaps a small, symbolic one, poorly aimed. For there is much here that is true, and much that goes against common sense. In response to the extreme utilitarianism of the Constructivists, who hailed the death of art and its rebirth as industry, Malevich sensibly recalled that there are indeed "two planes" and that humanity needs something more than table, chair, and dish. But in affirming a "non-objective technical school" that has "no aim," he mixed the two planes and approached nonsense.

Within the very private world of contemplation and image-making, as Malevich discovered, there is initially no aim other than inner availability. A quite new and unforeseeable aim may disclose itself when the contemplative artist abandons old aims and accepts the emptiness from which, in Malevich's terms, "art emerges as such, faceless. . . ." But this intimately creative episode of loss and discovery is part of a longer process that includes the use of technical skills to render a vision on canvas or in brick and mortar. Malevich at times confused vision with the whole of art, and in so doing called down a hail of stones.

In this sense, the Constructivist critique of Malevich is accurate and resonates even now as a challenge to "mysticism" that lacks both intellectual rigor and a Benedictine regard for manual labor—for plain and simple work. In Malevich, the spiritual in art attempted to stand naked, without wrappings; it openly declared its contemplative nature and enigmatic procedures. But it failed to be simple and workmanlike when being so would have served it well. Extraordinary at times, it didn't know how to be ordinary.

It was unfairly attacked. "There are [artists]," wrote Osip Brik in *Lef,* a prominent Constructivist review,

who do not paint pictures and do not work in production—they "creatively apprehend" the "eternal laws" of color and form. For them the real world of things does not exist. . . . From the heights of their mystical insights they contemptuously gaze upon anyone who profanes the "holy dogmas" of art through their work in production, or any other sphere of material culture.[58]

It was, however, fair game.

Had Malevich been a surpassing sage rather than the volatile man he was, he would surely have failed in any case to develop an acceptably Soviet art from the kernel of Suprematist ideas and experiences. His critique of the Constructivism of his era was also accurate. "Constructivism can never kill Art," he wrote to the German artist Kurt Schwitters in 1927. "But however strange this may seem, the Constructivists have been conquered by the automaton."[59]

The conquest, in fact, proceeded not only through the Constructivists' own renunciation of art but also through the gradually narrowing scope of activity available to Constructivists in an increasingly controlled society. Rodchenko in time became a graphic artist of originality in his handling of photomontage and typography for periodicals and posters. Tatlin, the potential creator of an Eiffel Tower for Petrograd, spent the later 1920s and the 1930s working in relative obscurity on industrial designs ranging from a marvelously tender infant's feeder to a Leonardo-like flying machine, all struts and taut cloth. His seems another deflected life, although scholars have treated his designs sympathetically as a natural progression from his interest in the unity of art and technology. The Constructivists who proved able to flourish and develop their art freely were those who emigrated to the West.

Malevich became at best a poor Communist. "Social conditions," he wrote,

> are determined by the sensation of hunger, they produce only corresponding things, they do not seek spatial norms, only material ones. They cannot create art, just as ants cannot manufacture honey. . . .[60]

Although his reputation and material opportunities seem to have slowly waned in the Soviet Union after about 1924, Malevich made a European tour in 1927 for exhibitions of his work in Warsaw and Berlin. His Bauhaus publication was arranged—a signal honor in the world of the international avant-garde—and he met many artists who wholeheartedly recognized his stature, including European Constructivists who had never wished for "the death of art," men to whom he could feel close.

He left behind for safekeeping with a friend in Berlin many works of art and manuscripts, to which he added the following sad note:

In the event of my death or permanent imprisonment or in the event of the owner of these manuscripts wishing to publish them, they must be studied and then translated into another language, for finding myself at this time under revolutionary influence, contradictions could arise with that form of the defence of art that I now hold, i.e. in 1927. I consider these decisions to be final.[61]

THE UNSEEN VICTOR: HEROIC REALISM

The Soviet government's openness to artistic experiment until the mid-1920s, and to innovative graphic arts for a number of years more, did not preclude a preference in high places for another sort of art altogether. "Art belongs to the people," Lenin had written.

> With its deepest roots it should penetrate into the very thick of the toiling masses. It should be understood by these masses and loved by them.[62]

Neither Constructivists nor Suprematists disagreed. Their hope lay in educating the masses to appreciate the innovative art and industrial design they offered. For his part, Lenin was uninterested:

> I just cannot consider the works of expressionism, futurism, cubism, and other "isms" as the highest manifestation of artistic genius. I do not understand them. I do not experience any pleasure from them.[63]

He acted on his conviction. In the winter of 1917–18, just months after the October Revolution, Lenin took first steps toward what became his Plan of Monumental Propaganda, signed into law in the spring of 1918. It was a plan for demolishing Czarist monuments across the nation and replacing them with sculpture and monumental inscriptions that evoked the Revolution. Karl Marx would figure prominently among the sculptural subjects, as well as predecessors in politics and the arts ranging from the predictable (Robespierre, Garibaldi) to the wholly unpredictable (Chopin). Lenin's intention, as interpreted by John Bowlt, was "a series of . . . three-dimensional posters recognizable immediately as historical personages to the mass spectator." [64] In fact the sculptors who fulfilled commissions under this program delivered a hodgepodge of works and styles, some clearly foreshadowing the realism of Stalinist art, others drawing from avant-garde sources. Punin, always an acerbic observer of the Revolutionary art scene, wrote in 1919:

Every day I walked past the Radishchev monument, but only on the eighth day did I notice that it had fallen over.[65]

Lenin's Plan of Monumental Propaganda, uneven as it was in execution, foretold the general direction that official art would follow as the government seized hold more tightly and made its own assessments of social need. In part encouraged by Krupskaya, Lenin's wife, an artist grouping known as the Association of Artists of Revolutionary Russia exhibited in 1922, and for the occasion issued a Declaration that can be considered the charter document of Soviet realism. Realism had never disappeared from Russian art, although it only now began to reassume prominence. "The Great October Revolution," stated the Declaration,

> in liberating the creative forces of the people, has aroused the consciousness of the masses and the artists—the spokesmen of the people's spiritual life.
>   Our civic duty before mankind is to set down, artistically and documentarily, the revolutionary impulse of this great moment of history.
>   We will depict the present day: the life of the Red Army, the workers, the peasants, the revolutionaries, and the heroes of labor.
>   We will provide a true picture of events and not abstract concoctions. . . .
>   The day of revolution, the moment of revolution, is the day of heroism, the moment of heroism—and now we must reveal our artistic experiences in the monumental forms of the style of heroic realism.[66]

And so Socialist Realism was born, and the style was launched that dominates official Soviet art to this day. Western people generally ignore this art because its style is imposed, and over the years the West has celebrated periodic revelations of "unofficial" Soviet art, some of it very beautiful. There are nonetheless fine craftsmen among the practitioners of the official style.
Malevich, in his time, looked on angrily:

> Artistic societies . . . have again resurrected themselves in Russia. They could be described as a great graveyard of painters . . . with the flag of the magic circle of death standing over them.[67]

The year 1934 definitively marked the end of the Russian avant-garde, with all that it had brought both of the spiritual in art and of the strident social conscience that could not find its relation with the more inward aspects of art. This was the year of the First All-Union Congress of Soviet Writers. At that conference, an exercise in humiliation for independent artists and writers, much was said that gives pause. Viktor Shklovsky, for example, formerly of the avant-garde periodical, *Lef,* said:

> We constructivists created a construction that proved to be non-constructive.[68]

Rather than lapse into an elegiac mood over the subversion of the grand adventure of the Russian avant-garde, we would do better to listen again to the impassioned voice of Malevich, striving to express one of the central truths of the spiritual in art:

> Empty space is a place where man wishes to find asylum and save himself from things and instruments. . . . In this empty space he wishes to stand outside views, images, and conceptions, outside struggle and existence which has shattered into little pieces like ice that hinders his movements, pushing him in different directions. . . . He seeks spaciousness . . . he will find a location that is without path. . . .[69]

We could reformulate Malevich's insight to conform more obviously with the Buddhist concept of *śūnyatā,* Emptiness, or with the Christian concept of *kenosis,* the emptying that precedes any possibility of grace. But there is no need to do so. Speaking in his own way, with his own good measure of torment and confusion, he spoke clearly enough.

RUSSIANS ABROAD, AND AN AFTERWORD

We have brought the spiritual life of Russian avant-garde art into focus by dwelling on the conflicting ideals of Malevich and the Tatlin/Rodchenko circle of Constructivists. Issues and individuals of real interest in this complex period have necessarily been overlooked, but the strife of ideas has made itself felt.[70] Most of the leading combatants whom we have discussed remained in the Soviet Union; others, unwilling to adapt to the climate of the times and the growing emphasis on industry, emigrated to the West—among them Wassily Kandinsky in 1921, the brothers Naum Gabo and Anton Pevsner in 1922, and Marc Chagall in the same year. El Lissitzky moved easily between Russia and the West in the 1920s, serving intelligently as a channel through which Russian avant-garde art and ideas became known, especially in

Germany. In Europe, the De Stijl movement under the exuberant political leadership of Theo van Doesburg, and for a time the artistic leadership of Piet Mondrian, recognized its kinship with Constructivism and opened the pages of its influential journal to Constructivist voices. Laszlo Moholy-Nagy, the Hungarian artist who replaced Johannes Itten at the Bauhaus in 1923, brought with him a fully assimilated understanding of the Constructivist and Suprematist approaches. Kandinsky brought no less to the Bauhaus, although his interests lay with painting and the theory of art while Moholy-Nagy explored three-dimensional construction and the principles of design.

From these roots, Constructivism spread throughout Europe and emigrated in time to the United States. Through the Depression, World War II, and the flourishing postwar period, Naum Gabo (1890–1978) steadily served as a living link with the history and ideals of the first Constructivism. Through periodic lectures and articles, he recalled its meaning and lasting importance, while in his art he singlemindedly pursued an evolving Constructivist vision. Concerned in the years around 1917 with planar constructions, he moved on to explore the aesthetics of science. His mature work often seems a translation into elegant abstract form of mathematical relationships that could be written as complex equations (Fig. 37). An art more of mind than of spirit, it is clean and sure of purpose. Knowing that Constructivism could easily become an intellectual exercise, he insisted throughout his life on a hidden ethic. "Far be it from me to advocate," he said in 1948,

> that a constructive work of art should consist merely of an arrangement of . . . elemental means for no other purpose than to let them speak for themselves. I am constantly demanding from myself and keep on calling to my friends [to convey] . . . not just some image, any image, but a new and constructive image . . . which by its very existence as a plastic vision should provoke in us the forces and the desires to enhance life, assert it and assist its further development.[71]

The destiny of Suprematism as an idea and a repertory of forms was more complex than that of Constructivism. While Constructivism entered the mainstream of European art with its name and general intentions intact, Suprematism never became a European art although its spirit moved in Kandinsky's work during his Bauhaus years (see chapter 13), and the Bauhaus paid Malevich the homage of publication. The individuality of Suprematism seems to have been submerged in the geometric vocabulary of European Constructivism, only to be re-

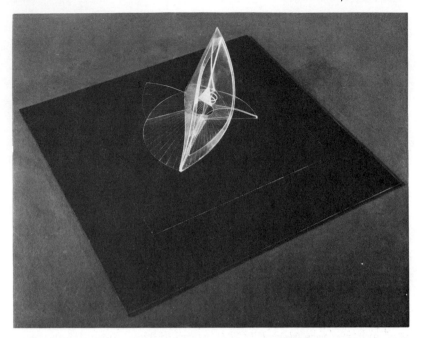

37. Naum Gabo. *Spiral Theme*. Construction in plastic. 5½″ × 13¼″ × 9⅜″, on base 24″ square. Collection, The Museum of Modern Art, New York. Advisory Committee Fund.

covered again after World War II, when a new generation of artists recognized a kinship with its extreme simplicity and scholars saw to the translations that Malevich had requested.

A short time ago I visited the New York studio of Luise Kaish, whose brilliant work in collage I have long admired (see chapter 21). Expecting to see highly colored, complex grids with telling details, reflecting a visual poet's exploration of image and experience, I was not disappointed. But at the far end of a studio wall hung a triptych of plain square canvases, carefully aligned, that took me by surprise. They depicted simple geometries—a circle inscribed in a square, an equal-armed cross, and a linear "seam"—through a combination of meticulous outline and spontaneously applied white paint. They were works of simple beauty. We spoke about them briefly, Kaish referring to the idea of archetypal symbolism, but she clearly had little wish to launch a prolonged verbal inquiry, and there was no need to do so. These works were Malevich again, not "copied," borrowed, or even necessarily remembered, but their eloquence was also his.

We have an art of our own. We speak it naturally, as a native language. It is, of course, not limited to the metaphysical geometries of Malevich or the bold physical structures of the Constructivists; these are only two complementary aspects of an art that includes much more. That these "signs" have survived and continue to challenge artists reflects the often unacknowledged stability of the art of our century.

11 PAUL KLEE: CLOSER TO THE CENTER

Paul Klee (1879–1940)—Swiss-born, mature in art by 1914, Bauhaus master in the great years of the institution, renowned for works of originality, wit, and depth—is the author of one of the century's few unerring statements on the spiritual in art. With Kandinsky's *On the Spiritual in Art* and Brancusi's aphorisms, Klee's 1924 lecture "On Modern Art" is all one need know to be certain that twentieth-century art conceived ideals that in their religious dimension would have been recognizable to Meister Eckhart and in their workshop dimension to Leonardo. The lecture, published years later as an essay, is available today in a familiar anthology of artists' writings.[1] Nonetheless, it is something of a Dead Sea Scroll buried in the mass of documents and works of the century, rarely offered to art students as a unique meditation that might positively influence their development over many years.

Modern time moves so quickly that an artist's words pronounced little more than sixty years ago, however penetrating and timeless, are immobilized in "history"; they do not feel like a timely message. The rapid recession of historical moments, each sealed off from the next, easily defeats the sense of kinship and shared enterprise that might link artists and concerned people from one end of the century to the other; the discoveries of one moment are "history" for succeeding ones.

We should leap over the obstacle. It is not impossible to enter into dialogue with Klee as if we were with him and he with us. History orders and distances the past; dialogue recovers it. Can we set out in the first part of this chapter to read his lecture as if it were new, stopping here and there to explore or emphasize, ignoring great chunks of it, hoping nonetheless to adopt into our repertory of ideas the essence of what he conveyed to his audience in 1924?

"I shall confine myself," he began,

largely to throwing some light on those elements of the creative process which, during the growth of a work of art, take place in the
subconscious.

Attitude and method are already apparent: Klee is taking a reasoned
view of experiences that move well past thought into the domains of
feeling and sensation, nonverbal domains that our era has chosen to
call "subconscious." References to process and growth imply at once
that, for Klee, laws similar to those governing orderly change in Nature also govern art.

To establish himself as a man who may have a special gift but who
nevertheless shares the common lot, he went on to describe himself as

> a being who, like you, has been brought unasked into this world
> of variety and where, like you, he must find his way for better or
> for worse.

To find one's way means generally to search for it, but Klee's expression betrays modesty. *Seekers* are sometimes proud of their activity,
however much it is at base motivated by humble need, while people
finding their way are just finding their way.

After these preliminaries, Klee introduces a major image to evoke
the artist's scope and role:

> May I use a simile, the simile of the tree? The artist has studied this
> world of variety and has, we may suppose, unobtrusively found his
> way in it. His sense of direction has brought order into the passing
> stream of image and experience. This sense of direction in nature
> and life, this branching and spreading array, I shall compare with
> the root of the tree.
>
> From the root the sap flows to the artist, flows through him, flows
> to his eye.
>
> Thus he stands as the trunk of the tree.
>
> Battered and stirred by the strength of the flow, he guides the vi-
> sion on into his work.
>
> As, in full view of the world, the crown of the tree unfolds and
> spreads in time and space, so with his work.
>
> Nobody would affirm that the tree grows its crown in the image of
> its root. Between above and below can be no mirrored reflection. It
> is obvious that different functions expanding in different elements
> must produce divergences.
>
> But it is just the artist who at times is denied those departures
> from nature which his art demands. He has even been charged with
> incompetence and deliberate distortion.

And yet, standing at his appointed place, the trunk of the tree, he does nothing other than gather and pass on what comes to him from the depths. He neither serves nor rules—he transmits.

His position is humble. And the beauty at the crown is not his own. He is merely a channel.

Klee's choice of image and his fastidious observation that no one expects root and branch to be identical reflect his lifelong study of Nature. Destined by temperament to follow the models of Leonardo and Goethe, he applied his mind and prodigious draftsman's abilities to exploring the forms and dynamics of Nature to a degree unequalled by other artists in our time. As Emerson once said of Thoreau, his "position was in Nature and so commanded all its miracles and infinitudes."[2] But as the simile of the tree makes clear, through study and absorption Klee transformed what he gathered "at the roots" into something new. It may be worth noting that even in 1924, before what must have been a well-informed audience in the university town of Jena, Klee felt the need to defend "departures from nature," i.e., the more abstract language of contemporary art.

In this passage, Klee ponders the delicate balance between impassioned perception and humble transmission. "Battered and stirred by the strength of the flow," artists often identify themselves with that flow and acquire eruptive, "inspired," egotistical characters. Infinitely more scholarly and, in his own words, unobtrusive than artists of this kind, Klee found his joy in allowing the movement from the depths to occur without self-attribution. To be a channel was not only enough, it was essential if the movement was to pass unhindered. "He neither serves nor rules"—a subtle formulation. Thought typically leaps from the idea of modesty to ideas of service or even subservience, but Klee proposes a rarer attitude. The artist's sensitivity "at the roots" and expressiveness and craftsmanship "in the branches" require so much of him or her that there is no time left over for sentimentality. In Hindu terms, Klee was a *jñāna yogi,* a seeker of knowledge with a disciplined gift for recognizing the irrelevant and freeing himself from it. Clearly, knowledge for him was not only idea; it was perception of all kinds.

After offering his vision of the tree, Klee moves briefly to cooler observations about the simultaneity of visual art; its many dimensions can be seized by eye and mind all at once, unlike words or music which unfold in time. We must, however, study separately the elements or "parts" of visual art without losing sight of the fact that they are parts of a whole. "Otherwise," he observes, again evoking the quest that underlies his art, our courage may fail us when we find ourselves faced with a new part leading in a completely different direction, into other dimensions, perhaps into a remoteness where the recollection of previously explored dimensions may easily fade.

This is the language of quest tales in which the hero needs courage to move beyond the known "into other dimensions, into a remoteness," where forgetting is an overwhelming danger. That remoteness drew Klee. He was a natural esotericist who sensed that more is hidden than shown and that one must seek the secrets of reality where they hide. "Nature loves to hide," said Heraclitus in the earliest formulation of this insight.

Klee's abiding concern for thoughtful observation and manual craftsmanship kept his inherent tendency toward abstraction in balance. He was both speculative and empirical, high-minded and handy. A long passage in his lecture lays out with precision the various formal means of visual art defined as measure, weight, and quality, manifesting through line, color, and the play of light and shadow. He admits the reader into his studio research, in effect grounding metaphysics in an earthly discipline of mind, eye, and hand. "Vagueness in one's work is . . . only permissible when there is a real inner need," he observes, echoing William Blake's demand for lucidity in art. The challenge of mastering workshop knowledge prompts him to evoke again the greater challenge that lies beyond it:

> I now come to the first construction using the three categories of elements which have just been enumerated.
>
> This is the climax of our conscious creative effort. This is the essence of our craft. This is critical.
>
> From this point, given mastery of the medium, the structure can be assured of foundations of such strength that it is able to reach out into dimensions far removed from conscious endeavor.

In this passage, "conscious" surely means reasoned and deliberative; Klee is speaking the *lingua franca* of our time by describing a subtle, nonverbal consciousness in action as "far removed from conscious endeavor." The words call to mind a form-finding, form-making intelligence that draws from the whole human being and moves more quickly than worded thought. In my view, thought describes such intelligence as "unconscious" because it doesn't quite understand its own role in that intelligence—and thus experiences itself as an outsider when, ironically, the purest faculty of mind is at work there.

Klee goes on to explore why artists of his kind first create forms and only later name them and, perhaps, acknowledge their relationship with familiar objects in the world. The artist brings together pictorial elements in an autonomous construction and *rediscovers* them as table, chair, face. By attention to the materials of art and the internal play of form rather than to external objects, the artist finds "tremendous possibilities for the variation of meaning."

> Color as tone value: e.g., red in red, i.e., the entire range from a deficiency to an excess of red. . . . Then the same in yellow. . . . Or colors diametrically opposed—i.e., changes from red to green, from yellow to purple, from blue to orange.
> Tremendous fragments of meaning!

The last phrase is one of Klee's great moments as an interpreter of art, although the brilliant translation departs widely from the idiosyncratic original *Stückwelten des Inhaltes*, literally "part-worlds of content." The phrase evokes the artist's acute responsiveness to color as such and his or her ability to start from color alone to build new meaning, just as writers build meaning not only from the sense but also from the sonority of words.

One must first understand and experience the autonomy of visual impressions in order to delight in art. In part, the viewer has to see works of art as a cat sees the world, thoughtlessly but ever so acutely. Many artists see in this way when they are working: without names, but with immense sensitivity to the pressure of each little variation. Nonverbal awareness is not a substitute for or improvement over discernment of mind—a hypothesis from the 1960s that hasn't worked out very well. They are in fact complementary kinds of intelligence, both needed for a connoisseurship of art and of things in general.

Klee's exploration of color and form, and his assertion of the artist's freedom to work with them as such without reference to the external world, leads him to restate in modern terms one of the most ancient insights about art and artist.

> . . . [the artist] surveys with penetrating eye the finished forms which nature places before him.
> The deeper he looks, the more readily he can extend his view from the present to the past, the more deeply he is impressed by the one essential image of creation itself, as Genesis, rather than by the image of nature, the finished product.
> Then he permits himself the thought that the process of creation can today hardly be complete and he sees the act of world creation stretching from the past to the future. Genesis eternal!

. . . Does then the artist concern himself with microscopy? History? Paleontology?

Only for purposes of comparison, only in the exercise of his mobility of mind. And not to provide a scientific check on the truth of nature.

Only . . . in the sense of a freedom which merely demands its rights, the right to develop, as great Nature herself develops.

The distinction so drawn is Aquinas's distinction between *Natura naturans* and *Natura naturata*—Nature "naturing" and Nature "natured." For Klee, the artist at best is Nature "naturing," one in kind with the creative force of Nature herself, although on a very different scale. The potential coalescence of Great Nature and the artist's nature leads Klee to a classic statement of the visionary artist's faith:

Presumptuous is the artist who does not follow his road through to the end. But chosen are those artists who penetrate to the region of that secret place where primeval power nurtures all evolution.

There, where the powerhouse of all time and space—call it the brain or heart of creation—activates every function; who is the artist who would not dwell there?

In the womb of nature, at the source of creation, where the secret key to all lies guarded.

But not all enter. Each should follow where the pulse of his own heart leads. . . . Our pounding heart drives us down, deep down to the source of all.[3]

What springs from this source—whatever it may be called, dream, idea or fantasy—must be taken seriously only if it unites with the proper creative means to form a work of art.

Then those curiosities become realities—realities of art which help to lift life out of its mediocrity.

For not only do they more or less revitalize the visible, but they also make secret visions visible.

Typical of Klee, and deeply moving, is his abrupt contraction from vision to a craftsman's practicality: only "the proper creative means" entitle visionary "curiosities" to become parts of life and enduring inspirations not just for the artist but for the community. The word curiosities (*Kuriosa*) is itself curious: Klee's innate circumspection reasserts itself, balancing his impassioned journey to the heart of creation with a probing attitude. As in myths and fairy tales, it is not enough to reach the treasure; one must bring it back.

The talk concludes with an extraordinary evocation of the interdependence of artist and public:

> Sometimes I dream of a work of really great breadth, ranging through the whole region of element, object, meaning, and style. This, I fear, will remain a dream, but it is a good thing even now to bear the possibility occasionally in mind.
>
> Nothing can be rushed. It must grow, it should grow of itself. . . .
>
> We must go on seeking it! We have found parts, but not the whole! We still lack the ultimate power, for: the people are not with us.
>
> But we seek a people. We began over there in the Bauhaus. We began there with a community to which we all give what we have.
>
> More we cannot do.

An artist of our time, supposedly a blasted time with no sound inspiration, has guided us on a remarkable journey. He has led us from the color wheel and the workshop to the source of all. He has counseled artists to develop technical craft to a superb degree *as preparation* for a movement beyond "conscious endeavor" into remote, fundamental realms of creativity. He has offered an image of the artist as a link between the hidden depths into which roots penetrate and the common light of day in which branches freely multiply; and he has asked us to recognize the artist as a questing seeker, both invited and bursting uninvited into the heart of creation. All of this he has stated with unquestionable authority, as one who not only imagined or admired these things but lived them. The word "spirituality" is too narrow to encompass it all.

With his appreciation for the concept of "Genesis eternal," Klee would not think that he had the last word or cut off later generations from the light by his own closeness to it.

JOYS OF THE APPRENTICE, SORROWS OF THE JOURNEYMAN

The sheer authority of Paul Klee's lecture brings back to mind questions initially explored in terms of guides, men and women who achieve broad visions and offer them to the community as a Way or discipline. Kandinsky's warmth softens the impact of his authority. First deliberate explorer of the spiritual in the art of our time, he also seems a friend—prone to error, more than willing to pick himself up and start again. Klee is different. A cool breeze blows through his art and writings—qualities of detachment and genius, more than a touch of irony. He traveled the remoteness, like the artist in an old Chinese tale who painted a scene and then entered into it forever. One's admiration of him can be tinged with self-doubt: is it possible to go as far as he did, possible to go further? Isn't it already *too late* to achieve the mastery of form in Nature, the workshop technique, the philosophical breadth that he achieved? One of the prices of association with genuine authority is bouts of self-doubt.

Whether or not the reader experiences Klee as an authority, it is probably time to consider the linked questions of authority and tradition. The spiritual in art cannot flourish at length and in fullness without an acknowledged tradition. Tradition, meaning "the given over," the passed on, implies teachers and students, mastery and apprenticeship, authority and receptivity. Artists in our time tend to have an *ad hoc* sense of tradition—feelings of kinship with certain artists of the past, personal loyalty to teachers who benefited them—but very little of the mystique of tradition.

The mystique of tradition is complex. It is made up in part of a sense of immersion in an enduring enterprise to which one comes as a neophyte, a learner and beggar. It includes a "sacred history" and heroic personages who dominated the epochs when that history was being constructed out of their wishes and deeds. It recognizes the difficulty of certain traditional ideas, which may require a lifetime to understand with the whole of one's being. It acknowledges the unconditional demand imposed by certain inherited practices or methods. Think, for example, of Cézanne's unending quest to "realize his sensations," as if he could never entirely succeed in transferring subtle perceptions onto canvas; he laid the groundwork for a code of creative dissatisfaction among some twentieth-century artists. In the 1950s, Georges Braque had not forgotten Cézanne:

> . . . Since Cézanne, talent is not enough. There is here an aspect that could practically be called heroic. To my way of thinking there is no master to equal Cézanne, who took risks and searched for himself all his life.[4]

Participation in a strong tradition is experienced as inviting, even as a necessity for one's life, but also as forbidding. Because there are standards, there is risk of failure. Because heroes have gone before, the aspirant must become a hero—and knows in sincere moments that this outcome is unlikely. The aspirant goes forward nonetheless, and this is the beginning of a modest sort of heroism.

The liveliest paradoxes emerge from a serious encounter with authentic tradition at any level. No one has illuminated these paradoxes and strains more clearly than Harold Bloom in his studies of literary tradition.[5] I am not certain that he caught the ecstasy of apprenticeship, but he certainly depicted with remarkable penetration the anxieties of a later stage, when the journeyman must emerge from under the master's shadow to establish his or her independence.

Apprentice, journeyman, master—these are the stages of initiation into craft traditions and, by extension, into any tradition that demands effort over long periods of time. When the aspirant has recognized the tradition to which he or she *must* belong and has obtained provisional acceptance as a student, the ecstasy of apprenticeship begins. The central experience is guided learning under the tutelage of an impressive teacher. A hitherto unknown world of ideas and methods is freely opened to the apprentice. The tuition and menial service associated with apprenticeship—the long vigils over white-hot kilns in the middle of the night, the hours spent redrafting a design that fell short—are nothing in comparison with the opportunities for learning. The abuse meted out to the apprentice for errors made and ideas misunderstood is nothing in comparison with the limitless joy of being given another chance. Learning itself is redefined as an assimilation not only of external methods and intellectual concepts but also of attitudes, customs, history, sensibility. The apprentice enters into a tradition as if into a great house with innumerable rooms, each to be visited and memorized, each containing a test of his or her substance and adding to it.

All of this occurs under the eyes of the *mentor* (from Indo-European *men,* mind; the mentor is the mind-maker). To be a child in such a house and of such a father or mother is a great thing, entailing only a child's limited responsibility. Needless to say, the apprentice's admiration for the mentor is boundless. Every word, every gesture has meaning. The poor mentor cannot tie a shoelace unobserved—as a wonderful Hasidic tale illustrates, even that simple gesture can be a teaching. Authority is not an abstraction in the actual experience of it; it is a personal influence intimately received.

The apprentice in time becomes the journeyman. Scarcely less joyful in its earlier stages, the journeyman's life is one of provisional companionship with the master and marked by the assumption of limited teaching duties, not so much to teach as to learn in greater depth. The journeyman knows many of the techniques of the craft, although there is still much to learn; knows the history and legends that define its ancestry; has acquired respect for it in the very cells of the body, so that he or she is well on the way toward *becoming* the craft and need not always look outside for a sense of direction. The journeyman recognizes with increasing clarity that the tradition exists only *in and through people,* not in the abstract, and that it must be carried on through a fragile human medium; hence a dawning sense of responsibility, well before the journeyman is capable of full responsibility. All of his or her attainments are provisional. The journeyman is uncertain, yet accepted; knows his abysmal ignorance, yet must stand forward.

The journeyman travels with the mentor, substitutes for him on occasion and is proud to be able to do so, however haltingly. But after hours the mentor mounts his attack, points out senseless errors, builds fires of retribution in the face of which the aspirant is nothing. The journeyman must now grow quickly to endure both the prestige of teaching and the ordeal of correction.

This duality in the end becomes a burden: the journeyman is neither a child nor an adult, neither joyously tied to the mentor nor wholly free. A dark time ensues. Admiration for the mentor is increasingly accompanied by unspoken recognition of his or her shortcomings, perhaps not in the craft itself but in other respects—and perhaps even in the craft because no one, finally, is all things. The growing awareness that human beings are the sole vehicle of tradition is paralleled by a new awareness of human flaws.

The relation between journeyman and mentor is by now old and well established; it easily survives these small depredations. More serious is the journeyman's uneasy sense of being overshadowed by the mentor, as if some maturation, only guessed, is impossible at close quarters. A heretical thought, it adds to the journeyman's burden, for the truth is and always will remain that the mentor is the giver of light—the man or woman who has illuminated the journeyman's mind, body, and world. If a potter, the journeyman knows himself to have been fired in the kiln with the mentor's pots. Likewise a painter: the journeyman can see only because the mentor showed him how. The journeyman moves efficiently in the pattern of the craft only because the mentor showed the movement and the pattern.

The mentor, seeing more than he or she lets on, leaves this miserable situation intact for a long time. It is the final fire. No amount of compassion can relieve it. Furthermore, the mentor himself experiences a subtle change of heart. He cannot help but see that his teaching has failed in many respects; the journeyman is acceptable, perhaps even shows mastery on occasion, but more often seems living proof that the teaching effort was clumsy and unworthy of his own teacher's example. It has quite logically produced a clumsy worker, an inexact thinker. The mentor feels humiliated. The journeyman feels humiliated.

At this stage of the drama, the mentor traditionally invites the journeyman to produce a ritual object known as the "masterpiece." Often a small object but intensely technical in nature, the masterpiece is intended to demonstrate to senior members of a craft guild that the journeyman deserves a place among them; it is a final examination. Judgment and acceptance of this object are not left to the journeyman's mentor alone, for he or she is not expected to be objective. For the occasion, a number of masters of the craft gather around. If all goes well, the masters induct the journeyman into the craft as a mature worker in whom they deem the full authority of the tradition to be intact.

Now a master, and prepared in turn to be a mentor, the former journeyman may discover what it was that remained beyond reach. The final level of mastery cannot be conferred by others.

If he succeeds in making that discovery, the tradition will continue to grow; if he fails to do so or forgets that it is needed, the tradition will begin, perhaps unnoticeably, to wither. For the goal of the drama just enacted is to bring individuals to the point where they not only sustain a tradition but add to it.

In any good teaching studio, today and always, mentors and their pupils are seized at moments by the archetypal pattern: differences in age, technical skill, and sophistication of sensibility catalyze it. What is missing in our time is not richly endowed people to live the initiatic adventure but a clearer sense of tradition. We need to rediscover the history of twentieth-century art as a tradition—that is, history that makes demands on the living.

PAUL KLEE'S ART

A photograph of Klee in his Bauhaus studio, taken in 1925, speaks to the difficulty of summarizing his art, and it illustrates how the man placed himself in relation to it. He stands in a painter's smock, arms soberly crossed, partly hidden by an easel in the background of a studio filled with the evidence of industry. I count six works in progress on the easels, others hung on the rear wall. The center of the photograph is not the man himself but low tables with brushes, paints, solvents—the tools of his trade. Klee is "standing at his appointed place," "unobtrusive," as he wrote for the Jena lecture given just a year ear-lier.[6] Other photographs show the remarkable intensity of his face and eyes, the eyes of a man devoted to consciousness. It was an intensity that served his work and entered into it.

Some eight thousand paintings, drawings, and prints came from his various studios between the turn of the century and his death in 1940. A 1914 trip to Tunisia had enormous impact on his sensitivity to color; from then on his work is virtually a continuum. Among his innumer-able creations, certain works naturally stand out. Up to a point there are "periods"—cycles of interests that emerge, submerge, and re-emerge, rather than definite ages to which there was no return. Above all, there was sustained vision and execution, few if any of the spells of laziness and self-delight that occasionally swamped Picasso and other prolific masters of our time. Klee's works are generally small or moder-ate in size, they do not trumpet their importance or ask to be consid-ered "monumental." Klee was an artist who loved movement and who remained in movement until his very last years, when a difficult ill-ness narrowed his exuberant vocabulary of forms, although not his intensity.

The range of theme and style is overwhelming, twenty artists in one. Klee's gifts from the very beginning—remarkable draftsmanship, vig-orous, original imagination, satirical wit—never failed him and only matured as time went on. To these he added over the years genuine mastery of color and atmosphere, a knowledge of pictorial construc-tion that was deliberately scientific and exploratory, and an intimate acquaintance with form and process in Nature which inspired his work rather than bound it into imitation. He further added an open-ness to what he called "curiosities"—imagery drawn without the Sur-realists' fanfare from the realm of the unconscious and dreams, imag-ery distilled from the art of children, the insane, prehistory, and tribal cultures. His intelligence held all of this together in one consistent fab-ric. His was an intelligence that moved across the full range of experi-ence, from minute observation of Nature and the technical means of art to the most distant metaphysical realm where, as he once wrote, "the light of the intellect is piteously extinguished."[7]

There was also an imperfection. This perfectly gifted artist was bur-dened with what seems a flaw, yet one that surely made its contribu-tion to his ceaseless imaginative energy. Something rubbed at him, like a bit of grit in the pearl oyster. To grasp that flaw in the larger context of his creativity we should look at a number of his works, a small selec-tion from a universe of equally arresting examples.

38. Paul Klee. *Battle Scene from the Comic-Operatic Fantasy "The Seafarer,"*
1923. Colored sheet, watercolor and oil drawing. 15″ × 20¼″. Collection
Frau T. Durst-Haas. © 1987 by COSMOPRESS, Geneva. Photo: Colorphoto
Hans Hinz.

A painting from midstream in his career, *Battle Scene from the
Comic-Operatic Fantasy "The Seafarer"* (Fig. 38), illustrates the elements of fantasy, technical control, and satirical humor so often present
in his work. Klee reconceived the archaic theme of a hero combatting
monsters as a droll encounter between a stick-figure knight burdened
by a voluminous, disabling helmet and quilted sea-creatures with confused, flounder-like eyes. Klee set this vignette against a beautifully
rendered gradation of blues and blacks, an abstract study that is as
much the theme of the painting as the mock-heroic encounter itself.
This work is not a classic expression of the spiritual in art; it demonstrates, instead, a wonderfully satisfying intelligence that gently
mocks the heroic. It is an icon that has taken an odd turn, depicting a
St. George who must do his best to slay the dragon with the odds ab-
surdly stacked against him. *The Seafarer* participates in the world of
traditional religious and heroic imagery through warm-hearted irony
and humor—at a distance.

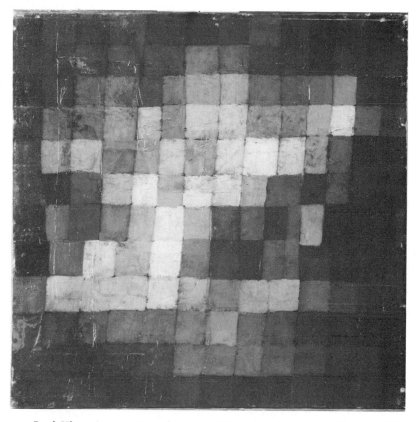

39. Paul Klee. *Ancient Sound*, 1925. Oil on board. 15″ × 15″. Öffentliche Kunstsammlung Basel, Kunstmuseum. © 1987 by COSMOPRESS, Geneva. Photo: Colorphoto Hans Hinz.

The colored grid in the background provided the subject for some of Klee's most beautiful work. During his trip to Tunisia, he experienced that "color possesses me. . . . Color and I are one."[8] Some years later as a Bauhaus professor, he developed an extraordinarily thorough course of study on color. The results of this marriage of passion and intellect show. In *Ancient Sound*, for example (Fig. 39), a grid of muted earth tones emerges from surrounding darkness with magical power. The title of this painting is all the comment that it really needs. The emergence of light, its continuing relation with darkness, and the diversity of its manifestation as color is theme enough, many themes in one like all truly expressive abstract art. The image takes the viewer into the realm of primary sensation—the seeing and sensing that we do negligently, and in front of this painting with greater awareness. It can also take the viewer into a realm of self-awareness where one's own life is experienced, not in words but in a compact recognition as if this chiaroscuro were one's own image.

This is the spiritual in art: an image with the ability to simplify and intensify the viewer who receives it. "Everything passes," wrote Klee,

> and what remains of former times, what remains of life, is the spiritual. The spiritual in art, or we might simply call it the artistic. In everything we do, the claim of the absolute is unchanging.[9]

Like much from his personal notebooks, the passage is a little cryptic, addressed to himself, rich in thought and feeling—and especially appropriate to a work titled *Ancient Sound*. He goes farther in his private notes than I am prepared to go, by equating the artistic with the spiritual. Gustav Klimt, the Viennese painter, comes to mind as an artist of uncertain spirituality but enormous imagination, skill, and passion—an artist of distinction, not a contributor to the spiritual in art. The difference need not be broken down.

A well-known image from Klee's *Pedagogical Sketchbook*,[10] the waterwheel and hammer (Fig. 40) suggests the brilliance of his graphic work, at which he excelled early. In context an illustration of active, passive, and mediating forces (respectively the falling water, the hammer, and the wheels and transmission belt), the drawing has its own delightful genius: the massive forces of industrial production have been miniaturized into an image childlike and wise. The viewer senses a *joie de vivre* in the drawing that goes far beyond its humdrum subject, as if in the very act of drawing Klee began spontaneously to play and to discover. Further, the hammer is about to strike an empty worktable and the whole apparatus is spindly—poetry pretending to be engineering. In this lies its extraordinary charm. Like so much else from Klee's hand it evokes largely, through modest means. The movement "from above," where the waters flow with tempestuous freedom, to the dry thudding "below" of a boxy hammer will suggest to some viewers a metaphysic of the degradation of energy. At whatever level one likes—as pedagogic illustration, as poetry, or as metaphysics—the drawing lives.

Already by 1903, Klee had shown an extraordinary gift for satirical images of humanity. The etchings from those early years—a pair of naked bureaucrats bowing to one another, a menacing head, an evil-looking "virgin in a tree"—are the forerunners of a gallery of human

40. Paul Klee. *Waterwheel and Hammer*. Print. Reproduced from *Pedagogical Sketchbook*, fig. 25. © 1987 by COSMOPRESS, Geneva.

beings who are by turns funny, confused, lost, strained, child-like, frightened, evil, but never restful and intact. A 1919 self-portrait, *Lost in Thought* (Fig. 41), can stand for hundreds of examples. Klee has rendered himself almost as an African totem, a blocky carved mass with cowrie eyes and a seed-case mouth. Great white spaces (forehead, cheeks, neck, and shoulders) contrast with compact, almost crowded detail; it is a sort of death mask, graphically brilliant and totally unsettling—not satirical, not laughing at all, but full of doubt.

The "flaw" lies somewhere here, an unrest with self or with the inevitabilities of human nature that gives a prevailing somberness to his images of man. Introspectively, in his diary, Klee probed this trait of character in the months after the wartime death of Franz Marc, who was a very different sort of man and a starkly revealing foil. Klee himself was on military duty as he wrote.

> While I was standing guard over the munitions dump . . . a great many thoughts about Marc and his art came to me. . . . When I tell what kind of person Franz Marc is, I must at once confess that I shall also be telling what kind of person I am. . . . He is more human, he loves more warmly, is more demonstrative. He responds to animals as if they were human. He raises them to his level. . . . In Marc, the bond with the earth takes precedence over the bond with the universe. . . .
>
> My fire is more like that of the dead or of the unborn. No wonder that he found more love. His noble sensuousness with its warmth

41. Paul Klee. *Lost in Thought*, 1919. Pencil on paper. 10⅝″ × 7¾″. Norton Simon Museum of Art, The Blue Four Galka Schreyer Collection. © 1987 by copyright by COSMOPRESS, Geneva.

attracted many people to him. He was still a member of the human race, not a neutral creature. . . . What my art probably lacks is a kind of passionate humanity. I don't love animals and every sort of creature with an earthly warmth. I don't descend to them or raise them to myself. I tend rather to dissolve into the whole of creation and am then on a footing of brotherliness to my neighbor, to all things earthly. I possess. The earth-idea gives way to the world-idea. My love is distant and religious. . . . Do I radiate warmth? Coolness??[10]

At the time, Klee was 37 years of age; these are not the reflections of a self-centered youth but of a man who could make a fair appraisal of his inner situation.

Events would, of course, release Klee from the loneliness of military service. After the war, as a Bauhaus teacher and increasingly celebrated artist, he would give abundantly to many men and women from his unique artistic and intellectual understanding. Nonetheless, something of what he wrote in isolation remained true to the end. He could participate in "Genesis eternal" as an artist, and he was a devoted friend to Kandinsky and many other peers and students. But there was a distance, a coolness in his nature that both helped and hindered him. It flowed into his extraordinary abstractions and fantasies, which move in a ceaselessly changing, self-renewing world; it must also underlie the somber, doubting images of man, which lack "noble sensuousness," just as he said.

To perceive this "flaw" implies no judgment. In a character as rich as Paul Klee's, no "flaw" strays at the edges or lingers in the depths, playing a purely negative role. On the contrary, the uneasiness of his relation with self and others must have urged him on to explore more deeply in the realms where he was at home.

In the years since Klee's death, scholars, family, and friends have pooled their efforts to publish his notebooks in both German and English editions.[11] Astoundingly rich in thought, image, and research, they are nonetheless partially closed to our understanding. I have pored through them on occasion with a sad sense that we have lost more than we have salvaged. A man's notes are not his thought; the pieces don't quite fit together as *he* must have fit them in the Bauhaus studio sessions for which many of these pages were preparation. This said, they still reflect the mind and hand of one of the great artist-metaphysicians of our time and of all time. The notebooks need living Rosetta stones, teaching artists capable of translating them from the page into the consistent studio discipline that they reflect.

The notebooks reveal a Goethean mind. Klee was a man who took all things as his province, ignored nothing, and drew all things together through the act of sustained observation. To conclude this brief study of Klee's contribution to the spiritual, let us listen to him thinking. This passage from the notebooks, apparently dating to 1922, seems addressed to students at the close of a course.

> The power of creativity cannot be named. It remains ultimately mysterious. What does not shake us to our foundations is no mystery. Down to our finest particles we ourselves are charged with this power. We cannot formulate its essence but we can, in some measure, move toward its source. In any case we must reveal this power in its functions, just as it is revealed to us. Probably it is only a form of matter, but one that cannot be perceived with the same senses as the kind of matter we are used to. Still, it must make itself known through the familiar kinds of matter and be at one with them in function. Merged with matter, it must enter into a form that is alive and real. And it is thus that matter takes on life and order, from its smallest particles to its subsidiary rhythms and its higher structures.
>
> Creation lives as genesis invisibly under the surface of the work.[12]

12   THE BAUHAUS: PART SHOOTING GALLERY, PART "METAPHYSICUM ABSTRACTUM"

The odd and evocative phrase at the head of this chapter is Oskar Schlemmer's description of a mechanical cabaret built for the first Bauhaus festival and exhibition in the summer of 1923.[1] It also describes the Bauhaus itself. Conceived during World War I and virtually never free of political and artistic controversy until its demise at the hands of the Nazis in 1933, the Bauhaus nonetheless pursued and realized high ideals. A point of collection and distribution for many of the artistic and spiritual currents that we have encountered, it forged an enduring link between the new art and society at large through its concern with architecture, industrial design, interior furnishings, and typography. Assembling under one institutional roof some of the most authentically creative men and women of the century, it was a place of contemplation and enthusiasm, of discipline and open-ended search, rare in any era.

There was no single Bauhaus style—Klee's visionary paintings were as much of the Bauhaus as were Marcel Breuer's tubular furniture. The school is closely identified with the emergence of machine-made goods in which form follows function, shapes tend toward simple geometry, and structures often reflect a Constructivist temperament that delights in revealed, even dramatized connections and fastenings. Building on the innovations of the Deutsche Werkbund, Frank Lloyd Wright, and other predecessors of the years before World War I, the Bauhaus simplified the twentieth-century living environment through its return to spare but eloquent form on every scale, from architecture to typography. It gave us our setting—a setting which, however much it is taken for granted in today's offices and homes, gleams with what Walter

42. Marianne Brandt. *Teapot,* 1924. Nickel silver and ebony. Height 7″. Collection, The Museum of Modern Art, New York. Phyllis B. Lambert Fund.

Gropius once called a "new, universal idea." The austere elegance of static geometry and dynamic structural forces bound into a whole is the identifying sign of Bauhaus design (Fig. 42). It is no less a sign of longing for a bright and simple life, satisfying without ostentation. The "mystique" of the Bauhaus, if one phrase could capture it, is luminous geometry: the fundamentals of form shined, as a contribution to a world that might also shine.

For many years, the Museum of Modern Art in New York has given pride of place to a painting by Oskar Schlemmer, teacher of wall painting, sculpture, theater, and dance at the Bauhaus (Fig. 43). Depicting students mounting the stairs of Walter Gropius' glass-walled academic building, Schlemmer painted it in the year when the school moved under duress from its home in Dessau to its precarious afterlife in Berlin. The artist himself had left three years earlier, glad to be "out of range of the Bauhausian racket for a while," [2] as he wrote a friend, but

43. Oskar Schlemmer. *Bauhaus Stairway,* 1932. Oil on canvas. 63 7/8″ × 45″.
Collection, The Museum of Modern Art, New York. Gift of Philip Johnson.

his powerfully nostalgic painting reflects an enduring relation.

Schlemmer's students, smooth mannequin-like figures of classical simplicity, give the impression not of a dehumanized schematism but of a statement of essentials. Walter Gropius (1883–1969), director of the Bauhaus, had written some years earlier, "In order to achieve precision here, we must consciously seek to make the personal factor more objective, but every work of art carries the signature of its creator."[3] Gropius was addressing the question of industrial design, but the aesthetic he favored operates in Schlemmer's somewhat impersonal yet felt image. The students move within a strict architectural geometry, but the warmth of light enveloping them and the mysterious figure of a dancer hovering on point at the landing make the image a haunting homage referring beyond its realistic theme. The power of symbols is nearby: the dancer is a disguised "psychopomp" or leader of souls—a witness and immaterial *genius loci* or spirit of the place—while the stairway mounted by impersonal figures echoes ancient images such as the Ladder of Ascent found in medieval manuscripts, on which monks toil toward heaven. That all of the students ascend, and none descend, reinforces the gently stated symbolism of the painting. Few works so successfully capture the blend of spiritual alertness and resolute worldliness of the Bauhaus.

Its story has been written many times, both as an institution and as the professional home, for longer or shorter periods, of outstanding artists. The concern of this chapter and the next is twofold: to touch on the ideals and evolution of the institution during the years when Gropius spoke for it, and to engage with the art and thought of certain Bauhaus "Masters of Form," notably Kandinsky who took refuge there in 1922 after the disappointment of his hopes for art in the Soviet Union. The Bauhaus is the only institution of which I am aware that unquestionably earned a place in the spiritual history of twentieth-century art; the rest is a history of partially shared ideas but individual research, of individuals loosely bound in communities of like-minded people. The Bauhaus embodied the great idea of School: a learning and research community with its own genius, solidly at the service of society and yet resistant to conventional thinking.

Institutions live under different laws than individuals. They may conduct their internal affairs discreetly, but the resulting policies and actions are by and large subject to public review. They generally derive their funds from public sources and are therefore answerable to the public in ways that individuals are not. They require well-organized processes for attaining consensus among many participants, failing which their internal conflicts often tumble out into public view and invite ridicule, loss of reputation, or coercive solutions. Individuals, on the other hand, may go through agonies of inner conflict without calling down the public. Institutional vulnerability to public opinion—mediated through government officials, experts on art and education, and so on—and the need to align the school adequately with society make the Bauhaus a unique study of the spiritual in twentieth-century art. A public institution from the outset (although it sheltered and encouraged some very unpublic men and women), it threw a bridge across the gap between the militantly modern artist dreaming of new forms of expression and the world at large in which people dreamed, on the whole, of other things.

Throughout this investigation I will cite documents from the period quite liberally. The Bauhaus knew how to speak for and of itself with economy and understanding. The cast of characters assembled by Gropius was astonishing: Kandinsky, Klee, Schlemmer, Johannes Itten, Moholy-Nagy, Lyonel Feininger, Gerhard Marcks, Josef Albers, Marcel Breuer, Herbert Bayer, and others as faculty, supplemented by friends and friendly rivals who lectured at the school, published in its monograph series, or cheered from the sidelines. Among the latter were Mondrian, his colleague and competitor Theo van Doesburg, and Malevich (first published in a European language by the Bauhaus). Our study cannot encompass all of these individuals; it is sufficient for our purpose to know that they were in or nearby this community guided with admirable skill by Gropius.

The history of the spiritual in twentieth-century art is no disembodied thing. Moving through individual men and women and receptive communities, it is the sum of their insights and demonstrated abilities. As described in 1923 by Feininger, Gropius combined intrinsic energy and intelligence with tireless activity in his exposed position as the director of an avant-garde school torn by internal and external conflicts.

He never complains, never seems exhausted or embittered. He works until 3 in the morning, hardly sleeps at all, and when he looks at you his eyes shine more than anyone else's! And he doesn't know, moreover, what he should do to make it all a success. . . . One can feel sorry for anyone who cannot, somehow or other, take heart from this man. Often enough I have quite positive criticisms to make against the whole project, I am often deeply unhappy about the way things are going; but there is certainly a power at work here. . . .[4]

Already a prominent architect by the war years, Gropius was invited by state authorities to propose the program for an innovative school, successor to an existing one, that would integrate training in architecture, fine art, craft, and industrial design. To the Grand-Ducal Saxon State Ministry in Weimar, where the school was founded, he was able to state the challenge of integrated arts education in terms that might well appeal to cautious officials.

> Whereas in the old days the entire body of man's products was manufactured exclusively by hand, today only a rapidly disappearing small portion of the world's good is produced without the aid of machines. . . . In the entire field of trade and industry there has arisen a demand for beauty of external form as well as for technical and economic perfection. Apparently, material improvement of products does not by itself suffice to achieve victories in international competitions. A thing that is technically excellent in all respects must be impregnated with an intellectual idea—with form—in order to secure preference among the large quantity of products of the same kind. . . . The manufacturer must see to it that he adds the noble qualities of handmade products to the advantages of mechanical production. . . . A working community [might well be] formed between the artist, the businessman, and the technician. . . . The artist possesses the ability to breathe soul into the lifeless product of the machine, and his creative powers continue to live within it as a living ferment.[5]

The position paper submitted to the ministry is a good deal longer, but we can easily judge from this excerpt that Gropius possessed strong and refined ideals, a clear sense of the historical moment in art and design, and a diplomat's grasp of strategy—hence his reference to success in international competitions.

In the first official publication of the Bauhaus upon its foundation in 1919, Gropius revealed something more of his thought and underlying feeling. A pamphlet designed to attract students (and perhaps faculty) to the new institution, it spoke a very different language that would in time kindle attacks from right-wing political circles as well as from people in the arts community who felt left behind. The pamphlet's cover, an Expressionist woodcut by Feininger (one of Gropius' earliest collaborators), depicts a Gothic cathedral against a miraculous night sky, filled with light from above and radiant stars (Fig. 44). The

44. Lyonel Feininger. *Cathedral*, 1919. Woodcut print. 12″ × 7½″. Collection, The Museum of Modern Art, New York. Gift of Abby Aldrich Rockefeller (by exchange). Copyright ARS NY/ADAGP 1987.

style of the woodcut, somewhat imprisoned by its homage to the il-
lustrious tradition of German graphic art, scarcely foreshadows the
suave imagination of Feininger's developed art. The early Bauhaus itself was similarly drawn by the past, as the text of the pamphlet amply
demonstrated. For this audience, Gropius passed over his interest in a
patnership between art and industry, stressing instead the foundation
of art in craft discipline and the participation of all visual arts in architecture. His concluding words are familiar to all students of twentieth-
century art.

> Let us then create a new guild of craftsmen without the class distinc-
> tions that raise an arrogant barrier between craftsman and artist!
> Together let us desire, conceive, and create the new structure of the
> future, which will embrace architecture and sculpture and painting
> in one unity and which will one day rise toward heaven from the
> hands of a million workers like the crystal symbol of a new faith.[6]

This translation of Gropius' last words, by now standard, misses a
nuance: he spoke of a *kommenden Glaubens,* a faith still to come—
echoing the prewar convictions of Kandinsky, Marc, and others. The
Bauhaus helped to formulate and impose disciplined methodologies in
design, architecture, and the fine arts. But in the early years especially,
alongside its rationalism was a current of hope that the future would
bring immense progress not only in the political and social spheres but
in intimate human understanding, the realm of the spiritual.

Externally organized as a state school with the usual burden of bud-
get reviews, formal memoranda, and so on, the Bauhaus was internally shaped in quite other terms. "No large spiritual organizations,"
Gropius told the students in summer 1919,

> but small, secret, self-contained societies, lodges. Conspiracies will
> form which will want to watch over and artistically shape a secret, a
> nucleus of belief, until from the individual groups a universally
> great, enduring, spiritual-religious idea will rise again, which finally
> must find its crystalline expression in a great *Gesamtkunstwerk.*
> And this great total work of art, this cathedral of the future, will
> then shine with its abundance of light into the smallest objects of
> everyday life. . . . We will not live to see the day, but we are, and this
> I firmly believe, the precursors and the first instruments of such a
> new, universal idea. Up to now, the artist has stood by himself, for in
> these chaotic times there is no rallying idea discernible which would
> spiritually and materially reverse the order of things. On the strength

of his visual gifts, the artist reads the spiritual parallels of his time and represents them in pure form. When such spiritual common property is lacking, there is nothing left for him but to build up his metaphysical element from his own inner resources. He stands aloof, and at best a few friends understand him. . . . I am dreaming now of the attempt to gather a small community from the scattered isolation of the individual; if this succeeds, we will have achieved a great deal.[7]

In keeping with the medieval concept of secret lodges and his emphasis on craftsmanship, Gropius borrowed titles for professors and students from Germany's rich medieval past. Students began as apprentices and advanced to journeymen and junior masters. Teachers were Masters of Form and members of the Council of Masters organized to administer the school's affairs. Some years later, when the forces at work in the Bauhaus had sorted themselves out more clearly, the archaic titles were challenged but retained. It is a matter of lasting astonishment that the Bauhaus began with a medievalizing, romantic self-image and emerged in a few short years as the principal artisan of design principles that are the essence of "modern" and the hallmark of our century.

"The unique structure of the Bauhaus can be perceived in the person of its director," wrote Schlemmer in his diary for 1923,

it is characterized by flexibility, adherence to no dogma, receptivity to anything new, with every intention of assimilating it. Also the intention of stabilizing this whole complex, of finding a common denominator, a set of standards. The result: an unprecedented battle of the minds. . . .[8]

Logic alone suggests that Gropius' desire to coordinate the school's activities with the practical needs of industry would in time conflict with his own romanticism and that of some colleagues whom he had called to the new institution. This particular "battle of the minds," reaching the point of crisis in 1922, was played out between Gropius and a teacher widely acclaimed for his brilliance, whom Gropius had invited to the Bauhaus at an early stage. It was Johannes Itten (1888–1967), creator of the *Vorkurs* or basic course through which all students passed before entering a specific studio—a course whose general approach remains influential to this day. Itten's 1963 publication on teaching method, which includes student work dating from the *Vorkurs* as well as later teaching appointments, reflects an extraordinary level of intelligent experimentation and technical skill.[9]

A well-known photograph of Itten depicts the young Master of Form, monk-like with shaven head, in special Bauhaus priestly robes of his own design, eyes lowered in contemplation, hands clasping an architect's tool in a reminiscence of masonic symbolism, standing before an image of the sun as if it were the emblem of an esoteric school. Itten was a power in the early Bauhaus years, thanks to his pedagogic gifts and personal zeal. He viewed the Bauhaus as a "secret, self-contained society" with spiritual goals. In his classes, he offered students the opportunity to practice relaxation, breathing, and concentration exercises intended, as he later wrote, "to establish the intellectual and physical readiness which makes intensive work possible." [10] Much ahead of his time, he was also an extremist during the Bauhaus years—traits not necessarily identical. For example, upon his return from a conference on Mazdaznan, a Zürich-based sect with Zoroastrian leanings, he managed to convince the Bauhaus kitchen that it should henceforth follow Mazdaznan principles of cuisine: vegetarian, with copious garlic eating as a measure of preventive medicine.

Institutional cooking was the least of Gropius' worries in the early years, taken up as he was with organizational and administrative problems. But in the course of 1922, he felt obliged to take an uncompromising stand about all of the issues championed by Itten. "Gropius contends," wrote Schlemmer in his private notes,

> that we should not shut out life and reality, a danger . . . implied by Itten's method. . . . Itten's ideal would be a craftsman who considers contemplation and thought about his work more important than the work itself. . . . Gropius wants a man firmly rooted in life and work, who matures through contact with reality and through practicing his craft. Itten likes talent which develops in solitude, Gropius likes the character formed by the currents of life (and the necessary talent). . . . These two alternatives strike me as typical of current trends in Germany. On the one hand, the influence of oriental culture, the cult of India, also a return to nature in the *Wandervogel* movement, and others like it; also communes, vegetarianism, Tolstoyism, reaction against the war; and on the other hand, the American spirit, progress, the marvels of technology and invention, the urban environment. . . . I affirm both possibilities, or at least I would like to see cross-fertilization between the two. Or are progress (expansion) and self-fulfillment (introspection) mutually exclusive? [11]

Itten precipitated the crisis of 1922 by embodying the esoteric and romantic aspects of the Bauhaus so militantly that he threatened to sever the school from its mooring in mainstream society. Gropius contended that "facing up to reality by no means has to result in compromise," [12] and from late 1921 he sought more actively industry commissions for design prototypes that could be developed in the Bauhaus studios to which Itten had so richly contributed. The conflict was resolved in favor of Gropius; the administration circumscribed Itten's responsibilities, and he eventually withdrew from the school.

Gropius' concern for the transformation of society, or at very least of its material culture, now suggested to him that Bauhaus graduates

> will be in a position, with the knowledge they have acquired . . . , to exert a decisive influence on existing [craft] enterprises and industrial works, if they will just decide to join these and exert their influence from within. [13]

The Bauhaus could not long sustain itself as a benevolent "conspiracy." The concept of the secret lodge thus opened out into the idea of dispersed adepts working within the system. The institution would not stand over against but would instead infiltrate the ordinary workplace and bring new values to bear on projects at hand rather than on imagined "symbols of a new faith." Gropius called at this time for a good deal more discretion and thoughtfulness where spiritual questions were concerned. As he wrote in a memorandum of early 1922 to the Bauhaus masters,

> . . . the terms "sacred" and "profane" . . . are so frequently confused in today's chaos of confused feelings. The dying religions conjured up the desecration of the sacred just as much as they have precipitated a real cult of the profane. There is one remedy for this mania: if the words "art" and "religion" were answered with silence. . . . [14]

The clarifications of 1922 did not meet with universal praise among the Bauhaus masters. "When Gropius need no longer fear the strong opposition of Itten, he himself will constitute by far the greater threat," predicted Schlemmer in June 1922. [15] And Feininger, in the fall of that year, wrote to his wife:

> *I see a new Gropi*—but, thank God, Kandinsky, Itten, and Muche preserve the pedagogic balance very well. . . . Gropi . . . wants the best, from the point of view of good craftsmanship, but in practice must compromise. . . . "Whoever cannot now show what he is worth can go to the Devil with his art," he said. . . . But Gropi has a clear grasp of realities, and that is something we others haven't. [16]

Toward the end of that difficult year, lived out against a background of runaway inflation in the German economy, Oskar Schlemmer formulated the new direction most succinctly:

> The idea of the cathedral has for the time being receded into the background and with it certain definite ideas of an artistic nature. Today we must think at best in terms of a house, perhaps even only *think* so, but in any case in terms of a house of the *simplest* kind. Perhaps, in face of the economic plight, it is our task to become pioneers of simplicity, that is, to find a simple form for all of life's necessities which at the same time is respectable and genuine.[17]

Through many dramatic turns of events, including forced exodus from its original home in Weimar ("an aerie of vultures who constantly strike at us"[18]) to incomparably better quarters in Dessau, the Bauhaus under Gropius flourished until his retirement from the school in 1928. Throughout these years, his controversial but powerful slogan, "Art and Technology—A New Unity,"[19] provided a general sense of direction that included and even partially relied on the noncommercial artistic and pedagogical research of Paul Klee, Wassily Kandinsky, and Schlemmer himself, who developed an innovative dance theater and continued his fertile work as a painter. "The Bauhaus wants to serve in the development of present-day housing," wrote Gropius, "from the simplest household appliances to the finished dwelling."[20] But meanwhile, Klee taught the fundamentals of form and wrote (for a Bauhaus publication) about man's position as "a creature on a star among stars";[21] Schlemmer rehearsed his wildly innovative *Triadic Ballet*, and Kandinsky taught an elaborate rationale for abstract imagery. And these were not the only Bauhaus masters of exceptional ability. People may have scoffed (a critic in 1923 said, "Three days in Weimar and one can never look at a square again for the rest of one's life"[22]), but Gropius and his colleagues had achieved a diverse and purposeful community, spiritual by all but the most otherworldly definition yet rooted in technical competence and service.

At the opening in 1926 of Gropius' new Bauhaus building in Dessau, he expressed the school's history and goals:

> The Bauhaus . . . set itself the task of investigating the entire field of spatial design, its means and possibilities. In that endeavor the Bauhaus followed the principle of collaboration, establishing a common level from which to work and beginning a search for exact, that is, objective, fundamentals of creativity, the validity of which

can be acknowledged by a large number of individuals. . . . Today one can observe with satisfaction that the ideas that were either gathered by or born in the Bauhaus have started an active movement which has become recognized beyond the borders of this country, a movement which bears the structure of our modern life. These results cannot be achieved by an individual—they evolved from the purity of an idea and from the strength of the common achievement of our Masters and students. . . .[23]

The spirituality of the Bauhaus was very nearly as diverse as the individuals who participated in it. Klee's Jena lecture (see chapter 11) and Kandinsky's search for a "science of art" (chapter 13) represent the Bauhaus no less truly than Gropius' intention to bring "a new, universal idea" to the lifeless products of industry. As an institution, however, the Bauhaus clearly furthered one dominant idea, in equal measures practical and spiritual—Gropius' idea, which elicited the loyalty of many in the Bauhaus community. As so often, Schlemmer in his private notes expressed it cleanly:

Do not complain about mechanization; instead enjoy precision!

Artists are willing to convert the drawbacks and perils of their mechanistic age into the silver lining of exact metaphysics. If today's artists love the machine, technology, and organization, if they aspire to precision and reject anything vague and dreamy, this implies an instinctive repudiation of chaos and a longing to find the form appropriate to our times, to pour new wine into the old bottles: to formulate them in a unique and unprecedented manner. That is saying and demanding a great deal.[24]

Behind this view, as the Bauhaus people well knew, is another and far more ancient one, the Platonic view of the perfection of geometry. The meaning of "exact metaphysics" becomes clearer in Socrates' words in the *Philebus,* cited in an early Bauhaus publication to evoke the impeccably Classical roots of the institution's seemingly unprecedented approach to design:

The beauty of figures which I am now trying to indicate is not what most people would understand as such, not the beauty of a living creature or a picture. . . . What the argument points to is something straight, or round, and the surfaces and solids which a lathe, or a carpenter's rule and square, produces from the straight and the round. . . . Things like that, I maintain, are beautiful not, like most

things, in a relative sense; they are always beautiful in their very nature, and they carry pleasures peculiar to themselves.[25]

Schlemmer's observations, with Socrates' behind them, allow us to
formulate the achievement of the Bauhaus in general terms. Curious as
it may seem, the Bauhaus succeeded in carrying a Platonic sense of
form and beauty into everyday life—not a heavily ideological Constructivism, but something simpler and more heartfelt. We still live today among "things straight and round," and while the spare geometry
of modern objects represents only one quality of form among many
equally possible and lovely, it is not without spiritual resonance. The
"exact metaphysics" of this type of design may be lost on many of us,
but the quiet beauty is not. This is the gift of the Bauhaus to this century, and it is an enduring one.

Walter Gropius, like many other Bauhaus masters, was destined to
become briefly a refugee and at length an American. Like Mies van der
Rohe, who guided the Bauhaus in its excessively difficult final years,
Gropius brought his genius and values to bear in the United States as a
teacher and working architect. Chairman of the Department of Architecture at Harvard (1937–1952) and a preeminent contributor to what
came to be called the International Style in architecture, he retained
the robust understanding, healthy pragmatism, and sensitivity that
made him such a resourceful guide in the Bauhaus years. His later architecture is currently eclipsed in reputation, as is the International
Style in general, but his leadership of the Bauhaus will survive his critics. In a late book, *Scope of Total Architecture,* Gropius stated his lifelong credo in cautious but moving terms:

> Since my early youth I have been acutely aware of the chaotic ug-
> liness of our modern manmade environment when compared to the
> unity and beauty of old, preindustrial towns. In the course of my life
> I became more and more convinced that the usual practice of archi-
> tects to relieve the dominating disjointed pattern here and there by
> a beautiful building is most inadequate and that we must find, in-
> stead, a new set of values, based on such constituent factors as
> would generate an integrated expression of the thought and feeling
> of our time.[26]

The concluding words distantly recall the *Gesamtkunstwerk,* the total
work of art embracing all arts, of which Gropius had spoken with such
enthusiasm at the beginning of the Bauhaus experiment. The ideal had
mellowed, not vanished; in 1955, it no longer conveyed the unmistak-

able flavor of *Gotterdämmerung,* triumph and catastrophe intertwined, as it did in the years just after World War I. It had evolved instead into a sound ideal, richly explored in the course of Gropius' later work and, like so many twentieth-century ideals, remaining somewhat unfulfilled and still promising.

13 KANDINSKY AT THE BAUHAUS: A BLOCK OF ICE WITH A FLAME INSIDE

Kandinsky created works of stunning beauty during his Bauhaus years, yet he thought about them for the most part rather narrowly. In some canvases, he was indisputably a religious artist in Apollinaire's sense (see Chapter 5), expressing the grandeur of metaphysical form and the reality not of sight but of insight. He depicted the mobile cosmos in vivid and lovingly imagined terms, and to enrich his imaginings he drew from little known spiritual and pictorial sources such as the Kabbalistic Tree of Life, Robert Fludd's Cosmic Monochord, and perhaps shamanistic images published by anthropologists in the 1920s. Yet other of his works seem, broadly speaking, to be poetic designs without precise meaning apart from the physical push and pull of forms. There is an obdurate, irrational core of signs in his pictorial world; they function as elements of design but resist being gathered up into a consistent scheme of symbolic expression. We shall look in this chapter at works varying from lucid metaphysical poetry to a language of design that is not altogether a language of the mind.

By working in part with signs that do not yield to symbolic interpretation, Kandinsky may have been instinctively protecting the primacy of color and form. As we have seen, many twentieth-century artists have perceived the nonverbal presence of color and form as a quality to be left intact and, if possible, heightened by the artist's skill. The keen vibration of paint, the dense "suchness" or *tathatā* of stone are not to be subordinated to schemes of intellectual meaning; to do so is to subordinate primary life to secondary reflection.

With meaning and legibility in mind, it is time to enter Kandinsky's pictorial world of the 1920s.[1] After seven years in wartime Russia and the emerging Soviet Union, Kandinsky accepted a teaching appointment at the Bauhaus and assumed his duties in the spring of 1922. He filled his Russian years with strenuous service to various new government arts agencies and institutions, including the People's Commissariat for Enlightenment and its Department of Visual Arts, the Free State Art Studios, the Museums of Painterly Culture, the Institute of Artistic Culture, the Higher State Art-Technical Studios, and the Russian Academy of Artistic Sciences. Kandinsky was teacher, administrator, curator, institution-builder—and somewhat less painter during these years of momentous change. He met increasing resistance to his values and, foreseeing the conscription of art by politics, found his way back to Germany, long his second home.

He brought with him the discoveries of the Russian avant-garde. Critical of the starkness and lack of expressive variety in Suprematism and Constructivism, he nonetheless acquired from them a vocabulary of geometric signs—circles, arcs, angles, grids, quadrilaterals—which became the ordering factor of his art in the 1920s. The liquid swirls of color and almost hypersensitive draftsmanship of his Munich years firmed up into clearly defined geometric figures enclosing planes of bold or subtle color. No less animated than before, his new work reflected in pictorial terms the geometrical aesthetic of the Bauhaus design studios.

And much more. Like many Bauhaus men and women, he both accepted and surpassed its mainstream vision. Soon after his arrival, he reportedly told a colleague that his artistic goal was to "proclaim the reign of the Spirit . . . to proclaim 'light from light, the flowing light of the Godhead, of the Holy Ghost.'" [2] In notes from 1925 for his course on design, Kandinsky wrote characteristically:

> Opposition to a materialist world: the supraterrestrial, the pursuit of a raison d'être, theosophy, astrology, the search for a reality above our all-too-narrow terrestrial sphere. [3]

In a letter from the same year, if further evidence is needed that Kandinsky remained very much himself, we find him again prophesying the riches of art in the future and sensing his own role as a precursor:

> The circle which I have been using so often of late is nothing if not Romantic. Actually, the coming Romanticism is profound, beautiful. . . , meaningful, joy-giving—it is a block of ice with a burning flame inside. . . . [4]

A number of Kandinsky's enduringly beautiful works from the Bauhaus years rely on the simple motif of the circle. A pair of canvases

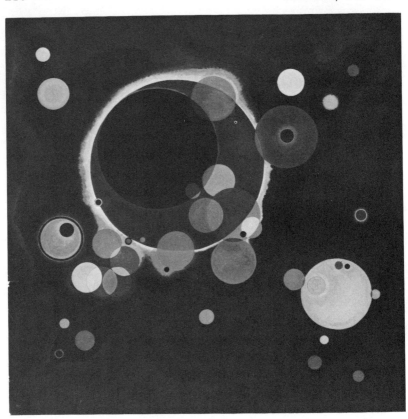

45. Wassily Kandinsky. *Several Circles*, 1926. Oil on canvas. 55¼″ × 55⅜″. Solomon R. Guggenheim Museum, New York. Photo: Robert E. Mates. Copyright ARS NY/ADAGP 1987.

from 1926, surely masterpieces, deserve attention. *Several Circles* (Fig. 45)—titled as if it were a cool Constructivist study, a modest geometrical exercise—is one of the most richly imagined and felt images of cosmos in the art of our century. In general, Kandinsky's titles both at the Bauhaus and earlier tend to emphasize physical elements of design or color and to camouflage metaphysical or psychological themes. In the world of the Bauhaus, he apparently preferred to underplay his philosophical and spiritual interests. Even in a letter to a close friend, later a biographer, he stressed the physical expressiveness of the circle and diverted attention from its traditional value as a sign of the heavens or of cosmic order:

You mention the circle, and I agree with your definition. It is a link with the cosmic. But I use it above all formally. . . . Why does the circle fascinate me? It is 1) the most modest form, but asserts itself unconditionally, 2) a precise but inexhaustible variable, 3) simultaneously stable and unstable, 4) simultaneously loud and soft, 5) a single tension that carries countless tensions within it. The circle is the synthesis of the greatest oppositions. It combines the concentric and the excentric in a single form, and in equilibrium. . . . It points most clearly to the fourth dimension.[5]

To all of which one might say "true," although some of his points seem so subjective that, like taste, they are beyond dispute. Evidently, Kandinsky was not paying only *pro forma* homage to Bauhaus rationalism; he was searching for a "hard" empiricism to balance and perhaps even justify his "soft" intuitive search for "a reality above."

Looking across from his cool letter to the illustration of *Several Circles,* the reader will find a symphonic image of the cosmos, its central motif a darkly shining solar eclipse amid a series of planetary worlds and moons drifting through a dark firmament, framed by a filmy serpentine nebula. This is not a cool "formal" use of the circle but an image of undeniable power: dark and foreboding at the center where solar energy is constrained, brilliant and cheery as soap-bubbles as the image develops to the edge, the whole immersed in inscrutable darkness. The overlapped circles in several areas of the painting, resembling illustrations for scientific color studies, add to its imaginative richness. One feels as if one is looking in on the origin of color or observing the Creator's trial studies in a universe become artist's studio.

The second canvas in this series, *Accent in Pink* (Fig. 46), has all the magic of *Several Circles*—and a comparably apathetic title that deliberately disregards the strength of its cosmological imagination. It is more richly painted, with a background firmament and central trapezoid marvelously varied in color and texture. One might describe it as an icon of cosmic renewal: new worlds pour from a central opening and float out into deep space to become a universe. Close to the center, a little version of the overlapped circles motif suggests the biological division of cells, as if the worlds in this canvas split off from an original unity. The canvas evokes in contemporary terms the ancient cosmology of Plotinus and others, which describes the derivation of the Many from the One through a series of degradations. Kandinsky borrowed the central trapezoid, dominating the painting and important to its compositional coherence, from the geometric vocabulary of Suprematism. But here it recalls the poetry of the *Book of Revelation* (6 : 14), from which Kandinsky had often drawn in earlier years: "And the heaven departed as a scroll when it is rolled together." It seems unlikely, however, that Kandinsky intended this canvas as an image of the End of Days: given to his wife on her nameday in 1930, it is filled with quiet, affirmative energy.

We can reasonably confirm that this pair of works proclaims "light from light, the flowing light of the Godhead," in keeping with Kandinsky's aspiration when he first came to the Bauhaus. These are religious works, enriched from many different sources: modern telescopy, the geometries of the Russian avant-garde, the sensuous colors and textures of Kandinsky's Expressionist years, the diagrams of scientific color research, and the long tradition of cosmological images reaching back from Vincent van Gogh's *Starry Night* to Early Christian dome mosaics and Roman palace decorations. However numerous the sources and kinships, the works themselves are whole and in the best sense original—the sources wholly assimilated, the statement fresh and compelling.

Unlike the Christian and late Classical mosaics to which they relate, Kandinsky's canvases adhere to no specific cosmology. Closest to the concept of the Many as an emanation from the One, they are not even remotely intended as doctrinal statements. Modern, individual, they are touched by traditional ideas and images but not determined by them. This is perhaps all that we can justly expect from artists of philosophical temperament in our time who experience the need to make images of the cosmos, our large home, but don't quite know what it looks like. The scientific picture of the cosmos changes from decade to decade and cannot be ignored; indeed, the concentric circles of ancient cosmologies reflected the science of their day. Science itself generates imagery, sometimes in collaboration with artists, to illustrate subatomic structures and inscrutable immensities such as black holes and binary star systems. Scientific illustrations are by intention utilitarian, but on occasion they evoke unexpected awe.

Artists of any era do not wait for science to tell them precisely how things look; given a few clues from well-informed sources (the priests of the temple at Karnak, the "priests" of Mount Wilson observatory), they imaginatively transform what they learn into images that can be felt—thus continuing the human dialogue with Nature and completing science with art. The goal of all cosmological art is to situate the viewer in the largest possible world, to wrest us from a room and place

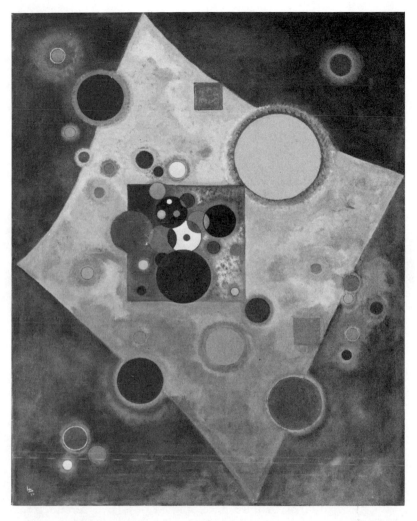

46. Wassily Kandinsky. *Accent in Pink*. Oil on canvas. 39⅜″ × 31½″. Musées nationaux, Paris. Gift of Madame Nina Kandinsky, 1976. Copyright ARS NY/ADAGP 1987.

us in a universe and help us remember, as Paul Klee put it, that we are creatures on a star among stars. This is one of the tasks of the spiritual in art.

Kandinsky's canvases abound with images that read as eclipsed suns, often accompanied by planets with enveloping atmospheres (presaging the astronauts' photographs of planet Earth). The eclipsed sun has a suggestiveness and poetry of its own, perhaps best understood as an oblique expression of Kandinsky's conviction in the mid-1920s that real culture was hampered and all but extinguished. In writing about this theme, he did not use the image of eclipse, but it coheres with the analogies he chose:

> . . . "today" is made up of two basically different parts—blind alley and threshold—with a great preponderance of the first. The predominance of the blind alley theme excludes the use of the term "culture"—the time is altogether without culture, although a few seeds of a future culture can be discovered here and there—threshold theme. This thematic disharmony is the "sign" of "today" which continually forces itself upon our attention. . . . "Today" human beings are completely absorbed with the external; the inner is dead for them. This is the last step of the descent, the end of the blind alley. In former times, such places were called "abysses"; today the modest expression "blind alley" suffices. The "modern" individual seeks inner tranquillity because he is deafened from outside, and believes this quiet to be found in inner silence. . . .[6]

Kandinsky's dry comparison of the poetic language of former times with the pedestrian language of the present shows him measuring the distance between his deep romanticism and the demands of his immediate environment. Just as he now gave the great speculative paintings modest titles, so he had learned with some irony to moderate his language.

The two paintings that we have studied possess a certain transparency; they are easily read and understood, although they are not superficial. Many paintings from Kandinsky's Bauhaus years are difficult, and to enter thoroughly into the topic we should engage with representative examples. We can understand their difficulty as a struggle between the artist's delight in form and the seeker's delight in meaning.

Transitional between the truly transparent visual language and the difficulties that lie in wait is a magnificent work, *Yellow Center,* also of 1926 (Fig. 47). We can read it almost completely without relegating its

47. Wassily Kandinsky. *Yellow Center,* 1926. Oil on canvas. 17¾″ × 14⅝″.
Museum Boymans-van Beuningen, Rotterdam. Photo: A. Frequin. Copyright
ARS NY/ADAGP 1987.

elements to the realm of "mere design," mere form perhaps physically eloquent but not necessarily informed by wisdom. In this work, what we can best describe as a primitive animal with a stiff tail and hard carapace moves from lower left to upper right. An abstract form, it nonetheless brings to mind a horseshoe crab or some comparable survivor from the early stages of evolution. It foreshadows Kandinsky's interest in later years in fantastic, gelatinous life-forms resembling microscopic protozoa. The "crab" moves through a spacious environment glowing with puffs of diffuse primary color and framed at the upper and right edges of the canvas by intruding planes that provide a sense of boundaries in an otherwise limitless pictorial world. In compositional terms, they tell the viewer where the picture ends but not where the world ends.

The "crab" or primordial life-form appears to be attacked, its tough carapace repeatedly pierced by shapes that seem fixed like harpoons in its body. And yet there is no pictorial sign of anguish or struggle to the death; on the contrary, one receives the impression of steady upward progress in spite of these incursions. The lances themselves are brightly colored, of one substance with the environment and the pool of bright color inside the "crab."

What story is Kandinsky telling here? What are we looking at? It would be pleasant, and efficient, to say a few words about Kandinsky's incomprehensible but seductive world of imagination, or to make a few historical remarks relating the style here to earlier and later works. We could also quote Kandinsky's interpretation of the perceptual dynamics of some of the forms and colors on the canvas—he was writing in these years what he hoped would be a scientific treatise on expression in art. In general, he disliked interpretations of meaning. In the 1930s, he wrote:

> I ask you to understand that my painting does not try to reveal "secrets" to you, that I . . . have not found "a special language" that has to be "learned" and without which my painting cannot be read. . . . The content of painting is painting. Nothing has to be deciphered. The content, filled with happiness, speaks to that person to whom *each* form is alive, i.e., has content.[7]

But his familiar strategy misses the point where this picture is concerned, and where many others are concerned. The point is that one senses *a story* being told here in abstract terms, a story that Kandinsky himself surely felt and intuited clearly, although he might have found words heavy. The danger of words is that we may lose the picture—

may find ourselves with a verbal formula but no beauty and no sense of discovery.

In any event, I have made no secret of my reading: a primitive, persevering life-form not only withstands attack but incorporates the harm that comes to it into the totality of what it is. Its upward thrust and the attacks it sustains become one whole, an image of survival in a vibrant but challenging world. Cloaked in the enigmatic language of abstraction, the image is eloquent, even heroic, a continuation in new terms of Kandinsky's early love of the image of the questing knight. Perceiving the "story" in this way, we can make sense even of the rectangular planes at the edge of the canvas: they threaten the creature, they bar its progress. It must find the way past.

Is this the spiritual in art, or a legitimate branch thereof? This question suggests itself again and again, because as modern people we have no traditional guidelines and no traditional repertory of images upon which to found secure judgments. If this is a St. George, it is an odd one.

And yet it is. Kandinsky was not the only twentieth-century artist to look backward toward archaic styles or downward to the realm of primitive life-forms to find icons of being in an era of enormous military and weak spiritual force. What do we have and what are we, if we *have* nothing truly secure and *are* nothing that has proved to be trustworthy? Some of our greatest artists—not only Kandinsky but Henry Moore and others—have answered: life itself, a core of unsophisticated vitality that may be infringed but will not be destroyed. Kandinsky's "crab" is an icon of this answer: a lower form of life but life nonetheless, calling to our life-affirming instincts at a level below words.

Kandinsky's late art, which we will not investigate in this book, centers on cheery protoplasmic creatures wriggling up and down ladders, inching across high wires, just relating to one another, or displayed like emblems—on the face of it, an odd vocabulary for art practiced in part during the dreary, dangerous years of the Nazi occupation of France, where Kandinsky lived after 1933. Yet it is not so odd. The art does not seem to me terribly effective, but it is the understandable late song of a man who believed in life and found little more than "dead ends" in the culture of interwar and wartime Europe.

The three paintings of 1926 are *intelligible*. The word is heavy, but it compactly expresses one's ability to penetrate the meaning of the marks on canvas and make them one's own—perhaps not correctly in all respects, but with a sense of recognition. These works make themselves felt as a seeker's poetry, a guess at the way the world works in its larger

48. Wassily Kandinsky. *Composition 8*, 1923. Oil on canvas. 55⅛″ × 79⅛″. Solomon R. Guggenheim Museum, New York. Photo: Robert E. Mates. Copyright ARS NY/ADAGP 1987.

dimensions, a guess not without philosophical underpinning. But Kandinsky's art is not always so intelligible. Let us take for example Kandinsky's large *Composition 8* (Fig. 48), a work of 1923 which, according to his friend and biographer Will Grohmann, Kandinsky viewed as the "high point of his postwar achievement." [8]

Much admired in formal terms—that is, in terms of its composition and chromatic vigor—*Composition 8* has not received fully satisfactory interpretation from critics and historians. Grohmann relates the work to a passage from Thomas Mann's *Dr. Faustus* in which the composer-protagonist states that every note in strict musical composition has significance; reason and magic become one. But from this provocative beginning, Grohmann goes on blandly to describe the physical dynamics of the composition—offering no revelation of "significance." The discussion of the painting in the general catalogue of the Guggenheim Museum provides a thorough overview of the meaning of the circle to Kandinsky and cites the artist and his critics on a number of other points, but it ventures no interpretation of the work as a whole. [9] The museum's most recent catalogue, *Kandinsky: Russian and*

Bauhaus Years (1983), devotes two pages to the work and probably collects all that can be said from a historical perspective about the meaning of *Composition 8*.[10] There we learn that it translates Kandinsky's prewar landscape motif into the geometric language of his Bauhaus period and, from passages such as the following, we can gather that it closely reflects the artist's theoretical and pedagogical writings of the 1920s: "For Kandinsky the combination of triangle and circle creates the strongest and most evocative contrast, exemplifying the power of abstract forms and their interactions."[11] The catalogue cites a Kandinsky article of 1929 on "the basic character" of a picture and the artist's effort (the words are Kandinsky's)

> to achieve the clearest possible expression of this basic idea (e.g., dark, warm, very controlled, radiant, introverted, restrained, aggressive, "disharmonious," concealed, overpowering, etc.). This is what is called "mood". . . .[12]

In sum, the literature from Grohmann's groundbreaking study in the 1950s to the most recent major catalogue adds little to Kandinsky's own way of looking at abstract form.

As artist and teacher, Kandinsky was fascinated with the expressiveness of abstract form, with what Henri Focillon called "the life of forms in art." As spiritual seeker, he was concerned with uncovering an order extending from this world to the "supraterrestrial," as he once put it, that includes human beings and confers a well-founded sense of purpose and belonging. Sometimes, not always, Kandinsky found it possible to fuse the artist and the seeker in himself; sometimes they split off. When the split occurred, his art suffered. It became mixed, more physical than metaphysical, more thing than thing of the spirit, good design but not good wisdom.

As landscape, *Composition 8* depicts a mountain toward the left, with a suggestion of sky and at upper left a heavenly body of ambiguous nature, eclipsed sun or planet with an attendant sphere. Other objects in the painting conform to some degree to a reading as landscape: bands of semicircles suggest clouds, streaks in the "sky" suggest plunging meteorites. In addition, a linear pattern reminiscent of the Orthodox Christian cross stands near the summit of the mountain, juxtaposed to a curved shape resembling a horn, as if they convey a common message. So far, a viewer might be content to identify this work as a geometric variation on the theme of Apocalypse, which preoccupied Kandinsky during his Munich years. The lonely cross, an apocalyptic angel's trumpet, and the darkening of the sun suggest a joining of traditional crucifixion imagery with the Apocalypse.

Virtually any concerned viewer would recognize these elements; they are parts of public knowledge requiring no special acquaintance with Kandinsky's thought. There is, however, another set of signs that cannot be interpreted without reference to Kandinsky's writings—and here we begin to encounter the question of intelligibility. If viewers must know his writings in some detail to understand the painting, then it speaks, in part, just what Kandinsky hoped it would not, "a special language." In traditional religious cultures, spectators or worshipers had little need to consult special texts to understand the major themes of icons: their knowledge of themes was fundamentally identical to the artist's, and the work of art was an occasion to share and deepen it. In our own time, we need a degree of deliberate cultivation to interpret the signs and symbols of abstract art which purports to be more than decoration. We need to be willing to learn from the artist, who is elaborating new signs, if not new meanings, within a culture that has long since abandoned traditional spirituality and its conventional signs.

On the other hand, if the new signs are unconvincing and somehow fail to make the passage from the personal to the interpersonal or even transpersonal domains—if they remain obdurately the *artist's* signs but not ours, and nothing to which the mind and heart gratefully respond—then we have to admit that the search continues, and the challenge of restoring the spiritual in art remains.

The discipline of paying close attention to the artist's work lies with the viewer, but the burden of proof lies with the artist: do these signs and pictorial dynamics, born in the privacy of the studio, carry into the world at large as a rewarding language? Willing viewers who care for the spiritual in art have no cause for embarrassment if they feel unmoved by work offered with obvious sincerity by an artist or with reassurances from a gallery or museum. The enterprise is new; we are only beginning to find our way.

In *Composition 8,* a great vertical triangle just to right of center reaches from bottom to top; it balances, one might say, on the T square below it. These are the most stable elements in the right half of the canvas, which teems with dynamic signs. A flying triangular wedge hurls in from the right, carrying circles and squares in its wake; a medley of geometric figures fills the space around and inside the major triangle. Along the right side of the vertical triangle, a compact assemblage of forms includes a pierced circle akin to the crab-like figure in *Yellow Center* (Fig. 47). On the left, beneath the sign that we have interpreted as a holy mountain, we find an odd trapezoidal grid with curious lumps appearing to grow out of it, like rubbery fungus from a tree. This is an unflattering association; on the other hand, one of the challenges facing artists is to channel our associations, so that we see just what we are supposed to see and have no cause for stray thoughts that strip the image of its dignity. Just above the trapezoidal figure, there is the caduceus-like sign of a "snake" coiled about a simple oblique line.

These elements resist being collected into an orderly understanding. Does the tumult on the right indicate "modern times," contrasting with the less cluttered lefthand region of religious and cosmic symbols? Does the aspiring triangle toward the center (recalling a metaphor developed by Kandinsky in *On the Spiritual in Art*) mark a unifying direction—an arising from this dichotomy toward a higher condition that includes them both? Does the strange trapezoidal grid with oval forms emerging from it represent a transition from the strict grids of modernity on the right toward the cosmic circles on the left? Perhaps; that may be it. But many details resist falling into place. One has the strong impression of being thrown into the role of a diviner. We had better turn to Kandinsky's major writing of the 1920s for whatever hints it offers.

Point and Line to Plane, his prestigious Bauhaus publication of 1926, was intended as a primer offering a few essential guideposts toward a science of art. "[Painting] has attained a level," he wrote by way of introduction,

> that inevitably demands a precise, purely scientific examination of pictorial means for pictorial purposes. . . . Our examination should proceed with painful, pedantic precision. This "tedious" path should be measured pace by pace—not the tiniest change in the substance, in the qualities, or in the effects of each individual element should be allowed to escape the attentive eye. Only by a process of microscopic analysis will the science of art lead to an all-embracing synthesis, which will ultimately extend far beyond the boundaries of art, into the realm of "union" of the "human" and the "divine." [13]

This "birth or rebirth of the science of art" which the book is intended to serve requires a new knowledge of what Kandinsky called the *Kunstelemente,* the basic constructive elements of pictorial art. *On the Spiritual in Art* had taken an adequate first step toward a theory of color. Kandinsky devoted this second treatise to just three elements of expressive geometry—point, line, and plane. While Kandinsky writes that their study must be pedantically systematic, the instruments he proposes to carry out the study differ from those of a pedant. He writes of an awakened sensitivity more closely related to traditional spiritual values than to hard science.

> The open eye and the open ear transform the slightest disturbance into a profound experience. Voices are heard on every side. The world resounds [*die Welt klingt*]. Like an explorer immersing himself in new, unknown lands, one makes discoveries in one's "daily round," and one's environment, normally mute, begins to speak an increasingly distinct language. Thus dead signs turn into living symbols. The dead comes to life. Naturally, the new science of art can only come about provided that signs become symbols and the open eye and open ear make possible the passage from silence to speech.[14]

What a wonderful passage. "Naturally," he writes—a "naturally" that in practice calls for decades of dedicated work from spiritual seekers, and even then is not guaranteed. *Die Welt klingt*—this was his faith from earliest days, based not on assumption or fantasy but on flashes of experience that deeply impressed him. But flashes of insight and the yearning to construct a new art from the living symbols they reveal hardly constitute a scientific methodology. To fulfill the plan of his book, Kandinsky turned for the most part to his artistic sensibility; on this he could rely.

Point and Line to Plane is neither a grammar of the spiritual in art nor an empirical textbook of design but a somewhat idiosyncratic collection of observations on the life of forms in art. For example, about the generation of line from the isolated point he wrote as follows:

> There can . . . exist [a] force, which arises not inside but outside the point. This force attacks the point as it burrows its way into the surface, forces it to emerge, and pushes it across the surface in one direction or another. This at once obliterates the concentric tension of the point, which itself perishes, and out of which comes into being a new entity leading a new, self-sufficient life and thus subject to its own laws. This entity is the line.[15]

The passage bears witness to Kandinsky's extraordinary sensitivity to form, sensitivity bordering on animism: he sensed the life of things outside of him and at times knew with great immediacy the animation of the seemingly inanimate. In this style, *Point and Line to Plane* offers Kandinsky's evaluation of many compositional elements. For example,

he examined his responses to the upper and lower portions of the picture plane (the rectangular canvas), and concluded as follows:

> "Above" conjures up an image of . . . rarification, a feeling of light-
> ness, of emancipation, and ultimately, of freedom. . . . This "rarifi-
> cation" negates density. . . . "Below" has entirely the opposite ef-
> fect: density, weight, bondage.[16]

Similarly, he assigned values on the basis of his experience to "right"
and "left," horizontal, vertical, and oblique lines, the point and clustered points—and so on. All of this is much in keeping with the simple
notions of structure and energy explored in chapter 2, but it does not
quite emerge as a body of knowledge separable from Kandinsky's personal sensibility. Kandinsky's book is not a failure; it points the way to
a grammar of twentieth-century art. Nonetheless, much is missing from
it. It does not offer, for example, anything approaching a full *explica-
tion de texte* for *Composition 8,* to which we might now briefly return.

Neither common knowledge nor consultation with Kandinsky's
own treatise on form has yielded a thorough understanding of the
painting, although we have pieced together an interpretation that
seems reasonable and in keeping with his world-view. A better scholar
would have fared better, and surely scholars in time will reach a satisfactory interpretation. But we can approach the point of concern
here—public intelligibility, the sharing of signs that we *know* to be
about ourselves and our aspirations—without exhaustive scholarship.
Although silent, images can convey what we mean and feel, orienting
consciousness and even conscience without chatter. Traditional religious cultures have always had texts and pictures to orient their participants; we do, too. But our culture is not whole, and our visual languages reflect the gaps.

By his own reckoning the highest achievement of his postwar years,
Kandinsky's *Composition 8* seems to me a work in which visual excitement overwhelms the steady labor to join sign and sense in a way
that is true to the artist's "inner necessity" yet accessible to others. I
cannot help but find that Kandinsky's sheer fascination with the dynamics of form and color often submerges his ideal of the spiritual in
art during the Bauhaus years. Two disjunctions, then: between artist
and public, and between artist and seeker—the first outward and societal, the second internal.

Great as Kandinsky's achievement was, precursor of so much twentieth-century art that attempts to acknowledge the spiritual, he too

had his confusions and lacks. Like us all, Kandinsky fell, obeyed the gravity that pulls us into one venture and another, one view of life but not others. By any standards, he fell well; he had much to offer, and he did not spare himself. As artist and seeker, he dared to make *complex* statements. That they are not always fully intelligible indicates only, as Coomaraswamy once said of himself, that he was still a wayfarer and not yet at journey's end.

A nostalgia for Knowledge, not just factual and technical but initiatic knowledge, appears again and again in Kandinsky's work. So too does a love of play that remained fresh and touching into his very last years. These traits appear together in numerous works of the Bauhaus period. *Lyrical Oval,* for example, recalls the solemn and truly impressive cosmic speculations of the seventeenth-century English physician and esotericist, Robert Fludd (published in 1921 in Germany, in any case well known).[17] But that painting is also playful: it is a great cosmic clockwork and a toy. Similarly, reflections of the Kabbalistic Tree of Life appear in a number of works from the period, such as *Fixed Points.*[18] These images were borrowings, not precisely *his.* He remained something of an amateur in the domain of spirituality, but amateur means "one who loves."

Paul Klee was speaking once to a colleague in the privacy of his Bauhaus studio. His own art, Klee said, reaches only to the "world in-between," but Kandinsky's art glimpses the "world of light."[19] It is a generous expression, and on occasion not only generous but true.

14 CONSTANTIN BRANCUSI: NEGATING THE LABYRINTH

With this chapter, we return again to the origins of twentieth-century art to become acquainted—or reacquainted—with one of its most luminous figures. A man of unshakable principle, a peasant prince by his own description, subtle of mind, radically modern in his work, Constantin Brancusi (1876–1957) brought to twentieth-century art a unique body of work and wisdom that command heartfelt respect. Through the many decades that he lived and worked on a quiet impasse adjoining a busy commercial district of Paris, those who called on him received the impression of virtually entering another world. The hand-carved furniture, the massive whitewashed fireplace and walls were old Romania, but the sculpture that he kept close around him embodied a stark and uncompromisingly new vision. A hospitable hermit, irritable with people who struck him as greedy or superficial but welcoming to friends and serious inquirers, he lived with unfeigned simplicity. His art and thought, on their own, would legitimate the art of our time as a language of the spirit. Like so much in twentieth-century art, both his person and his work will be reasonably familiar to many readers, but just past the knowledge that we typically have of him begins another knowledge.

He wrote almost nothing. A few letters have appeared in print; he published a brief folk tale in 1925 that sounds on the page like spoken language and has nothing detectable to do with art—it must have pleased him to make his debut as an author with a cheerful tale about why hens gobble when you approach them on the nest. There are a few formal statements, too rare. But from the 1920s, his words were prized. Described variously as aphorisms, *propos,* and conversation, his penetrating sayings were collected by visitors and friends, and found their way piecemeal into writings about him. By way of "artist's statements," he permitted little collections of his sayings to be included from time to time in exhibition catalogues. A Romanian scholar has recently gathered a great many of his aphorisms and statements, and traced the loose-jointed but consistent philosophy to which they sum up.[1] These materials are his writings—and the best guide to his work that we could hope to have. No less than Paul Klee's 1924 lecture, they belong to the spiritual charter of twentieth-century art. It is not too much to say that the integrity of our art is bound up with Brancusi's work and thought.

THE LIFE AND ART

More than for other artists who figure strongly in this book, we need to consider not only Brancusi's art and thought but also his life. Entering the mainstream of twentieth-century art from a more distant origin than other artists, he brought with him intact the view of life that prevailed among thoughtful people where he was born and spent his youth. We would mistake the value of his ideas if we regarded them as wholly individual; Brancusi was "many men deep," as William Morris liked to say of medieval artists who drew from long tradition. Brancusi spoke brilliantly for himself, but also for a world. Yet he was not just a unique intruder from a more archaic world, who proved able to convey its values. A man who read little but read well, he was drawn in his maturity to a small number of classical Western, Taoist, and Tibetan Buddhist writings that gave him a universal insight and language. In this regard, he showed what it means to assimilate by deep affinity rather than to borrow and display. As an older man, he spoke for more than one world.

Lives conducted with passion and clear intent tend to have the quality of legend even as they are being lived, as if the individuals pare the accidental from their days and restore the essential. Born to a well-to-do peasant family in the rural Oltenian region of Romania, Brancusi spent his childhood in circumstances now difficult to imagine. The roots of the richly traditional peasant culture of Eastern Europe extend into Neolithic times; its view of Nature and man, its values, tales, customs, and superstitions, its handmade tools and homes constituted a *whole* world. The quality of that world is reflected in many of the sayings collected in the second part of this chapter. Peasant Romania gave Brancusi his aphoristic turn of speech. It also gave him common sense and a firm grounding, attributes that served him well as he reached for the spiritual in art.

He learned early in life to be free. "I don't like fame," he said in later years,

I have known fame. I'm sorry that I'm not a tramp singing by subway entrances. I love to sing; I even make up rhymes.[2]

As a child, Brancusi was far from happy—he ran away from home several times to escape a poor relationship with his father—but in later years he looked back on his youth as a charmed time in a charmed place. If his birthplace Hobitza was a mixed blessing, the small city of Craiova where he took refuge was a place of unmixed joy and intense learning. "Life was happy, without quarrels or sicknesses, because the civilization that makes things false had never come there,"[3] he said.

I was born in Hobitza, in Pestishan, but in Craiova for the second time.[4]

From the plenitude of my sunny province, I built a reserve of joy for my entire life; only in this way was I able to resist.[5]

His first after-school assignment in life was to be a shepherd in the Carpathian mountains where his village was situated. People who knew him well in later years felt that he drew from this experience his lifelong closeness to animals and communion with the stuff of Nature, wood and stone. He must also have learned many of the songs and stories that visitors heard years later in his Paris atelier, and he received the indelible impression of a settled order of life:

Among us in Romanian villages, a decision is never made when the old ones sit and the young ones stand.[6]

But at the age of eleven, he left his parents' home for good. Passing through a series of employments in small cities, he discovered his innate skill as an artisan.

It is because of a violin that I came to sculpture. I was eleven years old, working in a cleaning and dyeing shop. I had straightened out and arranged everything so well in the shop that the owner said to me, "I know something you will not be able to do—make a violin." I started working and made a violin. I discovered the secret of Stradivarius, I hollowed out the wood, I boiled it. The violin made a wonderful sound. After I made the violin, the owner said to me, "You must be a sculptor."[7]

This farsighted employer and others who recognized his promise helped the boy to enroll in the provincial Craiova School of Arts and Crafts, a trade school that gave him his confident skills with materials and tools. In later years, he sometimes described his view of life and art as "the laws of Craiova"[8]; it was his Eden, the place where everything cohered and had meaning.

From Craiova, he went on to the Bucharest School of Fine Arts, where he received a sophisticated education. His student work from the years around 1900—portraits, figures, studies on classical themes, a remarkable anatomical study—gives evidence of a thorough assimilation of high European sculptural technique. For example, a lifesize rendering of the flayed man, a motif going back to Renaissance medical texts, is a model of anatomical accuracy. When he spoke so fiercely in later years about the uselessness of nudes in art, described Michelangelo's work as "beefsteak" and nude statuary as corpses, he knew whereof he spoke; he had dissected enough cadavers during his Bucharest schooling to master the intricacies of the flesh. When he left that city, he was both a skilled sculptor and an accomplished artisan. He had not yet come into his own.

Many years later, speaking with a countryman, he evoked another aspect of his early experience. He had known and been impressed by peasants who worked the land and practiced the craft-based trades; he had also encountered traditional artists of a kind that once flourished throughout Europe.

> I met icon-makers during my youth in the country. I remember that an icon-maker before starting to paint, or a maker of wooden crosses before starting to carve, would fast for a few weeks in a row. They prayed continually that their icons and crosses would be beautiful. Before it is begun, the creation of any artist needs a pre-established orphic atmosphere. Today painters work with a beefsteak and a bottle of wine by their side. The sculptor holds a chisel in one hand and a glass in the other. The vapors of alcohol and rich food come out of the artist's mouth and pores like the fetid emanations of a horrible corpse. This kind of thing is no longer pure art; it is art governed by the earthly forces of alcohol and over-eating. I am vegetarian, maybe even because of the memory and example of the icon-painters and cross-makers of long ago.[9]

He was vegetarian, but he was not constrained by the Northern asceticism that we encountered in Mondrian. Brancusi was a lover and a man of passions, one of which was the search for truth. Even his austerity had a wholehearted, infectious cheerfulness to it (although, like Mark Twain, Brancusi is said to have had spells of bitterness in later years when his health and creative powers were diminished).

From Bucharest, the young Brancusi was drawn to Paris, probably by the compelling need to see and experience the work of Auguste

Rodin, whose reputation at that time reached across Europe. Brancusi made his way to Paris largely on foot, by way of Munich and Basel. From published sources, it is difficult to piece together a satisfactorily vivid account of this trip in the spring and summer of 1904. Its length and arduousness measure the distance between the archaic rural culture of his origin and the modern urban culture to which he would in time contribute so richly. An anecdote that he liked to tell reflects the bright attitude with which he must have undertaken his journey.

> One day, in Switzerland, in front of a beautiful mountain there was the most beautiful of cows, and she was contemplating me in ecstasy. I said to myself, "I must be someone if even this cow admires me." I came closer; she wasn't looking at me, and she was relieving herself. That tells you what you need to know about fame.[10]

The first years in Paris, where he arrived in 1904, were meager: he attended the Beaux-arts on small scholarships provided by the Romanian government, sang for small wages in the choir of the Romanian Orthodox Church, washed dishes, worked on his art, studied in the museums, opened himself not only to the example of Rodin but to everything around him. A photograph from these years shows the extraordinarily handsome and contained young man dressed in the silk liturgical robes of his church. Speaking later of this period, he said, "Every day I would model a new sculpture, and in the evening I would destroy it."[11] These were years of search and dissatisfaction, marked finally by a turn toward himself and away from the very influence that he had ventured to Paris to assimilate.

There is some uncertainty among historians regarding detail, but it is a matter of record that Rodin knew the young sculptor's work and had been urged by prominent people, including the Queen of Romania, to accept Brancusi as an apprentice in his studio. When the renowned master offered to do so, Brancusi refused. Years later he explained, "Nothing grows in the shadow of great trees." "My friends were very disturbed," he went on to say,

> because they didn't know how Rodin reacted. When he learned of my decision, he said simply: "All things considered, he's right, he's as stubborn as I am." Rodin had a modest attitude in relation to his art. When he finished his *Balzac,* he declared: "Now I'm ready to start working."[12]

In the same brief statement published in 1952, Brancusi paid an extraordinarily graceful tribute to Rodin that implicitly identifies the older sculptor as his father in art; a father refused, but a father nonetheless.

Looking down the corridor of European history, Brancusi seemed to perceive only two sculptors, Michelangelo and Rodin, against whom he could measure himself and whose energies, however differently directed, challenged his own. "Since Michelangelo," he wrote,

> sculptors wanted to create grandiose works. They succeeded only in creating grandiloquent works. In the nineteenth century, the situation of sculpture was deperate. Rodin came and transformed everything. Thanks to him, man became the measure, the module by which the statue is organized. Thanks to him, sculpture became human again in its dimensions and content. Rodin's influence was and remains immense.

The passage is interesting in itself, but even more so because one of Brancusi's key acts of self-discovery was his transformation of a classic Rodin theme, *The Kiss* (Figs. 49, 50). Rodin's version of the theme now seems inevitable, perfect: incomparably svelte and powerful, his lovers entwine in a passionate embrace stilled by sheer perfection of form and surface. In contrast, Brancusi carved his lovers with deliberate naiveté. Forcibly discarding the high technique and repertory of forms that he had mastered, he began again on the basis of essential feelings and the memory of an art beyond the pale of sophisticated art, the art of peasant Romania. He also affirmed the importance for his own practice of "direct carving," that is, working stone or wood himself with the traditional tools of sculptor, mason, and carpenter. From his experience of stone- and woodcarving over the years came some of his most penetrating aphorisms about art and man's relation to Nature.

Like many other motifs, the simple image of *The Kiss* traveled with Brancusi for years after he evolved its basic form. He worked literally for decades on a select number of motifs. In time, his folkloristic early treatment of *The Kiss* issued out into much more abstract designs developed for *The Gate of the Kiss,* a monumental arch completed in 1938 (Fig. 51). In its early form, the motif is a personal declaration of independence from high European tradition and a sign of Brancusi's intention to draw from personal resources; in its most evolved form, thirty years later, the motif is an impersonal sign of unity in diversity.

By 1912, some four years after *The Kiss* first took shape, Brancusi came fully into his own: his work acquired the distilled form and metaphysical content that characterized it in later years. It became a statement not only of essential feelings, cleared of learned rhetoric, but of the forces, seen and unseen, that move the world and man. This is his

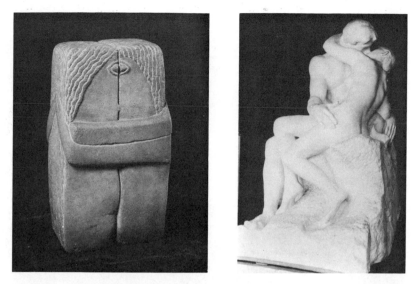

49. Constantin Brancusi. *The Kiss,* 1912. Limestone. 23" × 13" × 10". Philadelphia Museum of Art: Louise and Walter Arensberg Collection. Copyright ARS NY/ADAGP 1987.
50. Auguste Rodin. *The Kiss,* 1888. Marble. Musée Rodin, Paris. Photo: Marburg/Art Resource, New York. Copyright ARS NY/ADAGP 1987.

own account of his progress toward what proved to be a radically new, abstract sculptural language:

> Everything—animate or inanimate—has a spirit. At the turning point in the development of my métier, I said to myself: I must express the spirit of the subject. The spirit will be alive forever. Or if you wish, the *idea* of the subject: that which never dies. It grows in the viewer like life from life. Starting with this thought, you naturally reach the conclusion that it is not detail that creates work but rather the essential. I worked hard to discover the means of more easily finding for each subject the key form that would powerfully sum up the idea of that subject. Certainly, this directed me to a non-figurative art; it is a result. But I never proposed to astonish people through something odd. I reasoned simply, as you can see, and I also reached something simple, terrible in its simplicity: a synthesis that would suggest what I wanted to represent. I reached the point where I could draw out of bronze, wood, or marble that hidden diamond, the essential.[13]

51. Constantin Brancusi. *The Gate of the Kiss,* 1938. Stone. Height 17′3½″. Public Park, Tirgu Jiu, Romania. Photo: Peter Voinescu—EFIAP (courtesy Romanian Tourist Office). Copyright ARS NY/ADAGP 1987.

The work most clearly showing that Brancusi had attained an art which was both his own and larger than any personal ownership is the *Maiastra (Magic Bird)* (Fig. 52). Existing in multiple versions, it is a theme that earned his persistent attention and only waned in his interest as he began to develop a related theme that he called *Bird in Space*. The Pasarea Maiastra (Master Bird) is a magical creature in Romanian folklore, a counselor and guide with whose help the hero can be a hero. Standing with ritual rectitude, pristine in its marble whiteness, the Master Bird emits an intent cry from its open beak and imposing thorax—one of the most piercing sounds in twentieth-century art, although an "inner sound" as Kandinsky would have said. Beneath the Maiastra, a pair of roughly carved, deliberately clumsy human caryatids huddle to provide what support they can for the heroic image surmounting them. One turns toward the other, pressing its face against his ear, while the other looks outward but without radiance. They are *indistinct*, hardly released from the stone. Their unfinishedness contrasts with the formed brilliance of the Maiastra, the massive cube between the two images dramatizing the distinction all the more. Their clumsy stance and anxiously constricted gesture, arms pulled tight to the

52. Constantin Brancusi. *Maiastra (Magic Bird)*. Version I, 1910. White marble, 22″ high; on limestone pedestal, 70″ high, of which the middle section is the *Double Caryatid*. Collection, The Museum of Modern Art, New York. Katherine S. Dreier Bequest. Copyright ARS NY/ADAGP 1987.

chest, make a suggestive contrast to the self-containment and outward address of the Maiastra. The juxtaposition brings to mind the South Indian image of Shiva Dancing: poised and triumphant, He dances— not contemptuously but with inevitability—upon the figure of a dwarf that lies virtually crushed beneath Him.[14]

Were we standing at the edge of an archaeological dig to unearth the *Maiastra*, we would know at once that it addresses us. It is "art," but that isn't the point: it is a message. The Master Bird impeccable in its vigor and aspiration, the caryatids heavy and earthbound: together, a portrait of man.

The *Maiastra* is misplaced in a museum, where it can be seen today. Brancusi himself had little regard for museums; he did not sculpt for them.

> I would like my works to be built in parks and public gardens, I would like children to play on them, as they would have played on stones and monuments born from the earth. Nobody should know what they are or who did them, but everybody should feel their necessity and friendliness, like something that is part of Nature's soul.[15]

Perched with splendor atop common clay, the Maiastra is the first of many animal images that Brancusi conceived and reworked over the decades to come. One of the most important of these is his *Bird in Space* (Fig. 53). Like all of his major images, *Bird in Space* exists in multiple versions. Philadelphia has two versions, one a yellow marble shaft. New York has a polished bronze. Still other versions found their way to India and elsewhere in the world. "The bird," he said in old age,

> I am always working on it. I have not yet found it. It is not a bird, it is the meaning of flight.[16]

More than the Maiastra, which retains a chunky robustness and folkloric charm in spite of its smooth elegance, *Bird in Space* epitomizes Brancusi's search to realize the *idea*, the inmost essence of his subject. The outward address of the Maiastra has been drawn in; *Bird in Space* is wholly dedicated to ascension. "It struggles . . . toward heaven," Brancusi once observed.[17]

The simplicity and depth of this work make extensive comment unnecessary. Nonetheless, excellent scholarship has been accomplished *around* this long series of sculptures: the various versions have been dated and compared; the essential form has been carefully observed; Brancusi's thoughts about the theme have been collected and analyzed;

even the unconscious, Freudian psychology of the conception has been a topic of speculation.[18] A bronze version of *Bird in Space,* imported by the photographer Edward Steichen to the United States in 1926, occasioned a comedy of manners in the United States Customs Court. At a trial recorded as *Brancusi* v. *the United States,* the American authorities vainly attempted to demonstrate that the work was *not art* and should therefore be subject to duty payment as industrial metal. *Bird in Space* was so original and abstract in conception that it fell outside the popular definition of art when first introduced ("Justice Young: If you saw it in the forest, you would not take a shot at it? Mr. Steichen: No, your Honor."[19]). But scholarship and anecdote cannot substitute for standing in front of this sculpture and receiving the impression of its nobility, perfection of form, and heavenward thrust. "Look at my works until you see them,"[20] Brancusi said.

Photographs made by him in his studio over the years provide clues as to how Brancusi himself saw the work. In one example, *Bird in Space* stands or soars—it is both—above a chaos of raw stone and wood, as if its clean aspiring form has been released from tumult. In another photograph, the elliptical "face" of the bird catches direct sunlight and

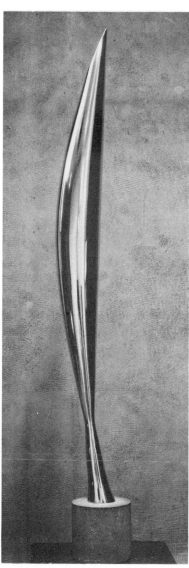

53. Constantin Brancusi. *Bird in Space,* 1928? Bronze (unique cast), 54". Collection, The Museum of Modern Art, New York. Given anonymously. Copyright ARS NY/ ADAGP 1987.

becomes a dazzling sun in turn. The photographs reflect a symbolic perception of the form, as if it traces an itinerary between unformed matter and immaterial light, and occupies the midpoint between matter and spirit.[21]

"Throughout my life," said the sculptor, "I have searched for the essence of flight. Flight, what happiness!"[22] The larger meaning of flight in Brancusi's art and thought is recorded in a comprehensive reflection:

> My sculpture *The Cock* is not a cock; and the *Pasarea Maiastra* is no longer a bird; they became symbols. I have always looked for the natural, for primary and direct beauty, immediate and eternal. I wish that my birds and my cocks could suddenly fill the whole universe and express the Great Liberation! The birds fly, but the cocks sing.[23]

I am uncertain of the date of this pronouncement; its retrospective quality reflects the later years. In any event, its reference to the concept of the Great Liberation, probably drawn from a Buddhist text, offers an occasion to think about one source of Brancusi's spirituality in his mature years. A book that he is known to have read year after year, from the time of its publication in 1925, was Jacques Bacot's translation of the thirteenth-century Tibetan *The Life of Milarepa*.[24] It has been described by a friend of the artist's as his bedside Bible, while others have minimized its legendary importance because Brancusi was after all *artist* not monk, and the separation between art and religion is defended no less scrupulously in our time than their unity was defended centuries ago.

The Life of Milarepa is a classic work of world literature, still little known in the West. Known as "Tibet's great yogi," Milarepa was earlier in life one of Tibet's great sinners. As a young man, he resorted to magical control of the weather to avenge the theft of his family's inheritance by rapacious relatives, in the process causing widespread destruction. Repentant, he turned to religion and was accepted as a pupil by the eminent scholar and sage, Marpa the Translator, who put him through such strenuous ordeals at the beginning of his education in religion that Mila fled in search of an easier path. However, even the subtlest teaching obtained outside of Marpa's circle had no effect on the rebel, and he was returned ignominiously to his teacher, under whose guidance he studied until the time came for the still more strenuous test of a hermit's life. As an itinerant cave-dweller, Mila passed through many spiritual and physical adventures until he achieved enlightenment, the Great Liberation to which Brancusi referred. Thereafter he became one of the most effective teachers in Tibetan tradition, cherished for his practical counsel and unique in his capacity for song. The "hundred thousand songs" of Milarepa have been fully translated only since Brancusi's lifetime,[25] but *The Life of Milarepa* as he knew it contains many poetic songs expressing Mila's search for truth and his observations along the way.

I dwell on this book because it is important to know what a man measures himself against. Michelangelo and Rodin, to be sure, but also—and more secretly—Milarepa provided Brancusi a touchstone of what it is to be fully alive, not only as an artist but as a seeker of truth. Of course, Brancusi was fully formed as an artist by 1925, the first year in which he might have read *The Life of Milarepa*. Not a formative influence on his development, it must have been more in the nature of a confirmation and nourishment for the values that Brancusi had adopted. He too was a cave-dweller of sorts; as the years went by, he tended to receive people at his studio rather than go out. Living alone with utmost simplicity, he had the chastity of those who don't make a fuss about their sexual lives, although he enjoyed the company of women throughout his life. He acknowledged in his way of life and in his work both this world and another that makes itself known through detachment and persevering search. "Buddhism isn't a religion," he commented to a friend in the 1930s,

> it is a morality and a technique through which one can come closer to the gods. Buddhism is my morality. I have neglected the technique.[26]

Strictly speaking, he neglected the technique if the phrase refers to formal study with a qualified teacher, but a number of aphorisms in the following section make clear that he understood the need to attune his consciousness to the task at hand, and the difficulty of doing so. They ring with the authority of experience.

Something more might now be said about *Bird in Space*. All versions (bronze, marble, and plaster studies) bring to mind a smooth seed liberated from its protective husk. The bronze version illustrated reads not as bronze but as gold, hence a golden kernel of life, pressing upward. Is this image a splendid individual invention or something more? An *Upanishad* text directs us to the realm of ancient symbols in which Brancusi was at home, if not learned in the scholarly sense:

> As a goldsmith, taking a piece of gold, reduces it to another and more beautiful form, just so this soul, striking down the body and

dispelling its ignorance, makes for itself another newer and more beautiful form.[27]

A related text reads, ". . . with a body of gold he proceeds to the heavenly light." [28] These passages take us close, I believe, to the essential theme of *Bird in Space,* which stands out in Brancusi's oeuvre and in twentieth-century art as a work of extraordinary depth. Its full meaning can be intuited but probably not grasped in a contemporary, secular frame of reference ("My new *I* comes from something very old," he once said[29]). Once we recognize that *Bird in Space* embodies timeless symbols of transcendance and immortality in a sculptural language of our own, the work comes to rest in the mind; it is "understood."

At an anxious moment, Milarepa and other disciples of Marpa resorted to dreaming for a presage of their future. Mila's dream included the image of a great vulture perched on a column; about to soar into space, it looked upward. Marpa interpreted: "Its glance turned toward the heights is a farewell to the world of creatures. Its flight toward the immensity of space is arrival in the land of deliverance." [30] Not a source of Brancusi's image, Mila's dream is a close parallel.

We can piece together the feel and tempo of Brancusi's life in his maturity from numerous memoirs. It was by all accounts an event to visit him at the impasse Ronsin; surprisingly often, people noted down their impressions later. On the other hand, his own life had few "events." He entertained people in his home and studio with what they perceived as Homeric bountifulness—creating unusual and fine meals, showing his work dramatically (one wasn't free just to poke around in the studio). There were travels—to India, at the invitation of a patron who had asked him to design a "Temple of Love" or "Temple of Deliverance" (an unrealized project for which preliminary designs exist); to Romania on a number of occasions, most notably to supervise construction of the memorial monuments at Tirgu Jiu; to the United States, where Brancusi continued to have one-man exhibitions from time to time. Clearly, he had his loves. He also had fairly serious illnesses that on occasion stopped his work. He was always one who liked to play— a visitor noted that he consecrated a new fireplace in the studio by doing a belly dance, claiming to have learned it at some exotic stage of his life. Carola Giedion-Welcker, author of an early study of Brancusi and his work, reported that he never freed himself from peasant superstitions and had what she called a "mediumistic sensitivity"—such that, for example, he found it easier to work on Sunday mornings because "most people were contented then, and many had left Paris. . . ."[31]

Sidney Geist, dean of American Brancusi scholars and a sculptor in his own right, reflects something of his superstition and extra sensitivity in the following story from the late 1940s. When Geist was on the point of leaving Brancusi's studio, he thanked him for his time. Brancusi said: "All this will pass." "What do you mean?" "All this will be crushed—you know [a large gesture with his hands, taking in all things], we're only between two ice ages."[32]

But none of this quite captures the man. Although it can be cumulatively felt in these reports and directly felt in some of his art and sayings, his quality of being escapes. Brancusi was one who didn't apologize to the world for what he was, yet was gentle; one who looked up and down the cosmos, sensed his belonging, yet retained solid common sense. His "I" had long ago launched its challenge to the ego sharing the same human residence—and shone with the light thrown off by the struggle. True, he posed artfully for photographic self-portraits. Looking intently into the distance with his patented white cloth hat pulled down to his brows, or slouched with casual majesty beneath a carved arch in the studio, Brancusi was not so selfless as to be unaware of his "style" as artist and man. But the awareness seems in him an innocence, as if he were playing with the reality of selfhood. The later self-portraits in particular convey a certain uncalculated grandeur and sincerity.

Among his later works, we should think briefly about the *Endless Column* (Fig. 54) and the *Table of Silence* (Fig. 55), both parts of the ensemble that he designed for the memorial park at Tirgu Jiu in Romania, where the *Gate of the Kiss* is also found (see Fig. 51). All sculpture must be directly experienced to be understood, and I have never had occasion to visit the ninety-six-foot-tall cast-iron realization of the *Endless Column* at Tirgu Jiu. However, the work can be appreciated to some extent through the eight-foot oak prototype exhibited at the Museum of Modern Art in New York. As sculpture, it yields little to the viewer: it has none of the physical finesse and thematic subtlety that one expects from Brancusi. As a monument pitched to awesome scale, a slender rhythmic procession of "beads" headed skyward, the photograph indicates that it must have great impact. Brancusi's intentions were clear:

. . . a column which, if enlarged, would support the vault of heaven.[33]

Let's call it a stairway to heaven.[34]

The *Endless Column* is the negation of the Labyrinth.[35]

The last comment has special resonance; it speaks for the whole of Brancusi's work. But what is the Labyrinth? Surely it is different for each person in detail but the same for all in substance: a complex prison that binds us as we wander it and releases us when we find the means to ascend. The *Endless Column* embodies that ascension. Scholars—notably Mircea Eliade, the historian of religions to whom this book owes much—have recognized the congruence between the *Endless Column* and the ancient idea of the *axis mundi*, the central pillar that upholds the cosmos and that exists within each person as the physical and spiritual axis of his own world.[36] Brancusi's statements, based less on scholarly learning than on his heritage and thoughtfulness, make clear that he was acutely aware of the symbol to which he gave form at Tirgu Jiu.

54. Constantin Brancusi. *Endless Column*, 1937. Cast iron. 96' 2⅞" high. Public Park, Tirgu Jiu, Romania. Photo: Romanian Tourist Office. Copyright ARS NY/ADAGP 1987.

Brancusi may have conceived the *Table of Silence* at the same site for use, but its scale and solemnity must discourage visitors to the park from laying out picnics on it. Built for a larger race of men, it evokes legends and sacred tales. Here one would expect not a casual event but rather the Passover meal of Jesus and his disciples or a latter-day convocation of King Arthur and the Knights of the Round Table. I know of few things more hopeful in twentieth-century art. Like the Arthurian sword embedded in stone that awaited its master and refused to give itself to lesser men, the *Table of Silence* conveys an impression of waiting. In his later years, Brancusi spoke of these values, which he seems to have discovered retrospectively as the underlying nature of the design became evident to him:

55. Constantin Brancusi. *Table of Silence*, 1937. Stone. Height 31½". Public Park, Tirgu Jiu, Romania. Photo: Romanian Tourist Office. Copyright ARS NY/ADAGP 1987.

Now, in old age, I finally see that the Table of Silence is another, a new Last Supper.[37] . . . The line of the Table of Silence suggests the closed curvature of a circle that gathers, rallies, and unites.[38]

We have looked at a number of Brancusi's works—and of course not looked at many others, some as brilliant as anything to which we have given time. But what cannot be overlooked in Brancusi's oeuvre is his thought, which moves well beyond the sayings and reflections that have already found their natural place in this account of his sculpture.

BRANCUSI'S THOUGHT: THE LAWS OF CRAIOVA

Brancusi's thought is well known and not well known at all. Everyone who cares for Brancusi's art has encountered aphorisms and sayings in specialized works and less frequently in general studies of twentieth-century art. Brancusi's admirers, as noted earlier, have long collected these *netsuke* of the mind. Their interest over the years makes possible a rich collection of aphorisms and statements, some familiar, others apparently never translated into English. These are the Laws of Craiova. Some to whom I have shown these sayings find Brancusi arrogant. It is true that the compactness of aphorisms and proverbs leaves little room for qualification; this alone gives them a touch of arrogance. Brancusi was aware of his achievement and earned authority, but his underlying humility—in any case, his great decency—seem beyond question. As he said, "Life is found below, on the earth."

On His Sculpture

Do not look for obscure formulas or mysteries. I give you pure joy. Look at my works until you see them. Those who are closest to God have seen them.[39]

They are imbeciles who call my work abstract; that which they call abstract is the most realist, because what is real is not the exterior form but the idea, the essence of things.[40]

In my sculpture, I do not like to represent strength and great muscles, but beings that are, in essence, ethereal.[41]

Sculptures are occasions for meditation. Temples and churches have always been and have remained sanctuaries for meditation.[42]

I made stone sing—for humanity.[43]

I am not Surrealist, Baroque, Cubist, nothing of this kind. My new *I* comes from something very old.[44]

His Search in Art

I would look intently at sculpture by others in the great museums, sculpture by people with sure talent—and then at mine. What was bothering me? Beautifully sculpted, beautifully carved, beautifully polished, meticulous, with details so well rendered—leaving almost nothing to say. Yes, but they were not *alive!* They looked like *ghosts! Petrified,* even! I wished to express movement and life, elan and pure joy. I was more and more disturbed by the crypt-like, funereal impression those sculptures gave me. Slowly, my way was defined.[45]

Once I was asked to create a monument to a dead poet. One of the figures was a woman. All of a sudden she looked too real to me. I felt like handling her roughly. I wanted to express prayer . . . with crossed arms. But then the woman looked as if she was cold. I cut off the arms. I understood then that realism was not essential to expression.[46]

I have been working on the "enchanted bird" since 1909, and it seems to me that I haven't finished it yet. I wish to present the imponderable in a concrete form.[47]

There has been no art yet; art has just begun.[48]

Aesthetics

Simplicity is not a goal in art, but one arrives at simplicity in spite of oneself by approaching the real sense of things.[49]

Inner proportion is the ultimate truth inherent in all things.[50]

Beauty is absolute equity.[51]

Art is reality itself.[52]

The work of art expresses precisely those things which do not die. It must do so, however, in a form that bears witness to the artist's own era.[53]

A well-made sculpture should have the power to heal the beholder. It must be lovely to touch, friendly to live with, not only well made.[54]

The Artist's Discipline

It is not difficult to make things, what is difficult is to reach the state in which we can make them.[55]

Art is not a chance happening.[56]

The artist is not a luxury animal but an austere animal. Art is performed only in conditions of austerity and drama, like a perfect crime.[57]

A monument depends on the precise place you choose for it, on the way the sun rises or sets on it, and on its surroundings. Only when you have these data can you choose your material and study the form most adequate to blend perfectly with nature and define the desired monumentality.[58]

Once a bird came into my studio. When it wanted to leave, it couldn't find the way and threw itself in confusion against the walls and windows. Another bird came into the studio, rested for a few moments on a base, and then flew off, easily finding its way to the sky. With artists, it's the same.[59]

Think that the oak before you is a wise and clever grandfather. The word of your chisel must be respectful and loving; only in this way can you please it.[60]

While carving stone, you discover the spirit of your material and the properties peculiar to it. Your hand thinks and follows the thought of the material.[61]

The Politics of Art and the Marketplace

I do not follow what is happening in art movements. When one finds his own direction, he is so busy there is no time.[62]

Those who let themselves be tempted to follow in the tracks of the competition at the same time allow their creative forces to degenerate.[63]

Artists have killed art.[64]

People take themselves much too seriously. Most of the time, they want to be *somebody*. But fame mocks us when we insist on achieving it, and the moment we turn our backs to it, it is the one that chases us.[65]

Religion in Art and Life

In the art of other times there is joy, but with it the nightmare that the religions drag with them. There is joy in Negro sculpture, among the nearly archaic Greeks, in some things of the Chinese and the Gothic . . . oh, we find it everywhere. But even so, not so well as it might be with us in the future, if only we were to free ourselves of all this. . . . It is time we had an art of our own.[66]

The humblest being is capable of finding the way to God.[67]

I hear talk today about all kinds of art movements. It is a kind of universal Tower of Babel. Art only developed in the great religious epochs, and everything that is created through philosophy becomes joy, peace, light, and freedom.[68]

We cannot ever reach God, but the courage to travel toward Him remains important.[69]

What you tie here on earth is tied also in heaven.[70]

On Self and Ego

The journey is really within oneself.[71]

There is a purpose in all things. To reach it, one must be detached from oneself.[72]

Michelangelo is too strong, his *moi* overshadows everything.[73]

My two last *Birds* . . . are the ones in which I came closest to the right proportions—and I approached these proportions to the degree that I was able to rid myself of myself.[74]

Whoever does not detach himself from the ego never attains the Absolute and never deciphers life.[75]

When you create, you need to join yourself with the universe and the elements. Yet to achieve something, you must be yourself and not destroy yourself. And you must always try to escape the masters.[76]

On Human Life

In my soul there was never a place for envy or for hatred, but only for the joy that you can collect anywhere and anytime. I consider that what makes us truly live is the feeling of permanent childhood in life.[77]

It is something to be clever, but to be honest—that's really worthwhile.[78]

A wise man makes from his own inner venom a remedy for himself or a healing precept for others.[79]

Sufferings strengthen a man, and are more necessary than any pleasure for the formation of a great character. And then, I always think that each is himself responsible for whatever happens to him.[80]

No moral energy is wasted in the universe.[81]

The Devil and the Good Lord are not separate in real situations; and they are neither here nor there, they are simultaneous and everywhere.[82]

Work and Aspiration

To see far is one thing, to go there is another. What counts is action.[83]

You must climb very high to see very far.[84]

Work is the most foolish thing, it's more a ways and means. But even God did not escape it.[85]

Create like a god, command like a king, work like a slave.[86]

On Intellect

We always want to understand something, but there is nothing to understand. Everything that you can see here has one merit only, that it is *lived*.[87]

Intelligence helps us if we give it the brakes of love and soul. Nowadays everyone is intelligent. It is a bad thing. Intelligence is fictitious.[88]

Naturalness and Nature

Self-content is established in your soul when you perceive yourself as a link in the endless chain of your ancestors, and when you do not wander even an iota from the prescriptions of unchanging natural truth.[89]

The ancients loved maxims, and our peasants preserve their proverbs. The *hoi polloi* today, the so-called bourgeois, do not recognize any norm. Rapacity and competitiveness have killed the age-old rules of naturalness.[90]

Did you really see those butterflies? When they left the studio, their wings were spotted with pollen from my marble.[91]

We will never be grateful enough toward the Earth that has given us everything.[92]

My laws are those of Craiova where I spent the decisive years of my youth.[93]

About Himself

What I am doing was given me to do. I came to this world with a mission.[94]

My life is the game I play.[95]

> During my childhood—I slept in bed.
> During my adolescence—I waited at the door.
> In my maturity—I have flown toward the heavens![96]

15 HENRI MATISSE: IN THE STUDIO WITH THREE FLOORS

"Matisse?" friends have asked. "Does he belong in a book on the spiritual?" The art and thought of Henri Matisse (1869–1954) gave our time a gentle vision dedicated more to balance, awareness, and acceptance than to self-abnegating rigor. His mature sense of man's identity and the world was not stridently metaphysical as in Mondrian, not feverish as in Malevich, not founded in a virile mysticism as in Brancusi, not divided by contrary impulses toward systemization and reverence as in Kandinsky. Matisse was a man of polished métier, a lifelong student and master of the means of art who rejoiced in clear expression. He spoke of serenity in art, and of repose. For him search meant almost always the search for a truer composition, a more thorough sincerity in the artist, a more refined equilibrium in the finished canvas.

His work itself, ranging from the first great originality of his Fauve period (1905–07) through odalisques and sun-filled interiors to the simplicity of the chapel at Vence (circa 1951), is clearly more concerned with refinement of *le bonheur de vivre,* as he titled a major early canvas, than with transcendental experience. To be vividly present to the work at hand—to experience "ardent moments of contact with myself,"[1] as he said late in life—was transcendence enough and a compelling sign that our lives are not at base empty. Although he spoke on occasion of working against his own anxiety and chaotic longings, at heart he accepted humanity, accepted himself, and thought there to be enough beauty and truth in things as they are—provided one is willing to look closely, to discipline imagination and body, to search tirelessly for a truer vision, to find the balance.

With these words and the life of effort they imply, we enter into the quietly demanding spirituality of Matisse. Publicly considered at the time of his artistic debut to be a fierce radical, he was in fact a man of scrupulously classical temperament who knew from within what the ancient Greeks meant by equilibrium, harmony, beauty, the Idea of things. He conducted his revolution in the early years of the century with stringent decorum, as a duty toward art and his own vision rather than as a picaresque adventure.

His was the prudent, reflective spirituality of a thoroughly sane man, Mediterranean by instinct if not by northern French birth, who was drawn both to lucidity and to a pagan capacity for celebration. In this respect, he had more in common with the old vase painters than with Raphael, although he knew Raphael's suave art intimately and had learned the many lessons of the Renaissance. If he seems now himself an Old Master remote from the late twentieth century, the distance is an effect of postmodernist anxiety. Postmodernism feels more akin to disquiet than to the invincible steadiness of Matisse, who did not consider anxiety to be a virtue. His conviction is an embarrassment; his views display no congenial trace of nihilism. "Painting is a serious and grave art," he said in 1949,

> [and] we still do not possess its entire soul, its whole principle; nor have we freedom, and this is what we most need.[2]

This is his voice, and these in part his values. Both imply a faith in humanity that comes hard today, as if we don't dare love what we are for fear of losing it.

Matisse deepened as he went along, yet from his first artistic maturity, reflected in his *Notes of a Painter* (1909), to his very last works and statements, there is a perfectly satisfactory sameness. He was aware of this natural steadfastness and once remarked on it with a touch of self-deprecation and innocent amazement:

> You know, each of us has only one idea, we are born with it, and we spend a lifetime developing this *idée fixe*, making it breathe.[3]

Matisse's art has been painstakingly studied for many decades, and his thought well documented in recent years.[4] Because his art is so familiar, we may do better first to explore his thought, which remains less well known, together with some aspects of his life that formed it. The sustained concerns and insights in the written record, when we come to know them, may refresh our vision of his art.

MATISSE'S THOUGHT: BENEATH THE SUCCESSION OF MOMENTS

In 1908 and for a few years thereafter, Henri Matisse maintained a studio school. Although he quickly found teaching duties an unwanted burden, he retained in his writings and interviews something of the objectivity and explicitness of a good teacher, and the school itself remained in his thoughts. Reminiscing in 1925 about his brief pedagogical career, he recalled an image, useful to him at the time, which still provides a resonant analogy for his art and spirituality:

> I had the habit of telling my students. . . . : the ideal thing would be to have a studio with three floors. On the ground floor, we would do a first study after the model. From the second, we would go downstairs rarely. On the third, we would have learned to do without the model.[5]

The three levels of his ideal studio correspond to levels of art about which he often spoke over the years—and correspond to the pattern of apprentice, journeyman, and master discussed in an earlier chapter. Matisse himself almost always started at the ground floor and lingered there. The model was literally his "ground"; things seen and the act of coming into contact with them were his discipline. No artist of our time has insisted more fervently on the need for a studio apprenticeship that includes not only thorough training of eye and hand but also eager receptiveness to the influence of other artists. Sensitivity to others' achievements is balanced in the best of students, he believed, by a capacity to assimilate influences and continue toward a fully personal vision; this had been his experience. An unbelievably ample workshop knowledge is reflected in Matisse's writings and interviews and in notes taken by Sarah Stein, a member of the famed Leo and Gertrude Stein family, who studied in Matisse's school. Through her record, readers can experience something of the intensity with which he conducted himself on the ground floor.

Matisse's assured movement from technique to the history of art to the possibility of fresh vision and back again to technique is part of his genius:

> Everything must be constructed—built up of parts that make a unit: a tree like a human body, a human body like a cathedral. . . . See from the first your proportions, and do not lose them. But proportions according to correct measurement are after all very little unless confirmed by sentiment, and expressive of the particular physical character of the model. . . . It was in the decadent periods of art that the artist's chief interest lay in developing the small forms and details. In all great periods the essentials of form, the large masses and their relations, occupied him above all other considerations—as in the antique.[6]

None of this is explicitly "the spiritual," but Matisse *assumes* certain values that condition his words and acts. They make themselves felt in his reference to "the essentials of form," and they emerge openly in the single most eloquent passage of his writings:

> I want to reach that state of condensation of sensations that makes the painting. I could be satisfied with a work produced in one session, but I would tire of it later. . . . Beneath the succession of moments that makes up the superficial existence of beings and things, and clothes them in changing appearances, soon vanished, one can search for a truer, more essential character to which the artist will dedicate himself in order to give a more enduring interpretation of reality.[7]

With these words, we reach the second floor of the ideal studio, midway between inspired freedom and "correct measurement" of the model. In phrases reminiscent of Cézanne, whom he described as "the master of us all,"[8] Matisse evokes his search for the truth underlying appearances, to which the artist penetrates by engaging with concrete reality again and again. To document appearances, however exactly, is insufficient. "What did the Realists do, what did the Impressionists do?" Matisse once asked impatiently. "Copies from nature," he answered.

> We wish something else. We are moving toward serenity through the simplification of ideas and form. The ensemble is our only ideal. Details diminish the purity of lines, harm the intensity of emotion, we reject them.[9]

He speaks here as a critic of style and composition, but his references to emotion and serenity point toward the raison d'être of his art.

Matisse has been taken to task over the years for the odd way in which he first expressed his raison d'être. Although he refined his expression as time went on, the gist of what he said remained. The passage is from *Notes of a Painter*, his earliest major public statement, already marked with the deliberation and certainty—and warmth—that characterized him in his years as an acknowledged master. In 1909, when *Notes of a Painter* was published, he was still subject to furious criticism and grateful for the farsighted collectors and dealers who had recognized him.

> What I dream of is an art of balance, of purity, of tranquility, with no anxious or worrisome subject, which would be, for all cerebral workers—for the businessman as well as the man of letters, for ex-

ample—a soothing, calming influence on the mind, something like a good armchair that relaxes his physical fatigue.[10]

Reading this passage today, people still wonder that he could compare the joyous refinement of his art to a *fauteuil*—a wonder easily shared. He must have wished to domesticate the art that critics had called *fauve* (wild, savage), and overdid it. The clumsy figure of speech nonetheless bears witness to Matisse's abiding concern with the home, the ordinary, the daily, the hopelessly bourgeois. Some of his finest works are transfigurations of the home, which becomes planes of light and color, abstract and raised, or else an intensely decorative setting in which the turmoil of family life yields to brightness and order. Decoration for Matisse remained linked with decorum; it was a surge of color and form, under control. Even his odalisques, generally comfortable European women in skimpy harem outfits, are safe; their eroticism reflects the private dreams of urban men more than the true grit of sexual passion.

No matter; Matisse was reaching through his references to balance and purity toward his ultimate concern. Later he would speak of "a sort of cerebral calm, a truce, a pleasant certainty—which will give peace and tranquility," [11] and he would say:

A picture must be quiet on the wall. It mustn't introduce for the viewer an element of worry and anxiety, but should gently guide him toward a physical state such that he doesn't feel the need to be more than himself, to depart from himself. . . .[12]

Matisse associated his deep instinct for serenity with two disparate sources: his own psychological need for quietness, and then something more general—the age-old Mediterranean atmosphere in which he lived and from which he drew nourishment. He once expressed his admiration for Northern painting but showed no sign of envying its psychological intensity:

My role, I believe, is to give a certain peacefulness. Because I myself need peace. Rembrandt's painting, obviously, goes very deep. It is a painting of the North, a painting of Holland, Flanders, which hasn't the same atmosphere that we have here in France or in the Mediterranean region. . . . The Mediterranean is very close to Paris, after all.[13]

Speaking of his own psychological struggles, he made clear that, whatever they were, they were private and not the stuff of art; he chose:

to keep torments and anxieties to myself and to transcribe only the beauty of the world and the joy of painting.[14]

This stance might be regarded as inherently insincere, deliberately blind to the tragedies of modern life. But Matisse did not evade the rough side; he chose, for example, to remain in France during the Nazi Occupation although he had been invited to Brazil and offered a teaching post in San Francisco. His wife and daughter, with him during the war, were imprisoned for Resistance work of which he was surely aware.

There are different missions; his was one of reconciliation. To "transcribe the beauty" is no small thing. The concept of sincerity was in fact central to his understanding of the artist's discipline. By sincerity he meant much more than honesty with others. The word evoked for him a willingness in younger artists to accept the influence of mature artists and absorb the lessons they offered. It evoked also the tendency to search oneself, to go ever deeper into what one is as human being and as artist. To be sincere is to know oneself privately and well, quite apart from the web of influences, however helpful. Sincerity provides the clarity and staying power to uncover internal resources, from which alone an independent art may grow. It is the key to fruitful relationships with others and a fruitful relationship with oneself. Because it grounds the artist in a psychological atmosphere closer to his or her true nature, sincerity grants relative immunity to praise and blame; it confers inner freedom. A disarmingly common word, sincerity signified for Matisse a power to see, a power to search, and a power to give form.

> I can't insist too much on the necessity for artists to be perfectly sincere in their work. This alone can give artists the great courage they need to accept their work in all modesty and humility.[15]

> One must be sincere, and the work of art only exists fully when it is charged with human emotion and rendered in all sincerity, not through the application of a conventional program. . . .[16]

Much of Matisse's workshop thought bears on the creative conflicts between the first and second floors of the ideal studio—conflicts between what has been intellectually assimilated as good practice and what is deeply felt; between the infinite detail of Nature and the synthesizing, dreaming, meditative power of imagination (the words are his, from various sources). And there is more still, a creative capacity sometimes experienced as other than oneself, sometimes experienced *as* oneself; unteachable, it belongs to the third floor of the ideal studio.

No doubt, one should paint as one sings, without constraint. The acrobat executes his number with ease and apparent facility. Let's not lose from sight the long preparatory work that has allowed him to reach this result. It's the same with painting. Possession of the means must pass from the conscious to the unconscious through work, and it is then that one attains this impression of spontaneity.[17]

If the third floor has much to do with spontaneity, it also has to do with an inalienable individuality to which Matisse once referred good-humoredly when recalling what must in fact have been an excruciating turn of events in his youth:

> I had the good fortune once to have Rodin's advice about my draw-ings, which were shown him by a friend. However, the advice he gave didn't suit me in any respect, and Rodin showed on this occa-sion only his nitpicking side. He couldn't do otherwise. For the best of what the Masters have is beyond them. Not understanding it, they can't teach it.[18]

Freedom, spontaneity, sureness, individuality so rooted in oneself that it cannot be passed on—these are signs of access to the highest floor, integrated by a discipline that goes well beyond what is ordinarily meant by attention. "When I am drawing," Matisse commented late in life, "naturally I try to empty my brain completely of all memory in order to receive only the present moment."[19] Speaking again of draw-ing several years later, he returned to that thought: "An emptiness ap-pears—and I become no more than the spectator of what I'm doing."[20] But he was not one to wrap himself in the prestige of "inspiration"; the clarity and perceptiveness that came over him were the result of long work, a grace yet also a result.

Matisse emerged from the same crucible that formed Picasso, Braque, Brancusi, and so many others: Paris in the years before World War I. "It was a period," he recalled late in life,

> when we didn't feel imprisoned in uniforms, and what one could discover that was bold and new in the painting of a friend belonged to everyone. . . . Fauvism, the exaltation of color; precision of draw-ing from Cubism; visits to the Louvre and exotic influences through the channel of the ethnographic museum at the old Trocadéro, were so many things that shaped the landscape in which we lived, in which we traveled, and from which we all emerged. It was a time of artistic cosmogony.[21]

For Matisse, to emerge meant to study diligently at the Beaux-Arts and to resent its limitations. "The Beaux-Arts masters told their students: 'Copy nature stupidly.' Throughout my entire career I have reacted against this attitude."[22] It meant to adopt and then set aside the anti-establishment styles of the late nineteenth century: "Working before an inspiring landscape, I thought only of making my colors sing, without concerning myself with all the [Divisionist] rules and prohibitions."[23] It meant finding a community of like-minded artists—André Derain, Maurice Vlaminck, and others—for whom the rediscovery of pure color, uninhibited by system, led to the rediscovery of art as a whole.

Acknowledged leader of the Fauve movement[24] in which they all participated, Matisse found his way past the bold but not always subtle Fauve experiment to the central revelation of color in modern art. In this aspect of art he, not Cézanne, was "the master of us all." Kandinsky was no less sensitive to color and equally eloquent about it in his writings, but Matisse's actual treatment of color on canvas as glowing, flat planes has exercised a much greater influence on the course of twentieth-century art. His simplicity, his concern for "purity of means," as he often said, struck the fundamental note that was needed.[25]

Matisse on color is the artist speaking of a force that he revered. There are many great passages on color in his writings and interviews; a few will serve here as signs of the rest. Matisse often recalled, for example, the Fauve years when he and his companions broke through. The following begins with one of the key formulations of twentieth-century art, a statement of acquired insight but also of the intention to explore:

> Color exists in itself, possesses its own beauty. It was Japanese prints that we bought for a few *sous* on the rue de Seine that revealed this to us. I understood then that one could work with expressive colors which are not necessarily descriptive colors. . . . Once my eye was unclogged, cleansed by the Japanese prints, I was truly ready to receive colors in terms of their emotional power.[26]

A more analytical comment, also from Matisse's late years, can help us to recognize what he meant by the emotional power of colors, quite apart from their ability to transcribe appearances from Nature to canvas.

> . . . Pure colors . . . have in themselves, independently of the objects they serve to express, a significant action on the feelings of those who look at them.

. . . Simple colors can act upon the inner feelings with more force, the simpler they are. A blue, for example, accompanied by the brilliance of its complementaries, acts upon the feelings like an energetic blow on a gong. The same with red and yellow, and the artist must be able to sound them when he needs to.[27]

Matisse abandoned modeling, perspective, and other time-honored means of binding color into a pictorial whole, but in recompense for these losses made color an independent force.

An empiricist to the core, content to leave the spiritual world largely undefined although sensed, Matisse was willing in relation to color to make one of his rare references to "the Spirit." It appears in a letter of 1948 to the curator of a planned retrospective in America:

If drawing proceeds from the Spirit and color from the senses, one must draw in order to cultivate the Spirit and to be capable of guiding color into the paths of the Spirit. . . . It is only after years of preparation that the young artist has the right to touch color—not color as a means of description—but as a means of intimate expression. Then he can hope that all the images and even all the symbols that he uses may be the reflection of his love for things, a reflection in which he can have confidence if he has been capable of carrying his education through to the end with purity and without lying to himself. Then he will use colors with discernment. He will place them in keeping with a natural design, unformulated and [yet] totally conceived, which will spring directly from his sensation; just what permitted Toulouse-Lautrec at the end of his life to exclaim: *At last, I no longer know how to draw.*[28]

Let us recall two further elements in Matisse's life and sensibility: a late Church commission, unique in his oeuvre, and the culminating self-examination which this commission brought about. Matisse had never been attached to the Catholic church or any other, had always been a free thinker with little interest in theology. Some souls don't require theology; they require only long enough lives to confirm their suspicions. The studio was his school and temple, and the sacred rose to meet him as he worked:

What matters the most to me? To work with my model until I have it enough in me to be able to improvise, to let my hand run free while respecting the grandeur and sacredness of all living things.[29]

"Do I believe in God?" he once asked—and responded with Gallic complexity:

Yes, when I work. When I am submissive and modest, I feel myself so helped by someone who makes me do things that surpass me. Still, I feel no gratitude toward *Him* because it is as if I were faced with a magician whose tricks I can't see through. I feel deprived of the profit of the experience that should have compensated my effort. I am ungrateful without remorse.[30]

Late in life, despite the vagueness of his religious views, Matisse accepted a commission to design and decorate the interior of the Chapel of the Rosary of the Dominican Sisters in Vence, a lovely town not far from Nice, where he had kept a studio for some years. Picasso, rival and friend, took him to task for working in a church context. In responding to him, Matisse found an opportunity to sort out the differences between formal faith and an underlying spirituality that requires no name to be real, provided that it is based on a real discipline:

For me, [this project] is essentially a work of art. I meditate, and let myself be penetrated by what I'm undertaking. I do not know if I have faith or not. Perhaps I'm somewhat Buddhist. The essential thing is to work in a state of mind that approaches prayer.[31]

As for Brancusi, the word "Buddhism" served Matisse to indicate a certain inwardness that must have struck him as rare in Western culture, an inwardness that he experienced but could not confirm against familiar cultural markers in the West. Like Brancusi, Matisse reached above all for a satisfactory *empirical* answer to the riddle of sacred art in an irreligious era. It would have to be enough in our time to work well and bring forth art "helped by someone," as he said. Sacred art requires no great elaboration of theory, but it requires a practice. He knew that the best he offered was spiritual in content even if it was not linked to a formal religion or path. He summarized this knowledge at one point in his meditations about the Vence Chapel:

Modern art is certainly an art intended to delight, but this in no way implies that it has no religious or spiritual content. I didn't experience the need to convert in order to execute the chapel at Vence. My inner attitude didn't change; it remained what it was, what it is in front of a face, a chair, or a fruit. . . . My only religion is that of love for the work to be created, love of creation and of great sincerity. I made this chapel with the single feeling of expressing myself *in depth*. I had the opportunity to express myself in the totality of form and color. This work, for me, was a teaching. . . .[32]

Matisse used the Vence commission to sum himself up to himself. Always in search of equilibrium and vitality in his work as an artist, he brought no less determination to finishing the composition of his life. "It was in creating the chapel at Vence that I finally awakened to myself. . . ."[33] The formal religious commission brought him to see clearly that his work, not excluding the luxurious nudes, had been inherently religious. In a sense, he had always known this; already in the 1909 *Notes* he had referred to the "so to speak religious feeling that I bear toward life."[34] Yet forty years later, there was a difference—greater breadth, greater conviction and simplicity, as if he were ready to start again.

Matisse also recognized that twentieth-century culture set limits on his own work and that of all artists. This recognition is recorded in a letter from the aged Matisse to the still more aged Pierre Bonnard, an artist of great charm.

> Giotto is the summit of my desires, but the road that leads toward an equivalent, in our time, is too long for a single life. However, the stages of it are interesting.[35]

Are these words moving only to committed students of art, for whom the simple, eloquent figures of Giotto are as familiar as family photographs? Conveying the aspiration to religious art with understated nostalgia, Matisse admits with exemplary dispassion that, while the goal is too high, the work toward it is "interesting." Above all, the road exists and there is traffic, however infrequent. Few artists of our time have struck such a knowing balance between the ideal of a fully realized sacred art and the experience of an era that scarcely knows its way to the sacred.

MATISSE'S ART: HAPPY THOSE WHO SING

A pair of works from Matisse's first artistic maturity encompasses much of what his art would be. *Bonheur de vivre* of 1905–06 (Fig. 56) is an icon of a world at ease, sensual yet innocent, ancient yet seen through a child's eyes—a world of music, dance, love, of the body freed. The word "icon" with its suggestion of fixed symbolic pattern is fitting because, in spite of the many figures that stretch and reach in the pleasant clearing, there is a stillness as if what we see has always been and will endure. *The Red Studio* of 1911 (Fig. 57) reflects *bonheur de vivre* in another way. From an icon of Nature and of humanity fear-

56. Henri Matisse. *Bonheur de vivre*, 1905–06. Oil on canvas. 68½″ × 93¾″. Photo copyright © by The Barnes Foundation, 1988. Copyright ARS NY/SPADEM 1987.

lessly at home in it, we turn to an icon of civilization; from a limitless exterior we turn to a limited interior where Nature is present only in oblique and tame ways—the rambling ivy in a jug, the landscape paintings. This is an orderly space, filled with the things of the mind. Even the most concrete objects—chairs, stools, tables—are rendered with a light, almost ghostly touch. The images on canvas, the imaginings, are more real than they. The great red field of color encompassing the entire canvas drives home the joy of having a room of this kind, dedicated to activities of this kind. In each of these paintings, Matisse created a paradise. "*Happy those who sing* with all their hearts, with upright hearts," he wrote late in life,[36] as if commenting on his own aspiration in language reminiscent of the Psalms.

Bonheur de vivre rewards close attention. Perhaps more than any canvas by Matisse, it has the quality of a deliberate credo—a statement of point of view, of loyalties, and of independence. It exists in a rich historical context. Matisse conveys the theme of a pastoral Golden Age through nude and lightly clad figures at rest, embracing, or playing

57. Henri Matisse. *The Red Studio,* 1911. Oil on canvas. 71¼″ × 86¼″. Collection, The Museum of Modern Art, New York. Mrs. Simon Guggenheim Fund. Copyright ARS NY/SPADEM 1987.

in a natural setting of great appeal. This theme moves back through Matisse's immediate predecessors, Cézanne and Puvis de Chavannes, to earlier masters of European painting—Nicolas Poussin, Giovanni Bellini, and Giorgione—and beyond them to the Greco-Roman and Biblical sources that implanted it in the Western imagination. Both the overall theme and many of the individual figures in Matisse's canvas reflect this long tradition, which perpetuated itself in part by passing from generation to generation a highly studied repertory of figure motifs.

The painting is, then, loyal to tradition in theme and composition—but radically disloyal in vision and style. The very fact that it quotes so closely but transforms so fully is its declaration of independence. Matisse rejected traditional European illusionism by foregoing the established techniques for creating perceptions of mass and space. His flat color, strong figure outlines, and summary treatment of recession into space, coupled with an indifference to detail, create a style incomparably simpler than that of traditional European painting, although not without a sophistication of its own. Its sophistication lies in the fluidity and power of characterization in Matisse's line, the harmony of his light-filled color, and the ease with which he carries the burden of the ancient theme. He strips away the conventionality of the theme to reveal the impulse that gave birth to it, a life-affirming joy that is both sexual and sensual—sensual in that merely to move, or pipe, or rest in this forest clearing is delight.

Bonheur de vivre is the first major reworking in the twentieth century of age-old Mediterranean imagery. Woven into the fabric of medieval art and deliberately cultivated since the early Renaissance, Classical imagery had become for the most part moribund academic convention by the later nineteenth century. Only in the art of Pierre Puvis de Chavannes (1824–1898) was there lingering eloquence: his statuesque figures and still landscapes, rendered in smoky color harmonies, convey a haunting mood of decline and valediction. The beauty of Puvis' work is autumnal. Hence the shock of Matisse's renewal of the Mediterranean theme. Matisse's Classicism knows nothing of decline; his setting is all spring, his figures prepare for a new day.

Matisse was not alone in recapturing the Mediterranean theme, which offered a powerful contrast to the urban living and anxious sense of self that became increasingly characteristic of the twentieth century. The dignity of the isolated figure, rendered with keen memory for its Classical antecedents, or a grouping of figures engaged in pleasurable tasks—or no task at all—would become twentieth-century icons, signs of something lost, signs of something underlying (see chapter 16).

The Red Studio calls for briefer discussion, although it offers no less delight. It has its own antecedents in the genre painting of bourgeois Europe—the warmly conceived, often surreptitiously symbolic scenes of home, tavern, and workplace represented earlier in this book by Chardin's painting of a boy blowing bubbles at the window (Fig. 1). Matisse is again transforming what had become a minor academic convention: his version of the artist's studio is a loving inventory of the tools and clutter of the workplace in the traditional manner, but it is also touchingly empty as if he cares most for the uncommitted space between objects. He allows everything to drift a little; it is all seen by a dreamer's eyes, yet sharply. "It was only slowly," he once said, that I succeeded in discovering the secret of my art. It consists in a meditation after nature, in the expression of a dream inspired always by reality.[37]

Dreamer, meditator—and child: objects and figures in Matisse's work are large and simple, apprehended without a dimming veil of thought. Matisse knew that a childlike openness served him as a deep resource; late in life he referred explicitly to "everything that was best in me when I was a child, which I have tried to keep throughout my life."[38]

The Red Studio is only one of many interiors painted in the groundbreaking early years of Matisse's artistic maturity and in the years to come—still lifes, interiors with a window open to the world, a model or models seated in a room without any activity other than to be there and to be seen. Linking them all are his uniquely vibrant color harmonies, characteristically fluent line, and unapologetic joy in pattern.

Drawn as he was to the commonplace ("The artist's role is only to take hold of current truths, to isolate the commonplace, which through him acquires a deep, new, and definitive meaning"[39]), Matisse ran the risk of failing to transform the commonplace into deep new meaning. This was the edge along which he moved, and in the course of such a long, productive life not an edge on which he or anyone could always remain balanced. While his work is never dull, it sometimes offers more sight than insight. Distinguishing his best work is a blend of magnificent seeing and quiet questioning, as if what is seen is a visible mystery, celebrated for its beauty, watched for revealing signs.

These qualities are powerfully evident in a work of 1911, *Goldfish and Sculpture* (Fig. 58), the title itself a mundane, almost evasive catalogue of objects rather than a statement of theme. The great poet in our time of the bourgeois condition, Matisse depicts merely a corner of his home but succeeds in evoking much larger sentiments than one could guess from an inventory of the objects and their setting. The world of his domestic interiors is vibrant in color and daring in its planar composition, but otherwise modulated and gentle. The nude at right, posed to reveal full breasts and hips, possesses in fact only a faint, remembered sensuality: it is only a terra cotta statuette, outlined without erotic insistence. Similarly, the three goldfish burn with orange-red intensity, but they are after all only goldfish drifting pleasantly in confinement. This is a sensory rather than sensual paradise, an ordered world in which passion and animal vitality take their place in the larger context of a peaceful home. The atmosphere is not one of com-

58. Henri Matisse. *Goldfish and Sculpture,* 1911. Oil on canvas. 46″ × 39⅝″. Collection, The Museum of Modern Art, New York. Gift of Mr. and Mrs. John Hay Whitney. Copyright ARS NY/SPADEM 1987.

promise or repression, but of equilibrium—the compositional and personal quality Matisse most prized.

Goldfish in a simple glass bowl became one of Matisse's recurrent motifs in these years. In one such image, a young woman looks on intently as the fish swims about; in another, the image of the fish is rendered twice, once through the glass and once through the water's surface where the refracted image appears. The motif conveys a gentle, intelligent meditation on equilibrium, the brilliant goldfish serving as a symbol of vitality, the clear water and spotlessly transparent bowl acknowledging the need for limits—limits without violence, permitting a true and durable equilibrium. The domestic interior, in turn, reads as a space for living under voluntary limitations.

The spiritual potential of equilibrium is easily overlooked. Nothing sticks out, no brows are furrowed, no weighty vows are taken, no grinding remorse is experienced. Yet the balance in Matisse's pictorial world is not slack or routine; it gives the impression of being earned over and over again by a return to first principles and rediscovery of wholeness. In his domestic works, Matisse seems a Baudelaire renewed in innocence.

Matisse much admired Baudelaire's famous poem, *L'Invitation au voyage,* from which he borrowed the titles of some early and important paintings:

> Là, tout n'est qu'ordre et beauté,
> Luxe, calme et volupté.

Nearly every word is recognizable to English-speaking readers, although the music of these lines defies translation. For Baudelaire, *there* is distant and imagined; for Matisse, order and beauty, opulence, calm, and sensuality are all *here,* provided that one can open to them. Matisse seems at times naive when he writes of this opening:

> To find joy in the sky, in trees, in flowers. There are flowers everywhere for those who are willing to see them.[40]

But he is not naive in his art, far from it.

Matisse's relation with Baudelaire goes a little further. In the same lyric, the poet evokes the rich interior *there,* where he and his lover will find heartfelt ease:

The gleam of furniture
Polished by the years
Would grace our room;
The rarest flowers
Mixing their perfumes
With the vague scent of amber,
The richly worked ceilings,
The deep mirrors,
The oriental splendor,
All things there would speak
To the soul in secret
Its sweet native tongue.

The lines read like stage directions for Matisse's interiors as he created them over the years, not excluding the "oriental splendor" that fascinated Baudelaire somewhat wickedly, and Matisse in all innocence during his middle years. But for the most part Baudelaire's dream of comfort *there* was found *here* by Matisse, found through loving awareness rather than anguish.

Any selection of Matisse's later works will reflect only a fraction of his sustained freshness, but three works come to mind that may fairly represent the whole. *La Blouse roumaine,* a work of 1940 (Fig. 59), is indelibly inscribed in the memories of all French schoolchildren and of the nation at large, through both the original in Paris and innumerable reproductions. It calls for little comment; its cheer and optimism, its pleasure in humanity and in the magical stuff of art—color, line, texture, decoration—are evident. That Matisse painted this work as Nazi troops assaulted Europe bears witness to an abiding faith, not in God but in some invincible goodness that cannot but find its way.

Much the same can be said of his Chapel of the Rosary at Vence, inaugurated in 1951, for which Matisse prepared not only the architectural plan but also stained-glass window designs, symbolic and narrative drawings for transfer to large ceramic panels, a bronze altar crucifix, and even liturgical vestments. His most ambitious single project, the ensemble is powerful and exact in those elements of religious art that Matisse could sincerely command: its gleaming white walls and bright ceramic murals collect colored light from the stained-glass windows to create a memorably springlike environment. "I want . . . visitors to experience a lightening of the spirit," he said.

59. Henri Matisse. *La Blouse roumaine,* 1940. Oil on canvas. 37½″ × 29¾″.
Musées nationaux, Paris. Copyright ARS NY/SPADEM 1987.

So that, even without being believers, they sense a milieu of spiritual elevation, where thought is clarified, where feeling itself is lightened. . . .[41]

However, Matisse was criticized—with justice—for his sketchy rendering of the Stations of the Cross, which were collected into a single ceramic panel and treated schematically as "signs" of the sacred events. They communicate little and seem, at this distance of years, to reflect the artist's uncertain relation with Christianity. He knew from within the purity of whiteness and the infinite appeal of color; he seems not to have known the Passion with the same sure inwardness and command. The chapel is nonetheless a small jewel, capturing the innocence of First Communion, not the universal drama of Calvary, and it occasioned a self-examination and renewed awakening in the artist to which few in any walk of life are privileged in their late years.

Renowned as painter and draftsman, Matisse periodically turned to sculpture and created in the medium a series of works that can truly be called masterpieces. Matisse completed four more-than-lifesize bronze reliefs, each titled simply *The Back* (Figs. 60, 61), in the period 1909 through 1930.[42] Like Mondrian's sequence of trees (see chapter 6), they record a search for form and meaning rather than progress along a preestablished route, although the logic binding one work to the next appears in retrospect to be inevitable and even obvious. No less than Mondrian's trees, this sculptural sequence demonstrates twentieth-century vision at its most powerful and sure; with almost pedagogical clarity, it unfolds both the modern aesthetic of purity and the metaphysic of a return to origins.

Albert Elsen has shown that the pose itself has only a few precedents in earlier European art, although the image of a woman seen from behind figures in the small Cézanne painting that Matisse owned and treasured for many years. The pose has an ambiguous quality of mixed pathos and impersonality. As Matisse moved from the earliest to the latest version, he moved also from a treatment that suggests ritual weeping or sorrow to a completely impersonal rendering of the gesture as pure movement, colored perhaps by a suggestion of masking the eyes so as not to be looking "out there" but instead to be entirely here.

The sequence begins with a *fauve* reinterpretation of Rodin's approach to the figure; a certain naturalism is challenged by a bold rendering of form as thick masses. The result feels unsteady, unresolved. Four years later, Matisse returned to the theme and recreated it in a more

60. Henri Matisse. *The Back, I–IV,* 1909, 1913, 1916, 1931. Bronze. Av. height 6'2". Collection, The Museum of Modern Art, New York. Mrs. Simon Guggenheim Fund. Copyright ARS NY/SPADEM 1987.

planar language influenced by Cubism, retaining nonetheless a sense of flesh and bodily structure. More than the other versions, *Back II* gives the impression of a massive sketch, an unfinished work. Another four years were to pass until Matisse again returned to the theme, this time nearly bringing it home through a radical transformation that abandons the feel of flesh and reforms the image as quasi-geometric masses drawn upward into an emerging architecture. The figure has actually risen, the head reaching past the rectangular supporting slab, the right leg losing the traditional flex used since antiquity to animate figural poses. Hair, neck, and spine, accentuated in *Back I*, have fused into a single strong vertical that both splits the figure and provides a unifying axis. In *Back III*, Matisse's quarrel with realism reaches its height; he seems to be searching for an altogether new image of humanity, one that defies photographic realism and speaks to some knowledge of human nature within us all.

61. Henri Matisse. *The Back, IV*, 1931. Bronze. 6′2″ × 44¼″ × 6″. Collection, The Museum of Modern Art, New York. Mrs. Simon Guggenheim Fund. Copyright ARS NY/SPADEM 1987.

The fourth version achieves that new image. The somewhat fragmented geometry of the third version is drawn into a continuous whole, and the figure fully assumes the tubular architectural form that had begun to emerge—but these words fail to capture the massive steadiness and presence of the final version. We witness a rebirth of the hero.

Consider the transitions as a series of releases or sloughings: the figure at first feminine and sensual, and at last neither feminine nor masculine but human, neither emotional nor cold but *there* with authority. We can also think in terms of a release or unwinding of history. The first version is easily recognized as an early twentieth-century reworking of inherited European form; it does not break the sequence, although it has its originality. The later versions recede to an archaism closest to pre-Classical Greek sculpture, although by no means identical; they break the sequence and, in stages, return to the origins of Western culture. As in his *Bonheur de vivre*, Matisse has sought new vision in the ancient world, but here he seeks past the sophistication of developed Classicism to a primal world in which Western humanity first took shape.

Aesthetically, the fourth version depends on our receptivity to abstract form. By 1930, when it was completed, the language of abstraction had been quite thoroughly explored. In our own time abstraction has become second nature to some people, who do not regard the figure as "distorted" in this version but simply reimagined and simplified under the inspiration of very ancient sculpture. Metaphysically, the power of this work and of the sequence as a whole depends on the equation "archaic = essential." Its evocation of archaic humanity can turn us not only toward historical memory but toward our essential being, that which we are before and despite the accidents and torments of history. The archaic in time is understood, by a poetic transposition, to correspond to the archaic within us now and always; and the archaic, in turn, is understood not as subhuman impulsiveness but as human being itself, the "I am" in each of us.

Four dominant types of archaic art have moved twentieth-century artists to investigate the equation "archaic = essential." The first, much studied by scholars and critics, is the tribal art of Africa and the South Pacific, which provided some of the impetus for Cubism and later for Surrealism and other movements. The second, children's art, was another sort of archaism valued by Kandinsky and his circle, and brought to fruition in the sophisticated art of Paul Klee. The third, somewhat more elusive, appears in Brancusi's work and in some Earthworks and sculptures of recent years (see chapter 21): it is a Neolithic current, a memory of the stone carvings and monuments of prehistory. Finally, there is the archaism to which Matisse responded so richly, and which Matisse is in good measure responsible for introducing into twentieth-century art; the archaism of the ancient Mediterranean. Its power is already evident in *The Backs,* but it needs further exploration in the following chapter.

Those who have searched in vain for a contemporary image of humanity that reflects our essence without irony can look to Matisse; it is here in *The Backs.* They are not works of complex symbolism, and know nothing of the celestial hierarchies or spiritual disciplines to which the traditional religious arts addressed themselves so fully. We do not find here an image of a god, a figure in meditation, or a dervish troubled and restless, marked with the signs of spiritual search. But *The Backs* address an emergence, a promising renewal. "Giotto is the summit of my desires," Matisse wrote, "but the road that leads toward an equivalent, in our time, is too long for a single life." Giotto must signify a wholly fresh yet spiritually sure and complete art. The freshness, the readiness, is here in what he and others have accomplished; the rest may follow.

Matisse was not one to make his own epitaph, but a paper cutout from his 1947 publication, *Jazz,*[43] provides something like one. Periodically confined to bed by illness in his old age, creative as ever, he developed a new medium based on the children's activity of cutting out figures and designs in colored paper. He brought some of these works together for the limited edition of *Jazz,* to which he added in longhand a series of views and cherished quotations. They offer a late, worthy counterpart to his earliest important statement, the 1909 *Notes of a Painter.* In *Jazz* he wrote, "Love sustains the artist"—but rather than let this sentiment trail off vaguely, he transcribed a lengthy passage from St. Thomas à Kempis which depicts love as an animating force born of God, a force that allows one to meet the challenges of life and to "fly, run, rejoice."[44] The passage is not a sign of conversion late in life but of an intuition, long with him, that could speak as well through the words of a Christian author as through painting or sculpture.

The epitaph-like image is not even remotely Christian but instead folkloric with vague roots in the pagan past, an image of Pierrot's funeral (Fig. 62). Pierrot, the harlequin clown of the Commedia dell'Arte, figured hardly at all in Matisse's earlier art (Picasso often used the motif), but late in life he explored his memories and came upon the

62. Henri Matisse. *The Burial of Pierrot*. Plate 10 from *Jazz*, Paris: Tériade, 1947. Pochoir, printed in color. 16¼″ × 25⅝″. Collection, The Muscum of Modern Art, New York. The Louis E. Stern Collection. Copyright ARS NY/SPADEM 1987.

circus image of a colorful chariot drawn by a prancing horse, bearing forth the mortal remains of Pierrot. The image is one of childhood and sheer joy; Pierrot's death is no tragedy but only a convenient way to get off stage. With characteristic gentleness, Matisse seems to have taken the measure of his death and responded with celebration.

16 THE MEDITERRANEAN ETHOS: FILL THE CUP AND AGAIN CRY

Classicism should have died altogether in the twentieth century, but it did not. The case against it was powerful. When artists born in the late nineteenth century left school behind, they generally also left behind the casts of "noble antiquities" and the rigid conventions of drawing and shaping that figured so strongly in their education. Artists of later generations often had no such education to overcome; it was rarely offered except in the diluted form of life-drawing classes taught without self-righteous standards. Henry Moore (1898–1986) spoke for many when he thanked his stars that he had begun art school rather late, thus avoiding prolonged exposure to a training that "deadened and killed off" fellow students who had spent too much time doing "humdrum copying from the antique."[1] Like a recessive gene, classicism went into hiding as the revolutionary arts of the twentieth century took form. But its influence reasserted itself from time to time, often veiled, on occasion fully realized and uniquely expressive, as if something had to be said which could only be said in that way. This "something" is not merely aesthetic, a matter of the pleasures of the eye and mind; it bears on reassuming an identity that twentieth-century history has battered. We are not noble Athenians, nor have we anything to say to the Senate and People of Rome, but we can be sensitive to imagery derived from their world that sheds light on our own.

Classicism in our time is no longer an academic convention, as it was in the nineteenth century. With the collapse of its automatic authority, it has regained expressive power in the hands of artists for whom it retained or recovered meaning. It can have magical effect, calling up the ancient in ourselves and asking us what we wish to remember. In this sense, twentieth-century classicism is a spiritual enterprise. It asks who we are, and answers that we are—however intact or bruised—what we always have been, and it shows us that image. But these words fail to capture the poignancy of a unique remembering. For some Western people, human competence and dignity remain curiously intertwined with the Classical era, as if we learned to stand, to observe, to think, to play, to take action, to meet fate in that era. For such people, classicism is not a historical reconstruction but a personal reconstruction. It is a lie, sheer illusion, but an instructive one capable of stirring collective memory.

Some definitions are in order. *Classicism* is a word of vast reference, encompassing not only the developed arts of Greece and Rome but also the Classical revival of the Renaissance, the great seventeenth-century art of Nicolas Poussin and others, the doctrinaire neoclassicism of the eighteenth century, and an entire sector of nineteenth-century art. Further, we speak now without hesitation of classical moments in Asian cultures, and by this we mean just what we mean in the Western context: the appearance of a powerful norm which thereafter provides a point of reference. The twentieth-century painters and sculptors who saw new possibilities in Classical forms and themes were acutely aware of the later European developments and learned from them, but their own classicism turned toward the origin—Greece and Rome. This aspect of their work has been designated neoclassicism by scholars and critics, but the cool historiographic flavor of that word says little about the thing itself, which is a deliberate but impassioned retrieval of ancient norms. For this reason, we might do better to think in terms of a Mediterranean ethos.

Ethos is now a scholar's term rare in everyday language, but it effectively evokes the total character of an epoch or culture. Ethos is the cultural climate within which a people lives and moves and has its being; housed immaterially in values and ideas, the ethos of an era is no less evident in institutions, monuments, poetry, fine art, and even in the physical bearing of men and women.[2] *Ethos* need not be a temporal term; it implies no recently arrived "neo" molded upon an authoritative original. On the contrary, it speaks to the enduring. Matisse in Corsica, in 1898, discovered the Mediterranean sunlight as it is and always has been. Barbara Hepworth (1903–1975), the British sculptor, sensed on Patmos "that the Greek idea had something of the will, the power, the ruggedness we need."[3] She reentered the Mediterranean ethos.

"Fill the cup, and again cry, again, again." This line from the early second-century poet Meleager captures the intense nostalgia that runs through twentieth-century classicism, as well as the earthiness that

Picasso and, to some degree, Matisse brought to the style. But the enchanting love poems of antiquity are too slight to capture two further aspects of our classicism, an imperturbable seriousness and a tragic view of life. "I have borne what cannot be borne," recites the Chorus in a tragedy of Aeschylus. Some of the strongest twentieth-century sculpture in the classical mode endows this sentiment with new force and makes it our own. At one extreme of sensibility, the Mediterranean ethos has sponsored the imagery of unashamed delight that we found in Matisse's *Bonheur de vivre* (Fig. 56) and that we will find again in Picasso. At the other extreme, it has provided stunning images of mankind nearly overwhelmed by fate and retreating into unbreachable solidity. For this, Henry Moore is principally responsible, although there are echoes of the mood in the work of Marino Marini and others.

In the middle ground between these extremes are further recastings of Classical form, ranging from the pristine abstract constructions of Ben Nicholson (see chapter 19), which reflect a Hellenic sense of equilibrium and proportion, to the overtly classicizing sculpture of Aristide Maillol, whose stubborn insistence on the female nude as the epitome of beauty seems, on occasion, not just sublimation but sublime. His perseverance in reworking woman into Woman transcends its origins in the polite art of the previous century. In the middle ground are also a number of haunting works dedicated, one might say, to the Delphic counsel "Know thyself"; it is again Picasso who best captured this theme.

As Western people we belong to Classical culture—it is our alma mater—but we belong still more strongly to the Judeo-Christian culture that washed over the Classical world, absorbing it, transforming it, and rejecting what it could not mark with its own sensibility. We belong more strongly still to our own era of science and unrest that makes every issue new again. Many of us live now with a mixed sense of utter failure and spontaneous hope—and it is difficult not to attribute the multiple disasters of the century, somewhat vengefully, to the Judeo-Christian culture by which, until August 1914, we thought we were living well enough. Some of the artists who turned to forms and themes that evoke pre-Christian, preindustrial antiquity explored in imaginative terms a world "other" and sweeter; in short, a world before the Fall. However, it isn't Eden; it is not a Judeo-Christian world at all. Our history has not happened to it; our morality has not constrained it. It is a world in which men and women, animals, land, sea and sky are restored to their original loveliness and sober integrity. Classicism allowed an imaginative leap outside of the Judeo-Christian world, with its sins which are our own, into an archaic and more civilized world which was also our own, and curiously remains so.

The word *world,* as used here, refers not only to outer setting but to the quality of persons. It may not be extravagant to think that every good culture acknowledges a distant Golden Age in which men and women were more. Socrates himself spoke of "the men of old, who were better than ourselves and dwelt nearer the gods."

Is the classicism of our time a rarified taste, appealing only to an older generation educated in Greek and Latin, for whom Gaul is still divided into three parts? Does it address only people who have enjoyed particular kinds of training or opportunities—artists, art historians, or tourists whose imaginations were kindled by visits to Athens or Pompeii? The reader alone can decide whether the classicism of Picasso, Matisse, Moore, and others is a living language.

MATISSE

We have already explored some aspects of the Mediterranean ethos in Matisse's art. *Bonheur de vivre* (Fig. 56), despite its clear debts to art nouveau and older European painting, recalls the sunny verve and style of Etruscan wall painting. *The Backs* (Figs. 60, 61) return progressively not to fifth-century Athens but to the Archaic period preceding it; the fourth recalls the cast of an Archaic kouros that Matisse kept in his garden and studio for forty years, of which he once said, "it marks the beginning of Greek feeling, from which we are descended." It marked for him the way to an essential image of humanity. The Mediterranean ethos in our time draws inspiration not only from High Classical and the later Hellenistic art but also from pre-Classical forms, which convey a sober sense of being, stripped of all excess—stripped even of the grace and variety of human personality. What remains, as in Matisse's work, is human being itself. Each artist found that part of antiquity that could give form to a particular insight about ourselves today and about self always. Brancusi, for example, retreated further into history than Matisse; he found "his" antiquity in the third- and second-millennium culture of the Cycladic islands, where marble was first shaped and polished into unforgettably elegant objects.

The selections from Matisse's oeuvre have not exhausted the repertory of works in which he recreated the ancient Mediterranean ethos in contemporary terms. Readers particularly drawn to his work will

63. Henri Matisse. *Study after Dance (First Version)*, 1909. Pencil. 8⅝″ × 13⅞″. Collection, The Museum of Modern Art, New York. Gift of Pierre Matisse. Copyright ARS NY/SPADEM 1987.

want to look carefully at least at reproductions of his large canvases of 1909–10, *Dance* and *Music,* once in the home of his Moscow patron Sergei Shchukin and now in the Hermitage. They are faithfully reflected in the *Study for Dance* in the Museum of Modern Art (Fig. 63). In these works, he searches for two "absolutes"—absolute ecstasy and self-abandon in the round dance, absolute sensitivity and self-collectedness in the grouping of musicians and listeners. As has long been recognized, the simplified color scheme recalls red-figure pottery, and the subjects, although treated with bare modern intensity, recall the festival and pastoral lives of antiquity. The quality of line in Matisse's figure drawings—somewhat "sketched," deliberately broad rather than detailed—exemplifies one of the ways in which twentieth-century classicism distinguishes itself from its antique models: there is always a marked *difference,* a deviation from complete fidelity to ancient style, and in that difference we can sense an encounter with antiquity rather than unthinking homage. In Picasso's etchings of the 1930s, his unmatched rendering of the human figure is on occasion deliberately "flatted" and "sharped" such that figures have odd articulations; similarly, he introduces absurdities into his Classical world, for example Surrealist or Cubist constructions. These deviations from the expected are signs, not just of the willful modern ego (although there is surely some of that) but of a questioning spirit. What is the shape of man and woman? And what is our inner shape, our identity? The best art drives toward these issues—with a question in periods of unrest, with an answer in periods of certainty.

PICASSO

Picasso's classicism draws from many periods and types of antique art: among others, early fifth-century Severe Style in sculpture, red-figure and white-ground pottery painting, engraved Etruscan mirror-backs reflecting the fluency of line and narrative power of Hellenistic art, Pompeiian wall painting, provincial sculpture. This inventory bears little relation to Picasso's actual procedure: a child prodigy who received a thorough academic training and never regretted it, he is said to have been endowed with a faultless memory for images that allowed him to see a thing once and assimilate its character.

Picasso's classicism falls into three major periods, each vividly interesting. In 1905–06, emerging from the famous Blue Period, he participated in what has been described as "a literary and cultural reaction in favor of the Mediterranean heritage and against the 'Gods of the North,' such as Wagner and Nietzsche."[4] In 1917–25, he again evolved a classical style, quite different in character. In the 1930s, he returned to the antique in a series of etchings that rival the ancient vase painters in clarity of line and force of mood. While these were the concentrated episodes of classicism in his enormously varied oeuvre, he drew recurrently from the antique heritage even for works that defy it in most respects—for example, in the fine Cubist drawing (Fig. 8) discussed in earlier pages, and in his world-renowned *Guernica*.[5]

A memorable work of 1906, *La Toilette* (Fig. 64), conveys the self-consciousness yet undeniable lyrical power of his early classicism. The nude girl is somehow felt as "modern" and of our time, while the stately woman, demurely gowned, is a quotation from antiquity. Her formal stance and masklike face contrast with the open pose and gracious tilt of head in the nude figure. The gesture they share—holding up a mirror as if enacting a ritual, arranging hair freely as if not bound by ritual at all—provides another contrast, enigmatic yet satisfying. The bare setting makes the viewer concentrate on the paired figures as image, and ultimately as symbol.

Like all effective image-making, this painting resists translation into

64. Pablo Picasso. *La Toilette,* 1906. Oil on canvas. 59½" × 39". Albright-Knox Art Gallery, Buffalo, New York. Fellows for Life Fund, 1926. Copyright ARS NY/SPADEM 1987.

words, although it is felt as a meaning and not only as a visual poetry. Despite their differences, the two women *are* one another; they could easily exchange roles. The image seems to state, without words, that women possess two natures: the one open, light, and of its time; the other more inward, deliberate, and ancient. The painting recalls a Greek altar that contrasts a nude flute-girl, all charm and relaxation, with an opaquely gowned priestess preparing to burn incense.[6] Picasso may not have known this work, but he had grasped the ethos from which such images flow.

Picasso's second exploration of the Mediterranean ethos began in 1917, at about the time he visited the antiquities of Rome and the Neapolitan region and saw the works of Michelangelo and Raphael in the Vatican. Historians have suggested that his interest in classicism reappeared in response to these new impressions but also as "a reaction from the excesses and brutality of the war, from the strident novelties of Dada and from the tameness of Picasso's Cubist imitators."[7] Particularly thought-provoking among these probable causes is his response to the war, whose shattering impact on the twentieth century can hardly be exaggerated.

During and just after the war, artists sought renewal, or at very least honesty and the ability to resume their work, along very different paths. Some of the Bauhaus masters, as well as the Mondrian circle and the Constructivists, found their way to an affirmation of human worth through rationality and purification of form. Picasso found his way to affirmation by the opposite route. Returning to the human figure without Cubist legerdemain, he created on canvas a new and monumental tribe of human beings—stronger, infinitely more self-possessed than the confused creatures that had participated in the Great War. Endowed with Michelangelesque size and seemingly carved features that bring to mind the qualities of provincial sculpture in the ancient world, these nude or seminude figures exist largely in a world apart. In some works of the period, Picasso defines that world ambiguously, as in *The Large Bather* of 1921–22 (Fig. 65). The heroic size and serenity of the nude evoke the ancient world, while the cloth that frames her and enters into her gesture is classical drapery reduced to service as a studio prop. There is a kind of wit here. Picasso's search for a heroic and ageless image of humanity is tinged with awareness of the conditions under which he searches—in a studio, in France, in the 1920s.

In another work, *The Pipes of Pan* of 1923 (Fig. 66), Picasso drops all reference to the modern world and creates one of the most intensely

65. Pablo Picasso. *The Large Bather*, 1921–22. Oil on canvas. 70⅞″ × 38⅝″.
Musées nationaux, Paris. Copyright ARS NY/SPADEM 1987.

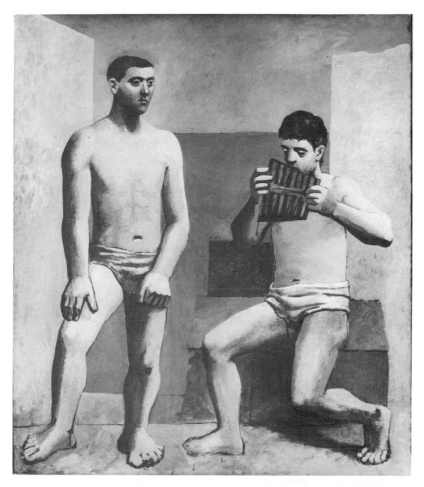

66. Pablo Picasso. *The Pipes of Pan*, 1923. Oil on canvas. 80¾″ × 68¾″. Musées nationaux, Paris. Copyright ARS NY/SPADEM 1987.

sober and memorable canvases of our time. A mercurial showman if ever there was one, he is all the more touching when he puts aside virtuosity, or so it seems, to construct an image slowly and painstakingly. In a bare setting of architecture, sea, and sky, the figures are impassive and solid, their poses intuitively believable; the viewer intimately senses weight and gesture. The entire image is suffused with a play of light and shadow that subtly reinforces our perception of substance, depth, and air. The figures are not doing a great deal—a little music, mere watching—but their relative inactivity is one of the strengths of the image, which projects an intuition of mankind as we are essentially and in our proper setting.

Like Matisse's sequence *The Backs,* this painting belongs to the modern spiritual in art. Speaking a transformed but wholly recognizable classical language, it is not a metaphysical statement but a simple witness to the human presence in this world. Further, it proposes an ethic of sorts, sobriety and attention to fundamentals. If there is a sermon here, it has to do with remembering the interwovenness of body and mind: these proud bodies, a little thickened and simplified for emphasis, are clearly also a thinking, sensitive substance. Inactive, they are active; active, they are also inactive. These odd words may capture something of the quiet thoughtfulness of the standing figure and the no less impressive quietness of the music-making figure. As in *La Toilette,* Picasso has contrasted two human attitudes to collect a sense of the whole. The Mediterranean ethos, this pagan current in twentieth-century art, is a spiritual current by virtue of its sober image of humanity and its acknowledgment of Nature. Its spirituality is not one of transcendence but of immanence, of presence to self and world. What we can relearn from the ancients is not their gods, their "other world," but their earth and their sense of being in and of it.

Many consider Picasso's third classicism in the 1930s to be his most delightful excursion into the ancient world. The Vollard Suite, etchings executed for the dealer and publisher Ambroise Vollard, includes both improvisations full of impromptu charm, and works carefully conceived and contemplative in mood.[8] Some have the slightly self-mocking humor and tenderness of the old Greek love poems. For example, in Fig. 67 a satyr has found his way by moonlight to a sleeping woman's room, but the scene of their encounter is not a rape; he admires her tenderly, reaches toward her with dignity of gesture. Like Picasso himself, he is a mixed creature, driven and yet knowing. The woman, all curves, cradling her head with a child's abandon, is sketched with remarkable feeling for gesture and pose. This work, like many in the suite, is not the spiritual, but it is nothing if not spirited and humanly interesting.

However, certain etchings reflect a self-inquiry that can become the viewer's own. Their setting is a sculptor's studio in antiquity, with a view to the sky and land; Picasso generally includes a few details to establish a sense of comfort and place—a patterned wall, a vase of

67. Pablo Picasso. *Faun Unveiling a Woman*, June 12, 1936. Etching and aquatint. 12'⁷/₁₆" × 16'⁷/₁₆". Collection, The Museum of Modern Art, New York. Purchase Fund. Copyright ARS NY/SPADEM 1987.

flowers, a bowl. The dramatis personae are generally the sculptor himself (bearded, in his prime, reflective, something of a worrier), the woman who is his model and companion, and various carvings they contemplate. In one fine example (Fig. 68), they recline together, nude; he holds her with a tenderness accepted and returned, and their eyes dwell on a carved female torso on a pedestal. It must be the sculptor's latest work. In a related image, the sculptor and his companion contemplate a carving on the violent theme of a bull attacking a horse, borrowed by Picasso from the modern bullfight but successfully transposed to an ancient setting. In still other images, the couple contemplates carvings on the theme of love—for example, a centaur passionately embracing a nude woman, who reaches up to him with equal passion—but the sculptor and his companion are themselves still, observant witnesses. In another etching (Fig. 69), the model enters the studio with a graceful double gesture, securing a garland around her neck with one hand while reaching with the other to touch the

68. Pablo Picasso. *Sculptor at Rest before a Small Torso,* March 30, 1933. Etching. 7⅝″ × 10½″. Collection, The Museum of Modern Art, New York. Purchase Fund. Copyright ARS NY/SPADEM 1987.

sculptor's knee. The sculptor sits meanwhile in a curiously bound posture, a brush or drafting tool in one hand, the other raised quizzically to his beard. Their encounter, tentative and tender, observant and already seized with desire, captures the endless ambiguities of human relationships. In still another example, the sculptor contemplates his companion and, perhaps as an enigmatic sign of the force of his observing eyes, her face and shoulders are darker and more closely detailed than the rest of her body. Nearby them, an antique portrait head is overturned in a melodramatic suggestion that the force of communion between the sculptor and his companion is stronger than art itself.

These scenes, romantic storytelling at one level, autobiography at another, belong also to the realm of the spiritual by virtue of their graceful but persistent examination of witnessing and doing, freedom and desire, life and its image, knowing and knowing oneself. The sculptor and his companion become our proxies as they step back

69. Pablo Picasso. *Sculptor with Standing Model*, April 7, 1933. Etching. 14⁷/₁₆″ × 11¹¹/₁₆″. Collection, The Museum of Modern Art, New York. Purchase Fund. Copyright ARS NY/SPADEM 1987.

from love and watch, step back from violence and watch, step back from art and watch. Their ease with each other allows them to turn their attention outward without losing touch with one another. But what they see is themselves: the love, the violence, the artistry are not just objects on pedestals but impulses in their natures. Their seriousness as witnesses conveys their awareness of this reflection back onto themselves. The theme of the Vollard Suite is self-knowledge. Its principal activity is *knowing;* hence the quietness of the images. Filled with lovely bodies, rendered with an extraordinarily fine and eloquent line, these images are also filled with mind.

MOORE

Henry Moore is universally acknowledged as one of the very great sculptors of our time. Like Brancusi and Noguchi, he fulfilled to the letter the sculptor's calling, which requires not only the image-making or image-finding ability common to all artists but also extra measures of physical strength, patience, and will. Sculptors need long lives. In general, their work evolves more slowly than a painter's; it concerns stone and bronze, and it shares their toughness. Blessed with a long life, Henry Moore reached sculptural expressions in his later years that unquestionably belong to the modern spiritual; their language is classical, their meaning poignantly of our time.

Born in 1898, one of eight children in a Yorkshire miner's family, he knew early that he wished to be an artist but was able only after World War I, during which he served at the front, to begin to realize his vocation. He entered the Leeds School of Art in 1919—where he was a comrade of Barbara Hepworth's (see chapter 23)—and in 1921 received a scholarship to the Royal College of Art in London. He studied as much in the British Museum as in the college studios. Ancient Mexican sculpture and primitive art opened him to worlds of form and meaning creatively at odds with the academic training that he diligently acquired, and which served him so well in later years. He became familiar with mainstream modern art, still largely unknown and little trusted even by educated Britons (his own reputation would build slowly against sizable odds). He traveled on the continent to see with his own eyes the masterworks of older European art, completing the groundwork for an exploration of sculpture that would extend and deepen over many decades. From his early years in Yorkshire, he retained a reverence for sheer unworked stone, the natural monument, and this too entered into the underground stream that fed his sense of form.

Like so many artists of our time, he gave little importance to traditional religious expression; what he knew of the spirit he learned through art:

> To be an artist is to believe in life. Would you call this basic feeling a religious feeling? In that sense an artist does not need any church and dogma.[9]

He found his themes early: mother and child, the female figure seated or reclining, and abstractions that spoke an "organic" language of form, as if the sculpture had grown into its shape or was partly worked by human hands and partly untouched. He seems rarely if ever to have actually left stone unworked, but he conserved something of the raw presence of stone as he carved. Countless drawings and carvings from the 1930s display a seemingly unlimited capacity for invention and variation. Whether he was juggling chunks of geometry in a Surrealist manner or stating and restating the long passage from head to foot in the reclining figure, he studied form more exhaustively and restlessly than any sculptor of his time. Like Picasso's, his drawing albums record ceaseless curiosity and improvisation.

A drawing of 1936, *Stones in a Landscape* (unfortunately unavailable for reproduction), reflects the recessive, almost dream-like continuity of classicism in the background of his activity. Great stones, anticlassical in character, Stonehenge-like, marked with smooth erosions and unaccountable nicks, dominate a grey landscape in which the whiteness of classical temple fronts is a vague presence in the distance. The drawing measures the attraction on Moore's mind of the primal as opposed to the civilized, the natural as opposed to the trained. He would have to find his way among these forces—forces, not just forms that he could casually adopt or dismiss. They were pressures from within his nature taking certain shapes.

Work of the late 1930s, such as *Reclining Figure* (Fig. 70), blends a sinuous, organic language of form with something of the bare presence of a boulder or cliff. The humanity of the figure—its personality and human verve—is eclipsed by a massive physicality, as if human consciousness is thin and volatile in comparison with the more fundamental fact of "being there." The consciousness of Moore's figures from the 1930s on often seems buried and immobilized; they look on without registering involvement. Yet this trait need not strike the viewer as

70. Henry Moore. *Reclining Figure,* 1938. Green Hornton stone. Length 55".
The Tate Gallery, London. Photo: Courtesy The Tate Gallery.

inhumane or apathetic; on the contrary, it imposes itself as a sign of
perseverance, of the will to endure. Something in these figures has resorted to hibernation; it is as if their thoughts have slowed. The trait
has a somewhat enigmatic appeal that may clarify as we look further
in his work.

"Until my shelter drawings during the war," Moore wrote,

> I never seemed to feel free . . . to mix the Mediterranean approach
> comfortably with my interest in the more elementary concept of ar-
> chaic and primitive peoples. [10]

His shelter drawings from early World War II (for example, Fig. 71)
were landmarks. Chalky, often crowded drawings that reverse the normal expectation of light—figures glow bleakly against the darkness—
they are a powerful imaginative record of the years when Londoners
took shelter in the Underground from nightly air raids. Initially at-

71. Henry Moore. *Women in a Shelter*, 1941. Watercolor. 22″ × 15″. The Museum of London. Photo: Courtesy John Freeman Group.

tracted by the pathos of the situation, Moore was also touched by the inadvertent sculptural presence of this impromptu gathering of people, who had little choice but to "recline" through the night while the bombs fell. He was soon formally commissioned by the government to continue his record of the event.

The shade of classicism makes itself felt a little more than before in these extraordinary drawings. Moore's figures are not just Londoners; there is little of the anecdotal or descriptive detail with which he might have loaded the drawings. The figures' dress is scarcely modern but seems rather a translation of antique gowns: blankets become drapery, rough shawls become himations. Yet Moore does not gloss over the restless, crowded misery of these figures and scenes. Their poses are more than occasionally reminiscent of Classical temple sculpture, but they are also "taken from life" without romance. Much of the beauty of the shelter drawings derives from the dialogue between the crushing character of the event and its elevation as art. The Classical ideal of dignified figures, moving with self-possession in the light and air, grates against the reality of human misery in the dimly lit Underground. The Classical antecedent helped Moore both to see what was before him and to see it again in larger terms.

His classicism, nascent here, was never a dream of a lost ideal that might be recovered if only we knew how. On the contrary, classical imagery became for him a standard against which he could better see the contemporary human condition—and a vessel into which he poured an extraordinary will to live. He originated an existential classicism, toughened and reduced; he rediscovered tragedy.

Although familiar early in his career with the Elgin Marbles and other Classical antiquities in European museums, Moore traveled to Greece for the first time only after the war. "I thought before going that I knew about Greek art," he wrote,

> because I'd been brought up on it, and that I might even be disappointed. But not at all, of course.

He sensed the sculptural power of the great architectural remnants, took knowing pleasure in the Mediterranean light—and recognized that he need have no disabling nostalgia for it:

> . . . in Greece the object seems to give off light as if it were lit up from inside itself. . . . The northern light can be just as beautiful as the Greek light and a wet day in England can be just as revealing as that wonderful translucent Mediterranean light. . . .[11]

Travel confirmed his growing regard for the expressive powers of Classical sculpture. He acknowledged that in earlier years he had thought that the Greek and Renaissance were the enemy, and that one had to throw all that over and start again from the beginning of primitive art.[12]

He had of course done so, but by "starting again" so thoroughly he could now return to a Classical sense of the figure with fierce creativity.

There is much to choose from among his works of the 1950s and 1960s. A *Draped Torso* of 1953 (Fig. 72) can serve to alert us to some of the formal values that enter into his new art although, as a deliberate fragment, it excludes important expressive values found in larger works. A bronze cast from a plaster original, the torso has an extraordinary authority that may seem illogical, given the abbreviated nature of the subject. The body as structure is profoundly believable; it is sensed directly, and so at once draws the viewer into the quintessential magic of sculpture, which is its power to appeal to the body. The forward thrust of the massive shoulders, the counterbalancing thrust of the arms, the tilt of the pelvis, the interplay of nervous, filamentous drapery and smooth surface make a single statement—in a sense abstract, yet alive with suggestion as if we have come upon a fragment of a powerful dramatic ensemble.

Something more might be said about the role of drapery in this figure and in Classical art generally. The topic is a tired war-horse if ever there was one; scarcely an art-history student in America has escaped class discussion of the evolution of drapery rendering in ancient Greek art and its continuation in Byzantium, Renaissance Italy, and Northern Europe, down to the very last draped creature that walked the earth, perhaps Isadora Duncan. Yet when such lectures are recollected in tranquility, they prove to have made quite an important point bearing not just on a nicety but on a fundamental of expression.

Drapery—read "clothing"—reveals and conceals; it therefore enters into any number of expressive scenarios, ranging from erotic suggestion to pristine withdrawal. Drapery can be a starchy case or a fluid envelope—in both instances introducing expressive values to complement or contrast with the figure itself. The rhythm, texture, and even volume of drapery express one meaning and mood or another. For example, in Moore's *Draped Torso* the veinlike texture of vertical folds gives the impression of streaming down the body—and conveys an almost imperceptible suggestion of weeping. That the folds cling so intimately makes us "read" them as mingled with the body: a perception of the body's integrity and strength blends with a suggestion of erosion, as if some force challenges it. The discreet striated drapery folds

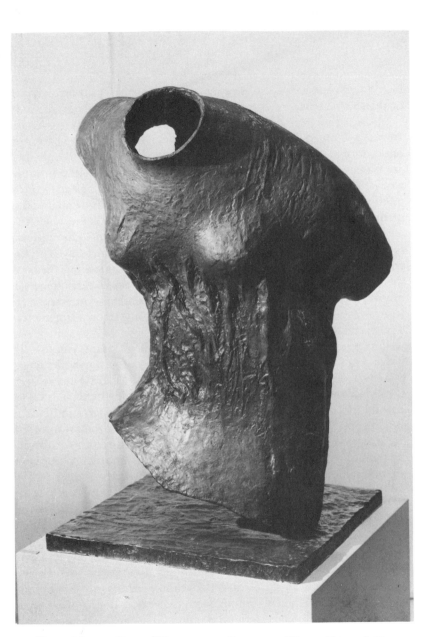

72. Henry Moore. *Draped Torso*, 1953. Bronze. 33½″ × 26″ × 19″. Ferens
Art Gallery, Hull.

around the shoulders and the smooth pelvic basin provide a quiet foil against which Moore can work out the curious, abstract, and potent drama of drapery form.

This language of drapery is new in his art, although foreshadowed in the shelter drawings. New also is a greater realism in Moore's rendering of the human body. While his realism in time again withdraws, his experience with it leaves behind a stunningly acute "feel" for the human body, so that in his later work even a figure resembling a cliff or rocky outcropping remains deeply and sensually human. His best works from this time forward stir and move from within; they have an animal presence, even when endowed with only a faint suggestion of animal form. All of these changes—truly gains and maturations—seem to have been catalyzed by Moore's experience of Greece and his reconsideration of Classical works known to him from his youth.

A nude *Seated Woman* of 1957 (Figs. 73, 74) takes us to the heart of Moore's developed classicism. In its simplicity, the pose is again reminiscent of ancient pedimental sculpture, although skewed from Classical balance by an anxious watchfulness, almost a readiness to flee. The odd and uncomfortable widening of the torso, the lengthening and thinning of limbs, and an almost brutal simplification of the face contrast with a practiced anatomical realism. The viewer senses this body as real and believably articulated from within, and Moore provides details such as a prominent vertebral column, bony elbows, and well-profiled muscle to strengthen the perception. He is Classical in his knowledge of the body, modern in his knowledge of emotion and circumstance. This figure with its stunned, almost unseeing eyes, its anatomical truth and uneasy distortions, is victim, witness, and survivor. She incarnates both the regal strength of the Classical ideal and the bruised, fearful reality of so many people in our time. This is the beauty of the work, and the essential beauty of many works from this period in Moore's creative life.

Moore was able to state this theme in terms of the male figure also. He has reported that the basic features of *Warrior with Shield* of 1953–54 (Fig. 75) were suggested to him by a pebble collected on a beach. The report makes clear that, however much he was now speaking a language of the figure rooted in an ancient and sophisticated culture, he remained sensitive to Nature as such. That sensitivity would return to sponsor another brilliant phase of his art in later years.

Warrior with Shield speaks for itself. The head, both helmet and wounded mass; the body rendered with poignant realism yet uneasily distorted; the defending gesture of a victim, dignified and harmed,

73. Henry Moore. *Seated Woman*, 1957. Bronze. Height 60″. Hirshhorn Museum and Sculpture Garden, Smithsonian Institution. Bequest of Joseph H. Hirshhorn, 1986. Photo: Hirshhorn Museum and Sculpture Garden.

erect yet falling—all of these traits again embody a twentieth-century classicism which is bitter, knowing, and to say the least, very touching.

The concluding note in Moore's recreation of classicism belongs to the 1960s. At the beginning of that decade, he immersed the narrative power of his art of the 1950s into abstract forms that recall the enigmatically nicked and contoured stones in the 1936 drawing discussed earlier. The masterworks of the period are two- and three-piece reclin-

74. Henry Moore. *Seated Woman,* 1957 (second view). Bronze. Height 60".
Hirshhorn Museum and Sculpture Garden, Smithsonian Institution. Bequest
of Joseph H. Hirshhorn, 1986. Photo: Hirshhorn Museum and Sculpture
Garden.

ing figures, beautifully exemplified by the *Reclining Figure* in the public plaza at Lincoln Center in New York City (Fig. 76).

New York City is privileged to have not only Moore's *Reclining Figure* to the west, but to the east his friend Barbara Hepworth's *Sculpture in Memory of the Late Dag Hammarskjöld* (see Fig. 121). Works
of eloquence and dignity, they convey messages without insisting.

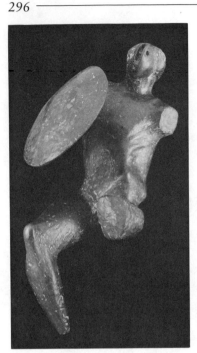

75. Henry Moore. *Warrior with Shield*, 1953–54. Bronze. 62" × 29" × 33". The Minneapolis Institute of Arts. The John Cowles Foundation Fund.

They demonstrate a very full understanding of the spirituality that can illuminate our art. Moore's two-piece figure can be "read" against the wounded warrior and, as well, the seated figure of a woman. Its truncated limbs, tensely stretched torso, and impenetrable head and face speak the same language as those works. There is again an acute sense of the living body moved from within. And of course something more: Moore has endowed the reclining figure with the imperturbable steadiness and longevity of an eroded seaside cliff. The torso seems to become raw stone, no longer human at all, as it descends into the water of a reflecting pool. The powerful form that stands apart from it reads as massive drapery from some angles and as a bony pelvic structure from others; it too is both remotely human and not human.

This work, when viewed with enough attentive leisure to decipher it, restates Moore's tragic theme in new and still more poignant terms. The human is reduced and harmed, it is almost infinitely distant from its origin in the harmonious Classical figure—yet it endures and, enduring, remains recognizable. The modern spiritual has few such monuments.

THE FUTURE OF THE PAST

Matisse, Picasso, and Moore represent the strongest response of twentieth-century artists to the Mediterranean ethos, a mixed heritage of sunny affirmation and tragic recognition, of essential values and charm. They were, of course, not alone: such a great heritage would hardly go unacknowledged by others. We have already mentioned Aristide Mail-

76. Henry Moore. *Reclining Figure,* 1963–65. Bronze. Length 30′. Lincoln Center for the Performing Arts. Photo: Mario Marino.

lol, the French neoclassical sculptor; his works, often for public places, are curiously bland and dreamy, but the dream is a pleasant one. Marino Marini (1901–1980) is among the strongest of Italian artists for whom the Mediterranean ethos remained vividly alive; his *Horse and Rider* bronzes rework the Classical equestrian theme into a touching image of instability and endurance. Like Henry Moore, although more limited, he found his way to an icon of modernity that asks to be seen and felt against antique counterparts. Gino Severini (1883–1960), originally a Futurist painter of no small power, later developed a nostalgic Mediterranean repertory of forms. His canvases can give the impression of assembled fragments of ancient relief sculpture in which gowned figures convey a hushed sense of survival and timelessness. Massimo Campigli (1895–1971) was yet another gifted Italian painter to whom the Mediterranean heritage, especially in its more archaic aspects, offered grounds for a decorative and nostalgic art. Ben Nicholson's classicism is discussed in chapter 19.

The future of the past is unpredictable. Contemporary society in general has little sense of kinship with the Classical world. Only specialists among us study the languages and literature; the art is greatly admired, from a distance. On the other hand, Classical scholarship has probably never been more exhaustive or creative in the questions it asks and the answers it elicits. The entire canon of Greek plays has been retranslated by numerous fine hands. Robert Fitzgerald's Homer is grand, a lesson not only in Homer but in the resources of modern English; Philip Wheelwright's pre-Socratic thinkers speak with a shockingly close voice. Artists throughout the century, relatively few in number but strong in their work, have created a classicism of our time. It can be recognized and claimed as an art of our own.

The root meaning of *epiphany* is a sudden disclosure of the sacred, as if it is shored up behind barriers and unexpectedly breaks into human awareness. Modern literature transposed the idea of epiphany from its religious context to the realm of personal self-discovery, a valid adaptation in the sense that some lives articulate around moments of massively liberating insight. Among American painters in the years after World War II, epiphany occurred at both levels. American art quite suddenly matured, fulfilling long, often genuinely difficult searches. Further, maturity for some meant that their art finally fulfilled in pictorial terms their preoccupying interests in religion, philosophy, psychology, and myth. The long flirtation in the early 1940s with concepts of myth and archetype, primal sign and the authenticity of the unconscious mind, issued out into an art that was largely free of such concepts although nourished by them. It was a new statement, in touch with raw energy and refined aspiration.

There has been uneasiness, at that time and ever since, whether this new vision needs unfailingly to be understood in terms of the spiritual in art. Key artists in the circle spoke of "the sublime," "the tragic," even of religious experience; others said nothing about such things or roughly blurted that their work had those dimensions although words—and wordy people—could not accurately apprehend them. Key critics during the formative years of the late 1940s and early 1950s developed ways of thinking about the new art that focused almost exclusively on issues of form and gesture, finding in the space, color, and structure of paintings and in the artists' dynamic approach to them grounds for a complex and satisfying critical perspective. Their point of view was richly humanistic—and somewhat caricatured by many later "formalist" critics who apply their method without their sensitivity to cultural realities. But they were reluctant to taint their starkly observant approach with a subjective, menacingly vague inquiry into religious or spiritual content. They were not wrong to stress aesthetic issues and let the rest, for the most part, take care of itself. Artists, critics, and a handful of dealers initially engaged in a classic battle to gain public and institutional acceptance for an art which they knew was exceptional. Such battles need to be won on aesthetic grounds; refinements of understanding can await easier days, particularly when the issues left in abeyance cannot be resolved once for all and may always be restated by another mind in another way.

It was Harold Rosenberg, however, one of those critics, who years later cleanly formulated the Americans' spiritual aspiration:

> In sum, what the new American artist sought was not a richer or more contemporary fiction (like the Surrealists), but the formal sign language of the inner kingdom—equivalents in paint of a flash, no matter how transitory, of what had been known throughout the centuries as spiritual enlightenment.[1]

The new art, broadly termed Abstract Expressionism, was a product of complex people immersed in complex personal and cultural circumstances. Yet they managed to shake free long enough to lay down image after image of indisputable aesthetic and, I would firmly say, spiritual power. Critics have spoken of the center of the art world shifting in the 1950s from Paris to New York. The center of the art world is located wherever artists ally aesthetic virtuosity with a sense of the sacred, no matter how uncertain, and some rigorous compassion for the human condition. For a time, this was New York.

The cast of characters in the first generation of the New York School will be familiar to many readers, among them Jackson Pollock, Willem de Kooning, Mark Rothko, Adolph Gottlieb, Barnett Newman, Robert Motherwell, Ad Reinhardt, Franz Kline, Philip Guston, joined by Clyfford Still in California—painters all. Some had met in the Federal Art Project of the 1930s, all were drinking companions, partners in adversity, coworkers in various avant-garde groupings and actions. They were people who spoke to each other often in the early years of Abstract Expressionism. The individual styles that emerged among them, however different from one another, owed something to the collective. The critics Clement Greenberg and Harold Rosenberg were no less key members of the loose collective, thanks to their ability to perceive and convey the life of the new painting. They influenced some of the artists privately (hence Tom Wolfe's classic satire, *The Painted Word*), and they influenced museums, collectors, and the public to look again at what initially seemed to be odd and difficult art.

A second generation of strong painters emerged in the 1950s, some continuing and expanding the new aesthetic, others contradicting it.

They were not all New Yorkers, although New York remained the artistic and commercial center to which they turned. Among them, I call particular attention to Morris Louis for reasons that will, I hope, become evident.

The period is difficult to approach and impossible to survey in a chapter. The artists are close to us in time and temperament; a few are alive today and working well. The period can be said "to belong" to certain American critics and historians who were direct witnesses, often friends of the artists. Apart from Greenberg and Rosenberg, who helped to shape the period, Irving Sandler, Dore Ashton, Barbara Rose, Lucy Lippard, William Seitz, and Thomas Hess come at once to mind as leading informants about the life, times, and achievements of these artists.

We had better plunge in, looking as always for the religious and metaphysical substance, however hidden, ignored, or denied, that sets the work of certain artists apart. The results may be curious. For example, we will little mention one artist who cared passionately for the spiritual in art. Although Barnett Newman (1905–1970) took keen interest in traditional spiritual ideas, possessed a sense of scripture, and contributed cogently to the endless murmur of conversation among American artists of the period, he never succeeded in giving eloquent pictorial form to his insights.[2] The austerity of his single vertical line, however much relieved by expressive brushwork or intense color, could not bear the weight of his intentions. His abstract *Stations of the Cross,* linked paintings on a sacred theme that should have been exemplary, is as disappointing as Matisse's version at Vence.

Robert Motherwell, a remarkable painter and one of few survivors from the first generation of Abstract Expressionists, recently assessed the historical situation of American art in the 1940s. "The problem for us was clear," he said:

> . . . the reigning painters in America were very parochial in relation to the international tradition. What held us together was our ambition to use the standards of international modernism as a gauge, not those of Thomas Hart Benton or Grant Wood. . . . We did have a terrible struggle, but not for success. It was to make painting that would stand up under international scrutiny, and all the rest was a byproduct.

Motherwell went on to relate his generation's struggle to the condition of art in the 1980s:

If there's something to be done now in the sense of a task like inter-
nationalizing standards, I don't know what it is—maybe to resist the
show-biz aspect of the contemporary scene, to protect the integrity
of painting. . . .[3]

The early years of Abstract Expressionism are evidently a touchstone
for Motherwell. They can be as much for us.

JACKSON POLLOCK:
WE'RE ON OUR OWN, GODDAMIT!

Born in Cody, Wyoming and raised in California, Jackson Pollock
(1912–1956) was trained in New York by Thomas Hart Benton and
took advantage of the multiple resources available to New York artists
in the 1930s and 1940s, from Mexican mural painters and museums to
the blurred but real wisdom of John Graham. Pollock was a seriously
troubled man. Apart from a few dry years coinciding, not at random,
with the height of his career, he was a confirmed alcoholic with no redeeming virtues under the influence. He was also a painter who cannot
be ignored. The conflicting energies inhabiting one and the same man
are vividly caught by the architect, Peter Blake, who knew him well,
and by Nicholas Carone, a highly gifted painter and young participant
in the New York School:

> . . . He was capable of incredible violence, and I think there were
> times when almost everyone in a given room was scared shitless by
> it. Jackson would come in and break up parties, appearing at ones
> he hadn't been invited to, come reeling in and make a pig of him-
> self. Later, when it got worse, people would flee on sight of him at
> the door.[4]

> The best I ever got was from him; it was an empathy out of a psychic
> relationship. I feel him. I can feel Jackson's presence. And his pic-
> tures—they're symbolic of a man who's alive; he's giving us a sort
> of energy.[5]

Pollock struggled on both sides of his nature—to overcome demons, to
project an original vision. Thanks to the help of a physician in eastern
Long Island where he and his wife, the painter Lee Krasner, made their
home after 1945, he conquered his alcoholism and lived the best years
of his life. Working with Jungian analysts, he took steps to understand

himself, becoming not a man at peace but one able to marshal his creative resources and use them in uncharted ways.

Pollock's intelligence was differently placed than in most men and women: it was above all an intelligence of the body. The trait is clear in a description of him at work by Betty Parsons, his first dealer, a painter herself, and an early friend of Abstract Expressionism:

How hard Jackson could work, and with such grace! I watched him and he was like a dancer. He had the canvas on the floor with cans of paint around the edges that had sticks in them which he'd seize and—swish and swish again. There was such rhythm in his movement. . . . [His compositions] . . . were so complex, yet he never went overboard—always in perfect balance. . . . The best things in the great painters happen when the artist gets lost . . . something else takes over. When Jackson would get lost, I think the unconscious took over and that's marvelous.[6]

A pair of works from 1950, *Number 32* and *One: Number 31* (Figs. 77, 78) may convey enough even in small reproductions to lead us into Pollock's art. *Number 32*, measuring almost nine by fifteen feet, is an enormous monochrome canvas, black enamel against white ground. A work from Pollock's strongest years, it embodies to perfection the rhythmic network of line, patch, and drip for which he was initially notorious and, in time, famous. In this monochrome version, the network appears as a layer of activity distinct from the neutral white space in which it exists. In more tightly woven works with multiple layers of varied color such as *One: Number 31*, the neutral space is nearly squeezed out of the skeins of paint, so to speak, but reappears as a relatively quiet frame for the intense activity within the network. In this respect, as critics have pointed out, Pollock's art recalls the early phase of Cubism, in which the complex interlocking planes thin and simplify toward the edge (see Fig. 9).

Pollock's style has been described as a modification of the Surrealists' automatic writing: he controlled the general character of events on the canvas, but obviously did not control the specific character of each and every mark. These are explosive works—"energy and motion made visible," as he wrote in a note to himself.[7] Yet one needs to spend time with them to grasp their visual and expressive subtleties. In *One: Number 31*, for example, closer observation shows networks of black and white paint mingling with drips and splashes of rosy brown

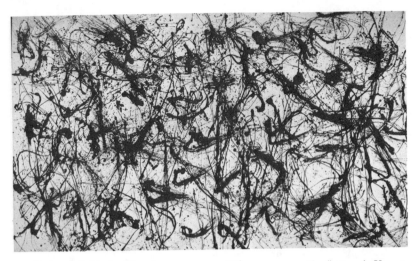

77. Jackson Pollock. *Number 32*, 1950. Oil on canvas. 8'10" × 15'. Kunstsammlung Nordrhein-Westfalen, Düsseldorf. Photo: Walter Klein.

and a rather soft blue, the black and white immensely active and kinetic, the brown and blue more quiescent, akin to the neutral ground or space against which one sees the whole image.

But description is not understanding. At best rhythmic and lucid, at worst clogged and frenetic, Pollock's canvases do not cohere intuitively with the works that we have grouped as the spiritual in twentieth-century art. Kandinsky's Munich canvases are a visible source, but those early abstractions, even at their most amorphous and swirling, move at a measurable Old World pace, while Pollock's American abstractions were literally flung onto the canvas and convey a sense of breakneck speed—oddly and beautifully superimposed on a sense of iconic stillness. What qualities, if any, align Pollock's works with those of artists whom we have recognized as heirs to the spiritual in art?

Is it their sheer energy? The spiritual is caricatured if we imagine it to be exclusively chaste and angelic—to be all silence and right view, right livelihood, right posture. Even within the Buddhist tradition from which these concepts of rightness stem, there were always nonconformists—irrepressible monks who broke the rules without major spiritual setbacks, artisans who surely cursed as they labored over the great temples and gardens. In our own tradition, we acknowledge the visionary energy of van Gogh's art and feel for the most part pity and

78. Jackson Pollock. *One: Number 31, 1950*. Oil and enamel paint on canvas. 8′10″ × 17′5⅝″. Collection, The Museum of Modern Art, New York. Sidney and Harriet Janis Collection Fund.

terror when we recall his fierce inner conflicts. We don't invariably sanitize creative people; Beethoven need never smile. Certain things exact a terrifying price.

On the other hand, energy can be fine or coarse, an energy of understanding or a ruckus. Many people to this day see in Pollock's art little more than a ruckus, but there is more to it than that. What, after all, is the picture *of*? Were we to say a complex, energetic intertwining within and against undifferentiated space, people with some knowledge of art history who have never seen a Pollock canvas might possibly imagine a page of interlace from an early Irish gospel or an intricate Koran frontispiece. Were we then to unveil a Pollock, that audience would almost certainly recognize his art as falling within the tradition of cosmological imagery depicting the wondrous complexity and order of Creation. But there is divergence, too—an anguish, a quality of near-chaos checked by the artist's sense of rhythm and very real apprehension of beauty.

"I *am* Nature," Pollock is said to have protested when Hans Hofmann, teacher of several generations of American painters, invited him to do some painting "after Nature" in the old man's studio.[8] Some of Pollock's words—about art, generally sparing—confirm the direction that we have begun to take in exploring his work. One of his friends recalled an exchange that took place in 1952:

Although Jackson was curious about religious institutions, he was judgmental. "Churches are okay if you got to belong to something to feel safe, but artists don't need that . . . they're part of the universal energy in their creating. Look—existence *is*. We're part of all like everything else, we're on our own, goddamit!"[9]

The thoughts are grandly contradictory: on the one hand a universal energy to which all belong and which artists on occasion know intensely; on the other hand all persons and things are alone. There are recognitions here of universal coherence and abandonment, of a redeeming force and its total absence, and of the artist's risk in relying on experience alone to reveal the larger pattern of things. The contradictions cannot be sorted out; they are in Pollock's art as surely as they were in his being. His vision is of a sacred universe but not a safe one.

There are other indications that Pollock was working in a religious mode with few intellectual formulations but considerable pressure of vision. The conversation is between Nicholas Carone and Pollock:

> "How the hell can you teach *art*, Nick? . . . it's got nothing to do with what I'm involved in, the cosmos." But I said the plastic language *can* be taught, and he said, "Maybe you're right, but if I had to teach, I would tell my students to study Jung."

Carone further commented on this rather cunning exchange:

> The artist is never happy until he finds the well of the unconscious; then, if he has a life force, there is engagement, an encounter, and he becomes illumined by the generating force as an icon. Jackson *knew*—we talked about this—and his statement is religious. He was a genius and a genius is a phenomenon; it is someone possessed and Jackson was possessed—absolutely.[10]

We have assembled a view of Pollock's art as an anguished *and* joyful representation of "the world"—the world as sensed and felt rather than the world reported by our eyes. We have identified the venerable tradition to which it belongs, that of cosmological imagery masquerading, in some instances, as decorative pages in liturgical books. There may be something more, deriving from Pollock's intensely troubled nature and equally intense capacity for aesthetic invention.

Much of the pain of life occurs not in the body at all but in the mind: wild thoughts, unhappy thoughts, fearful thoughts, thoughts running on and on. Lord knows what Pollock's thoughts were, but surely the intricately patterned windings of his art reflect something of his inner experience—reflect and raise it. The speed and clutter of the modern mind are evident in his art, but at best they are transmuted: obsessiveness becomes keenly constructed pattern, anger becomes bright energy, imprisonment opens out into spaciousness. I am suggesting that Pollock did indeed depict the modern mind, just as his least friendly critics said. He also transfigured it to the very limit of his understanding.

Jackson Pollock killed himself in a one-car accident in 1956, taking also the life of a passenger whom he had only met recently and hardly knew. It was a perfectly miserable ending, but he had accomplished what he set out to do as an artist. In a much-quoted phrase, Willem de Kooning said that "Pollock broke the ice."[11] He generated a powerfully original art, inspiring other American artists to gather their resources and do as much. Aesthetically it was new, and it not only met but overwhelmed "international standards." Spiritually, it was the trace left by a dancer sometimes moved by the universal energy, more often desperate and on his own.

MARK ROTHKO: THEY ARE NOT PICTURES

The spiritual in art requires strategies for its protection. It is easily debased, or simply mislaid, by too many or incorrect words. It can become a burden for artists who acknowledge a metaphysical dimension but do not wish to be construed as "spiritual," as if they were wearing clerical garb and must behave. And then, no matter how "spiritual" the artist, his or her struggle is to achieve a sensuous sign astonishing in its own right. The work of art may point beyond itself, but it points to itself as well. "Sensuality," Mark Rothko said, "the basis for being concrete about the world."[12]

The mature work of Mark Rothko (1903–1970) is one of the great spiritual realizations of twentieth-century art in any medium. It catches up the buoyant geometry of Malevich, the saturated color of Matisse, and Mondrian's chaste orderliness in a new and powerful figuration. At best it stops one in one's tracks, grandly suggests that the world as we know it daily is ringed by something more, and makes one feel akin to that "something more." Rothko's art briefly reinserts us into some large drama from which, who knows how, we have been exiled. Quite apart from such high matters, it endows the simple processes of perception—of absorbing impressions of color, weight, relationship—with a new quality of wonder. Consciousness rediscovers its subtlety, thanks to the artist's subtle work, and beyond that is reminded of a larger dimension which the paintings do not attempt to *define:* they make it visible and felt. There is an agnostic spirituality, one that does not presume to know—but nonetheless knows. Rothko's was of this kind.

In the years before he was able to formulate this art, Rothko spoke rather freely of the transcendental. In years after, he rarely if ever spoke of such things in public. He rankled when critics approached his art in spiritual terms, rejoiced when they stressed the physical concrete character of his paintings. Privately, he was different. Studio visitors and friends who listened well heard occasional undisguised remarks. He would briefly set aside the machismo of the painter, the no-nonsense artisan, to reveal the person underneath—a seeker, a literate man at no loss for words, in no way naive about the age-old task of art to relieve the grinding physicality of human life through a larger, and true, vision.

All of this was epitomized in the late 1950s when Rothko was hard at work on a series of enormous panels commissioned for a luxurious restaurant in New York. The restaurant never did see the panels, which in time found their way to The Tate Gallery in London (today they are the outstanding permanent exhibition of his art). His huge New York studio was a former indoor riding ring with the skylight darkened by a parachute silk. There were works in progress on the walls when Dore Ashton, an old friend and an art critic of commanding intelligence, paid a visit.

> Rothko had no lights on, and the great space was as dim as a cathedral. . . . I felt as though I had walked into a theater, or into an ancient library. The only perceptible object in the huge space was a table, very small in its isolation. Rothko watched my reaction as I examined the arrangement of large canvases and said, "I have made a place." . . . It was a long visit, with intermittent conversation, and at the end, as I was taking my leave, Rothko said: "They are not pictures." [13]

The few words are simple, but they are not ingenuous. The burden of art, at its best, is to still words by bringing other kinds of perception to the center of awareness. We will look in these pages for an understanding of the "place" that Rothko made and of the contrarian wisdom of his claim that his pictures are not pictures.

Born Marcus Rothkowitz in Dvinsk, Russia, the boy emigrated with his family to Portland, Oregon, where other family members had settled earlier. He lived a surprisingly respectable American adolescence, culminating in two years at Yale College. The cancellation of his Yale scholarship, mysterious since he was doing quite well, contributed to his decision to discontinue formal education (years later the university conferred an honorary degree on him). He moved to New York in 1924 and enrolled in the Art Students League, where he worked primarily under the direction of Max Weber. In 1928, the year of his first group exhibition, he befriended Milton Avery (1893–1965), an American painter of serene charm whose work has achieved due recognition only in the past decade or so. Through Avery, the young Rothko came in touch with Matisse's approach to color. It was a lesson that he would deliberately intensify as time went on.

The 1930s were no kinder to Rothko than to any of the artists who became the core of the New York School after World War II. Through artists' groupings and the Federal Art Project, he met his peers and formed key friendships with Adolph Gottlieb, Barnett Newman, and others. His art in these years was unimpressive, typified by subway scenes peopled with compressed, lengthened, and above all lonely figures. Toward the end of the 1930s a new theme emerged from his love of Greek mythology, to which Nietzsche's *The Birth of Tragedy* may have led him. But these works, too—*The Omen of the Eagle, Sacrifice of Iphigenia*, and so on—are plainly awkward. In the mid 1940s, responding to the influence of the Surrealists who had taken refuge in New York from Nazi Europe, he found a more accomplished art that explored imaginary organisms with whiplash tendrils and translucent bodies, immobilized against background washes of color that begin to resemble his mature work. But Miró-like organisms in Masson-like swirls were not the endpoint of Rothko's search.

In statements at the time, he and his friends were speaking of the authority of primitive and archaic art, and of the power of mythic motifs. Some of their thinking pointed toward the future. In 1942, Rothko wrote that the mythic motifs collected in a canvas of that year "merge into a single tragic idea."[14] In a 1943 letter to the editor written by Rothko with Adolph Gottlieb and Barnett Newman, they argued that

> there is no such thing as good painting about nothing. We assert that the subject is crucial and only that subject matter is valid which is tragic and timeless. That is why we profess spiritual kinship with primitive and archaic art.[15]

In a radio broadcast following on from their controversial letter, Rothko and Gottlieb asserted that the true portrait of man in our era has a new character:

> Today the artist is no longer constrained by the limitation that all of man's experience is expressed by his outward appearance. Freed from the need of describing a particular person, the possibilities are endless. The whole of man's experience becomes his model. . . .[16]

Some of this thinking would fall away over the next years—the explicit connection with primitive art, the understanding of "subject matter" as recognizable objects—but the gist would remain: yearning for the tragic and timeless, and for contact with "the whole of man's experience" rather than anecdotes about one or another aspect. The "single tragic idea" had not yet made itself known in Rothko's art, but his need prepared the way.

The transition, taking 1946 through 1949 to complete, began with an unfocusing. The bizarre Surreal objects in the world of his mid-1940s paintings were absorbed into the background, while the background itself—formerly organized into tidy horizontal bands—dissolved into unpredictably shaped patches of color with cloudlike, permeable edges (Fig. 79). The nervous energy of Rothko's Surrealist period dissipated. His color patches seem to drift across the canvas, fusing with each other, repelling each other, moving on—toward an order that has not yet appeared. Some of the earlier paintings from these transitional years suggested that a rectilinear order might emerge, and by 1948 this was clearly so, although the precise nature of that order was still variable and ill-defined.

As Rothko entered this transition, color became incomparably more arresting to him—and to all of us who engage with his paintings. The aerated, light-suffused planes of color in Matisse's art were his source, more deeply absorbed than ever. Rothko explained in later years that he spent great lengths of time in front of Matisse's *The Red Studio* (see Fig. 57) when it was first put on permanent exhibition at the Museum of Modern Art in 1949; he attributed his new art to it.[17] He became a master colorist, the phrase implying not just a remarkable eye for color but also a great deal of painterly métier. Underpainting, thin scrims of dilute paint, dry feathered layers—Rothko drew from the centuries-old tradition of European painting, not excluding a rabbit-skin sizing boiled up in the studio to prepare his canvases.

Technical skill is one of the consolations of the artist, just as grammar and syntax are consolations of the writer. It requires no imagina-

79. Mark Rothko. *Number 18*, 1948–49. Oil on canvas. 67¼″ × 55⅞″.
Collection Vassar College Art Gallery, Poughkeepsie, New York. Gift of
Blanchette Hooker Rockefeller, '31. Photo: Paulus Leeser.

tive powers, no creativity; it is just the right way of doing things. It can provide a formidable rest, allowing one legitimately to postpone or disengage from the uncertain encounter with "a generating force," as Nicholas Carone said in relation to Pollock's art. Métier is also plainly necessary, if one is reaching as high as Rothko began to reach in these years.

"You have to remember that Mark did not want to be a great colorist," recalled an artist friend. "He wanted to be a visionary."[18] In 1947, when his transition toward a visionary art was already well launched although the destination was of course unknown to him, Rothko contributed an article to the one and only issue of *Possibilities,* an artists' and critics' journal now perceived as a landmark for the history of the New York School. This was the last exhaustive public statement that he would make until 1958, and certainly the last in which he spoke openly of "the transcendental." Some of his remarks looked backward to his concerns of the early 1940s, others foreshadowed the art to come. The following excerpt is much abridged:

> The romantics were prompted to seek exotic subjects and to travel to far off places. They failed to realize that, though the transcendental must involve the strange and unfamiliar, not everything strange or unfamiliar is transcendental.
>
> The unfriendliness of society to his activity is difficult for the artist to accept. Yet this very hostility can act as a lever for true liberation. Freed from a false sense of security and community, . . . transcendental experiences become possible.
>
> I think of my pictures as dramas. . . . Ideas and plans that existed in the mind at the start were simply the doorway through which one left the world in which they occur. . . . The presentation of this drama in the familiar world was never possible, unless everyday acts belonged to a ritual accepted as referring to a transcendent realm.
>
> Even the archaic artist . . . found it necessary to create a group of intermediaries, monsters, hybrids, gods, and demigods. The difference is that, since the archaic artist was living in a more practical society than ours, the urgency for transcendent experience was understood, and given an official status. . . . With us, the disguise must be complete. The familiar identity of things has to be pulverized in order to destroy the finite associations with which our society increasingly enshrouds every aspect of our environment.
>
> Without monsters and gods, art cannot enact our drama. . . . When they were abandoned as untenable superstitions, art sank into melancholy. . . . For me the great achievement of the centuries in

which the artist accepted the probable and familiar as his subjects were the pictures of the single human figure—alone in a moment of utter immobility. . . .

I do not believe that there was ever a question of being abstract or representational. It is really a matter of ending this silence and solitude, of breathing and stretching one's arms again.[19]

The article is rich enough to demand close reading. The artist's interest and goal, without question, is to forge a connection with a transcendent realm. That realm is now distant, but it has always been distant: even in archaic societies with strongly sanctioned religions, artists had to create an intermediary, imagined world between their world and that in order to feel linked. Those imaginings were a disguise of sorts, but "with us, the disguise must be complete." At this point in his reasoning, Rothko reacts to the strident materialism of twentieth-century culture with stridency of his own: "The familiar identity of things has to be pulverized," the shroud of limiting thoughts with which society wraps all things must be destroyed if transcendent experience is to become possible again. There was, however, some residual strength in the secular European art of recent centuries; "the single human figure—alone in a moment of utter immobility" seemed to Rothko a particularly arresting motif—and one that, in time, would enter unseen into his developed art.

In an abrupt reference at the end of the article to "this silence and solitude," Rothko assumes that if we have followed him so far we can follow him farther. The silence and solitude cannot be other than the condition of modern life in which "the urgency for transcendent experience" is misunderstood and the environment shrouded off from contact with "the transcendent realm."

These are not thoughts to which one can easily be indifferent. They help us to understand the unfocusing in Rothko's art. The imaginary organisms in his canvases of the mid-1940s were hopelessly unable to bear the weight of his intentions; they were not gods and demigods, or even proper monsters. He was looking, with the Surrealists, toward the marine world and the world of microscopic creatures for inspiration, but there was precious little there. God is not an amoeba—at least, not only an amoeba. The unfocusing, the migrant planes of unshaped light-filled color brought Rothko back to himself and to a new creative source.

The classic composition that emerged in 1949 (exemplified by Fig. 80) could hardly have been structured more simply: two or more stacked rectangles hover against—and partially mingle with—a back-

80. Mark Rothko. *Untitled (Number 13),* 1958. Oil and acrylic with pow-
dered pigment on canvas. 95⅜″ × 81⅜″. The Metropolitan Museum of Art,
Gift of The Mark Rothko Foundation, Inc., 1985 (1985.63.5).

ground that reads as space, air, and light. The rectangles are almost
never opaquely painted but open and variable in tone and texture,
with freely brushed permeable edges. They are like nothing so much as
clouds, the most vagrant and variable of things, mysteriously conforming to a rational order. Narrow bands in the gaps between large rectangles in some canvases read in a number of different ways, depending on the overall composition—as transitional elements in a simple

architectural order, as light flashing, as vapor that has wandered into the gap.

The contrast between the predictable geometry of the rectangles and the variable brushwork across their surfaces and around their perimeters is a source of vitality. A gently stated but real order associated with a gentle but real randomness has immense aesthetic appeal, perhaps based on a deep awareness that our own lives represent a constant interplay—not always gentle—between order and randomness.

This classic composition is not a passive presentational device for Rothko's virtuousity with color—it has its own life—but color is nonetheless the stronger "voice" in his new formulation. The colorless word *color* hardly does justice to Rothko's expressiveness in this domain: it is astonishing. For once color *is* a music, as Kandinsky had hoped and Rothko himself had wished. Whether one takes Rothko's color as a melodic sequence or a simultaneous chord, it is often rich beyond expectation and, like music, somewhat inexplicable. Just as there are certain notes in Beethoven or Stravinsky that one remembers as infinitely "right" and piercing, without really knowing why, so in Rothko's color harmonies many passages are "right" and piercing for reasons that defy explanation. Somewhere here is the doorway to another world of which he had written in 1947. It is not a world beyond human awareness, but certainly a world whose facts can be more readily grasped by nonverbal intelligence—by eye and body and feeling—than by reason. The intensive play of color encompasses the entire canvas, both rectangles and background, and it is not severely zoned: as often as not, colors permeate one another. The entire canvas, varied as it is, is sensed as one whole.

Rothko had expressed admiration for "the single human figure—alone in a moment of utter immobility," and it is not farfetched to sense the presence of that figure in this totally abstract composition. The verticality, segmentation, and distinctiveness of the primary image endow it not with a literal human presence, but with a resonance to what we are. Similarly, there is a resonance to simple, archaic architectural orders—to the stacking of well-cut stone. This needn't be surprising: classical Greek sculpture is architectonic, classical architecture is sculptural. Rothko, a better classicist than most, seems to have intuitively recovered that relationship in his art.

The great majority of Rothko's canvases are monumental in size. "I realize," he said in 1951, that historically the function of painting large pictures is painting something very grandiose and pompous. The reason I paint them, however—I think it applies to other painters I know—is precisely because I want to be very intimate and human. To paint a small picture is to place yourself outside your experience, to look upon an experience as a stereopticon view or with a reducing glass. However you paint the larger picture, you are in it. It isn't something you command.[20]

He was relying on the large simple image with potent color harmonies and a half-material, cloud-like consistency to "pulverize our finite associations." The word *pulverize* seems out of keeping, now that he had found his art. In fact viewers feel invited to enter his almost featureless pictorial world, to dwell in it imaginatively, responding to the sensuality and unexpected impact of its colors, the contrasting austerity of its forms, and the curiously rewarding way in which each thing is separate and yet blends with the whole.

There are various testimonies as to how Rothko himself thought about his art. Robert Motherwell, a superb painter under the modest curse of possessing a historian's sense for his era, remembered Rothko explaining that "the main criterion for his work was ecstasy—that was the only subject he was concerned about."[21] Selden Rodman accosted Rothko at a Whitney Museum Annual, announced to him that he regarded Rothko as a colorist, and provoked a testy but valuable reply:

I'm interested only in expressing basic human emotions—tragedy, ecstasy, doom, and so on. . . . The people who weep before my pictures are having the same religious experience I had when I painted them. And if you, as you say, are moved only by their color relationships, then you miss the point![22]

In conversation with Harold Rosenberg, Rothko said simply:

I don't express myself in my painting. I express my not-self.[23]

By his own account, and the testimony of so many critics and ordinary mortals who perceive a potent spirituality in Rothko's art, there is something at work in his classic image that we have not yet grasped in these pages. To find our way, I know of no other means than to think about the symbolism of the cloud. Much as Rothko's image stands fiercely apart from tradition, and is well and truly a twentieth-century abstraction, it has hidden roots. In what follows, I do not wish to imply that Rothko's image is a deliberate reflection of any ancient symbol or idea. But it does recover certain symbols and meanings in a new form, a form of our own.

The God of Israel never appeared directly to the people. He appeared as a fire or veiled by a cloud.

> Moses went up on the mountain, and the cloud covered the mountain. The glory of the Lord settled on Mount Sinai, and the cloud covered it six days; and on the seventh day he called to Moses out of the midst of the cloud. Now the appearance of the Lord was like a devouring fire on the top of the mountain in the sight of the people of Israel. And Moses entered the cloud, and went up on the mountain.[24]

The God of Israel is not ensconced behind or within Rothko's hovering clouds. And yet . . . there is some undeniable epiphany in the greatest canvases. One cannot help but feel that a presence is mingled with and concealed by the clouds. They present a closed "facade," as some have said, but not just any facade. It bears a relation, however oblique, to the impenetrable facade that enveloped Moses for six days before the Lord addressed him.

Rothko had written somewhat enviously in 1947 of the imagined beings that ancient artists had freely placed between themselves and the transcendental realm. He lamented the disappearance of such imaginings. Perhaps here, in his aerial clouds, he recovered that intermediate realm in a new and abstract form. It is not a direct image of the transcendent; it is certainly not an image of anything earthly; it lies between.

The Biblical text is revealing. Without overdosing on interpretation, viewers who greatly appreciate Rothko's art may find in it an ancient analogue to their own experience. A later text is well worth noting to widen our appreciation of the ancient roots of Rothko's image. It is *The Cloud of Unknowing,* a classic work of spiritual direction written by an anonymous fourteenth-century English monk.[25] While it has been more or less continuously in print since 1912, I have no evidence that Rothko knew or valued it, nor is there any need for such evidence. The point is to find analogies that obliquely explain the power of Rothko's art—not to explain it away.

In *The Cloud of Unknowing,* the Biblical image of the cloud has been passed through the transforming filter of early Christian mysticism and is now internalized as two barriers, one existing "above" the contemplative by the will of God, the other placed "below" the contemplative through his own effort.

. . . it is not called a cloud of the air, but a cloud of unknowing, that is betwixt thee and thy God. . . . And if ever thou shalt come to this cloud and dwell and work therein as I bid thee, thee behoveth as this cloud of unknowing is above thee, betwixt thee and thy God, right so put a cloud of forgetting beneath thee; betwixt thee and all the creatures that ever be made. . . . Travail fast awhile, and beat upon this high cloud of unknowing, and rest afterward. . . . Do on thy work, and surely I promise thee He shall not fail in His. . . . Then will He sometimes peradventure send out a beam of ghostly light, piercing this cloud of unknowing that is betwixt thee and Him; and shew thee some of His privity, the which man may not, nor cannot speak. . . .[26]

The words may seem altogether alien, but I strongly suspect that they would not seem so to Rothko, who had written about pulverizing the familiar identity of things and looking toward a transcendent realm that lies beyond artists' imaginings.

This is the universe of discourse in which Rothko's art moves. It represents a meeting of twentieth-century expressive means—the lessons of Malevich, Matisse, and Mondrian—with a philosophical and religious temperament of very considerable depth. "With us the disguise must be complete," he said. And so it was, or very nearly.[27]

Rothko's art went from strength to strength in the 1950s and early 1960s, and with it his reputation. There were odd and even funny events—for example, he was employed as a painting instructor at Brooklyn College in 1951 and denied tenure by his colleagues in 1954, at a time when the extra income and the niche in life might still have been a comfort. They found him anything but a team player; he found them largely dominated by a bloodless version of Bauhaus design. In 1958 he worked on the restaurant commission that led to the extraordinarily stately ensemble at the Tate Gallery. In those paintings he succeeded in a task that came hard to him: a valid modification of his magical composition (Fig. 81). As Dore Ashton has suggested, he transformed his rectilinear format into a series of dark, archaic gates;[28] the center of the composition opened, but the somber light in the canvases suggests a troubled and difficult voyage. His "single tragic idea" is nowhere more palpable.

His own voyage was increasingly troubled. Fame didn't sit well with him, money was both an obvious good and a miserable addiction. A

81. Mark Rothko. *Black on Maroon*, 1959. Oil on canvas. 8'9" × 15'. The Tate Gallery, London.

sensualist always, he drank too much, smoked too much, took too many pills for too many ills. He was subject to depressions. The great gifts of this man did not extend to living the ordinary life with reasonable grace, particularly in the later years. His major commission of the mid-1960s, an ensemble of paintings for what came to be called The Rothko Chapel in Houston, was elaborated under these mixed circumstances and remains controversial: some find in it the fulfillment of his art, others find a waning.

There were other factors at work, all attacking his well-being. His gallery relationship with Marlborough Fine Arts became increasingly invasive and domineering. Always fastidious to a fault about the exhibition of his work, he had given up much of his control to Marlborough in return for dollars. In addition, a serious medical incident in 1968 signaled approaching death, although he made a good recovery.

Rothko committed suicide in his studio in the winter of 1970. Soon after, his estate became embroiled in a scandal and ultimately a criminal trial in which his dealer was convicted of fraud. It was a perfectly miserable end, but in light of his accomplishments nothing to dwell on and curiously stripped of instruction. He simply botched the end.

"The dictum 'Know thyself,'" he said in 1958, in his last major public statement,

is only valuable if the ego is removed from process in search for truth.

According to the notes of Dore Ashton, who alertly knew at this public meeting what she was hearing, he went on to say:

> art is not self-expression, as he had thought in his youth. . . . "A work of art is another thing." The notion of self-expression . . . was proper to the vanity of a beautiful woman or a monster, but not an artist. "For an artist, the problem is to talk about and to something outside yourself."[29]

The words are forthright where they evoke the cloud of forgetting, vague where they touch on the cloud of unknowing. But exact enough, and as exact as we can be.

MORRIS LOUIS: VEILS

It is difficult now to reconstruct, let alone convey, the delight occasioned by a recent comprehensive exhibition of paintings by Morris Louis (1912–1962). The rooms of veil paintings in particular (see Fig. 82) seemed an impromptu temple; one could rest there in a vision that was monumental without arrogance, beautiful without irony, lucid although abstract. Louis's art was religious in the unique way that twentieth-century abstraction can be—without the secure underpinning of scripture, instinctive and felt as opposed to intellectual, but marked with strong recognitions of mystery, scale, and beauty. It is rare when one can give oneself unreservedly to visual art, as one can to a symphony performance. This was such an occasion.

I was therefore surprised to read in a leading art periodical the following commentary on the exhibition:

> . . . hopelessly square and dumb, in the way unique to past styles that in their heyday too confidently held themselves to be transcendent. . . . the last great stab at a contemporary Beaux Arts-type orthodoxy, an art stamped with "quality" (like prime meat) for consumption by an ambitious class: the retro-bourgeois sector of '60s wealth and power, appalled by Andy Warholian cultural democracy and craving a secure, genteel, parental style. . . . [Louis's] historic importance is limited . . . to having popularized some technical possibilities of acrylic paint.[30]

This is not criticism, it is invective—driven, it seems, by a need to dismember the constellation of images, artists, critics, aesthetic ideas, and values which together created an American art that knew something of the spirit. The "retro-bourgeois sector," whatever that is, ignored

82. Morris Louis. *Russet,* 1958. Synthetic polymer paint on canvas. 7'8¾" × 14'5⅝". Collection, The Museum of Modern Art, New York. Given anonymously.

Louis in his lifetime—he worked in relative isolation, encouraged by a few artists and critics. His reputation and "prices" soared after his early death, but it is no blemish that the strength of his work was in time widely recognized and his estate deftly handled. While some critics have thought about Louis's art in terms of "the transcendent," the major studies have generally explored his development and milieu and taken a formalist approach to the paintings. For example, John Elderfield's catalogue for the recent exhibition stresses art-historical and formal issues, and treads very lightly where the transcendent is concerned.[31]

The explosion of negativity in this review illustrates the precarious position of the spiritual in art in the mid-1980s. For some critics, it is a highflown idea promulgated by Modernist pioneers and prolonged by the Abstract Expressionists, which died the death it deserved. They have no desire to think about it or even provisionally to respect its premises. Morris Louis's *faith*—in color, in simple and eloquent form, in art itself as a blessed thing—can seem dated, and those who share his faith can seem wishful.

Born Morris Louis Bernstein in Baltimore in 1912, the son of Russian-Jewish immigrants, Louis studied at the Maryland Institute of Fine and Applied Arts and, in 1936–43, was yet another participant in the Easel Division of the Federal Art Project. Moving to New York in

1936, he stayed through the early 1940s and met a number of artists of his generation who would soon figure in the New York School. Known even then as a retiring person, he returned to Baltimore at some point, married, and settled in Washington, D.C., where in time he took up a teaching post at a private art school. All of this is unpromising, and little seems to be on record about the man behind the ordinariness, although Elderfield notes his intense efforts in 1947–51 to explore the mainstream styles of contemporary art "from Joan Miró to Pollock."[32] He had as yet nothing visibly his own.

In 1952, at the hinge year of forty, his life began to open. Forging a rich friendship with Kenneth Noland, a fellow teacher at the Workshop with strong links to New York, Louis made an expedition to New York with him in the spring of 1953 that changed everything. He was introduced to Clement Greenberg, the celebrated critic who had the Socratic capacity to elicit the best from those with whom he really concerned himself. Over the next years, Greenberg's encouragement and critical insights helped Louis stay on course. Greenberg saw to it that the visitors called on Helen Frankenthaler, one of the most lyrical painters of our time. In her studio, they saw a large work created by means of an innovative technique developed a little earlier by Jackson Pollock but not fully explored—a technique whereby thinned paint was stained directly onto unsized, permeable canvas. The result was delicate washes of pure and overlapping color, at one with the canvas itself.

Louis and Noland returned to Washington in an uproar; they had seen something they couldn't overlook. Over the next weeks they ran tons of experiments, worked side by side and sometimes on the same canvas in what Noland later called sessions of "jam painting, like jazz."[33] From this fine crisis emerged new directions for both artists, Louis turning wholeheartedly toward exploration of the staining technique, Noland toward both staining and the strict geometries that led to his signature "target" paintings first shown in 1959.

Louis found his way in stages to a personal technique and vision. The vision proceeded from the technique itself, but it was not merely a mechanical elaboration of observed possibilities: there was a stroke of genius here. Thoroughly private, scarcely speaking even to his wife about his secluded studio ventures, he left no record of the working method he evolved. It has been deduced from the canvases themselves. Diane Upright, author of the Louis catalogue raisonné, writes:

> He worked with his canvas tacked to a work stretcher; variations in the angled placement of the stretcher, the tautness or slackness of

the canvas, the viscosity of the paint, the amount of paint poured, and the direction of the pour became his creative means.[34]

He destroyed much work as he learned to pour and stain—in effect to draw with color on a monumental scale—but a batch of paintings from 1954 passed muster and remains today to document an art that had not quite been brought to maturity. He had found the veil form, a curtain of seemingly translucent paint that floats freely down from the top of the canvas or rises from the base, fanning slightly in a way that conveys ease and expansiveness. But he hadn't yet found the precise shape of the veil or its relation to the unstained canvas framing it. In some examples the outline wanders, with irregular seepages and splashes toward the edge of the canvas; in others, the veil flows across the entire canvas, leaving no neutral ground as a quiet foil for the intense color patterning and mass of the veil itself. He also hadn't decided whether the veil should fall freely from the upper edge of the canvas or rise like a transparent cliff from the lower edge. A good deal of magic would be released by that decision.

In the 1954 canvases, he had already found much of what he would ultimately find with respect to color, although without the seemingly effortless control that became possible later. Much of the art lay here, in choosing colors that would state themselves purely, change in arresting ways as they encountered other colors, and blend into the continuous surface of the veil. His multiple pourings generated a multiplicity of small chromatic changes across the veil, itself a large and simple shape. These complementary features of his developing image offered the possibility of exploring the age-old aesthetic—and metaphysical—theme of the One and the Many.

Louis's sensitivity to color was simply grand. Critics have spoken of the "seductiveness" of his color harmonies, the word implying chaste recoil. In one of few recorded statements, Louis expressed delight in the seductiveness of color: "Paintings should produce a delicious pain in the eye," he said, "make the viewer gasp—knock him down and seduce him."[35] His metaphor is sexual, recalling the common origin of our words *rape* and *rapture*. *Something* has to lift the mind in worthwhile art, to be intense enough to create a sense of passage. For Louis, the subtleties and vibrancies of color were that element, and the primary source of his visible image of the invisible. He would not have stated his goal in these terms, which are borrowed from Paul Klee; he worked for paintings that would make him gasp, and in turn the viewer, owing to their physical beauty and "rightness." The rest ful-lowed, by virtue of the man he was and the largely unspoken motives that guided him.

Between 1954, the year of his initial experiments with the veil form, and 1958 when the form reappeared, Louis put himself through something of an ordeal as he sought another image altogether,[36] as Diane Upright has shown. He later destroyed most of the canvases produced in those intervening years; the few that survive seem rather violent, with high-contrast colors swirling or dripping across the canvas. It was apparently Clement Greenberg who helped Louis to abandon that approach and return to the "continuity of simple pattern and slow motion"[37] of the veils. The words are Louis's own, to my knowledge his only recorded description of the art for which he is now remembered.

The developed veil is a singular creation. Pitched to the monumental scale of much Abstract Expressionist art, a typical canvas may be seven by twelve feet or more: it commands attention. Its simple outline against a neutral ground of unsized canvas conveys a sculptural presence, while its translucent, glowing colors suggest immateriality. The form rises from a rounded base or root and follows enough of the laws of botanical growth—widening as it "grows," with a veined internal structure—to suggest that we are looking at an organic form, unspecified and "essential" in Brancusi's sense. However, there is more: the ability of abstraction to layer suggestion upon suggestion is keenly at work here. The form is also a cliff, a great towering mass with sheer drops; it is a fountain in which water rises and falls again with uncanny ease. A ripple at the top suggests just this rise and fall, while in some examples watery mist cascades down the sides of the central mass. In many examples, the form is also "read" by the eye as an array of harmonious color, a rainbow not in shape but in impact. Finally, of course, the form is a veil, an insubstantial apparition rising freely as if it knows nothing of the pull of gravity. All of these associations dissolve in the single image, none truer than another, all there.

Louis's color harmonies are generally muted and gentle, ranging from sunny yellows and oranges to bronzes achieved by flowing a dark transparent scrim over the underlying hues. In both modes—sunny and positive, shadowed and more withdrawn—the veils can be immensely impressive. Like Rothko's classic image, they impose themselves as nonobjective icons, endowed with both physical beauty and metaphysical suggestiveness. Almost apologetically, Greenberg spoke of a later Louis motif (the stripes) as "pillars of fire." As for Rothko, the Old Testament reference is not inappropriate. The veils are not identifiable "graven images," yet they are many images in one and seem, as much as any psalm, to praise Creation. The intuition behind them has something in common with Pollock's pantheism, but both the man and the work are far less troubled. The veils are rich in the fundamental quality of *tathatā* or suchness: images of life itself—complex, simple, grand—they rear up before the viewer and defeat any impulse to comment or withdraw.

There is no complex metaphysic here, nothing that Schoolmen would linger over. There is, however, an epiphany: a unified image that dares us to love the color, form, substance, and space of the world that we more often experience in parts, not wholes, with mistrust, not love. The archetype underlying the image may well be the Sacred Mountain, where life originated and where man and God meet, but Louis spontaneously rhymed that image with many others to give us our own version of the ancient theme.

Louis found three further veins of imagery to work in 1959–62, before his rapid death from cancer as his fiftieth birthday approached. Evolving just after the veils, the florals are gorgeous exercises in color, in which he dissolved the stern order of the veil into freely arranged petals of color. They seem to reflect an interval of rest and play before the artist resumed his search for an image with underlying severity. They are winning, beautiful, rarely "serious," signs of an inward and contemplative holiday that the man was taking in his studio.

They led on to the unfurleds, works that many critics have taken to be the height of his art. In canvases larger still than the veils, rivulets of varied color meander diagonally from the upper corners to the lower edge, creating roughly symmetrical triangles of banded color at left and right, while the center remains white and open. Louis in effect reversed the veil image by leaving the wedge-shaped zone of the veil open and flowing paints into the white space surrounding the veil. The effect is lovely, but empty. The stripes, his concluding image, come much closer to the genius of the veils, although here too he fell short of their high standard. As the name implies, he laid down stripes of pure color side by side, generally rising cleanly from the bottom of the canvas and terminating in a soft ripple at the top. The image is most effective when the stripes terminate in drips or slightly brushed shapes suggesting a candle's flame, the stem of a fruit, or a thickening as in a shaft of bamboo. Louis may have been temperamentally drawn toward simplification; however, his work reached its astonishing best when he accepted a good deal of complexity within the simple outline of the veil.

That these later periods were not as rich as the veils need not give pause. Louis's life ended abruptly. Given a longer life, he might have found more still. What he did find is unforgettable.

AD REINHARDT: LATE AFTERNOON ABSORBENT TWILIGHT

While the last chapters of this book were being written, the exhibition "The Spiritual in Abstract Art: 1895–1985" moved from Los Angeles where it originated to Chicago where I was fortunate enough to see it. It was eye-opening in many respects. Well-known paintings from European collections were there, works that anyone drawn to twentieth-century art would be happy to see in reality rather than reproduced in a book. The exhibition clarified the kinship of the modern spiritual to Renaissance and later cosmological diagrams through what amounted to a rare book library annex. But the event was nonetheless oddly disappointing: large exhibitions, by nature, merge one thing with one another and reduce receptiveness. The works themselves reflected not only a spiritual search but also a lack of common language and concepts: the vitality and confusion of the century were simultaneously evident. This was hardly an iconostasis, an orderly gathering of images of spiritual beings toward which one could look for a taste of heaven.

Until the very end. In what seemed a deliberate culmination, the curators ended the long suite of works with a *Black Painting* by Ad Reinhardt (Fig. 83) and a dark late work by Mark Rothko—side by side as if to convey a conclusive common message. These works at once "settled" the exhibition, brought it home; one could feel again that there *is* a modern spiritual, and these works demonstrated it. One responded to their simplicity and quietness by becoming like them. One sensed the truth of the dark sign each was, as if all things emerge from this sort of quiescence and return to it. Malevich's *Black Square* was reborn with the spiritual expressiveness that he long ago intuited in it.

Ad Reinhardt (1913–1967) was a man of utmost intensity and compensating humor. As a painter, he moved from undistinguished abstraction in his earlier years to a compelling vision elaborated from the colors of twilight and night. His nocturnes are among the most original and sheerly beautiful works of the modern spiritual. He was a thinker of undeniable scope who typically delivered his thought in a style recalling both Joycean wordplay and Buddhist litany. A polemicist

83. Ad Reinhardt. *Black Cross*, 1967. Oil on panel. 11″ × 10″. Philadelphia Museum of Art: Given by the Kulicke Family in memory of Lt. Frederick W. Kulicke, III.

of untiring energy and sharp perception, he occasionally plunged with relish into obvious absurdities which he himself would surely have denied, had they not served his argument's purpose. His public persona of later years was itself a work of art: he deliberately suppressed much of his personality in order to dwell on the "one thing needful" as he perceived it. One could say that he painted himself into a corner, but he found that outcome suitable and contentedly signed his name. He was perhaps more than we deserved in American art at mid-century. No one questioned more than he: "Art cannot exist without permanent condition of being put into question,"[38] he inscribed in the verbal shorthand of his voluminous private notes.

Born in Buffalo, he attended Columbia College from 1931 to 1935, where he was a student of the uniquely gifted art historian Meyer Schapiro, and a close friend of boisterous Tom Merton, later the Trappist monk and author whom we have already encountered in these pages (see chapter 1). It was surely at Columbia that both Reinhardt and Merton acquired their taste for punning, intricately knit language. They remained friends for life and in their correspondence over the years addressed each other in part as they had in their youth, with a mocking raillery that hid a great deal of fondness.

After Columbia, Reinhardt studied painting in New York, joined the American Abstract Artists association, earned something of a living as a designer and illustrator, and found employment like so many other New York artists in the Federal Art Project. These were his apprentice years, traced with scholarship and sensitivity by Lucy Lippard.[39] After a brief stint in the navy toward the end of the war, he managed to transform the generic educational opportunity offered by the GI Bill into an extensive program of art-historical study with Alfred Salmony at the Institute of Fine Arts in New York. Continuing to paint independently, he equipped himself for a teaching career in studio art and art history (primarily at Brooklyn College) which assured him a reasonable livelihood during the sometimes unreasonable years ahead.

Salmony, a fine Orientalist of speculative temperament, introduced Reinhardt to the writings of Ananda K. Coomaraswamy. These in turn became fundamental to Reinhardt's point of view not only on art but on religion and symbology. Reinhardt also returned to Columbia in the early 1950s to attend D. T. Suzuki's seminars on Zen Buddhism. His later writings reflect considerable literacy in Buddhism; he cites scripture with an ease born of genuine familiarity and unfanatical acceptance. Like Coomaraswamy—and probably modeled on him—he also recognized the illuminating analogies to Eastern thought in Western religious authors, particularly the late medieval mystics. Their formulations flowed into his later writings, not as matters for analysis but as "givens" or cultural landmarks to which he could refer.

Almost by-the-by, in the sense that his calling never ceased to be painting, Reinhardt assembled a sophisticated education in the linked realms of Asian art, philosophy, religion, and symbology, with a keen sense for Western parallels. In a letter of 1962 to Merton, he listed "my favorite religious writers"—Coomaraswamy, Suzuki, Tillich, Maritain, Buber—and jokingly suggested that from his point of view they were no longer as "all right" as they once were.[40] Perhaps he had outgrown them; he had certainly grown intellectually and spiritually thanks to them. This education, acquired in the earlier 1950s when Reinhardt's first great paintings were made, was one of the sources of his mature art.

Yet his art was not primarily about ideas. When an interviewer in 1966 suggested this possibility to him, he at once affirmed his allegiance not to ideas, not even to the materials of art, but to something far more abstract:

> [My painting] has nothing to do with materials any more than it has to do with ideas. Whatever I do has come from doing and only relates to what's done.[41]

This is Reinhardt's mature voice, somewhat circular in reasoning, on occasion enigmatic, always stubborn, but illuminating and unique among his peers.

Literally and figuratively a member of the Club—a familiar of the other major artists in the New York School—Reinhardt was left behind when Pollock, de Kooning, Rothko, and others became celebrities and, in most cases, began making serious money. He had important exhibitions, but there were also hurtful exclusions, for example from a 1958 Museum of Modern Art exhibition, "New American Painting." The Museum bought a *Black Painting* in 1963, the first Reinhardt in its collection, and in 1966 the Jewish Museum gave him a major retrospective. But by then—sadly close to the end of his life—he expected only moderate public recognition; his values lay elsewhere. He generally made good use—one might almost say predestined use— of his ambivalent "insidership" and "outsidership," both in his art and in his stiff criticism of the change in artists' values since the heroic days when the American epiphany was new, in the late 1940s and early 1950s. He referred to himself willingly as "the Great Demurrer in This Time of Great Enthusiasms"[42]—a phrase both true and funny, transposing as it does a nineteenth-century (and vaguely Buddhist) formality into the melee of the New York art scene.

The Great Demurrer, also known as the Black Monk, was capable of marvelous humor. In the mid-1950s he emitted occasional guides to the art world in the form of diagrams such as "A Portend of the Artist as a Yhung Mandala." But the Great Demurrer was also an angry man. "What's wrong with the art world," he wrote in his private papers, is not Andy Warhol or Andy Wyeth but Mark Rothko. The corruption of the best is the worst.[43]

In an interview of 1966, he saw it otherwise but no more brightly:

> There's a kind of moral prestige that an artist has, like a priest in a sense. . . . [But] there isn't anything that doesn't go on now. The artist community is completely dissolved and artists aren't even talking to each other. . . . The Pop artists exploded the thing. They really did. They really ran all those meanings into the ground. Pollock wanted to become a celebrity and he did. . . . De Kooning is living like Elizabeth Taylor. . . . But finally it was Andy Warhol. . . . He ran together all the desires of artists to become celebrities, to make money, to have a good time. . . .[44]

His protest was not only *against;* it was also voiced on behalf of an austere, essentially religious view of art which he had realized in his painting and thought to be paradigmatic, truly binding—if only the bonds could be recognized by others for what they were. It is to this art, and the often remarkable words that accompanied it, that we will now turn.

By 1953, Reinhardt had developed a number of approaches to the stark geometric composition inaugurated by Mondrian. Often working in powerful, saturated monochromes on large canvases, he would create for example a simple rectilinear pattern in brilliant closely keyed reds, or a simple equal-armed cross in deep blues.[45] Curiously, the paintings gain character as the palette darkens. A canvas in the Whitney Museum (*Abstract Painting [Number 17]*, 1953) beautifully exemplifies the trend: its palette of dark reds, blues, and yellows, presented in an irregular grid, is a poetic and compelling work. It is as if the natural palette of twilight—"late afternoon absorbent twilight" as he wrote[46]—has been seen, purified, and conveyed.

Reinhardt was about forty years old, a classic age of self-discovery, when he found this palette; the moment did not pass him by. By 1956, according to Lippard, he had decided to concentrate on dark paintings alone.[47] Some were "Black Paintings" properly speaking—works executed entirely in shades of black, such as Fig. 83—while others through the 1950s explored his enormously effective palette of twilight colors.

The magic of these paintings has little to do with their composition, which is really no more than a clean presentational device: as he was dimming color, so he was in effect dimming composition. But we can experience the magic of the twilight palette all the more strongly in the paintings because there is no compositional business. For many people, twilight is a time of spontaneous collectedness and heightened sensitivity. The waning of "the plain light of day" allows something not so plain to make itself felt—a natural inwardness, sometimes accompanied by oddly unfocused hope and remorse, as if these paired emotions are just beneath the surface waiting for their chance to make themselves known. Connoisseurship of the time of day, rare in Western aesthetics, is extensively elaborated in the Indian theory of musical *ragas*. Somewhat comparably, in cultures where the orthodox pray at set intervals throughout the day, the atmospheric difference between, for example, prime and vespers—between the rush of new light and the retreat of light—is acutely recognized. We live now in a largely secular culture, but all of those people sitting quietly on their porches at twilight, with eyes spontaneously attentive to the least change in light, are surely responding to an objective quality of the moment—a natural call to self-possession or prayer.

It is this, I believe, that gives such poetic and, finally, spiritual power to Reinhardt's paintings in a twilight palette. Had he remained in this mode, his work would no doubt have been more widely regarded as beautiful and approachable. But Reinhardt had another mission, bound up with the Black Paintings to which he dedicated himself exclusively from the later 1950s until his death in 1967. From 1960 on, he in fact found another simplification, to which he adhered with no less passion: just as he had chosen to limit his palette to shades of black, he chose from that time to limit his format to a five-foot-square canvas—a square of rather imposing size—and, compositionally, to a simple equal-armed cross. This was not, he insisted, a Christian motif, but a noncomposition, a neutral division of the canvas.

The experience of Ad Reinhardt's Black Paintings varies enormously, depending on light conditions and one's own condition. They are curious paintings: in a room filled with the colorful splash of his peers' work, they may initially seem dour and empty. Yet if one takes time to see them, allowing one's eyes to gather in their fine distinctions between plum black and blue-black, for example, they can be most impressive. In 1959, Reinhardt sent a Black Painting in small format, comparable to the one illustrated in Fig. 83, to Thomas Merton at Gethsemani, the Cistercian abbey in rural Kentucky. Merton kept it in his hermitage, a cement-block cottage with a comfortable porch isolated from the main abbey. It is in such circumstances that the expressiveness of a Black Painting can best be apprehended; Merton's letter of thanks to Reinhardt for the canvas vividly conveys his response to it:

It has the following noble feature, namely its refusal to have anything else around it, notably the furniture etc. It is a most recollected small painting. It thinks that only one thing is necessary & this is time, but this one thing is by no means apparent to one who will not take the trouble to look. It is a most religious, devout, and latreutic small painting.[48]

Ad Reinhardt's own description of the five-foot-square "standard" Black Painting can introduce us to the extraordinary process of pondering and valuing into which the strict decision to paint only Black Paintings plunged him. The "one painting," achieved through "one ritual, one attention," as he wrote, gave rise to an amazingly diverse process of perception: one painting, many thoughts. Perhaps it was this intellectual diversity that allowed Reinhardt to paint one painting with small variations again and again in his last years. There was more variety than he admitted; his mind was teeming with ideas, his perceptions were rich. The description reads:

> A square (*neutral, shapeless*) canvas, five feet wide, five feet high, as high as a man, as wide as a man's outstretched arms (*not large, not small, sizeless*), trisected (*no composition*), one horizontal form negating one vertical form (*formless, no top, no bottom, directionless*), three (*more or less*) dark (*lightless*) no contrasting (*colorless*) colors, brushwork brushed out to remove brushwork, a matte, flat, free-hand painted surface (*glossless, textureless, non-linear, no hard edge, no soft edge*) which does not reflect its surroundings—a pure, abstract, non-objective, timeless, spaceless, changeless, relationless, disinterested painting—an object that is self-conscious (*no unconsciousness*), ideal, transcendent, aware of no thing but art (*absolutely no anti-art*).[49]

While much in his words invites comment, I will limit myself to Reinhardt's reliance on negatives. Just as the Black Painting eliminated nearly everything that had previously been considered the inevitable means of art, so Reinhardt's mind was exploring the power of negations to clear a space for something that is no-thing—for an unnameable unknown at the core of things. The procedure, while somewhat unfamiliar, derives from Asian and Western religious thinkers whose works Reinhardt had absorbed in the earlier 1950s. It is the *via negativa*, as Coomaraswamy expounded it, the negative theology of Nicholas of Cusa and others, and in Buddhism the movement of discrimination formulated in the classic phrase *neti, neti*—not this, not that. The phrase recalls the insistent process by which consciousness can strive to liberate itself from "objects" in order to uncover the objectless awareness which is identified in Buddhist tradition as the home ground of consciousness. The motivation is on the one hand to be free of illusion and ephemera, on the other hand to cohere with an overwhelmingly fertile quality of consciousness which is as fulfilling for the artisan as it is for the contemplative.

Reinhardt evolved a studio practice and aesthetic principles that reflected the deliberate narrowing and intensification of the *via negativa*. His occasional articles on "Art-as-Art Dogma," published in art journals and read out at artists' meetings, were explorations of the aesthetic, spiritual, and practical aspects of the Black Painting conception. One of them reads, in part, as follows:

> There is just one truth in art, one form, one change, one secrecy.
> There is just one artist always.
> There is just one artist-as-artist in the artist, just one artist in the artist-as-artist.
> There is just one art process, just one art invention, just one art discovery, just one art routine.
> There is just one art work, just one art working, just one art nonworking, one ritual, one attention.
> There is just one painting, one brushworking, one brushoverworking.
> There is just one painting everytime.
> There is just one direction, one directionlessness, one size, one sizelessness, one form, one formlessness, one formula, one formulalessness, one formulation.[50]

And he continues in this manner: just one simplicity, one complexity, one spirituality, one uselessness, one meaninglessness. There is hardly an aspect of the spiritual in art which is not, in one way or another, evoked in lines such as these.

It has to be recognized that Reinhardt negated religion just as thoroughly as he negated other conditioning influences. "I have been called," he said,

> a Zen Buddhist, a neo-Christian, a Calvinist, a Hindu, and a Muslim, simply because there were people that wanted to read the paintings as symbolic of those religions. The only thing about the parallel to religion is that it is more respectable than other businesses, but painting really has no relation to any of the religions nor ever has.[51]

The need to negate religion, at least in its exterior forms, was not overlooked by the religions themselves—a classic Zen story depicts a chilly monk contentedly burning a wooden statue of the Buddha. Reinhardt managed to retain the values of contemplative Buddhism without being seized into its rituals:

> The fine artist should have a fine mind, "free of all passion, ill-will and delusion."
> The fine artist need not sit cross-legged.[52]

But there is no need to encircle Reinhardt's position with reassurances from tradition, to the effect that what he thought and did fell acceptably "within the pale." He had found it necessary to stand apart from everything—from the traditions which had nourished him, from his own inevitable trivia, from his New York School peers who had flashed forward into what he bitterly regarded as "the hero-whoreo-artist-man-of-the-world role."[53] To stand apart was deeply in character, and it led to one of the authentic manifestations of the spiritual in our art.

Reinhardt's character and his relative isolation prompted him on occasion to insist too much—for example, his deadpan certainty that he was "merely making the last painting which anyone can make"[54] was pedagogically interesting but factually false. The idea of the end of art, which we first encountered in Mondrian and later in Constructivist thinking, is irritating when taken seriously rather than as an intriguing thought-experiment. He also insisted often, too often, on the unique virtue of his own art and studio practice; there was a touch of obsession in some statements that goes beyond the good-humored insistence of his manner at other times. Similarly, his contention that art comes from art alone served to emphasize the internal resources of art and the need to perceive works of art purely, but in its extreme form the contention is irrational. In the following chapter, Noguchi gracefully responds to this argument—and makes just as much sense.

Readers will need to find Reinhardt's art on their own—it reproduces badly and in any case calls for direct experience. What we can share here, by way of conclusion, is the man's mind.

> Nothing to win, nowhere to go
> Debase by verbalization
> Describe by negations, definable only through itself.
> Mark it off, to keep it holy, not to be mistaken for ordinary. . . .
> Fewer beliefs, more belief. . . .
> Artist, one who works upon forms and whom forms work upon[55]

And as he wrote in an undated note: "Sanctuary is invisible."[56]

18 ISAMU NOGUCHI: TO COMFORT US WITH THE REALITY OF OUR BEING

Here and there across the world—Tokyo, New York, Paris, and Jerusalem, Yale University and the corporate headquarters of IBM—are stone gardens and atriums endowed with special intelligence. They are the work of Isamu Noguchi. Modern architecture promised a world in which living and working space would enrich the sense of self and community, but kept that promise spottily. Noguchi's gardens and atriums fulfill it. In contrast to the severe intelligence of International Style buildings, which dominate modern cities and for most of us typify twentieth-century architecture, Noguchi's settings are freely conceived yet guided by precise perceptions of form and meaning. Massive architecture comes under a hundredfold more economic and structural constraints than gardens and interior patios. But Noguchi's aesthetic, elaborated over some sixty years, stubbornly suggests an architecture that might have been and might yet be—varied in its forms, acutely sensitive to materials, alert to symbolic expression, yet grounded in awareness of pure matter and space. In few modern places is it a privilege simply to be. A designer of children's playgrounds in one phase of his activity, Noguchi created contemplative gardens for adults in his architectural settings, where one can look away from preoccupation into harmonies of space and stone, sometimes water and plant. The word *harmony* reflects a quality of these settings: they have the perfection of a freshly tuned piano.

Such closely designed places have not been his only concern. Noguchi is centrally a sculptor, and his art, deepening over the years, has never been stronger than in the recent decades of a career that began in the 1920s. Visitors to the American pavilion at the 1986 Venice Biennale, the international exhibition which remains a solid benchmark in the fluid world of art, found a presentation of Noguchi's work, *What*

84. Isamu Noguchi. *Ojizousama*, 1985. Andesite. 18″ high. Photo: Shigeo Anzai.

85. Isamu Noguchi. Second version of *Ojizousama*. Photo: Shigeo Anzai.

Is Sculpture? The exhibition catalogue featured a remarkable stone sculpture in two versions (Figs. 84, 85). The first version, with a silk veil conferring something of the presence of a woman in purdah, has a fascinating Surrealist quality of unexpected juxtaposition; one's eyes linger over it. But the simpler version provides a better starting point for exploration.

The unveiled stone recalls in part the classic portrait of Daruma, founder of Zen Buddhism: typically hooded or bald with a great bare cranium, he is present by association in Noguchi's abstract composition in granite. The disk cut cleanly through the surface of the stone to a second layer deeper down establishes a sense of inner and outer—of visible, partially visible, and invisible—and suggests an unrevealed core. Conceived within the Japanese cultural universe, the recessed circle recalls the Zen *ensō*—a brush-drawn circle on paper, mounted reverently as a scroll. The drive, pauses, spontaneities, thickenings, and gaps of such a boldly brushed circle are, from the hands of a master, all the symbol one could wish of the multiplicity, wholeness, and essential emptiness of life (emptiness understood in the Buddhist manner, not the Existentialist, as *śūnyatā*, refined positive energy in touch with everything, trapped by nothing). In Noguchi's sculpture, rough stone itself conveys the vital irregularity of the brush stroke.[1]

He might have stopped there; the work is already magical, although austere. A meditation hall would be fortunate to have such an ornament, which is Daruma and *ensō*, raw stone and delicate thought all in one. But he added the veil, in a gesture both Eastern and Western in character. From the Western point of view, the veil is a Surrealist gesture, as suggested earlier—a juxtaposition that shocks the viewer's routine sense of order. From the Japanese point of view, the veil and cord tenderly hung about the stone recall the Shinto tradition of *iwakura*, sacred boulders typically festooned with cords and paper talismans. Just as the recessed circle partially reveals what lies within, so the veil partially conceals what was revealed. We enter here into a play of "shown-unshown," in the compact phrase from Hindu scripture:[2] the concealed revealed, the revealed enigmatically concealed in a way that forces search for an "answer" to this *koan* in stone. *Koan* are the irrational, riddling questions given Zen students for solution; the answers may take years to find.[3]

Noguchi's stone *koan* admits of no easy answer. It seems to address the powers of penetration of human consciousness and to favor vigorous use of that consciousness while recognizing that our discoveries are incomplete, reality going far beyond us. *Consciousness* here must mean not just thought but something more like total intelligence or attention. The deliberate veiling becomes a playful yet reverent sign of acceptance both of our power and of our ignorance.

GREAT GOOD FORTUNE

Born in Los Angeles in 1904, son of the noted Japanese poet Yone Noguchi and his American wife Leonie Gilmour, a teacher and writer herself, Noguchi spent much of his childhood in Japan attending Japanese and Jesuit schools.[4] Early photographs reflect his mixed background—in one he is a handsome late-Victorian youngster with a fine straw hat and fetching curls, in another he is a Japanese child immersed in a glum class portrait with other boys and girls. He was fortunate in his parents—Leonie in the early years and Yone later. Leonie "farmed him off," as he said, while still very young to a country carpenter for training over and above his school obligations. He acquired at an early age the respect for materials and tools that would never leave him.

Somewhat ill at ease in Japan, where children of mixed parentage were rare, he was sent by his mother to an experimental school in Indiana in 1918, and after further adventures found himself finishing high school in La Porte, Indiana, supported emotionally and intellectually by astute parental surrogates. Expressing interest in a career as a sculptor, he was apprenticed briefly to Gutzon Borglum, sculptor of the Mount Rushmore presidents, but Borglum discouraged him from pursuing a career in art. He undertook premedical studies at Columbia University. At his mother's urging, however, he resumed his study of sculpture by enrolling in a private New York school directed by Onorio Ruotolo. Under Ruotolo's capable guidance, Noguchi's prodigious innate skill asserted itself. Within a very short time he became an accomplished academic sculptor; a photograph from the early 1920s shows him with a marble carving of a serpentine female nude, a technically splendid, potently sexual image. He was clearly destined to be a sculptor—but where his skills, acquired so quickly, would lead was uncertain.

An exhibition of Brancusi sculpture in New York in 1926 marked the beginning of a key passage toward himself. "I was transfixed by his vision," Noguchi wrote years later.[5] He understood through Brancusi that abstraction was the essential language of our time, or so it seemed to him. He soon applied for a Guggenheim Foundation grant that would permit him to widen his horizons and, among other things, study in Paris. That grant application, luckily preserved, introduces us to the mind of a preternaturally sophisticated twenty-two-year-old; it formulates ideas that he would only realize decades later.

> It is my desire to view nature through nature's eyes, and to ignore man as an object for special veneration. There must be unthought of heights of beauty to which sculpture may be raised by this reversal of attitude. . . . Indeed, a fine balance of spirit with matter can only concur when the artist has so thoroughly submerged himself in the study of the unity of nature as to truly become once more a part of nature—a part of the very earth, thus to view the inner surfaces and the life elements. . . . As yet, I have never executed any of these ideas. I have rather been saving them as sacred until such time as I should have attained technical confidence and skill. . . .[6]

In various writings and interviews over the years, Noguchi has evoked the events that followed immediately on his arrival in Paris as a

Guggenheim Fellow. Predestination was at work with effortless precision. At the Cafe Sélect, where (in one version) he stopped alone for a drink, an American who happened to be sitting nearby leaned over and, striking up a conversation, asked him what he would like to be doing in Paris. Noguchi answered that he would like to meet Brancusi, and the well-connected American replied that it could easily be arranged.[7] Within days, at a meeting in Brancusi's studio, some quality in the young man must have touched Brancusi, who disliked teaching and guarded the privacy of his working hours. He invited Noguchi to work in his studio as an apprentice. Noguchi continues:

> Great good fortune such as this has something of the divine and inevitable. . . . He spoke no English and I no French. Communication was through the eyes, through gesture and through the materials and tools to be used. Brancusi would show me for instance precisely how a chisel should be held and how to true a plane of limestone. He would show me by doing it himself, indicating that I should do the same. Certainly I was no help to him whatsoever in the beginning. . . .[8]

Writing a few years later, Noguchi added:

> I was privileged . . . to observe Brancusi in mid-career, at the height of his powers, most generous to me, and always with his eyes smiling. He was by then fully established as the person he remained to the end. All white. . . . Brancusi tried to din into me the need of tedious and exacting work. "Concentrate and stop looking out the window!" he would shout. Or, "Whatever you do, it is not for fun or for study. You must treat it as the best thing you will ever do."[9]

Noguchi's experience with and *of* Brancusi was formative. Later friendships and working collaborations would influence Noguchi deeply—he has always been both original and receptive. But Brancusi remained in a category apart as both the master with whom he apprenticed and the predecessor who, more than any, haunted him. Sons and daughters in art choose their fathers and mothers in art (or feel themselves to be imperiously chosen by them), as Harold Bloom has taught—so creating for themselves both a resource and an anxiety.[10] Brancusi initiated Noguchi into the language of abstraction and the avant-garde. He also initiated him into a view of art and craftsmanship that was timeless and placeless, although Noguchi was to find it more intact in Japan than in the West, when he sought assistants to help him with his later work.

Returning to New York after a year and a half in Paris, Noguchi formed a friendship with Buckminster Fuller, who was already in the late 1920s a visionary architect, engineer, and planetary planner. Fuller complemented and nourished the American side of Noguchi's nature, a side that had no fear of sheet metal, technology, and industrial tools. Noguchi accepted and worked comfortably in a Constructivist language that valued bold but harmonious forms rendered in modern materials by modern methods. Even late in life, when the center of gravity of his work had shifted toward a Japanese aesthetic, he occasionally produced works of Constructivist inspiration, sometimes to massive scale, which would have been comprehensible and congenial to Tatlin or Rodchenko (Fig. 86). There was a simple and touching symmetry between Brancusi and Fuller, each avant-garde in his own way: Brancusi searching beyond established norms for the essence of Nature, Fuller searching beyond established norms for supremely logical approaches to fundamental needs such as shelter and locomotion. It was Noguchi who built the clay models for Fuller's bizarre three-wheeled Dymaxion Car at a factory in Bridgeport, Connecticut, during the Depression. Noguchi was, of course, aware of the complementary nature of his apprenticeship with Brancusi and his friendship with Fuller:

> . . . in Paris . . . I had come under the great influence of Constantin Brancusi. . . . But I should say that after returning to New York I was in a sense in revolt against his too-idealizing influence. Bucky was for me the truth of structure which circumvented questions of art.[11]

Noguchi was fortunate to earn his living early by his art, in years when few artists could. He paid a curious penalty for his ability: in the Depression years, when many American artists were linked together in the fraternity of the Federal Arts Project, the New Deal program supporting both studio arts and art for public places such as post office murals, Noguchi was excluded from the program because he had other income. It was his fluent ability to catch a likeness in portrait busts that served him in these years. On the strength of his earnings, he was able in 1930 to make his first return to the Far East as an adult, studying painting in Beijing and later pottery in Kyoto with a noted artisan. In Tokyo, he reencountered his father, who proved willing after a gap of many years to introduce him to the cultural life of Tokyo and lay the groundwork that would allow his son to function as a Japanese artist. Years later, remembering his apprenticeship in Kyoto, Noguchi wrote:

86. Isamu Noguchi. *Horace E. Dodge and Son Memorial Fountain,* Detroit Civic Center Plaza, 1972–78. Stainless steel with granite base, electricity, and water. Height 24'. Photo: Balthazar Korab, courtesy of the artist.

I have since thought of my lonely self-incarceration then, and my close embrace of the earth, as a seeking after identity with some primal matter beyond personalities and possessions. In my work I wanted something irreducible, an absence of the gimmicky and clever.[12]

There were other promising beginnings in the 1930s. On his return to New York, his American home, he forged a working relationship with Martha Graham and designed over the years a considerable number of stage sets for her new dance productions. They were not just passive backdrops but active participants that provided shapes, platforms, spatial structures around which Graham composed. Noguchi regards his work for the stage as a training that directly contributed to his gardens and other public settings in later years. In 1933 he designed on paper and in plaster a pair of large-scale land sculptures that we would now call earthworks.[13] *Play Mountain,* an abstract, multitiered environment resembling an ancient amphitheater, was the precursor of many designs for children's playgrounds. All creative people seem to need at least one implacable adversary, and Noguchi had his in Robert Moses, the celebrated New York public works manager. He prevented the realization of a Noguchi playground in New York, although Noguchi offered a number of designs over the years with the support of highly respectable allies.

Noguchi had his early public success in New York, however, when he won a competition for a relief sculpture to surmount the entrance to the Associated Press building at Rockefeller Center. In 1938–39 he created the massive stainless-steel plaque which is there to this day. In a heroic, simplified style learned in part from the Mexican muralists with whom he had worked for a time in the mid-1930s, it depicts an airborne swarm of journalists writing, telephoning, photographing, typing. Best viewed as a period piece reflecting the taste of an era unready for stridently innovative art in public places and yet unwilling to be blatantly conservative, it is a Depression-era Correggio that doesn't come off very well. There is almost infinite distance between its heaviness and the subtlety of Noguchi's Chase Manhattan Plaza stone garden further downtown in New York, from 1960–64 (Fig. 87). Referring to the traditional Japanese garden through its carefully selected stones and sculpted, patterned pavement, while drawing from twentieth-century abstraction in the overall freedom of its composition, the Chase Manhattan garden is both ancient and modern—and so, to a degree, timeless.

87. Isamu Noguchi. *Chase Manhattan Bank Plaza Garden,* 1961–64 (Skid-more, Owings & Merrill, architects). Photo: Arthur Lavine, courtesy of Chase Manhattan Archives.

How did he move from the one to the other, from work narrowly of its era to work of much larger scope? Between the Rockefeller Center relief and the confirmed maturity of the Chase garden, much had to happen. One of Noguchi's most interesting "periods" occurred in the mid-1940s, when he assembled thin slabs of polished stone as if they were parts of a vertical jigsaw puzzle into intricate, formally intriguing works. Brilliant as they were, they owed a great deal to earlier Picasso drawings and did not yet fully declare Noguchi's own identity. The key episodes in a remarkable transformation occurred in the 1950s, begin-ning with Noguchi's return to postwar Japan. He had received a num-ber of demanding commissions, among them the sculptural aspects of a pair of bridges in Hiroshima and a garden for the Reader's Digest building in Tokyo. Transformation and maturation will always remain a partial mystery. Much as one can trace an emerging vision in a se-quence of works, one cannot fully trace the internal life that sponsors and needs it. One day, artists find themselves thinking a new thought, making a new gesture.

Noguchi's new gesture occurred in a Japan to which he was linked by blood and culture, and whose plight in the postwar years could not help but stir him. "[People] wanted to look to me," he reported in 1950,

> to show them how to function again after the long years of total-
> itarian misdirection of all energies, and I found it a duty to do what I
> could to help prime the pump of their renaissance. . . . Many Japa-
> nese, having seen much of Western culture, turn appreciatively to
> their ancient heritage. But, of course, old things cannot, and should
> not, be copied because no copy ever resurrected anything. There is
> only birth or no birth, and birth is that total thing that comes from
> within. . . . So the new Orient must come fresh born of itself. . . . An
> innocent synthesis must rise from the embers of the past.[14]

Always fortunate in his teachers, Noguchi went "down into the mud" for the Reader's Digest project, as he said, to learn garden design from a professional artisan who understood how to search for appropriate stones, how to assess their individual natures, how to design with stone and plant, water and space. His work and thought from this time forward are marked by this experience of mud and metaphysics, which was extended when he accepted the commission to create a Japanese garden for the UNESCO building in Paris. On this occasion, he worked with a master Japanese garden designer who took him to distant wilderness sites in search of stones.

Noguchi's work in the 1950s marks his coming of age—not as an artist (his technical skill and imaginative powers were evident by the early 1930s), not even as an artist of international stature (he was already recognized), but as a contributor to the modern spiritual. The UNESCO garden (Fig. 88), perhaps his finest work of that decade, combines some of the norms of the traditional Japanese garden with a Constructivist sense of geometry and a forthright use of modern structural materials. The result is not pastiche but something new and whole. One photograph captures little of it: there is a kind of perfection in *this* stone, *that* pattern, *this* transition, *this* detail, *that* emptiness. It all exemplifies what Noguchi meant years later when he spoke of "the brilliance of matter."[15] The weight and texture of stone, the mobility of water, the infinite variety of plants, and the transparency of space were his compositional elements in the UNESCO garden, and they were well served. It is also worth noting that the design pays homage to Brancusi in the stark geometry of its outdoor seating; Noguchi did not forget Brancusi's park setting at Tirgu Jiu.

88. Isamu Noguchi. *UNESCO Gardens*, Paris, 1956–58. Photo: courtesy of the artist.

Noguchi reasons effectively and economically about discoveries made through his work. In *The World of a Sculptor*, his autobiography, he spoke of his passage from traditional norms to their application and modification in the UNESCO garden:

> To learn but still to control so strong a tradition is a challenge. My effort was to find a way to link that ritual of rocks which has come down to us through the Japanese from the dawn of history to our modern times and needs. In Japan, the worship of stones changed into an appreciation of nature. The search for the essence of sculpture seems to carry me to the same end.[16]

I think it significant that he describes the Japanese as a channel for age-old perceptions rather than as the sole author and, in effect, owner of those perceptions. Noguchi succeeded in transferring the traditional Japanese garden aesthetic into this century as an art of our own, Japanese yet international, obviously traditional yet obviously modern. "Contrary to most Japanese gardens," he told an interviewer,

> the UNESCO garden is intended to be walked in. The vista constantly changes and, everything being relative, things suddenly loom

up in scale as others diminish. The real purpose of the garden may be this contemplation of the relative in space, time, and life.[17]

From this point forward in Noguchi's career, there is an embarrassment of riches. Readers will have already recognized that his version of the sculptor's calling includes but goes well beyond the production of works for exhibition. After the UNESCO project, there was a steady stream of commissions for art in public places, ranging in character from the superb geometer's courtyard at Yale University[18] to the Constructivist bravado of the Detroit fountain (Fig. 86) to the somewhat traditional Japanese stepped foyer for a Tokyo school of flower arrangement—an "interior mountain," as he called it, produced in collaboration with the architect, Kenzo Tange.[19] In the early 1950s, Noguchi also launched a business adapting the traditional skills of Japanese paper lantern-makers to the needs of modern electrical lighting. His designs in translucent paper and light, which he regarded as sculpture, remain to this day objects of simple beauty and no great expense, easily enough obtained. "I often craved," he wrote in 1968,

> to bring sculpture into a more direct involvement with the common experience of living. At such times I felt there must be a more direct way of contact than the rather remote one of art. . . .[20]

In an interview also of that year, when a retrospective exhibition of his work in New York commanded much attention, he added vividly to this thought:

> At one point . . . , when I became disillusioned about my function in the art world, I decided I would work in some other field—but still as an artist. And so I did furniture and lamps, and things like that. . . . I don't consider myself a high priest of art. . . . I am a practical artist.[21]

Sam Hunter has commented on the difficulties with art critics that Noguchi's diversity earned him.[22] Disguised by its modern setting and sculptural language, his performance has been that of a "Renaissance man." He has demonstrated the diversity of application of a single well-furnished mind to which the phrase refers; he gives it new and solid meaning.

ONLY STONES

Yet he has enjoyed all the fame an artist could wish. In 1980, two prominent New York galleries celebrated his seventy-fifth birthday with simultaneous exhibitions and a handsome catalogue that focused for the most part on recent work in granite and basalt—hard stones not typically attractive to sculptors. He had been led to them by his garden projects, and they came gradually to dominate his later work, although he periodically relaxed his preoccupation with hard stone by working with modern processed materials and geometric forms, reflecting his affinity for Buckminster Fuller's thinking. His stoneworks reflect in their own way a dialogue between ancient and modern. "The presumption to work as I do," he has written,

> comes from the ability of new tools to incise our will upon matter—like a meeting from the opposite ends of time to resume on another level the continuity that has gone on for eons.[23]

He achieved the smooth cylindrical borings, even seams, and apparently effortless cutting strokes of his later work in hard stone with the help of the diamond saws and drills of modern quarry technology. The tools have not mastered the man.

Much of Noguchi's thought in later years has revolved around the intrinsic qualities of stone, the process of working it, and the perceptions that gather as he works. It was an old attraction, dating to his apprenticeship with Brancusi, renewed from time to time in the intervening years. In 1957, in a brief review celebrating the opening of the Museum of Primitive Art in New York, he dwelt on the power of stone to evoke religious feelings:

> There are only stones exhibited in the room we enter. Is this why a vibrant power fills the place? . . . If this is a chapel, it is not one for any known religion.[24]

A pair of works in the seventy-fifth birthday exhibitions (Figs. 89, 90) can help us to see as he did. *Double Red Mountain* of 1969 is one of a series of "Landscape Tables" exploring the poetry of relationship between a generally smooth, polished plane and one or more forms rising from it like a mountain or wave. The best of these works, although not large, possess extraordinary silence and monumentality. One feels oneself in the presence of a highly significant object, not dedicated to "any known religion" but dedicated nonetheless—to the Earth. *Double Red Mountain* is an American conception—the isolated cliffs of Monument Valley lie somewhere in its background—but it also evokes the towering mountain landscapes of classical Chinese painting. Without anecdotal foolishness, it evokes as well the breasts of the Great Mother, Earth itself, no less than the age-old image of the Sacred Mountain (Sinai, Olympus, and Kailasa) and the emergence of

89. Isamu Noguchi. *Double Red Mountain*, 1969. Persian Red Travertine. 30″ × 40″ × 40″. Photo: Wernher Krutein, courtesy of the artist.

terra firma from the waters, with all the promise that Noah perceived in that saving emergence. These condensed references lie easy on the object, so to speak; the sculpture is not a homily on archetypal symbolism but a work of art with its own integrity. In visual terms, Noguchi has achieved a great deal through the simple contrast of polished and seemingly weathered surfaces. The tautness of the rectangular plane and mountain summits contrasts vividly with roughened zones implying growth, movement, and the erosions of age. The work has the compactness and intensity of a traditional Japanese tea house piece—the single work of art or flower placed in an alcove at the entrance to the tea house.

90. Isamu Noguchi. *Intetra,* 1979. Aji Granite. 16½″ × 24½″ × 23″. Photo: Michio Noguchi, courtesy of the artist.

Double Red Mountain meets an intimate criterion of excellence in sculpture: it prompts the realization that one has been asleep—asleep to real values, to beauty, and to one's own physical presence, which awakens in response to the physical presence of the sculpture. The analogy of sleep and awakening is intrinsic to Noguchi's vision, as the following section will make clear, but it is not too soon to listen as he evokes the mysterious relation between primary earth materials and our own natures.

Sculpture may be made of anything and will be valued for its intrinsic sculptural properties. However, it seems to me that the natural mediums of wood and stone, alive before man was, have the greater capacity to comfort us with the reality of our being. . . .[25]

Noguchi was moving in these years at a fundamental level in his art. At its frequent best, his later work has the capacity expressed with such originality in this passage.

A more modest work, easily overlooked, is his *Intetra* (Fig. 90). Basalt shaped again into a mountain form, its appeal depends on a number of simple contrasts: the organic, life-swollen quality of the overall form in contrast to the meticulous seams, the rough skin in contrast to the smooth and quiet opening into the stone, the overall triangular mass in contrast to the tetrahedra and central triangular space generated by the pattern of cuts. This is a Philosopher's Stone; one may well be impressed and stilled by it—yet wonder what it is about. Mid-twentieth-century art criticism would answer that it is about nothing apart from what we see: it is about these forms, these textures, and their interaction. But that answer leaves one hungry; there must be more. Noguchi himself has declared his freedom from that style of observation:

> I'm more interested in *what* I'm *expressing* than how I express it. If I became too involved with how, the work would become separated from the fundamental question of art—which for me is the *meaning* of a thing, the evocative essence which moves us.[26]

The evocative essence here must be the perennial mystery of relationship between the whole and its parts, associated with a visual meditation on the balance between symmetry and asymmetry in the order of Nature. These words are cold, but the sculpture itself is not cold: there we can see a whole subtly divided into parts without loss of integrity, and a play of geometry that is quite regular yet curiously irregular—like life itself. In effect, Noguchi gives sculptural form to Mondrian's concern with "dynamic equilibrium," the coming together of unequal forces in a whole and peaceful pattern. "Nature is that forever changing indeterminacy which is everywhere in asymmetric triangulation,"[27] Noguchi wrote by way of explanation—nicely obscure—in his notes for the 1986 Biennale exhibition. Clear in this compact, Mondrian-like remark is an acute awareness of change and order bound together in Nature and, by extension, in ourselves.

Both *Double Red Mountain* and *Intetra* are highly worked pieces in which the artist has entirely reshaped the natural stone. Many of Noguchi's later works represent a dialogue with stone that leaves it partially unworked—a dialogue of "chance no chance," he has written, of "mistakes no mistakes."[28] The sculptor's interventions are crucial and often extensive, but they leave intact much of the stone as it was pried from the quarry. The distant but unforgotten Western source for these works is Michelangelo's *Prisoners,* figures only partially released from the stone; the Eastern source is, as so often, the garden in which stones are aligned to human purpose without being altered in their own natures. Noguchi's works in basalt can be especially magical, owing in part to the contrast between the weathered outer skin of the stone and the pristine dark interior revealed by the sculptor's tools. This simple visual cue conveys a dramatic sense of two forces fusing in the work of art: the sculptor's shaping intention and the inherent strength of the stone itself. "Through the artist's hand," Noguchi has said,

> we arrive at a different epoch in the history of the primordial stone. All that I do is to provide the invasion of a different time element into the time of nature. My marks and modeling are a kind of definition, in an undefined nature, of our incursions. It represents a contract between myself and nature.[29]

Great Rock of Inner Seeking (Figs. 91, 92) is a truly commanding abstract sign, part stone calligraphy, part Easter Island head of massive size and presence. Its front and back differ entirely from each other, the front a forcefully carved but peaceful calligraphic sign, the back an intense pattern of drillmarks, pecking, and planes of relief that suggests the cloak—and character—of a Zen or Taoist patriarch. The two sides of the stone reflect two dominant aspects of "inner seeking" that, in many people's experience, need to be reconciled over and over again: a certain detachment and a certain passion, a cool metaphysical attitude and a willingness to suffer. The sculpture is, of course, not an allegory or illustration, it is grandly abstract. But it does suggest ideas of this order without imposing any idea at all.

The powers of stone are evident here, powers that Noguchi has not tired of investigating in his work and in after-hours conversation.

> [Stone] is a direct link to the heart of matter—a molecular link. When I tap it, I get the echo of that which we are—in the solar plexus—in the center of gravity of matter. Then, the whole universe has a resonance![30]

This is Kandinsky's intuition—"the world sounds"—in a sculptor's physical version.

In 1986, Noguchi opened the Isamu Noguchi Garden Museum in

91. Isamu Noguchi. *Great Rock of Inner Seeking,* 1974 (front view). Basalt. Height 10′7⅞″. National Gallery of Art, Washington. Gift of Arthur M. Sackler, M.D., and Mortimer D. Sackler, M.D.

92. Isamu Noguchi. *Great Rock of Inner Seeking,* 1974 (back view). Basalt. Height 10′7⅞″. National Gallery of Art, Washington. Gift of Arthur M. Sackler, M.D., and Mortimer D. Sackler, M.D.

Long Island City, an industrial neighborhood just across a bridge from Manhattan. Its building was his studio for many years, and he retains studio space there, but the majority of its expansive, unheated halls, adjoining an outdoor garden for stone sculpture, is dedicated to preserving and showing representative works from every period. That he conceived the idea of a museum at all is, of course, audacious. In the gesture there is not only a high estimate of the value of his work—in my view, justified; there is Brancusi. Brancusi bequeathed his studio to the French national museums on condition that it be preserved just as he left it and, although the studio was eventually moved, it has in fact been faithfully preserved. Something of his gesture is reflected in Noguchi's. Between artistic children and parents, as between spiritual sons or daughters and their parents, there is a lifetime of dialogue which continues in total disregard of physical disappearance.

In the entrance to the Noguchi Museum, and here and there in its rooms and garden, great stones stand guard. However varied in outward form, they have in common a peculiar silence and solitude which are the signature of Noguchi's mature work. Noguchi's art at its best is saturated with consciousness—aesthetic consciousness in the sense that the forms are entirely *seen,* even those left untouched; metaphysical consciousness in the sense that his work speaks simultaneously of meaning and emptiness, symbol and sheer being. This is no small achievement.

What does his phrase mean, "to comfort us with the reality of our being"? It must depend on the perception that human nature is a blend of awarenesses and faculties, always moving or so it seems, subject to profuse illusions—yet building on something hidden and enduring, unchangeably itself. Stone, for Noguchi, recalls the imperishable in Nature and in man.

THE INVOCATION IS STILL TO GOD

We have entered reasonably deeply into Noguchi's art and thought, but a number of his essential concerns have not yet found their place. The recurrent question of this book regarding the relation between art and teachings—and between artists and the teachings they may encounter—comes into sharp focus where Noguchi is concerned. Japanese-American, bilingual, so genuinely at home in both cultures that he has for years maintained homes and studios in both countries, he was uniquely placed among artists to undertake formal Zen practice. To the best of my knowledge he did not do so, although his mature work is saturated with the specific atmosphere and values of Zen: the adherence to Nature, the genius for abstraction, the meticulousness, the ability to evoke a sense of transcendent order through aesthetic gesture without heavy doctrinal reference. Something of Noguchi's mind remains to be discovered—not for the sake of biography, but because it is exemplary both for what it includes and for what it excludes.

Noguchi's mother raised him on the poets of the Irish Renaissance,

William Blake, and Greek mythology. These were the first layers of enlightened dreaming. The second was Swedenborgian thought, encountered as an adolescent through Samuel Mack, pastor of the local Swedenborgian church in La Porte, Indiana, with whose family Noguchi
boarded for three years. It seems not to have greatly marked him, although he has commented that Blake came up again in this context,
owing to the poet's preoccupation with Swedenborg. Another layer of
dreaming—its enlightenment doubtful—was occasioned by his first
serious art teacher, Onorio Ruotolo, director of the Leonardo da Vinci
Art School in New York and a committed "spiritist."

> Ruotolo was a very interesting man, a Neapolitan, very handsome,
> who had done various heads such as Caruso and Helen Keller. He
> was interested in the avant-garde of the mind. At that time, New
> York was overflowing with interest in Houdini and in psychic mani-
> festations, and Ruotolo became interested. We attempted table-
> turning, levitations, things like that. A group of Italian doctors was
> interested in the subject, and I accompanied them to seances. In fact,
> I was charged to take photographs of whatever appeared, the ecto-
> plasm. My photographs were developed in a drugstore and, sure
> enough, there it was. The tables moved, I swear I saw a pencil get up
> and write on a pad. . . . This groaning and what-not took place be-
> hind a black screen. . . . The medium's name was Nino Palendino.
> Ruotolo always claimed that he taught me psychically. . . . As for
> myself, I didn't feel I was working hard, I was merely in a kind of
> daze, doing things, you know. . . .[31]

There seems to be no substantial influence at all of these early psychic
escapades in Noguchi's maturity. Yet he remembered; a passage in his
autobiography charmingly describes the artist as a medium of the old-
fashioned kind:

> What is the artist but the channel through which spirits descend—
> ghosts, visions, portents, the tinkling of bells?[32]

A fourth layer of influence that he absorbed cannot fairly be described as enlightened dreaming. It was the direct influence of one of
the cardinal teachers of the century, D. T. Suzuki, whom he met at Columbia University seminars in the 1950s—and perhaps knew already
in the 1930s. After the war, Suzuki was a discreet yet immensely influential figure, whose expositions of Zen reached right across America,
from John Cage in music to Thomas Merton in monastic Catholicism
to Jack Kerouac in literature and to Alan Watts in what would soon

become the human potential movement. "He was a much older man," Noguchi has remarked, "much older than anyone. . . . He was not a stranger, but I came to see him more in Japan." "I am not a beater of the more obvious links of art to the spirit," he went on to say—but it seems a fateful coming together that Noguchi had access to Suzuki in the 1950s at the time when he was learning garden design, closely linked to Zen, from traditional artisans. This was the mud and metaphysics that helped to form his mature art.

Obviously not naive about the content of formal Zen teaching, Noguchi seems to have felt at home with the scholarly version offered by Suzuki and with the direct apprehensions made possible by practical work in the garden tradition. "With Zen," he has said,

> there is a more direct linkage [to art] than through other mystical forms. It is the spiritual as direct appreciation of the thing itself. It is like a reverse linkage: you can't say whether art came from the spiritual, or vice versa.

This emphasis on direct appreciation allowed Noguchi to steer a course around Zen, insofar as formal Zen practice makes substantial demands on an individual's time and elicits some degree of sectarian thinking. Asked whether art without the support of a spiritual teaching is an adequate means of refining the individual, Noguchi responded in terms that acknowledge Zen without identifying with it.

> I don't think that art comes from art. A lot of artists apparently think so. I think it comes from the awakening person. Awakening is what you might call the spiritual. It is a linkage to something flowing very rapidly through the air, and I can put my finger on it [*he raises his finger as if to connect with something above him*] and plug in, so to speak. Do artists need a spiritual way or do they need art? You can say that one is the same as the other. Everything tends toward awakening, and I would rather use the word *awakening* than a word derived from some system—because there are many systems.

"Something flowing very rapidly" is the prime mover, which can be experienced by the artist and creative people but not closely defined without loss.

> I would say from my own experience that the motivation [for art] doesn't come from religious formulations or anything of that kind. These formulations are, in a sense, refractions of the main flow which comes from something else. It always comes from something

else, indirectly, in a flow. With some people, it comes with less obstruction.

Here, in the idea of obstruction, Noguchi recognizes the artist's most intimate work: working *with* himself or herself, and working *against,*

> . . . to break away from barriers like habit and convenience and fear and accommodation—barriers which afflict everybody, not just artists. But the artist tries to overcome such barriers, especially barriers of the self and what one thinks about art, for instance. Everything becomes in time a barrier. Everything becomes in time an opportunity. I don't try to speak in riddles, but that's the way it is.

Eastern and Western, modern and ancient in methods and aesthetic, religious without affiliation, Noguchi emerges preeminently as an individual who has tested values, and tested himself, through his art. Art was the focus, early and late. In 1949, in a lecture at Yale University, he all but predicted the character of his art in years to come and renewed the challenge that he had inherited directly from Brancusi, indirectly from Kandinsky. It was a challenge he met.

> If religion dies as dogma, it is reborn as a direct personal expression in the arts. I do not refer to work done in churches . . . but to the almost religious quality of ecstasy and anguish to be found emerging here and there in so-called abstract art. Using the ever more perceptive truths of nature's structure, the invocation is still to God. I see no conflict between spirituality and modern art as some do; rather it opens another channel to our non-anthropomorphic deity.[33]

19 MODEST MASTERS

German art history has the charming word *Kleinmeister*—little master—for skilled artists who remain somewhat in the background. Living in periods of imaginative or technical innovation, *Kleinmeister* add to the general lustre of their times without drawing a great deal of attention to themselves. Their style may be a little old-fashioned, their imaginative concerns slightly out of step, their workshops in provincial centers; nonetheless they make their mark.

The modest masters in this chapter possess some of these characteristics. Unlike *Kleinmeister,* most of them enjoyed international fame, but they were personally retiring, unwilling for the most part to cut a public figure or engage in prolonged controversy. Their art is quiet and richly contemplative, an exercise in awareness as much as in style. They often worked the same vein for years, sure that there was more to be discovered in a simple still life, a landscape that others might not notice, or a certain quality of gesture.

One was something of a hermit; another scarcely left the region where he was born, as if he had taken a vow of stability; a third remained discreetly out of sight during the long years when his government meddled with the arts. A few were miniaturists in spirit or in fact. One found her art early and, hardly changing for decades thereafter, was serenely indifferent to the avant-garde. Two found their most memorable art late in life and will be remembered for what they were as older artists beyond the pulls of fashion or ambition. Their biographies differ, but they have in common dedication, penetrating intelligence, and love of simplicity. Their work imposes itself for these very reasons.

BEN NICHOLSON: ABSTRACT ART— POWERFUL, UNLIMITED

Ben Nicholson (1894–1982) is not often considered a master-artist of the age. Prominent, yes; interesting, surely; but second tier. Yet his work would fit easily, and justly, in any of three chapters in this book. His decades-long series of shallow reliefs (Fig. 93), a form of collage, participated richly in the Mediterranean ethos. He worked in a refined Cubist language from the 1930s forward, much of his best work occurring in the 1960s when Cubism was supposed to be a thing of the past. He was unquestionably a modest master whose first loyalty was to a quiet, exquisitely studied art that nourishes those who see its strengths—and that seems uncomfortably plain to others.

The son of two British artists (his father William was well known in his day), Nicholson studied briefly ˙ ˙ the Slade School of Art but only began to find his way in the early 1930s. Sharing a studio in those years with his second wife, Barbara Hepworth (see chapter 23), he began to assimilate the lessons of Picasso, Braque, Mondrian, Brancusi, and Arp, all of whom he had met under more than casual circumstances. The art that emerged—a new approach to collage and a wiry, taut draftsmanship—was well tuned by the mid-1930s, although it brought him widespread and deserved recognition only after World War II.

We have had occasion to recognize that the Cubist collage was—and continues to be—a visual sonnet, a refined mutual adjustment of elements within the limited world of the picture. Practicing a kind of alchemy, the artist combines handmade elements with castoffs from the world at large—bits of newspaper, theater tickets, anything at all of arresting texture, color, or shape—and works them into a new and harmonious whole. There is much fulfillment in this simple act for both artist and viewer, the artist exercising aesthetic faculties with great intent, the viewer experiencing the results as a welcome call to attention. Collage is a Western *ikebana*, an art of arrangement, and like Japanese flower arrangement its aesthetic impact can go far beyond the separate impacts of the materials it employs.

Woven into its aesthetic dimension, collage has ethical, political, and spiritual dimensions. On the ethical plane, the making of small, studied worlds affirms the human need for order in an era hardly satisfactory in that regard. In relation to politics, collage and its cousin photomontage have long been effective media for communication and protest through their potential for stark juxtapositions; they offer opportunities for dynamic *dis*harmony. More intimately, collage permits exploration of the guiding powers within the self and fosters reawakened sensitivity to small differences. It can serve as a meditation for the artist who patiently assembles an unexpected order, and for the viewer

93. Ben Nicholson. *Decor for 7th Symphony Ballet (4th Movement). White Relief, Version 1,* 1939. Oil on carved wood. 15¼″ × 19½″. Norton Simon Art Foundation.

who is led to reexperience his or her own sense of order. At best, art occasions this kind of sharing—the artist leading into a realm, the viewer following but just as much at home there as the artist, who has the imaging gift but no exclusive privilege.

Thin lines of light and shadow, pristine circle and square, surfaces with the feel of old architectural stone—these are the elements of Ben Nicholson's art of shallow relief. One of the quietest arts of the century, it subverts ideas of "greatness" and glamour by making them seem superficial in comparison with its pure intensity. It is an art of memory, appealing to people who are sensitive to nostalgia for ancient times, places, and moods. Collecting above all the forms and sensations of Greek architecture and relief sculpture, not literally but in essence, it delivers them into the miniature world of the collage.

Nicholson's work may seem sheltered, distant, cool—criticisms well taken, but in no way infringing upon the integrity of the task in art that Nicholson made his own: to create works that call and enrich attention through subtle relationships of form, color, texture, space, and light. Looking with care at a simple but accomplished example of his art such as the relief illustrated here, the viewer cannot help but rediscover the force of his or her own attention moving over the surface of the work, savoring the clean lines of light or shadow, stepping psychically from plane to plane as if through a curiously bare but well-proportioned garden. This awakening of attention surely responds to the artist's studio experience; his work often bears witness to an experience of attention as the fundamental creative force, virtually a religious force. "Painting and religious experience are the same thing," Nicholson wrote in 1937,

> and what we are all searching for is the understanding and realization of infinity—an idea which is complete, with no beginning, no end, and therefore giving to all things for all time.
>
> Certainly this idea is to be found in mind and equally certainly it can never be found in the human mind, for so-called human power is merely a fantastic affair. . . . Painting and carving is one means of searching after this reality. . . .[1]

Nicholson's language is somewhat idiosyncratic, but it is clear that he defined his art in terms of a subtle process in the studio that brought him in touch with a new sense of reality. To speak of this as an awareness of "infinity" is no doubt exaggerated, but his art at best breeds confidence in the shaping power of human attention; it stirs up an odd faith that to exercise this power well is one of the finest things of all. Casual reality is countered by an intentional search that changes the seeker and the overall "feel" of life. Surely experiencing this more than once in the studio, Nicholson could write: "'Realism' has been abandoned in the search for reality. The 'principal objective' of abstract art is precisely this reality."[2]

A man who took joy in fine distinctions, Nicholson could be irritable with run-of-the-mill intellectuals. His work had been rejected often enough by critics and others who failed to grasp the refined intellectuality of its formal structures.

> This language is comprehensible to anyone who doesn't set up barriers—the dog and cat set up no barriers and their eyes, whiskers, and tails are alive, without restriction, but the whiskers of an intel-

lectual do not give off the necessary spark, and contact cannot be made.

I think that so far from being a limited expression, understood by a few, Abstract Art is a powerful, unlimited, and universal language.[3]

In museums across the world that show one or two pieces by Nicholson in rooms largely dedicated to more acclaimed artists, his work nonetheless stands out. Modest, soft-spoken, precise in its effects, conveying restrained ecstasy, it is at best a touchstone by which the quality of other art can be known.

GIORGIO MORANDI: A MEDITATION ON VISIBILITY

Through the ages, certain painters in Asia and the West have explored visibility. Visibility recalls the discriminating attention that scans the physical world, probes its fine phenomena, and governs the brushwork that records what is seen. It also evokes something of the physical world itself, which offers to whoever looks closely both kaleidoscopically changing appearances and a steady impression of the substantiality and shapeliness of things. The act of looking and the answering gift of intense visibility are mystery enough for those rare painters who find in them all the theology they need and their lifework. They love visibility, and they typically explore it with a certain selflessness, as if the grandeur and subtlety of the act of seeing, and of things seen, leave little room for a demanding ego. Giorgio Morandi (1890–1964) was a painter of this kind.

Morandi gave few interviews, but when he did so he spoke with a deliberation and clarity that make a biographical sketch largely unnecessary.

I have been fortunate enough to lead . . . an uneventful life. Only on very rare occasions have I ever left Bologna, my native city, and the surrounding province of Emilia. . . . When I was in my twenties, my highest ambition was to . . . study art in Paris. Unfortunately, the material difficulties involved were too great. . . . Later, I had too many responsibilities, with my teaching and my family. . . .

I have always led a very quiet and retiring life and never felt much urge to compete with other contemporary painters, whether in terms of productivity or in terms of exhibitions. . . .

I am essentially a painter of the kind of still-life composition that communicates a sense of tranquility and privacy, moods which I have always valued above all else.

When most Italian artists of my own generation were afraid to be too "modern," too "international" in their style, not "national" or "imperial" enough, I was still left in peace, perhaps because I demanded so little recognition. My privacy was thus my protection and, in the eyes of the Grand Inquisitors of Italian art, I remained but a provincial professor of etching, at the Fine Arts Academy of Bologna.[4]

After World War II, he was recognized internationally as something more than a provincial professor. Paintings from these later years—modest in scale, repetitive in theme, technically astute but never vain—are among the treasures of twentieth-century art.

When Morandi was starting out as a painter, Italy was loud. The Futurists, mixing genius with showmanship, were making their break *viva voce* from the academicism of nineteenth-century Italian art. Among them, Umberto Boccioni (1882–1916), who died in the war, achieved a memorable vision of structure and movement. Like Mondrian, another non-Parisian, he understood better than most of the artists working in the shadow of Picasso and Braque how to draw out the implications of Cubism. Also making their debut in Italy at the time were a number of so-called Metaphysical painters, precursors of the Surrealist movement, who were exploring the expressiveness of teasingly enigmatic motifs and a cleansed approach to form and space reminiscent of early Renaissance painting. Briefly associated with both groups, Morandi largely went his own way, perhaps more concerned than any to assimilate the art of early Italian masters from Giotto to Piero della Francesca, as well as the intimate art of Jan Vermeer and the work of French painters from Chardin to Corot, Seurat, and Cézanne. A list of celebrated names is hardly instructive, but it serves to illustrate that Morandi found an extensive natural lineage and did everything necessary to learn its lessons in depth. A thoroughly schooled painter, he nonetheless viewed pictorial tradition as a resource that needs to be absorbed and then forgotten for the artist who wishes to find his or her own truth:

The victories of artists who have preceded us are of interest to art history and not to the artist, be he painter or sculptor. Each one of those masters resolved the problem which his individuality had imposed on him, thus discharging his most noble duty.[5]

Morandi had few themes: the still life with bottles, pitchers, vases, cups, or canisters; landscape vignettes from the region of his summer home near Bologna; a few self-portraits and other themes, mostly from his youth. Regardless of medium—he was fluent in oil painting and etching—he remained faithful to this narrow range of themes throughout his career. The still life became his meditation on visibility. Visitors to his studio—just a room at the back of the apartment he shared with three unmarried sisters—remarked on the undisturbed, somehow poignant layer of dust on the objects that he rearranged for canvas after canvas. He was not a worldly man, but a man who had found his own world.

The meditative mind risks becoming muffled or dour. To turn away from the energy and pace of life in society can leave one empty until another quality of life makes itself known with some abundance. In his middle years—sad and dangerous years in the Italian national life— Morandi had already achieved the tranquility of his later art but not its exquisite light. In the postwar years, his canvases began to glow with a pale white light tinged with color; they gained an almost healing power, born of some new maturity and freedom. It is for the work of these years that he will long be remembered.

The Hamburg still life illustrated here (Fig. 94) beautifully represents his later years. Viewers with a knowledge of earlier European painting will instinctively assess the closely grouped bottles and pitchers as an abstract *sacra conversazione,* the typical altarpiece composition of the Renaissance in which saints and donors cluster around the Virgin and Child in a wordless "sacred conversation." Even without this association, the grouping is enough like a gathering of human beings to evoke subtle sympathy. Morandi establishes the group both as a unity and as a collection of separate objects. A continuous shared outline, uniformity of hue and intensity, soft contours suggesting transitions rather than breaks between objects, and an uninsistent spatial construction work together to define the objects as one mingled whole. But they are also clearly distinguished and free to conduct a little drama among themselves, deriving from their shapes, relative positions, and colors.

The placid axial order of the composition—four bottles across, pitchers in foreground and background—contrasts with subtle variations in light and color. The material presence of each object is both

94. Giorgio Morandi. *Still life,* 1957. Oil on canvas. 11″ × 16¼″. Hamburger Kunsthalle.

affirmed and softened or altered, so that each object *is* without violence. One's gaze rests gently on each. The dark wine bottles, for example, are affirmed as such, but their strolling outlines and receptive surfaces draw them into the poetry of visibility. The tall pitcher, half-seen behind, plays a compositional role, solidly closing off the group and reinforcing the central axis, but also plays a larger role by introducing a note of mystery. Ambiguously placed so that one can't fully imagine how it rests on the table, its oddness may prompt the viewer to reconsider the entire composition as a thought or metaphor.

The ambiguity of this passage in the painting and Morandi's delight in the geometry of the object-world recall the Cubist vision, to which he brings much. Placing us imaginatively at a midpoint between pure unchanging form and ceaseless change, he obliges us to sense both acutely. Further, he implicitly teaches us to savor small differences, to find unity among unlike things and distinction among like things—in a word, to see consciously.

Speaking of Cézanne and Monet, Morandi remarked that they were able even through simple objects to convey "a majesty of vision and an intensity of feeling to which we immediately respond."[6] As his interviewer, Roditi, recognized at once, the thought applies as much to Morandi as to his much-admired predecessors. Nowhere in Morandi's thought is there a formal metaphysic, an emphasis on spirituality as a concept, or any trace of need to go beyond art to find satisfactory depth of meaning. Like Ad Reinhardt, although without Reinhardt's anguished pressure, he thought in terms of "art as art." Depth of meaning was present in the process that he pursued and in its results. "I have always avoided suggesting any metaphysical implications," he said. "I suppose I remain, in that sense, a believer in Art for Art's sake rather than in Art for the sake of religion, of social justice or of national glory."[7] Within those limits, he found an affirmation of human awareness that recalls the simplicity of a Desert Father or early Greek philosopher who looked at experience with few concepts but keen attention.

To express what is in Nature, in the visible world, is my greatest interest.

The educational mission possible for figurative art, particularly at the present time, I believe to be that of communicating the images and feelings aroused in us by the visible world. . . . The creation or invention of an artist . . . has the capacity to break down the barriers, the conventional images that interpose themselves between oneself and things.

Remember Galileo: the true book of philosophy, the book of Nature, is written in letters foreign to our alphabet. These letters are: square, circle, sphere, pyramid, cone, and other geometric figures. I sense Galileo's thought in my long-standing conviction that the feelings and images aroused by the visible world, which is a formal world, are very difficult to express, or perhaps inexpressible in words. They are in fact feelings that have no relation, or a very indirect one, with daily emotions and interests, inasmuch as they have to do with forms, colors, space, light. . . . For me nothing is abstract; or rather, I think that nothing is more surreal and nothing more abstract than the real.[8]

With these words, Morandi carved out his domain and left no doubt that it can be approached only through a cultivated sensitivity to physical and visual experience. But he did not merely "see what was there." The reciprocity between seer and seen—between who one is and what one sees—is felt strongly in his work. Bringing a profoundly serious nature to bear on ordinary objects, he transformed them into what he was: silent, receptive, luminous, solitary yet bound into the whole.

JULIUS BISSIER: FALLING INTO ONE'S OWN ESSENCE

The art of Julius Bissier (1893–1965) is typically viewed as a footnote to the grander achievements of more celebrated artists. Both his own slow creative development and the wretched course of German history contribute to this limiting assessment. Warmly praised and clearly "promising" in the 1920s, he lost his university teaching post in his native Freiburg-im-Breisgau at the beginning of the Hitler regime and retreated into obscurity. He and his wife moved in 1939 to a village on the shores of Lake Constanz, where he continued secretly to pursue his work but showed nothing. By contributing decorative designs to his wife's weaving shop, he was able to help her bring in some income during these extremely lean years. This was the era when art that did not conform to the regime's preferences was considered *entartete*—degenerate—and artists in Germany were obliged to choose among conformity, obscurity, emigration, and persecution (not all were afforded even this range of choices). After the war, Bissier was overlooked until the mid-1950s, when a perceptive German museum director, Werner Schmalenbach, "discovered" him and brought his work to public attention through a major retrospective in 1958.[9] From that date until his death not many years later, Bissier was recognized, even beloved.

Advanced in age and confirmed in his taste for privacy, Bissier did not become a public figure, but his work—enchanting, light of touch, easily accessible yet profound—made its way around the world. Extracts from his diary of the 1940s, critical years in his creative development, were published in books and catalogues dedicated to his art. His words were striking, weighty; one glimpsed through them a struggle in the spiritual and aesthetic realms that had been conducted with total honesty, broad culture, and religious insight strengthened by modesty.

Then his moment was over. Bissier died, well-deserved homage was paid through retrospective exhibitions and books, and life moved on. His art and thought are now matters of historical record. But to what part of our history do they belong? By standard criteria, his work has been correctly identified as beautiful but secondary, not of the mainstream. However, in terms of the quest in this postreligious era for the spiritual in art, his work is both beautiful and primary. The mainstream flows a little differently when viewed in this light; it passed right through his studio.

"Pictures must come like breathing,"[10] wrote Bissier in his old age. But to reach the freedom which these simple words imply had cost a lifetime of effort. His first art, a rather dour realism with roots in the so-called New Objectivity of the 1920s, was compelling enough to win an important prize and government purchases in 1928, but when these encouraging events occurred he had already begun to move on. Bissier's world in these years was Freiburg, a small medieval city with a great intellectual tradition centered on the university. From 1929 to 1933, he taught drawing and composition in the university studios, as well as scientific drawing in zoology and dissection programs where he often worked from microscopic imagery. At the university, Bissier particularly befriended Ernst Grosse, an orientalist and author of a study of Far Eastern ink painting. The deeply formative exchange between them introduced Bissier to the Far Eastern sources that renewed his art when realism no longer held his attention.

Professionally committed to teaching traditional studio skills and exact drawing, Bissier totally revised his art in private after 1928. He experimented with various languages and themes until he settled in 1931 on monochrome ink brushwork—the classic Far Eastern medium—and on an evolving repertory of symbolic and calligraphic signs as his thematic focus. His first period of "inks," as he called them, extended from 1931 to about 1936. They encompassed heart-rending events in 1933–34, when he was dismissed from the university, suffered the death of his seven-year-old son, and lost all but a few of his paintings and drawings in a fire. What remains of his art from these years is mixed in nature: some sheets represent explorations of the ink-and-brush medium through simple landscape renderings; some toy with Surrealist motifs borrowed from Picasso and others; while others, derived from the historical research of J. J. Bachofen, explore antique symbols, some of a funerary character that must parallel the artist's search for reconciliation to his son's death.

Around 1934, Bissier began moving toward the Far Eastern calligrapher's classic use of ink. The uninsistent three-dimensional illusionism of his first years of experimentation flattened into brushed signs, while the brushwork itself became freer and more varied in character. Opacity versus translucence, smoothness versus raggedness,

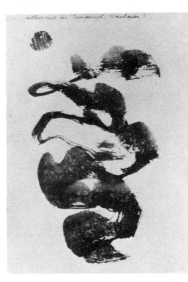

95. Julius Bissier. *Tellurisch bis lunarisch (Bachofen) 37/38,* 1938. Ink on paper. 9⅞″ × 6½″. Kunst-sammlung Nordrhein-Westfalen, Düsseldorf. Photo: Walter Klein. Copyright ARS NY/ADAGP 1987.

gestural speed versus deliberation, legibility versus abstraction, containment versus openness, and so on—all of these elements from the traditional repertory of the Far Eastern calligrapher entered into his art, which became more sure and spontaneous with the passing years (Fig. 95). His works from the late 1930s through the 1960s are remarkably satisfactory. The brushed sign stands against its white ground as a bold Zen gesture, a flash of life that does not disturb the void, or it gives a cheery eccentric testimony to the vitality of simple things—a row of bottles, a pair of fruits.

The Far Eastern aesthetic that engaged him was a good deal more than skin deep. Naturally, although no doubt also impelled by the threat of Nazi interference, Bissier acquired a love of solitude that he himself felt to be monastic in character. With dry humor, he would refer to himself as a monk and to his work in later years as *Monchsgeschäft*[11]—monkish business. But his developing inner life and his sense of the artist's calling were, without irony, dedicated. In the diary for 1944, he evoked his aim:

> . . . to realize the unprepossessing ideal of stillness in small and even smaller pictures. The vastness of things, the vastness of silence, the uncombative, the undramatic—that is all.[12]

In another entry, he measured the distance between the studio as he conceived it and the marketplace (see chapter 22):

> It goes without saying that artists are the most solitary of people—if they view their occupation as a calling. Above and beyond all, an inner peace must pervade their souls and their workshops. If he, the artist, is corrupt, if he is motivated by the market, then the world around him is corrupted. Because he creates the world, he inter-

prets his time and is a symptom of it. If he refuses, he adds to the disorder.[13]

Bissier was displeased when critics regarded his work as nothing more—or less—than skilled Far Eastern calligraphy fused with a Western abstract vision, but he acknowledged with humorous self-deprecation in 1944 that, however accomplished, his art remained tied to its Asian source:

> How long I have been searching for a way to free the inks from their Japanoid entanglement.[14]

His embrace of Far Eastern technique and aesthetic was virtually unique in his time. As Schmalenbach has pointed out,[15] only the American Mark Tobey, whom Bissier befriended years later in Ascona, engaged in a comparable Asian apprenticeship that led in time to an independent art, "original" by Western standards. But the "Japanoid entanglement" left Bissier unfulfilled; he searched on, recording his observations as he progressed.

The issue facing him in the mid-1940s is difficult for nonartists to appraise in terms of difficulty and importance: the transition from monochrome to color. Lay people would advise the artist simply to use color if he so desires, but it isn't so simple. More than a decade of disciplined work had defined for Bissier an art that was reliable, sober, yet inventive; further, his art was linked to an Asian spiritual tradition of indisputable depth, and Bissier was far from indifferent or illiterate in this respect. He had found in brushdrawing much of what he needed. But his mastery of the poetics of the calligraphic brush seemed increasingly a station on the way elsewhere. A diary entry for 1945 reflects both his love of color and his confidence that the monochrome inks possessed values that should not be left behind lightly:

> Working like mad. . . . Pleasant splashing in colors and lines, on themes like those of the inks. The feeling a bit sinful, more shallow: an escape from the holy earnest of the inks. . . . Whether the moral value is the same I cannot tell now. . . . The "inks" unquestionably have something sacred about them—the new works are late *peinture*, that much is clear.
>
> *Late at night:* The monk will renounce that little transgression into the flowering fields of life. He will return to God![16]

The tone is again gently self-deprecatory but cheerful. It is clear from this passage and others that he wished at all cost to avoid *peinture*, a word that conveys his mistrust of much European painting. To skirt the superficiality of *peinture,* he experimented with color monotypes, a method of transferring color from a plate to a surface rather than applying it directly with the brush. He often believed that he had found a new medium perfectly suited to his needs; then disbelieved and withdrew.

> Each print more beautiful than the next. Could the synthesis have come at last in secrecy and silence, like health?[17]

Printing never fully satisfied him. However, it allowed him to explore color in a reassuringly technical external setting, just as his diary allowed him to explore internally his responses and ideals. "Color to match the sense of my works," he wrote in 1947,

> must be festive, grandly original, without aestheticizing adornments. In other words: large reds, whites, blacks, greens, browns, etc. See the hues of multicolored stones, of green leaves, of the wilting autumn foliage, the great light of sunrise and sunset, the steelblue to purple of the sun's play on the lake. . . . He who bears witness to life must have the courage to speak with the language of life, to show the images of life unvarnished, and first of all and above all: to create with the intensity of life.[18]

And in the following year:

> Once more working in a state of grace. One sheet more radiant, more festive, more flowery than the next. Such days find me full of heartfelt thanks to fate. These new works *must* be successful: they haven't a trace of the gloom of the inks that menaces the Germans.[19]

Bissier needed to be reasonably certain that were he "to speak with the language of life" in full-blown color he would not lose the underlying sobriety and thematic strength that had given such life to his inks. He measured himself not only by local standards—those of his time and place—but by everything that he knew of Asian and Western art. And then, he measured himself by the standards of the spiritual in art that he absorbed early from the writings of Kandinsky, who had greatly appealed to Bissier's generation.

> I am aware again and again of the heritage of my predecessors. The quest for a sacred, ritual art becomes more and more clear, firm, and unequivocal through intensive engagement with it. What good to me is the pursuit of a formalistic aesthetic without content?[20]

96. Julius Bissier. *30 July 59*, 1959. Egg-tempera and goldleaf on canvas. Kunstsammlung Nordrhein-Westfalen, Düsseldorf. Photo: Walter Klein. Copyright ARS NY/ADAGP 1987.

It was only in 1956, at the ripe age of sixty-three, that Bissier's search came to term. The emergence of his "colored miniatures" (Fig. 96), the numerous masterpieces of his late years, signaled some great relaxation and receptivity to joy that had never been his before. Technically, these works are either watercolor on paper or egg-oil tempera on irregularly shaped, unstretched canvas, generally small. Spiritually they defy description, although their values are not at all esoteric or heady and make themselves readily known.[21]

The viewer may note first their spaciousness despite their typically small scale. The resonant white space of the calligrapher's page, against which signs can become all the more powerful, followed him into his new art. Bissier's signs in the miniatures seem innumerable: simple geometric figures, bottles, vases and cups, letters of the Roman and Greek alphabets, little bright blocks resembling mosaic, patches of goldleaf, seeds, stones, colored planes defining areas and colored washes defining atmospheres, abstract brushwork imported from his earlier work, vaguely animate forms that might be snails or wings, abstract shapes that have no name. He gathered all of these protagonists in the world of his new art in loose but not careless compositions, as if they had been turning in a kaleidoscope and briefly configured to please the artist. There is no trace here of strenuous "composition," no Golden Section or other stern device; on the contrary, there is utter relaxation, as if an infinitely sensitive but undemanding awareness had allowed all this to happen. In terms of color, the minatures have the variety and unexpectedness of flowers, just as Bissier had predicted years before in his diary entry about the "flowering fields of life," which seemed threatening at that time. This is Bissier's *Monchsgeschäft*—a new sort of monkish business, all joy, not even remotely frivolous.

Bissier signed and dated the miniatures prominently in a floating, tentative hand that adds a concluding note of intimacy, as if they were letters addressed to the viewer. Schmalenbach, who spoke often with Bissier and surely understood him well, related this element of Bissier's art to the artist's notion of *kairos,* the moment of grace at which the work of art makes itself known. "Whenever a picture or a sheet was successful," Schmalenbach recorded,

> Bissier felt he had been presented with a gift and he was grateful. This corresponds . . . to his concept of passive "reception," a notion of creativity which he insisted upon and which encompassed the idea of a "giver." [22]

Bissier himself raised this issue—in somewhat complex terms—in the diary that predates the miniatures:

> It's always the same. Refuge resides only in the thought that nothing depends on the individual, but rather that everything is established by the eternal, law-abiding change of the stuff of the world, entirely guided by Spirit, and all of our opinionated plusses and minuses are merely subjective values. [23]

Bissier's miniatures help us understand something of the essence of "late periods" in artists' creative lives. Just as elderly people typically say what they want when they want—praising when the spirit moves them, vehemently criticizing without a trace of politeness—so artists toward the end may enter a "free zone" that has none of the old constraints. Whatever discipline they instilled into their art remains intact, but the rules, the anxieties, the ingratiation drop away, leaving a less elaborate being, truer to itself. For many older people, the process is sadly reductive; the person was, after all, not very rich in inner life and becomes more impoverished than ever. For one of Bissier's internal strength, the stripping away is a gain:

> I advanced consciously to the highest simplicity of expression. . . . The inner command was obeyed still more frequently: to allow oneself to fall into one's own essence.[24]

The concluding phrase is striking, simply worded but marked with a wisdom that craves few words to convey its meaning. What it implies took Bissier nearly a lifetime, and few find their way so far. He was not always free—of course not. Late in life he still felt vulnerable to gnawing depressions and sorrows. But in his art, to which he returned daily—and surely in the meditations that surrounded his art and give it even today such stillness—he was as free a man as any.

GEORGIA O'KEEFFE: CUTTING SHARPLY TO THE CENTER

Georgia O'Keeffe (1887–1986) was a modest master by virtue of her solitary way of life in later years and her lifelong passion for simplicity. She was also the toast of the town in the 1920s, when her annual New York exhibitions were both well received and controversial, and by 1939 she was "the most famous, most successful woman painter in America."[25] Thoroughly and triumphantly American, O'Keeffe brings to mind Walt Whitman. Although she had a priestly reticence and he was a great psychic spendthrift, each spoke of American things with an American voice, and succeeded in making those things important to the world at large. Exposure to new European art during her student days catalyzed her development, but when her art matured around 1919, it had little in common with the European avant-garde. It was more naive, far less complex, with no background of worried thought. She went right for the "one thing needful" as she perceived it: the cultivation of a pictorial style that could reflect the beauty of Nature directly and forcefully. What she loved she loved well: landscape and flower, stark objects in stark settings, the endless variety of color, the poetry of simple things.

Like her art, O'Keeffe was direct, stripped to essentials, and forceful. Her spirituality, rooted in feeling and sensation, was unshakeable. She did not gather "on high," like Mondrian, to bring the universal downward; she raised earthly things. The badlands of New Mexico, faithfully observed, became in her art a figure for the universal, for what *is* after the nonsense has subsided. She lived what she felt and saw, gave it great intensity in her art—and little intensity in writings and interviews. Her words are separate brushstrokes.

Once established, her style changed little. The act of painting was her way of making contact with self and world, and it never became stale. "Making your unknown known is the important thing," she wrote to Sherwood Anderson in the 1920s,

> and keeping the unknown always beyond you—catching—crystallizing your simpler clearer vision of life—only to see it turn stale compared to what you vaguely feel ahead—that you must always keep working to grasp—[26]

O'Keeffe's life had the force of legend. It has been told well, and it will be retold decades from now when her extensive correspondence is opened to scholarly research. I will not attempt a serious biographical sketch, although we need to be aware of certain times, places, and relationships to enter into her art. Born to a Wisconsin farming family, educated first in Madison, and later in Virginia where her family resettled in 1902, she decided early to become an artist and sought training in the major teaching institutions of the day, including the Art Students League and Columbia Teachers College in New York. A position in 1912–14 as supervisor of art in the public schools of Amarillo, Texas, laid down her love of the American southwest that became such an important condition for her art and life. In 1914–15, she studied with the gifted Arthur Dow in New York, resuming her teaching career in autumn 1915 in South Carolina. This was the time and place of her first awakening.

O'Keeffe's teaching career seemed assured, but she was striving to realize herself as an independent artist. She had been trained by William Merritt Chase and others in the traditional skills of drawing and painting; she had been introduced by Dow and others to the uncharted freedom of the European avant-garde, including Kandinsky's *On the Spiritual*. But she herself had not yet emerged. One day, to gauge her progress, she hung a little retrospective of her work around her room. Periodically in years to come, she would remember the impact of this experiment:

. . . as I looked around at my work I realized that each painting had been affected by someone else. I wondered why I hadn't put down things of my own from my own head. [I thought:] "I have things in my head that are not like what anyone has taught me—shapes and ideas so near to me—so natural to my way of being and thinking that it hadn't occurred to me to put them down." I decided to start anew—to strip away what I had been taught—to accept as true my own thinking.

I . . . found myself saying to myself—I can't live where I want to—I can't go where I want to—I can't do what I want to—I can't even say what I want to—. School and things that painters have taught me even keep me from painting as I want to. I decided I was a very stupid fool not to at least paint as I wanted to and say what I wanted to when I painted as that seemed to be the only thing I could do that didn't concern anybody but myself—that was nobody's business but my own.[27]

The art that emerged, rooted in Nature and in her own inwardness, was spontaneous, careless of rules, and explosively original. At their strongest (Fig. 97), her early watercolors are unforgettable. Here the land and the magic of the evening star are joined in one flow, conveying with ease—and without metaphysical formalities—the embrace of "higher" and "lower." Her first watercolors range in subject from this poetic image to childlike expressions of joy (for example, *Chicken in Sunrise*), to stark, preternaturally skilled abstractions. Exploring abstraction in the isolation of South Carolina, just a few years after Kandinsky and others had begun their explorations in Europe, she leaped into the avant-garde with unaccountable grace and clarity.

I was alone and singularly free, working into my own, unknown— no one to satisfy but myself.[28]

It fell to Alfred Stieglitz, the famed photographer and champion of new art (see the following chapter), to inform her of her achievement in worldly terms. Shown some of her work by a friend who had been instructed to share it with no one, Stieglitz almost at once hung examples in his gallery without permission—and so drew the outraged O'Keeffe to his side. It was spring, 1916; O'Keeffe, again studying with Arthur Dow at Columbia Teachers College, visited Stieglitz's gallery to correct the situation as soon as she caught wind of it.

The love affair of urbane, middle-aged Stieglitz with the headstrong young artist from the Midwest is a rich, largely untold story. Their

97. Georgia O'Keeffe. *Evening Star, III,* 1917. Watercolor. 9″ × 11⅞″. Collection, The Museum of Modern Art, New York. Mr. and Mrs. Donald B. Straus Fund.

marriage in 1924 seems only an incident in a larger tale, by no means always joyous, that lasted from their first meeting until the death of Stieglitz in 1947. It does not demean O'Keeffe's fierce independence to acknowledge Stieglitz's contributions to her development. As a gallery director, he promoted her reputation effectively. As friend and for a time as mentor, he encouraged the flowering of her vision and style. By 1919, she had achieved her mature style and staked out many of the themes that would be hers for decades to come, however enlarged and varied as time went on. She was a better painter than "the men," as she called the artists whom Stieglitz showed at his gallery and championed in the critical arena. But living around them through the late 1910s and 1920s gave her the chance she needed to sharpen her vision and skills in a highly concentrated atmosphere. In 1929, she began living a part of each year in New Mexico, where she eventually found a home of her own. The desert themes foreshadowed earlier came to dominate her art.

O'Keeffe's developed art (Fig. 98) asks the viewer to see with sim-

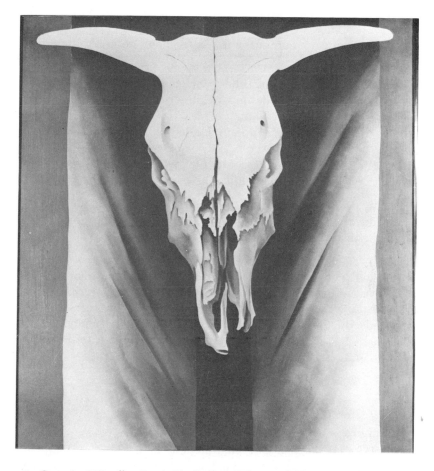

98. Georgia O'Keeffe. *Cow's Skull: Red, White and Blue*, 1931. Oil on canvas. 39⅞″ × 35⅞″. The Metropolitan Museum of Art, The Alfred Stieglitz Collection, 1949 (52.203).

plicity and penetration, to forego details in order to apprehend the larger presence of objects and places. One's gaze glides through an O'Keeffe canvas as it encounters and appraises smooth contours and slowly changing color gradients; her pictorial world is typically crisp, clear, and abstract. From the 1930s, her paintings of bones and skulls—the "found objects" of her desert home—exemplify the vision. "I have wanted to paint the desert," she wrote in 1939, and I haven't known how. The bones seemed to cut sharply to the center of something that is keenly alive on the desert even tho' it is vast and empty and untouchable—and knows no kindness with all its beauty.[29]

More compactly than in any other passage, she speaks here to the essence of her art. Its value lies in its ability to connect us directly with something keenly alive in Nature. It proposes a spare but heartfelt vision as the truth, preferable to any kinder, more elaborate version of things.

For O'Keeffe, seeing and recording the world were a sacred service that she could never entirely fulfill. She owed the effort:

> . . . my painting is what I have to give back to the world for what the world gives me. . . . What I have been able to put into form seems infinitesimal compared with the variety of experience. . . .[30]

Living by and large alone in her desert home for many years, although with good friends and neighbors, O'Keeffe found the rigorous simplicity that others find in monasteries or demanding spiritual communities. She may not have known or cared for the hierarchies of knowledge and the multiple states of being of traditional contemplative literature—but she came to know *this* world with extraordinary directness and respect, and through her art showed its natural holiness.

ET AL.

The four "modest masters" discussed in these pages should in all justice be joined by many others, although the chapter is already long. By way of homage to others skilled in hand and vision who have contributed to the modern spiritual through long careers, I wish to call attention to Leonard Baskin, Anton Music, and Bernard Childs.

Leonard Baskin (b. 1922), the American teacher, sculptor, and printmaker of dark yet humane vision, is a master of his crafts. His lurching emperors, predatory creatures, and God-fearing, God-singing Hasidim are among the richest imaginings of our time.

Anton Music (b. 1909), a Yugoslav painter long resident in Italy, for years sent his herds of archaic horses through rich and simple landscapes of the heart. The loving spirit of his work, reminiscent of Franz Marc's, should not be forgotten.

Bernard Childs (1910–1985), American painter and printmaker,

99. Bernard Childs. *Outrider*, 1972. Oil on canvas. 62″ × 51″. Private Collection. Photo: Clara Aich.

was an exquisitely refined image-maker who worked in a language closest to Kandinsky's. He was also one of the most original portrait artists of our time. The finesse that he brought to *Outrider* (Fig. 99) gathered around those who sat for portraits. The likenesses he captured are sharply characterized but translucent, as if the sitters had been visited by a spirit, and that spirit was their own. His distant ancestors were icon-makers in Yaroslavl; he was an icon-maker in Paris and New York.

"We are unused to such attention in modern times."[1] The words are Harold Clurman's, written of Alfred Stieglitz (1864–1946) in 1934, when the old man's career was beginning to be seen in retrospect. They offer an essential clue about the transformation of a mechanical device—film and camera—into a source of images that added unmistakably to the spiritual in twentieth-century art. Because the camera "sees all" and renders what it sees with faultless draftsmanship, photographers eventually had to reexamine the value of their own seeing. Because it sees in a moment, photographers had to reconsider the meaning of the moment. Because the camera is ruthlessly materialistic and records only physical images, photographers had to reexamine the larger expressiveness of realistic images and the nature of symbols which, following Stieglitz, some called "equivalents." And because the portrait could as well be of suffering humanity as of patrons or friends, photographers found themselves exploring the human condition in a bare new way. Camera work became a new way of giving attention to the world.

The person behind the camera may be a seer or a voyeur. The one penetrates to the meaning of things seen with awe, compassion, or aesthetic sensitivity; the other fills an emptiness. The one records with joy or sorrow, the other with desire. Both are keenly observant. Between seer and voyeur there are of course many stations; one and the same photographer probably visits them all in the course of a career.

The mechanical aspects of photography forced the rediscovery of attention. Spawning a popular hobby on the one hand, it generated on the other an intense inquiry into what it means to see. The legendary Stieglitz was largely responsible for this structuring of photographic art. From before 1900 until his death, he took upon himself the fate of photography, sometimes high-handedly, more often with vision, and his influence has passed down a living chain to men and women working today. Like so many idealisms, his idealism is now out of date. His ferocious belief in photography and its near-sacred mission are the very opposite of the cool eye that now tends to dominate the art. Stieglitz wrote for the preface of a 1921 exhibition of his work:

> I was born in Hoboken. I am an American. Photography is my passion. The search for Truth my obsession.[2]

This is hardly calculated to please the postmodern sensibility; it does have a drumbeat to it. But Stieglitz is the patriarch, undeniable.

Born in Hoboken, educated in Germany, Stieglitz was drawn early to photography. Working in Berlin in the 1880s with technical pioneers whom he challenged and even bested with his extensions of the technique, he also educated himself thoroughly in philosophy, music, art, theater, and literature at a time when Berlin offered them richly. He has been described as a "one-man university"[3]; his niece (and biographer) noticed that he dipped into Goethe's *Faust* every summer throughout his life. This is not to praise the man for a refined education, which others also had, but to surmise one of the sources of his fervor. Just as Emerson decades earlier had given German Romanticism a native American voice, Stieglitz married it to the pragmatic new medium of photography.

Stieglitz joined a warrior's temperament to the philosophical concerns of a born sage. ". . . Without a break, from 1883 in Berlin on, I was fighting for photography. . . ."[4] The ideal with which he returned from Germany to New York in 1890 was the "straight photograph." As he recalled in 1919,

> . . . always back of my head there was photography—always the Photographer—without tricks—subterfuge—self-seeking of any kind—the search for Truth—Beauty—Order. Everything straightforward—in broad daylight—no secrets—no diffusion lenses nor confusion printing papers—no artiness—frankly a photograph. . . .[5]

His early photographs in New York, such as *The Terminal* (Fig. 100), are among his most memorable; they actualize what he would eventually describe as "seeing." Without artiness, he saw as an artist. Of the innumerable views that he might have taken, he chose the one that makes space intensely real, owing to the zigzag recession of the horses and trolley toward the facade that closes off the image like a stage. Of innumerable moments, he chose one when the driver, hosing down his horses, leans out of axis with the image—and so seems, although the image is still, to be active and somehow solicitous of his horses' well being. Stieglitz saw the momentary poetry of the steam rising off the

100. Alfred Stieglitz. *The Terminal*, 1892. Gelatin-silver print. 4¾″ × 6⅜″.
Philadelphia Museum of Art: Given by Carl Zigrosser.

horses' flanks and didn't shy away from recording the foul slush un-
derfoot—not that his camera could avoid taking the image in, but
darkroom techniques could have taken it out. This is a "straight photograph," but governed as much by acute perceptions of narrative,
form, and atmosphere as by the mechanics of correct exposure and the
intention to make "frankly a photograph." Writing years later about
this image, Stieglitz remembered that he had felt lonely and out of
place since returning to America from Germany. The loneliness of the
scene and the driver's redeeming solicitude had moved him: it was an
image close to his own heart at the time.[6]

This is not the spiritual in art, it is urban poetry of a kind that had
been familiar since the Impressionists took to the streets. But it illustrates some of the values that came together in Stieglitz's concept of
seeing: the search outside for an image that brilliantly embodies the
photographer's inwardness, a frank and uncensorious relation with
outward detail, a crisp approach to photographic mechanics combined
with immensely high standards, such that darkroom work becomes a

search for perfection and not a routine. To be present at a significant moment or event, to recognize it fully, and to record it cleanly—these things were bound up, for Stieglitz, with an endlessly improvised philosophy of life that turned around a few core ideas.

Stieglitz was a gifted and charismatic organizer. Internationally renowned for his photographs by the early 1900s, he was impatient with the pokey people who, for the most part, made up New York photography. In 1902 he brought together a group of superb photographers as the Photo-Secession (named in homage to the Vienna Secession) and in 1903 founded *Camerawork*, one of the great twentieth-century art journals. Until its final issue in 1917,[7] it captured most of the important things in photography and visual art worldwide. Recognizing the relation between photography and avant-garde European painting and sculpture—all innovations fighting for acceptance—he opened a gallery in New York known as 291 where, with the prescient help of his comrade and later rival Edward Steichen, he gave the first American exhibitions to Picasso, Matisse, and Brancusi.

Stieglitz's forum was 291 and its successors. In these settings he championed photography, promoted and nurtured a small number of avant-garde American artists, behaved with classic ambiguity where *selling* art was concerned—and discoursed as if he had strayed from the Athenian agora to midtown New York. In such people, one thing matters: Have they something to say? Alfred Stieglitz did.

At 291, The Intimate Gallery, and An American Place—his galleries over the years—the talk was often extraordinary. It justifiably attracted not one but two faithful recorders at different periods, Herbert Seligmann and Dorothy Norman.[8] Stieglitz was almost always there; if not there, then he was in the apartment that he shared with O'Keeffe when she was in New York. As often as not surrounded by people in both places, he would speak at length and then go on to dinner to continue. His gallery was a port of call; he could be immensely generous to people—and contemptuous of gallery visitors who didn't seem to grasp what was on display. He had a nineteenth-century reverence for authentic art and authentic artists, now difficult to reconstruct in its fervor and certainty.

Stieglitz's words, passed on by his recorders and preserved in correspondence, vary between fundamental truth and a more self-centered heroism that leaves one uneasy, as if he has said the right thing but somehow wrongly. "I refuse to identify *seeing* with *knowing*," he once said.

Seeing signifies awareness resulting from inner experience. Not by way of the experience of another. Not through institutionalization of ideas, not theorizing.[9]

It is not *art* in the professionalized sense about which I care, but that which is created sacredly, as a result of deep inner experience, *with all of oneself,* and that *becomes* "art" in time.[10]

If only each will permit himself to be free to recognize the living moment when it occurs, and to let it flower, without preconceived ideas about what it *should* be. And if the moment is not permitted to live—is not recognized—I know the consequences. . . .[11]

I do not make "pictures" . . . I never was a snap-shotter. . . . I have a vision of life and I try to find equivalents for it sometimes in the form of photographs. It's because of the lack of inner vision amongst those who photograph that there are really but few *true* photographers. . . .[12]

These are the blameless statements of a seeker. Such words, and many others wilder in content and imagination, helped to form the conscience of American photography. Ansel Adams has written:

Stieglitz taught me what became my first commandment: "Art is the affirmation of life."[13]

A man of restless mind, Stieglitz was constantly seeking new formulations of his old commandments—for example, in conversation with the Russian émigré artist David Burliuk in 1925. The two men were looking at Stieglitz's photographs of clouds (see Fig. 101):

"They are so simple," said Burliuk, "as to be almost mystical." Here Stieglitz broke in to say that it was strange Burliuk should use those words since utter simplicity held something bordering on the mystical for him. He drew a diagram making adjacent dark spots. "Here," he said, "is reality. When that is seen it is so close to the mystical that the dividing line is almost imperceptible." He drew a line between the two spots. "That is the line of my life running between them."[14]

The formulation is attractive. Behind the play of ideas we can sense some irreducible experience that came over Stieglitz when he was photographing at his best. That experience was the engine driving the man, the fleeting but impressive guarantee that what he had to say was at base true, and that his photographs were true. The keener attention

101. Alfred Stieglitz. *Equivalent, Mountains and Sky, Lake George*, 1924.
Gelatin-silver print. 9½″ × 7½″. Philadelphia Museum of Art: Given by
Carl Zigrosser.

that reveals the world as real and solid is magically bound up with a recognition of something beyond it. "Looking beyond" begins, for some people, with looking here and now.

Stieglitz photographed clouds from his Lake George home in the 1920s as a challenge to his art and mind. "I wanted to photograph clouds," he wrote,

> to find out what I had learned in 40 years about photography. Through clouds to put down my philosophy of life. . . .[15]

He titled one series *Music*, another *Equivalents*. In these works, some bland, others richly expressive, he was feeling his way toward a photographic analogue to abstraction and toward a new landscape vision, perhaps moved by earlier work of Paul Strand's, surely moved by the art that he had exhibited over the years. *Mountains and Sky, Lake George* is a powerful study of landscape and skyscape, and beyond that a renewal of the religious imagery of light and darkness, vertical and horizontal, higher and lower.

Such works of the 1920s are a link in the chain uniting nineteenth-century landscape painting, with its reverence for the natural scene, to the mid-twentieth-century photography of Ansel Adams, Minor White, and others who gave new life to landscape art.[16] While landscape photography was already practiced in the nineteenth century, Stieglitz renewed it through his larger vision and technical crispness. Much of what he meant by *seeing,* so evident in this photograph, is evident again in a passage from a letter to Sherwood Anderson in 1923. He wrote it in late November; he and O'Keeffe had stayed on at Lake George, where they witnessed "a day of days—a blizzard":

> the moon came out clear—& I stood watching the barns—& trees—& ground—& hills—the sky—an unbelievable dignity. Gosh what a small thing man is with his capers. I'll never forget the barns that I saw in the moonlight. Talk about the Sphinx & pyramids—there was that barn—nothing could be grander—The austere dignity of it. Flooded with light. . . .[17]

For photographers in the Stieglitz tradition, *seeing* implies both a transforming recognition of the ordinary and a sharper, grander vision of the extraordinary. They move in the world as if it might at any moment emerge from routine and reveal itself with utmost power. The barn—by certain light and weather—is grander than the "Sphinx &

pyramids." But so too are the Grand Teton range, Yosemite Valley, a simple bell pepper, a nautilus shell, and the human body. Whatever the subject, the metaphysic is roughly that of Stieglitz, appreciative of the physical world, sensitive to something more that makes itself felt through it. And the ethic is to see, to give attention to the world and to oneself moving responsively through it.

In Stieglitz's time, seeing was a humanistic discipline. The proper function of the artist-photographer was to see richly into the nature of things and to record starkly, without elaboration. For a time in the 1960s and 1970s, under Minor White's influence, photographic seeing became a deliberate spiritual discipline, an emptying out of the ordinary person so that a strong, almost impersonal attention could perceive truly and record well on film. Shortly after White's death in 1976, the mystique of seeing seemed irrelevant to many photographers, while others continued with fewer references to spiritual tradition but with no lesser intent. Elaborated as in White or largely unspoken as in Paul Caponigro, the roots of this approach are firmly planted in Stieglitz's ideals. "Today in talking to a visitor to the Room," recorded Seligmann in 1926,

> [Stieglitz] said: "Unless I can feel God in the palm of my hand, unless my touch is sensitive enough, then God does not exist for me. I have always believed that."[18]

This is the credo of a man for whom the physical world was immensely real.

Paul Strand (1890–1976) visited 291 with his school class sometime after the turn of the century—shepherded by Lewis Hine, a humble school photographer at the time whose later documentary work in Manhattan's Lower East Side and elsewhere is now universally admired.[19] Strand fell in love with photography, did what was necessary to learn the art, and in time brought his work to Stieglitz for criticism. He became an intimate friend, and his work quickly evolved to the point that the older man could learn from it. While Strand's work goes far beyond the illustration on the opposite page (Fig. 102), this photograph can help us to continue our informal meditation on seeing and attention in photography.

The subject is perfectly ordinary—a wild mushroom, grasses, and leaves—but Strand's vision and technical command transform it into something perfect and extraordinary. This is Blakean art, seeing in-

102. Paul Strand. *Toadstool and Grasses, Maine,* 1928. Gelatin-silver print. 10″ × 8″. Collection, The Museum of Modern Art, New York. Gift of the photographer. Copyright © 1950 by Aperture Foundation, Inc., Paul Strand Archive.

finity in a grain of sand; Blakean also in its valuation of clarity and focus. Focus in the image becomes a proxy for attention, while the humble subject serves as a proxy for "all things," the whole of Nature. The orderly finned ellipse of the mushroom becomes a cup of light against which the randomly bent stalks of grass and warm shadows contrast in pattern and intensity. At the literal and expressive center of the composition, the stalks cut into the mushroom: that detail reveals seemingly perfect forms as both fragile and mysteriously related. The two parts of the composition join in a way that is perfectly ordinary and perfectly extraordinary—ordinary because it happens all the time, extraordinary because Strand's attention and technical skill reveal a small event as a parable of firmness, change, and almost unseen unity.

That a toadstool glows with such light and has such an admirably fine structure is nothing—or something. That grasses surrounding it create warm patches of darkness and streaks of light is nothing—or something. That grasses pierce the flesh of the toadstool so quietly, leaving its structure intact and binding the overall image into one, is nothing—or something. The photograph invites the viewer to focus on small events and common textures, and find in them an opening to a large sense of Nature and self.

Ansel Adams (1902–1986) is, to my mind, the oustanding landscape artist in any medium in the twentieth century. His greatest photographs join an Emersonian reverence for Nature and a keen sense of place and moment with overwhelming technical command of the medium. They have an unschooled but persuasive spirituality that should not be forgotten when the soul of this century is put in the balance.

The art historian Barbara Novak has brilliantly reconstructed the pictorial repertory and philosophical background of the nineteenth-century American landscape tradition on which Adams enlarged.[20] Well educated in San Francisco but not an insistently learned man, Adams surely never undertook a systematic study of the art and writings to which she refers, but deliberate study is not the only route through which influences pass. Adams knew his Emerson, no doubt directly but also through the writings of John Muir, the turn-of-the-century wilderness author and conservationist who lobbied successfully for the designation of Yosemite Valley and the surrounding high country as a national park. Yosemite was Adams' "place" from his youth, Muir its unforgotten partisan.

A small historical test shows uncanny continuity between Emerson, Muir, and Adams. The following passages from their writings, dated

1844, 1912, and 1932—make their unity of thought and even language all the more surprising.

Emerson:

At the gates of the forest . . . is sanctity which shames our religions, and reality which discredits our heroes. Here we find Nature to be the circumstance which dwarfs every other circumstance, and judges like a god all men that come to her. . . . The incommunicable trees begin to persuade us to live with them, and quit our life of solemn trifles. . . . These enchantments are medicinal, they sober and heal us. . . . We come to our own, and make friends with matter. . . . The mind loves its old home. . . .[21]

Muir:

. . . the Valley, comprehensively seen, looks like an immense hall or temple lighted from above.

But no temple made with hands can compare with Yosemite. Every rock in its walls seems to glow with life. . . . Down through the middle of the Valley flows the crystal Merced . . . , reflecting lilies and trees and the onlooking rocks; things frail and fleeting and types of endurance meeting here and blending in countless forms, as if into this one mountain mansion Nature had gathered her choicest treasures, to draw her lovers into close and confiding communion with her.[22]

Adams:

. . . contact with fundamental earthy things [gives] a startling perspective on the high-spun unrealities of modern life. No matter how sophisticated you may be, a large granite mountain cannot be denied—it speaks in silence to the very core of your being. There are some that care not to listen but the disciples are drawn to the high altars with magnetic certainty, knowing that a great Presence hovers over the ranges. . . .[23]

Working in the tradition of Emerson and Muir, Adams worked best with his camera. One of his well-known photographs (Fig. 103) embodies the unique blend of natural fact and unspoken metaphysic that gives such dignity to his work. In the foreground is a randomly strewn, forbidding zone of boulders; one cannot help but sense how exhausting it would be to pass through this terrain. In the background, rising

103. Ansel Adams. *Mount Williamson, Sierra Nevada, from Manzanar, California,* 1944. Gelatin-silver print. 19″ × 15⅜″. Copyright © 1985 by the Trustees of the Ansel Adams Publishing Rights Trust. All rights reserved.

from the rocky floor without transition, is a range of lofty peaks capped with storm clouds and enveloping shafts of light—an epiphany of sorts, another Sinai. The scene itself is superb, the moment equally superb, and Adams' technical control captures both. Sharp focus throughout the field of vision again serves as a proxy for attention, the ability to see what is and see its meaning.

Adams is a realist and symbol-maker at one and the same time. The viewer needn't think in terms of Desert, Holy Mountain, and an epiphany of Light to appreciate the image as a dramatic rendering of what Adams called the natural scene. The foreground boulders transform, at moments, into the troubled mass of Israelites, cloaked and bent before the miracle of Sinai. Adams knew those values were there, but he was never stuffy about it. A hiker in close touch with the earth, he was not given to intricate formulations, although he did speak well from the heart:

Art is . . . both the taking and giving of beauty, the turning out to the light the inner folds of the awareness of the spirit. It is the recreation on another plane of the realities of the world; the tragic and wonderful realities of earth and men, and of all the interrelations of these.[24]

As might be expected of a vastly gifted photographer who had been helped as a young man by Stieglitz's example and personal friendship, Adams took the concept of photographic seeing one step further. Seeing became for him both a movement of the total understanding and a technical discipline of previsualizing the finished photograph in terms of receding zones of light and dark. Adams' technical approach to photographic seeing, the Zone System, is still widely taught. The following passage from a 1944 article reflects its underlying point of view:

. . . "seeing," or visualization, is the fundamentally important element. A photograph is not an accident—it is a concept. It exists at, or before, the moment of exposure of the negative. From that moment on to the final print, the process is chiefly one of *craft*. . . . Truly "accidental" photography is practically non-existent; with preconditioned attitudes we *recognize* and are arrested by the significant moment. The awareness of the *right moment* is as vital as the perception of values, form, and other qualities.[25]

Adams did not live only in the Pure Land, although he sometimes saw and recorded it. He earned his living for years as a commercial photographer, ran a studio and workshops at Yosemite, and explored new technologies such as the Polaroid system for a fee. Some of his transparencies were enlarged as Coloramas for New York's Grand Central Station, which to this day has huge photos advertising Kodak products ("aesthetically inconsequential but technically remarkable," he commented[26]).

I struggled with a great variety of assignments through the years. Some I enjoyed and some I detested, but I learned from all of them. . . . I have little use for students or artists who . . . scorn commercial photography as a form of prostitution. I grant that it is not difficult to make it so, but I learned greatly from commercial photography and in no way resent the time and effort devoted to it.[27]

But that was his living, only a part of his life. As one looks today through the "75 images by which he wished to be remembered,"[28] one finds in them a very great faith and faultless artistry. It is Emerson's

faith in Nature, rendered crisply, with twentieth-century technical finesse. And it is Stieglitz's faith in seeing, the intrinsic act of consciousness. Adams' aspens shining against a dark grove, his little town of
Hernandez crouched beneath an enigmatic sky, his image of Yosemite
half-wrapped in a winter storm are classic works. Each captures an
extraordinary moment as an emblem of a world that Adams found extraordinary. "Expressions without doctrine,"[29] he called them, "images of the endless moments of the world." But he was not quite so
neutral or embraced in the Tao as his words imply. As he wrote to a
friend in 1947:

> What I call the Natural Scene—just nature—is a symbol of many
> things to me, a never-ending potential. . . . The relatively few au-
> thentic creators of our time possess a resonance with eternity. I think
> this resonance is something to fight for. . . .[30]

The grandeur of the natural scene, as photographed by Stieglitz,
Adams, White, Caponigro, and others is one face of the spiritual in
twentieth-century photography; the other face is often darker. Stieglitz
had insisted on "the straight photograph" because it was true to the
medium—and because he was not immune to the seductiveness of art
for art's sake. The documentary photograph was straight photography
with a vengeance. There was art in it often. Its goal, however, was to
report on man to man.

Dorothea Lange (1895–1965) began her career as a studio portrait
photographer in San Francisco, but when the Depression took hold
she found herself questioning the value of comfortable studio work
when millions of lives were in turmoil.[31] She was drawn into the streets
to record breadlines, union meetings, and strikes, and soon teamed up
with sociologist Paul Taylor (later her husband) to document the self-
help cooperatives through which some workers were trying to meet
their needs. In 1935, her photographs came to the attention of Roy
Stryker, an economist in the Resettlement Administration (RA) who
was beginning to document the conditions of migrant workers as a
part of the government's effort to improve their lot. She was hired as an
RA photographer, and by the end of 1935 Stryker had assembled a
team of roving photographers who in short order redefined the scope
and power of documentary photography. They included Arthur Roth-
stein, Carl Mydans, Walker Evans, and Ben Shahn.[32] In 1937, with an
expanded staff that included the brilliant photographer Russell Lee,
Stryker's group was absorbed into the Department of Agriculture

under the name with which their work is now commonly associated, the Farm Security Administration (FSA).

There was nothing of the voyeur in what they accomplished, although one can mistake Walker Evans' cool eye for place and shape for indifference to the men and women making their lives there. Their photographs are participatory; they tell the story of Depression-era America to Americans more effectively than any other medium, and they remain both powerful period pieces and a new sort of epic, visual not literary, comparable to a sequence of narrative wall paintings. The hero is everyman and everywoman, and the odds are against them. The emotional range embraces quiet dignity and humor, love, anger, despair, arrogance and foolishness. The collective work of these photographers can be regarded as a twentieth-century observance of the commandment "Love thy neighbor as thyself."

Among many images that might epitomize FSA photography, Dorothea Lange's *Migrant Mother, Nipomo, California* (Fig. 104) comes insistently to mind. It was recognized almost at once as an image in the Madonna tradition. Other photographs of the woman and her family made by Lange on that occasion are documentary in the narrow sense—honest reports on person, time, and place. This photograph is clearly more; it transcends its documentary mission to become one of the few valid Holy Family images of our time, not in a sectarian sense but in the larger sense captured by Edward Steichen in his famous photographic exhibition, *The Family of Man*.[33]

The spiritual in art is not exclusively directed toward the higher or the more inward, toward the essential released or the individual liberated—nor toward the paths that lead to them. Now and always, it also looks toward the human condition. Giotto's early fourteenth-century storytelling at Padua is a sacred narrative but also a loving commentary on the quality of ordinary people in his time and place. The sufferers whom St. Peter cures by his shadow in Masaccio's fresco are unforgettable images not of the transcendental but of circumscribed humanity, whom Masaccio sees with stunning clarity and compassion. Even in the grandly transcendental cycles of Hindu sculpture, one finds vignettes that speak to the common condition—memorably, for example, a monkey family grooming peaceably and nursing a baby while mythic events roar unnoticed around them in the main sculptural ensemble.

Both contemplation and compassion are easily undermined. The contemplative impulse can become abstract and juiceless. Compassion degrades into sentimentality or voyeurism. However, in their authentic

104. Dorothea Lange. *Migrant Mother, Nipomo California*, 1936. Photo: Library of Congress.

forms, contemplation and compassion are the deep capacities out of which the spiritual in art has been elaborated. Most traditions recognize that they complete each other: fulfilled *jñāna* bears *bhakti* somewhere within it, and vice versa; in Luke's gospel, Martha and Mary are sisters. In plainer terms, human beings need to think and feel at one and the same time to make their way with something approaching *common* sense.

From this general point of view, the work of Dorothea Lange and other concerned photographers is a branch of the spiritual in art, no less legitimate than Brancusi's search for an image of pure aspiration or Rothko's vision of the holy cloud. This perception can be put to the test through war photography—to our misfortune a required skill in the twentieth century. Some of the most heartrending images of any era have been made by combat photographers. Among Americans, Eugene Smith, David Douglas Duncan, and Robert Capa come at once to mind, but there have been others, including a photographer from the Soviet Union in World War II who was responsible for at least one timeless photograph.[34]

Robert Capa (1913–1954), born André Friedmann in Budapest, became a frontline photographer in the Spanish Civil War and photographed every major conflict until he lost his life in Vietnam when the French phase of the war was unwinding. He was not only a combat photographer, although his character and personal courage drew him into that role again and again. A founding member of Magnum, the photographers' collective that included Henri Cartier-Bresson and other top photojournalists, he had a perfectly extraordinary eye for human gesture, the telling moment, the unique scene. His art, of which there was much, was entirely at the service of conveying the look, feel, and meaning of a circumstance.

His photograph of a Spanish Republican soldier's death in battle (Fig. 105) captures a fleeting moment, one that could exist, so to speak, only in the camera's eye. But Capa's speed of perception and forceful eye for composition make it an icon of our time. Against a vast sky and almost featureless landscape, the soldier's body is flung open by the force of a bullet. The utter strain in his face, the fall captured midway, the oddly unforgettable relaxation in the release of his grip on the rifle, the simplicity of the total image in which the figure is alone—all of these features build to a sacred image, not sweet but necessary: a crucifixion suited to its era.

105. Robert Capa. *Death of a Republican Soldier,* Spain, 1936. Gelatin-silver print. 10" × 6¾". Photo copyright Robert Capa Magnum.

The great cycles of narrative art in traditional religious cultures include scenes of human and divine suffering. Those who love traditional art and despise twentieth-century art ask where anything comparable to those cycles can be found in the art of our time. One element is here. The compassionate mind has been at work in this century, as in every richly endowed era. Capa was a tough sort of man, with Hemingway-like machismo and flash; in point of fact, he and Hemingway were friends. It is hard to imagine another sort of man taking this photograph or, for that matter, accompanying the first wave of troops to the beach on D-Day (another of Capa's assignments). In a not very spiritual era, the spiritual in art has many disguises. One of them is combat photography.

For many years, Dorothea Lange posted a sentence from Francis Bacon on her darkroom door:

> The contemplation of things as they are, without substitution or imposture, without error or confusion, is in itself a nobler thing than a whole harvest of invention.[35]

It is a ringing truth, as it must have been for her. It can, however, become untruth when used as a weapon against those who no less resolutely explore "things as they are" in the psychic and spiritual realms where war and peace begin. Art that responds effectively to crises in human affairs can make other art seem pale. Solzhenitsyn's *The Gulag Archipelago* and Elie Wiesel's writings leave one doubting that anything more can or should be said. Only by remembering that there is no need of war or social catastrophe to live fully can we accept, after Lange and Capa, the softspoken works with which this chapter concludes.

Jerry Uelsmann's collage-like photograph, *The Poet's House* (Fig. 106), is a supple symbolic work conveying an awareness of the high adventure of daily life. The scene is ordinary and, obviously, not ordinary. Small in the distance beside water that feels like a river, a house is gripped between higher and lower "forces"—the luxuriant crown of a tree hovering enigmatically overhead, a threatening stubble below resembling the roots of an overturned tree. Nearly caught in this odd vise, the house itself is immersed in the shoreline woods and hemmed in by an unaccountable fanning reflection of branches in the water. The poet in that house would seem tiny, if he or she were to step out for a breath of air.

What may appear at first glance to be a peculiar fantasy slowly takes shape into a superb evocation of the unpredictable vitality of all things and of our small but conveniently central place in the scheme. The image is of a poet's world, and of our own: promising, threatening, strange, familiar, perfectly grand. The composition, with its axial forms that lend themselves to symbolic reading, will remind viewers who are familiar with traditional religious symbolism of much that they know in other contexts. But such knowledge is unnecessary to appreciate the image, and it represents only an informal source for the photographer, who is a gifted dreamer and explorer unready to bind himself to any canonical approach. "It seems to me that life abounds with mystery," Uelsmann has written,

> that it is central to life, that when you are alive there are many kinds of questions. . . . It is the challenge of the questions that makes life exciting.
>
> I think of my photographs as being obviously symbolic but not symbolically obvious. There isn't any specific correlation between the symbols in the image and any content that I have in mind.[36]

106. Jerry Uelsmann. *Poet's House (first version)*, 1965. Gelatin-silver print. 13 13/16″ × 9 13/16″. Collection, The Museum of Modern Art, New York. David H. McAlpin Fund.

The Poet's House exemplifies Uelsmann's language, developed in the early 1960s and pursued to this day, often enough with remarkable results. He owes various debts—to nineteenth-century narrative photography that used multiple exposures, to René Magritte and other Surrealists—but when the debts are tallied, Uelsmann's language still seems fresh and productive. There is a real intelligence here, not one that compels images to conform to an intellectual plan, but one that welcomes the unusual, wanders freely, and—by some acquired or innate sense of balance—generally returns with an image that opens out our plain world without distorting it angrily or recklessly.

> Often, confident that we have the right answers, we fail to ask enough questions, and then our seeming confidence fogs our vision and the inconceivable remains truly unconceived. . . . It is important to realize that all aspects of the photographic process carry the seeds of revelation.[37]

In spirit, skill, and pedagogic gifts heir to Alfred Stieglitz, Minor White (1908–1976) recast in original terms the conviction that photography can be a visionary medium and its practice a spiritual discipline. Sought after as a teacher both in workshops across the country and at Massachusetts Institute of Technology, where he directed a photography program for some years, he influenced many photographers active today for whom camerawork is a dedicated calling. It is interesting, then, that a 1984 publication, *Minor White: A Living Remembrance*, elicited a major review entitled "The Fall from Grace of a Spiritual Guru" that tore the man apart. The reviewer regarded White as "consigned to the dust-bin of history . . . almost forgotten"—and for the best of reasons: he found in White's work

> little sense . . . of the artist's life as an ordinary mortal, as an individual living in an age of uncertainty and ambivalence. . . . One suspects that his compulsive adoption of a number of mystical philosophies . . . served the cause of repression as much as the cause of enlightenment. . . . In today's milieu . . . , there is no longer a moral figure of unimpeachable authority who stands ready to lead us into the light—nor, indeed, does there seem a need for one. There is no apostle for the creed of photography as a spiritual inquiry, no wise man to sing the epiphanies of photographic seeing, no replacement for Alfred Stieglitz. It would seem that Minor White, for all his flaws, was the last of the line.[38]

The bristly either/or attitude of the reviewer may help us to look with new eyes at White's work. Just as Lange's photographic record of Depression-era America was not merely a documentary exercise, so White's landscapes and abstractions from Nature—the strongest parts of his work—are not merely aesthetic exercises that ignore the human condition. From his writings, no less than from his photography, it is clear that White took a Platonic and Upanishadic view of the human condition: human beings begin in ignorance and blindness and make their way toward knowledge and illumination, if they make their way at all. More is to be gained from an art that looks toward the light, toward "displaying the infinite which was hid" in William Blake's words, than toward the darkness. White and photographers like him are hunters of the revealing moment, the shining detail, the perspective that unites a local place with the universe. "A fool sees not the same tree that a wise man sees," wrote Blake. White took him at his word.

White's strongest work represents moments when he was able to see the tree with rare vision. Rather than an evasion of human nature, as the reviewer believed, his art is a passionate exercise of its finest competence. White does not imply through his art that suffering is best ignored. He was one who "looked beyond" at his best and happiest times, but he knew where he stood.

A photograph from 1964 (Fig. 107), made at the height of his powers, transforms what must have been a bit of wall covered with cracked and weathered paint into a dark lacquer landscape in the Far Eastern tradition. "Landscape," "mountains," perhaps "trees" and "mist" glow beneath a no less enigmatic, elliptical "moon" and starless "sky." The linear pattern of cracks branching horizontally through the image contrasts with mysterious vertical washes of grey light. The image as a whole seems consummately fashioned by a Zen artist, perhaps of the period when an eccentric spirit entered landscape painting. The illusion of night and land is complete, yet the actuality of the eroded wall remains visible; hence the power of this work, which combines an almost painfully exquisite recognition of form with a salute to the ordinary.

The photograph is hushed and may prompt the viewer to quieten. It does not ignore the human condition; it changes it. For Minor White, whose life was full of uncertainty, this change had much to do with the purpose of art.

"The camera lures, then compels, a man to create through seeing,"[39] White wrote in 1952, toward the beginning of his mature career. The thought is close to Stieglitz's, whom White met near the end of the old man's life, and from whom he received a small token that served well

107. Minor White. *Moon and Wall Encrustations, Pultneyville, New York,* 1964. Gelatin-silver print. 9¼″ × 12⅛″. The Art Museum, Princeton University. The Minor White Archive. © 1982 by Trustees of Princeton University.

in later years—a reminder to participate, not to be a voyeur behind the camera.

As White's thought and experience developed, he increasingly related camerawork to spiritual disciplines—Zen and others—that he understood more deeply as time went on. His insights were not well ordered and expressed on every occasion, but the gist of what he said made sense. In the 1960s, the workshop emerged as an original teaching vehicle in various disciplines, including photography. White was quite a master at conducting workshops. Such small, voluntary gatherings dedicated to a single pursuit for a weekend or more helped to generate a strikingly intimate, fresh approach to the practical aspects of a skill. One can hear something of workshop intimacy in White's suggestions about creativity:

The state of mind of the photographer while creating is a blank. I might add that this condition exists only at special times, namely when looking for pictures. . . . For those who would equate "blank" with a kind of static emptiness, I must explain that this is a special kind of blank. It is a very active state of mind really, a very receptive state of mind, ready at an instant to grasp an image, yet with no image pre-formed in it at any time. . . . "Blank" as the creative photographer's state of mind is, uncritical as it is while photographing, as sensitized, as prepared for anything to happen, afterwards with the prints safely in hand he needs to practice the most conscious criticism.[40]

This may strike the reader as clumsy Zen—but it *is* Zen, and were it more elegantly expressed, the approach might not have been clearer to White's workshop listeners. On the whole, much of what Minor White said probably needs to be said again, but his finest photographs need not be made again, nor could they. They are perfect of their kind.

For people concerned with the spiritual in art, photography cannot help but have an odd poignancy. It is an essentially mechanical process. It presents the world as a solid. It cannot depict angels or any creature of the religious imagination without a good deal of costuming. Yet in certain hands—quite a few in the course of the century—it has repeatedly transcended its limitations. By making the world immensely real, it prompts a penetrating love of place, a brilliant confrontation with objects, and a longing for keen awareness. By reporting on the human condition, it can move us to recognize ourselves in the photograph and to awaken to what we are.

21 SEEKERS AND BRATS: ART IN RECENT YEARS

The spiritual and aesthetic adventure of twentieth-century art has not ended. The roaring success of Pop Art in the 1960s challenged the high seriousness of Abstract Expressionism, and Pop Art has continued to flourish both in the marketplace and intellectually as a devil's advocate. Andy Warhol (1928–1987), who did much to define its character, moved for decades in the art world and the public eye as a memorable, slightly corrosive Oscar Wilde—dispassionately witty, truth-telling in many respects. He was also a portrait of Dorian Gray: his boyishly sardonic face, effeminate ways, and dedicated pursuit of surface values held up a mirror to the art world that it found either irritating beyond measure or seductive. His art was dull, but he was a superb adversary, as necessary as the "contrary" was to Cheyenne warriors, years ago. The "contrary" had a genius for throwing the values and certainties of the tribe into question: he would wear women's clothes, ride into battle backwards, dip his hand with apparent delight into near-boiling water, pretend to swim on the waterless prairie—to the benefit of all concerned. But the "contrary" did not set the agenda, he challenged its rigidity; whereas Warhol and others with less flair have tended to set the agenda of contemporary art, at least in the marketplace. They are brats; he was the best of them.

Despite the rise of brats to fortune and influence, individual artists of merit have extended and deepened twentieth-century art in recent years. The best of their work bears comparison with the best of earlier twentieth-century art and shines quite brightly in the larger context of the history of art. Seekers and brats cohabit the art world—and cohabit, in some instances, one and the same person.

To divide contemporary and near-contemporary artists into seekers and brats is simplistic but to the point. Dualism haunts the galleries where one is so often rolled, so rarely nourished. Brats can be clever, keen-eyed, entertaining, intriguing, but their art is not serious even when solemn. Unlike solemnity, seriousness can include cascading good humor and sharp-edged Duchampian absurdity, but underneath the surface, however sparkling, there is a hidden tide in serious art—a question, an unrest, a knowledge trying to achieve visibility, an astonished apprehension of beauty, a sober assessment of ugliness that needs to be faced.

Some brats are taken very seriously by critics, collectors, and museums. Their work will be permanently inscribed in the history of art. It has made its mark in time; it is part of the fabric of action and reaction, and generates intriguing social and cultural insights. However, this chapter concerns seeking artists who have acknowledged and extended the spiritual in art. Those discussed here are representative. Our purpose will be served if these pages make clear that concern for the spiritual in art has survived into the 1980s, where it is, I believe, reaching for a still more knowing and vigorous realization than in the past.

The work of contemporary and near-contemporary artists has no patina. It may have the glamour of "brand-name" recognizability, but that is not the same at all as age and distance. Even Paris 1910, Dessau 1926, and New York 1950 have acquired patina of a kind that art of more recent decades cannot have. Knowing the weaknesses of our culture—particularly the spiritual uncertainty—and not expecting artists to be wholly free of them, viewers may mistrust contemporary art that *seems* to be spiritually informed merely because it is contemporary.

We need provisionally to trust the artist to be a channel. Years ago, Klee wrote that the artist "does nothing other than gather and pass on what comes to him from the depths. He neither serves nor rules—he transmits. . . . He is merely a channel." Few believe this of artists today, and few believe that it could be so. Most believe that artists are by and large egotists, channeling primarily their own notions and passions. A little more generosity is in order. When an artist *seems* to know and has found a marvelously winning expression, it will do no harm to acknowledge the achievement and allow that—perhaps, for a fleeting moment—he or she was transparent to what came from the depths. We cannot reasonably expect "much, much later, the *pure art*," as Kandinsky wrote, without some sign of it today.

The roster of contemporary and near-contemporary artists in this chapter begins with Robert Smithson, a highly dedicated and celebrated artist who died too young to fulfill himself. It concludes with Setsuya Kotani, a Japanese-American little known outside of art circles

in the southeastern United States where he lives. It includes living artists who enjoy acclaim and others who have abandoned hope of public
recognition, artists with substantial university posts and others who
make do. What they have in common is more important than their differences: they are seekers—and finders.

The Earthworks movement that emerged in the 1960s united rejection
of the conventional art market with ecological concern, self-protective
irony, and immense nostalgia for ancient religious monuments. Some
Earthworks, collage on a massive scale, retrieved waste material and
abandoned sites and transformed them—not precisely into temples or
sacred places but into something of that kind.

Among the Earth artists of that decade, Robert Smithson (1938–
1973) was a pioneer. Killed in an air crash while surveying a colossal
work in progress in the American desert, he was accorded a hero's
honors and remains now a legend, a *puer aeternus* forever hiking
in lonely places, worrying and dreaming. Smithson put his greatest
efforts into transforming the landscape in places that few connoisseurs
would be likely to visit and still fewer could own. "The new aesthetics," he wrote in 1968, "sees no value in labored sculpture or hand-
painted paintings."[1] On the other hand, documentary reflections of his
Earthworks—preparatory drawings, photographs, film—were made
available to the art market and helped to support his work. During his
eight years of increasing prominence in the American avant-garde, he
also wrote for art journals not only about his own work but about
other art and the world at large. As a writer and thinker, he recalls the
Beat Generation: his words can be howls of protest, leaping from
thought to thought, image to image, untidy, willful, and obscure, but
just as often brilliant. Unlike most members of the Beat Generation, he
exercised a meticulous scientific temperament both in ironic forms—
for example, in narratives crammed with empirical trivia—and in absolute sincerity.

The poetry and anger in his writings and the vigor of his return to
the scale of ancient monuments set him apart as one of the artists of his
generation most sensitive to the threat of an art emptied of meaning.
His was an idealistic mind caught between a thirst for meaning and the
recognition that the twentieth century is defined more by industrial
wastelands and urban chic than by some utter sincerity that he felt to
be necessary. The culture of the marketplace seemed to be driving toward entropy, as he put it—a motionless endpoint drained of energy.

In passage after passage in his writings, he evoked the fall into entropy in a grimly poetic style that masks discomfort with cool detachment, as if he were a reporter from elsewhere.

> . . . we gain a clear perception of physical reality free from the general claims of "purity and idealism." Only commodities can afford such illusionistic values; for instance, soap is 99⁴⁴/₁₀₀ percent pure, beer has more spirit in it, dog food is ideal; all this means such values are worthless. As the cloying effect of such "values" wears off, one perceives the "facts" of the outer edge, the flat surface, the banal, the empty, the cool, blank after blank; in other words, that infinitesimal condition known as entropy.[2]

Smithson echoed this passage, from a review of Minimalist art, a year later in one of his finest essays, "A Tour of the Monuments of Passaic, New Jersey," in which he narrated and recorded in photographs a mock-heroic odyssey by bus and foot along the industrially blighted shores of the Passaic River. His stately title recalls the literary excursions of other eras, such as Thomas Browne's antiquarian wanderings and Thoreau's *A Week on the Concord and Merrimack Rivers,* which Smithson transforms with irony and underlying sorrow. He photographs a bridge and identifies it as "The Bridge Monument Showing Wooden Sidewalks." He captions a child's sandbox "The Sand-Box Monument (also called the Desert)."

> Under the dead light of the Passaic afternoon the desert became a map of infinite disintegration and forgetfulness. This monument of minute particles blazed under a bleakly glowing sun. . . . This sand box doubled as an open grave—a grave that children cheerfully play in.[3]

There is educated wit in Smithson's writings, undeniable sensibility and intellectual scope—and more than a touch of sophomoric, self-regarding angst. But apart from these traits, which he shared with many of our generation, there is also a powerful, individual instinct that eventually drove him into the desert to make monuments that more nearly satisfied his unspoken longing for the pure and ideal—for coherent, purposeful action, not entropy.

From this venture came the *Spiral Jetty* (Fig. 108). Smithson later narrated his discovery of the site on the shores of the Great Salt Lake and his realization that the project he had been nurturing for some time would have to be a great jetty wheeling out into the water. His

108. Robert Smithson. *Spiral Jetty,* Great Salt Lake, Utah, 1970. Mud, precipitated salt crystals, rocks, water. Coil 1500′ in length, approx. 15′ in width. Photo: Gianfranco Gorgoni/Contact.

comments combined Whitmanesque poetry with the factuality of an engineering project description. The desert, so important to the imagination of Malevich fifty years earlier, became for Smithson a real working environment.

> . . . the valley spread into uncanny immensity. . . . Slowly, we drew near the lake, which resembled an impassive faint violet sheet held captive in a stony matrix, upon which the sun poured down its crushing light. An expanse of salt flats bordered the lake, and caught in its sediments were countless bits of wreckage. Old piers were left high and dry. The mere sight of the trapped fragments of junk and waste transported one into a world of modern prehistory. The products of a Devonian industry, the remains of a Silurian technology. . . . As I looked at the site, it reverberated out to the horizons only to suggest an immobile cyclone while flickering light made the entire landscape appear to quake. . . . The site was a rotary that enclosed itself in an immense roundness. From that gyrating space emerged the possibility of the Spiral Jetty. No ideas, no concepts,

no systems, no structures, no abstractions could hold themselves together in the actuality of that evidence. . . . No sense wondering
about classifications and categories, there were none.

    After securing a twenty year lease . . . , and finding a contrac-
tor . . . , I began building the jetty in April, 1970.[4]

With the help of dump trucks, a tractor, and a front-loader, the jetty
began to take shape. Smithson continued inwardly to move among
powerful psychological forces—on occasion perceiving the jetty and
the algae-pink lake as symbols linked in complex patterns with the culture he had amassed, on other occasions perceiving them as neutral
things. He could list their attributes with an obsessive nominalism absorbed from the writings of Ad Reinhardt and Samuel Beckett:

> North—Mud, salt crystals, rocks, water
> North by East—Mud, salt crystals, rocks, water
> Northeast by North—Mud, salt crystals, rocks, water[5]

Both his stolid refusal of meaning here and his supercharged layering
of meaning in other passages possess a restless, uneasy quality, as if
neither voice speaks for Smithson, not quite. Neither a Beckett nor a
Walt Whitman, yet drawn to the attitudes each typifies, Smithson was
torn and vitally at work during the construction of the *Spiral Jetty* and
in writing about his experience retrospectively.

    The monument itself can be understood as a twentieth-century
homage to archaic Earthworks and temples—to the Serpent Mound of
Ohio, the Nazca Lines of Peru, the great Neolithic temple in Malta,
and other monuments created by human beings more certain of their
worlds and their gods than we can be. The *Spiral Jetty* is dignified by
its simplicity and intent—and by a certain naiveté. Smithson poured
into it his ravenous need for meaning, for a comprehensive sign that
defeats "classifications and categories" and reaffirms the sacredness of
the Earth and of ourselves. But the jetty also embodies his question:
Can the Earth, and man who harms it, escape final entropy?

    In his writings, Smithson showed little hope of a joyful outcome, but
as an Earth artist he went on from the jetty to envisage further projects
full of his fervor for decency. For example, he sought corporate spon-
sorship to reshape an abandoned strip mine and other industrial wastelands into purposeful Earthworks. Had they ever come to be, these
projects would surely have reflected the idealism and hope that he concealed, for the most part, beneath cool rejection.

> . . . purity and spiritualism and esotericism and hermeticism . . . ab-
> straction, all those things . . . idealism . . . all those imponderables

. . . metaphysics. There's just a great storehouse, as I call it, at the end of this junkyard, metaphysics, you constantly dispense purity, ideals, spiritualism.[6]

This inventory of the junkyard, metaphysics, is clearly knowledgeable. Up to a point, he had explored it—enough to know that contemporary life and ancient ideas are tenuously related at best. His work represents a first attempt on his part to link them convincingly. As it happened, an unforeseeable rise in water level submerged *Spiral Jetty* a few years after its construction. It is, for now, invisible. The strange pathos of its disappearance can only underscore a perception of the dignity and fragility of Smithson's work.

Like the work of Robert Smithson although with greater sophistication, Beverly Pepper's recent sculpture (Fig. 109) evokes the gnawing need in contemporary culture for a sense of the sacred, a rediscovery of primal dignity in what we are and where we live. Working in a Minimalist, geometric language from the late 1960s until about 1978, Pepper acquired superb skills as a metalworker in factories and foundries in the United States and Italy. Her art in those years, while intriguing, laid the groundwork for a new departure that is more than intriguing.

Writing a few years before the new art emerged, Pepper said:

. . . the abstract language of form that I have chosen has become a way to explore an interior life of feeling. . . . Put briefly, I wish to make an object that has a powerful physical presence, but is at the same time inwardly turned, seeming capable of intense self-absorption.[7]

Her polished geometries of the earlier years did not fully capture that intention, owing to a bravura quality of controlled performance and a Minimalist schematism that tend to be chilly rather than accepting and meditative. But she conceived the desire to be a sculptor at Angkor Wat, and in time the values that must have moved her at that great temple site found their way into her work more explicitly. "For many years," she told an interviewer in 1981,

"I thought monumentality was only about scale, and there was no need for us to make monuments. There were no heroes or events to celebrate, so we have made no monuments." That changed one day in Rome [*the interviewer continued*], when she sat in a piazza and really looked at the commemorative columns and arches around her. "They were monuments to special events or heroes, yet for me

109. Beverly Pepper. *Basalt Ritual*, 1985–86. Basalt. Height 7′11″; diameter of base 4′11″. Photo: courtesy André Emmerich Gallery, New York.

the work had an enormous meaning beyond the historical moment. I decided I had been incorrect. A monument could be to a whole people. . . . A monument transcends time. It doesn't have to be physically big, but it should be able to have something you get from primitive art, a spirituality. The meaning of it is . . . man saying: "It exists; I still exist."[8]

This insight was joined by another, gleaned from the massive old tools and machine parts that she had often seen in Italian foundries. Like David Smith before her,[9] Pepper found them arresting and suggestive beyond their utilitarian function; such tools have the magic of an intimate archaeology as if, digging up our own culture ahead of time, we find its remnants to be just as exotic as artifacts from a proper dig. There is a crafted honesty and enlivening ambiguity in tools made during the transition from the preindustrial world of handwork to the world of machine production.

Pepper found her way in the late 1970s to a new art monumental in scale, and in form inspired initially by the shapes of old tools. The hard gleam of highly polished metal gave way to the earthy patina of cast iron and subtly integrated washes of paint on satiny steel surfaces. The expressive scope of her art ranges now from the archaic anonymity of *Basalt Ritual,* which seems to have survived from an early era of religious certainty, to baroque shafts with intricate detail and painted elements resembling the finials of a processional chariot or ritual posts from an unidentified culture, not our own. *Basalt Ritual* is a grouping, nearly a *sacra conversazione,* in which the pillars seem to engage with each other in some infinitely slow way.[10] Pepper is exploring here a terrain of form and meaning previously visited by Brancusi and Noguchi, but with a vigor and sincerity denoting independence.

The difficulties of the spiritual in twentieth-century art remain what they were. Franz Marc could write in 1914 about art that "belongs on the altars of a future spiritual religion"; he saw such art around him. It is still here—Pepper in fact describes some of her metal sculpture as "urban altars." The religion prophesied in 1914 by Marc and in 1985 unforgotten by Pepper continues to be unidentified, and unidentifiable. The forms of *Basalt Ritual* evoke the ancient past, but they are presented into our technological world—where they are widely received with a shock of recognition. Pepper's growing reputation confirms that some substantial segment of the public for art feels benefited by her work and wishes to share in the affirmation: "It exists; I still exist"—not "I," the mundane ego, but "I" deeper down.

Both Smithson and Pepper carried something of archaic religious worlds into our own world, stripped of specific references and all the more expressive for that reason. While the spiritual in art need not refer back, the images, doctrines, and atmosphere of traditional religious culture remain capable of evoking powerful nostalgia. Twentieth-century artists who are sensitive to that nostalgia and who go to the trouble of learning ancient forms and techniques have a struggle on their hands to bring those forms and techniques forward without ceasing to be of their own time—and without denaturing the very things they value by repeating them in an alien context. This explains why I have not drawn Georges Rouault, a French artist of considerable poetic power, into this book; his work relies on a painterly evocation of medieval stained glass and is, for all its warm beauty, retrospective in orientation—not a leap toward an art of our own but an extraordinarily comforting remembrance.

The work of André Enard, a French émigré now living in New York City, provides a rich context to continue this line of thought. Trained as a painter in the atelier of Fernand Léger after World War II (where Beverly Pepper worked for a time), he also designed stained glass in the years when church windows lost in the war were being replaced across the country. Enard supported himself in the 1950s by stained-glass commissions and distanced himself from Léger's strong influence. The mobile calligraphy of the American Mark Tobey and the energy of Jackson Pollock's work entranced him. His art followed suit, but parallel to his informal American apprenticeship, he continued an eclectic exploration of traditional religious imagery and underlying technical procedures that ranged from Orthodox Christian icons and Islamic patterning and calligraphy to Hindu painting in its more abstract, geometrical phases. The integrated art that emerged in the 1970s can be ravishing; a black-and-white reproduction (Fig. 110) is only a pale reflection of an art that, for all its borrowings, has a life of its own. Against a black ground, a meticulously detailed cellular gold mesh winds its way through a triangular frame flanked by semicircles. Axial and central points within the frame are emphasized, while a "frame within the frame" reads as a shell or seedcase sheltering a central kernel. The image has a tidy coherence and remarkable flash owing to its juxtaposition of black and gold, as in old Hindu painted cloths.

What are we looking at? A geometry that recalls both the Platonic "perfect figures" and Tantric designs, the image of the labyrinth rendered as a looping intestinal pattern, gestational images of seed and egg—drawn into a whole by craftsmanship that brings to mind the

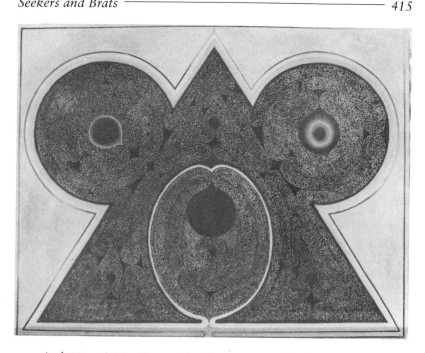

110. André Enard. *Number 27*, October 8, 1975. Oil and goldleaf on wood, 30″ × 24″. Private Collection.

skills of jeweler and icon-maker. Has this anything to do with our own culture? That, of course, was the question Enard worked through in this series of images.

These works are treasures. No one, to my knowledge, has more diligently gathered up the skeins of traditional forms, symbols, and materials to create twentieth-century icons of such intensity. They can make a chapel out of a game room. On the other hand, they are fervently and deliberately retrospective and for this reason leave open the question of an art of our own.

Enard's thinking about art and spirituality promises new explorations. He writes with the blend of passion and deliberation that we encountered in Paul Klee, to whom he feels akin. "Most manifestations of art today lack good common sense," he has written,

lack relation with a higher reality, and lack spiritual purpose.

What can there be of value without a search into oneself, linked to essential knowledge?

Isn't the ultimate desire of human beings to perceive an order of laws that surpasses us yet is also within us, and to participate in that order?

Isn't the role of the artist to reflect on and to reflect back something of this greater order, for the sake of stimulating the viewer to reconstruct the original idea?

Isn't this quest the purpose, conscious or unconscious, of all artistic effort?

To try to grasp the soul, that which animates each thing at its source!

Finally, what seems most important in the process of painting is the quality of feeling that the artist conveys by doing what he does, no matter what subject he chooses; and then, the care he takes and the quality of attention he communicates, which may arouse the same quality in the viewer.

When that quality of energy is there, it can be felt—it is palpable, visible in the canvas. It has an action; one is touched, and one can glimpse the reality behind appearances.

The act of painting can be understood as a work of contemplation, of meditation, through which the artist can rediscover and remember what is laid down in his deepest nature, his primal consciousness—and by that very means summon the same in response from the viewer.[11]

The work of Cynthia Villet, a South African-born artist who has lived in many parts of the world (Barbados, Jerusalem, Vancouver), exemplifies the hiddenness of the spiritual in twentieth-century art. While Villet has exhibited for several decades and achieved a *succès d'estime*, like many highly gifted artists she is shy of the art market and unwilling to put time into self-promotion. Her work can nonetheless be found in New York and elsewhere, and it is often very beautiful—intensely felt yet rigorous, soft-spoken but sure. Her style is cultivated; her spirituality, like a wildflower, seems given.

Villet has acted as if twentieth-century art is a tradition. Her sources, long meditated and well understood, are primarily the Cubist collage, Klee, Bissier, Nicholson, Tobey, and Morandi—the "modest masters." Not captured by them, but learning from them at earlier stages of her career, she has long since struck off in independent directions without losing touch. Even now her work resonates back through that lineage of quiet, musical artists, miniaturists in spirit if not always in scale. This pattern of kinship and freedom is surely one criterion for a valid tradition.

111. Cynthia Villet. *Pythagoras No. 3*, 1985. Oil wash on canvas. 12″ × 11½″. Private Collection.

Pythagoras No. 3 (Fig. 111) is a splendid example of Villet's current work. Like Enard, she is drawn by ancient signs. Here the classic geometrical figure that demonstrates the Pythagorean theorem is immersed in a fluid environment of calligraphy and parchment-colored washes. Suggestions of antiquity and of a primal rationality, tinged with religious awe, are balanced by bright spots of color that tumble freely like balloons or puffballs in the solemn atmosphere. The canvas is magical, a meditation on ancient things made light and surprising by a few childlike marks that have the gaiety not of childhood but of childhood recovered, innocence renewed. It conveys in quiet pictorial terms the only message of this book: kinship and freedom, disciplined apprenticeship and unworried spontaneity.

A charcoal drawing of a bottle (Fig. 112), executed originally enough on a square of sandpaper, typifies Villet's approach to a theme that has preoccupied her over the years—one with an honorable history dating from Cubism. Bottles have provided Villet a fertile meditation on figure and ground, substance and atmosphere, line and texture, assertion and reticence, Nature and imagination. This drawing, like a number of others in her oeuvre, conveys a further set of complementaries: solidity

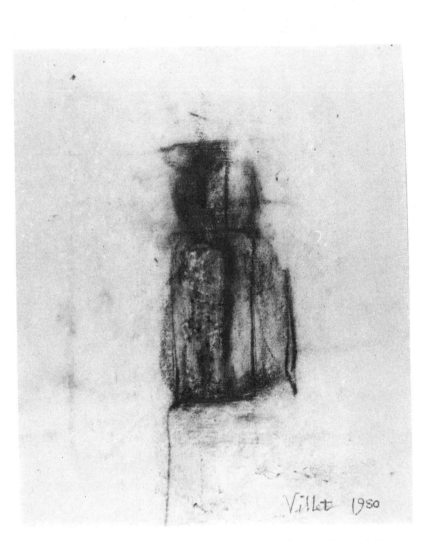

112. Cynthia Villet. *Bottle*, 1980. Charcoal on sandpaper. 8″ × 10″. Private Collection.

and transparency, poise and precariousness, presence and absence. With unerring authority of gesture, it asks the viewer to share in a vision of change.

There is a natural mysticism, not learned or aggressively pursued. It represents simply a point of view on life experience that unfolds in its own way, and seemingly without strain includes unusual perceptions of energy and structure. It is a rather solitary consciousness, not one that benefits much from orderly spiritual teachings with their inevitable suggestion of progressive attainments, their intimidations and triumphs. The barriers are thinner for the natural mystic. Something of this creative and risky condition seems reflected in Villet's art.

Recently pondering her "main thoughts and guiding rules" where art is concerned, she wrote with clarity and robustness about the things that matter:

Aesthetic Honesty
Aesthetic honesty is a goal to be pursued and, when discovered, treasured.

For instance, the intentional combining of particular colors—e.g., the proximity of a certain red to a certain blue—will arouse a particular emotional response in the viewer. By introducing a certain shade of purple (the combination of red and blue), or adding the complementary yellow which the purple craves, a drama of color occurs.

Other dramas, of preconceived intent, are enacted with the appearance of other colors. The same rules apply with the use of form. Weight and balance take the place of color or interact with it.

The Accidental Discovery, the Unexpected, and the Free Gift
Sometimes colors or forms are accidentally splashed or dropped— and have a magical quality, indefinable, seldom attained through striving logically. This to me is the Free Gift.

The process of making art is much like fishing. Beneath the fluid and enigmatic surface of the water, anything may occur—and who knows what might be brought to the surface when the line is reeled in. How one looks forward to the joy of the Accidental Discovery and the Unexpected.

Curiosity
I am always, above all, curious. Saying—"What would happen if I put this color next to that one, remove this form and substitute an-

other, enlarge this area and diminish its neighbor," and so on. I am always expectant of a miracle.

> The change from the old to the new,
> The worthless to the valued,
> The lost to the found.

The Magic Studio
When entering my workroom, I am usually expectant and a bit fearful. It would not surprise me if, on opening the door, the work of the day before started to hum, sing, or give off light.

Stillness
A pot is spinning on the wheel, perfectly centered, its clay walls brought to the form desired by the potter. The wheel gradually begins to turn more slowly until it comes at last to a stop. The pot is complete.

Just so in my work, there comes a moment when time seems to slow down, the work and I seem to blend together, until everything including time stops. There is stillness, and the work is finished.[12]

There must be an emblem—a charged image that provokes heightened attention—but it needn't be exotic or ancient. While some contemporary artists have legitimately looked toward ancient symbols and atmospheres, others have found an understated but real spirituality much closer at hand. Hence the Pythagorean figure but also the bottle in Villet's work; hence the ordinary workman's tools (Fig. 113) that recur in the paintings, drawings, and prints of Jim Dine.

Ohio-born, and a born seeker, Jim Dine began his career in New York as a brat in the late 1950s. He participated in Allen Kaprow's Happenings and devised performance pieces of his own that earned a good deal of notoriety. He created roughly painted canvases with attached objects in the manner of Robert Rauschenberg and Jasper Johns, his elders in the generation that was challenging Abstract Expressionism. Taken up by the media, praised as an innovative Pop artist before he had in his own opinion accomplished much, Dine took a leave of absence in 1967 and lived in London with his family for a number of years while rededicating himself to painting. Returning to the United States in 1971, he found a farm in Vermont and thereafter divided his time between city and country.

Dine embraced the most sober discipline of all, drawing—sheer drawing, sheer seeing translated to the sheet of paper with affection for

113. Jim Dine. *Untitled Tool Series (5-Bladed Saw)*, 1973. Charcoal and graphite, 25″ × 19⅞″. Collection, The Museum of Modern Art, New York. Gift of the Robert Lehman Foundation, Inc.

the object and for the process of rendering it. Among a number of re-current themes in the 1970s and 1980s, his renderings of familiar tools are unforgettable. Like Villet's drawings of bottles, Dine's tools take us into the artist's confidence and allow us to share a search for lucid yet felt seeing. In the rendering of a multiblade saw illustrated here, the interplay between realism and a poetry of light and dark is remark-able. There is an unbiased attention at work, as willing to explore the reality of a shadow as to render hundreds of sawteeth with equanimity. There is as well a telling poetry, rooted in Cubism and Malevich, that turns on the assertion and dissolution of form; the saw is "real" and not real, the blades fanning to the right are asserted by highly legible lines and defining shadows and dissolved by what amount to erasures. "I'm not interested in realism," Dine has said.

> I'm not interested in realist painting. I'm not interested in illustrative painting. I'm not interested in depictive painting. I'm interested in painting that's about painting.[13]

The circularity in this statement is true to his experience. It is a cir-cularity that we have encountered before, memorably in Ad Reinhardt's writings. But if his painting is about painting, and his drawing about drawing, then what are painting and drawing about? When they have the purity and intentness of Dine's best work, painting and drawing are about the process of consciousness: the seeing; the physical trans-lation of things seen into representations; the feelings, thoughts, and instinctive recognitions about the world and ourselves that cannot help but appear as the artist works—and cannot help but find their way onto the sheet of paper or stretched canvas.

Not explicitly spiritual, Jim Dine's work suggests a relation with ex-perience based on attention that goes beyond the ordinary. This is surely the basis for any authentic spirituality; speculative systems that "go off into the blue" err precisely because they lack attention to the real. Dine's drawings, the record of a probing, relentless attention at work, are more true to the spiritual in fact than many neotantric geometries, ethereal atmospheres, and other odds and ends that are brought forward from time to time as the spiritual in art. "It's the greatest thing that's ever happened to me," Dine has said,

> I can now say to myself . . . , I am real. I am there, I am real. This literal mark I make is made by me, it's real.[14]

This is not a finished spirituality, a completed whole, but it is no small thing. Dine seems to have come to it in a moment of epiphany. Briefly evoked some years ago, it remains poignant:

> . . . in the beginning I had to struggle against a tendency in my work toward the banal. Then one day I simply decided to *celebrate* the banal.[15]

Celebration, as he understands and practices it in his best work, is not a Happening; it is a contact with reality full of poised attention, sustained by the will to remain "there" and "real." Having taken the time to establish himself in this practice, Dine has earned the right to be critical of much that passes for art today:

> The great failure is the lack of drawing. [Some] would say that there's no need for it in modern art, but I think that's the weakness in the art. The automatic quality of everything, the manufactured quality. What everyone thinks is great freedom is a lack of draughtsmanship. And the forced ugliness is true ugliness, I think.[16]

The superb art of William Bailey (Figs. 114, 115) will allow us to continue exploring the issues raised by Jim Dine's drawing—and enter on quite new ones. Kingman Brewster Professor of Art at the Yale University School of Art, Bailey is recognized for his technical and imaginative strengths, and he has earned a fiercely loyal following among collectors. This is European painting in the grand tradition of Piero della Francesca, who perceived the inherent geometry of all things without losing touch with their suppleness; of Ingres, whose crisp draftsmanship and sense for the eggshell-like delicacy of surfaces are timelessly fresh; and of Corot, who combined a stately, monumental sense of form with intimate brushwork willing to perfect the smallest passage of a painting. Bailey has acknowledged admiration for these artists and several others, not least Giorgio Morandi in whom he finds a belief, like his own, "in the power of the mute object."[17] But Bailey's art is of our time, and a learned inventory of sources cannot reveal it.

It is, again, an art of attention. Whether the subject is a still life or a poised young woman, Bailey perceives it with a clarity and a will to discover pure form in a purified setting that invite the viewer to share the artist's enterprise. It is an art tinged with sadness, as if the objects were being recorded for the last time: art in a minor key. The quiet

114. William Bailey. *Manhattan Still Life,* 1980. Oil on canvas. 40″ × 50″. General Mills Art Collection, Minneapolis, Minnesota. Photo: courtesy Schoelkopf Gallery.

attention that assembles a horizontal flow of objects or isolates a figure against a textured expanse of wall is enormously responsive. He notices every detail of contour, of surface, of light and shadow, and of formal relations, holds them in the mind, and records them with Mondrianesque precision. While the subjects are "realistic," the art itself is not realistic in the ordinary sense. "I don't understand a lot of realist painting," Bailey has said.

I don't know why anyone would do it. I think that all painting is abstract.[18]

The mood of objects and of persons becomes acutely perceptible when we grasp their physicality not just once in a flash but at length with persistence. The tempo of Bailey's art is slow; one's eye moves slowly through and across the canvas. "I want to make work that is silent," he has commented, "that unfolds very slowly."[19] For the viewer

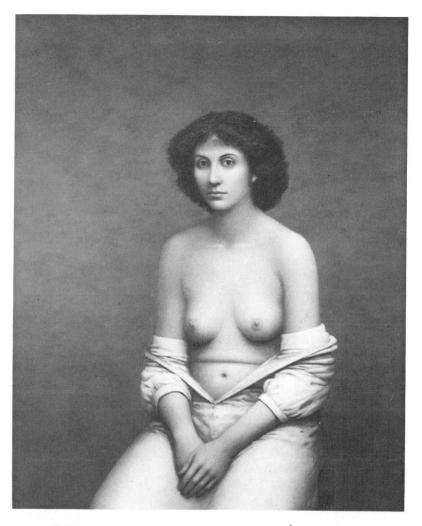

115. William Bailey. *Portrait of S.*, 1980. Oil on canvas. 50″ × 40″. University of Virginia Art Museum, Charlottesville. Photo: courtesy Schoelkopf Gallery.

as no doubt for the artist, seeing acquires the quality of ritual and gradually reveals a somewhat enigmatic mood.

This mood, finally, is the theme of the paintings. There is more here than dedication to seeing and virtuoso craftsmanship. There is anxiety, subtle confrontation with doubt—as if the artist, testing the substantiality and durability of things, finds them fragile and mortal. The formal purity and solidity of his objects have something of the character of a protest, an assertion of substantiality against an implicit threat. Similarly, the vibrant psychological life of the young woman and the tender nakedness of her torso are challenged, one might say, by the odd restriction of her arms. She is not only a beauty presented with loving attention, she is also subtly constrained and, in the large featureless space that surrounds her, a little lost. The magic of Bailey's art derives as much from its quiet "living with" the unseen fragility of things as from its masterful rendering of their visibility. Seemingly an academic art, a professorial art, it is in fact a contemporary poetry that brings the viewer freshly in touch with the ancient theme of the beauty and transiency of all things.

That theme is aesthetic and in the best sense humanistic, but it is also a perennial theme of spiritual teachings. Like many of his peers, Bailey is said to dissociate his work from the spiritual in art, and rightly so if the spiritual is understood, as it often is, to substitute wooly thinking for a direct encounter with sensuous experience. That is not Bailey's spirituality. His paintings convey a stripped-down spirituality of the kind we have already encountered in Jim Dine's work: a reverent attention that reveals both how the world is and how the artist is before it. This spirituality is not an "answer" to the enigmas of experience; it is a concentrated willingness to question, observe, and feel the state of affairs. There is more true nourishment in these paintings, where there is no definitive answer, than in many works that claim a metaphysical prestige.

Speaking recently about his creative development, Bailey recalled a key transition that occurred in 1960, when he had just returned from a world trip and had begun to distance himself from the influence of Abstract Expressionism—which haunted any young artist who trained as he did in the 1950s.

> I . . . realized that American painters, using Picasso as a role model, believe artists must constantly change and amaze. I decided that that kind of innovation was not a primary virtue at all. It may have been for Picassso, but it wasn't for a number of painters that I most ad-

mire in the history of art. The key was to stay with something and keep making it better, cleaner, more resonant, more intense.[20]

Hence the long series of still lifes and figure studies, dating back to the early 1960s, that have graced this artist's career and provide an imposing counterbalance to the turbulence and superficiality of much else in contemporary art.

An abrupt return from the crystalline world of Bailey's art to painterly abstraction will enforce the obvious truth that twentieth-century art is exceptionally rich in valid languages. The abstract collage-paintings of Luise Kaish carry into the 1980s a series of concerns dating back through the beautiful colored grids of Anne Ryan to those of Paul Klee, and through the deliberately reckless brushwork of Rauschenberg and Johns to Kandinsky's generation. Kaish's daring brushwork and meditative temperament yield paintings endowed with brilliant surfaces and an understated contact with age-old symbols and patterns of meaning, in which the language of abstraction comes to life again and speaks to the human condition as clearly as ever.

Lover's House I (Fig. 116) appears rough and unfinished in a black-and-white illustration; it depends a great deal on brilliant color and, further, on contrasts between smooth and gritty passages of paint. Like Jasper Johns' *Numbers* paintings—genuinely philosophical works little recognized as such—it projects the steady order of a grid and challenges it with the fluidity of paint. This "house" is one of order and disorder, cleanly drafted lines and seemingly random trickles and smudges. The pattern of a central cross is picked out on the grid, flanked at right by a cool zone of blue flecked with red and yellow, at left by a hot red zone with yellows, oranges, and smudges of blue. There is a hint of the yin—yang concept—the cool zone visited by warm colors, the warm zone visited by cool, the whole structured and unified by the "colorless" white cross articulating the grid. At the top of the image, there is a suggestion of the sun's rays illuminating only the warm side of the grid.

Is this an icon, a condensed and deliberate statement that points beyond itself? I believe so. By pure painterly means, the canvas depicts order and disorder, structure and energy wholly mingled with each other, and contrasting energies bound into one. It remains pattern and paint, fascinating in its careful construction, no less fascinating in its rhetoric of carelessness. It digs deeply into the viewer's sensibility, asking to be recognized as a meditation on experience.

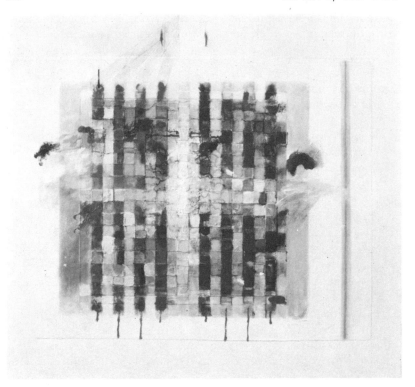

116. Luise Kaish. *Lovers' House I*, 1983–84. Mixed media on canvas. 28" × 30". Private Collection.

Is this the spiritual in art, in one manifestation? Arguably so. We can restate its theme in terms that would be congenial to pupils in the Hermetic schools of late antiquity. For example, "The Two are One; the Third is neither the First nor Second, yet allows them to be One," etc. The restatement is intentionally ridiculous, but it serves to illustrate the underlying abstraction of abstraction. Most of us surely prefer the vitality of the picture, which allows us to experience many levels simultaneously: form and color, the feelings they arouse, and perhaps some unspoken acknowledgment that the design of reality pits complementary energies against each other which need to be reconciled again and again.

Kaish is a maker of abstract icons, a metaphysical artist almost despite herself, in the sense that her work resonates with larger themes without setting that aim. A metaphysic does not need to be devised conceptually where it emerges naturally. She has discovered in twentieth-century abstraction a language of the spirit that is also a keen pictorial experience.

Kaish served until recently as Chairperson of the Division of Painting and Sculpture at Columbia University School of the Arts, where she remains a professor. Like William Bailey, she is associated with a distinguished institution; and like him, she has not lost what Coomaraswamy called "the art of thinking in images," which can make "the verbal logic of philosophy" seem pale.[21]

The drive to change and amaze, as Bailey put it, has been quietly ignored by many gifted artists, who find their study and pursue it through thick and thin. Erik Koch is one such, a Danish artist now living in France, who studied with Hans Hofmann in Provincetown in the years around 1950. Koch has done everything that he should not have done. In years when massive paintings were the norm and paintings of moderate size were considered unsure, he became for the most part a miniaturist. His diminutive works (Fig. 117), measuring often five inches square or less, could not have been more out of step. In the decades when the marketplace was thriving successively on dramatic Abstract Expressionist works, the cheerful commonplaces of Pop Art, the retinal assaults of Op Art, the expensive austerities of Minimalism, and the imposing impasto of Neo-Expressionism, Koch was simply not on board. He had a vision that was not of the marketplace, and he persisted in it. This was a miserable business strategy, but his art was very good and remains so.

In historical perspective, Koch's art is a meditation on the pictorial discoveries of Matisse and Mondrian. The *colour-poems,* as he calls his decades-long series of miniatures, explore the infinite range of color and color relations through the simple compositional device of a variable grid. He may dynamize the grid into a highly irregular pattern, as in the illustrated work, or treat it plainly as sets of intersecting perpendiculars; in either case, the focus is color itself. The results are often nothing short of ravishing. Like the ragas of Hindu music they are tone poems reflecting the intrinsic qualities of moments and places. Their frequently literary titles tie them to the artist's experience, as if they are the distillate of changing circumstances.

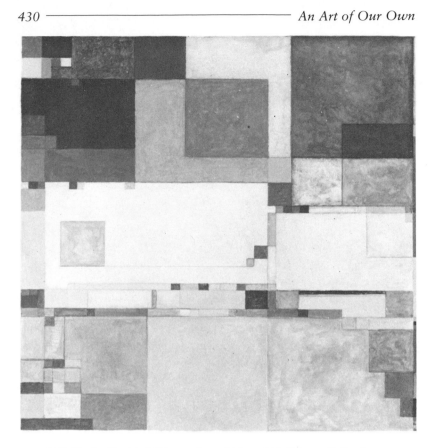

117. Erik Koch. *Untitled.* Watercolor. 7¾″ × 7¾″. Private Collection.

Simple as they are, and asking only to please by taking the viewer into an ordered and sensuous world, they nonetheless have rather complex intellectual and spiritual roots. The thought behind them is Mondrian's concept of pure plastic art, and beyond that P. D. Ouspensky's *Tertium Organum,* which Koch has long admired. The *colour-poems* are Koch's solicitations, day after day, year after year, of an awareness that reaches past the obvious to a more fundamental awareness, aesthetic and spiritual. What Schmalenbach wrote of Julius Bissier's colored miniatures can be said here: the *colour-poems* are a "book of hours," an intimate diary in pictorial form.

In my work, I search for central nothingness. From there colour-poems are born. I am working on open endgames, that is the way.[22]

"Open endgames"—the phrase is altogether satisfactory. In chess, endgame is the final stage: defeat is imminent for one or the other player. What is an open endgame? It must be a stage of art and life played out in recognition of imminent defeat but without tension, with no loss of finesse or spirit. The *colour-poems* themselves are no defeat. They figure among the lost works of twentieth-century art.

The art of Setsuya Kotani disappears in black-and-white reproductions; it even disappears behind framer's glass. I have included two illustrations (Figs. 118, 119) as a basis for discussion, but readers will not find anything approaching the finesse of the originals.

Born in Japan, Kotani accepted his family's rather daring offer of an American college education in Hawaii, and he later earned his MFA— passport to a teaching career—at Columbia University. He is now a professor of painting and ceramics at the University of North Carolina, Greensboro. In his work, the spiritual in art is at home. He has explored in recent years two imaginative worlds. One is all atmosphere, endlessness, and mystery; the other blends rigorous Constructivist patterning with the hushed color harmonies of his atmospheric works. In the first, energies predominate over structure; in the second, structure predominates over energies.

The first is an aerial world defined provisionally by vibrant spaces, levels, and flows of energy from one level to another. It gathers up some of the hard-won "signs" of the Abstract Expressionists—Rothko's atmospheres, Barnett Newman's vertical line, the color fields of Motherwell and others—into a new figuration of such beauty and meditative stillness that one forgets the past and sees the painting. Twentieth-century art is a nascent tradition, and Kotani's work (like Villet's) illustrates the power of that tradition: he speaks an established language, but with an eloquence and individuality that make it new again.

In the second phase of his art, Kotani explores the mainstream geometric language that passed from its implicit form in Cézanne through Cubism, Mondrian, and the Constructivists into the general vocabulary of twentieth-century art. It becomes again in his hands a language of the spirit, pitching obvious axial orders against strong diagonals, thus assembling in Mondrian words a "dynamic equilibrium" in the image of the world and of ourselves. The bold geometry of these works is stilled by washes of color borrowed from the "late afternoon absorbent twilight" of Reinhardt. Stillness is the genius of these works; the

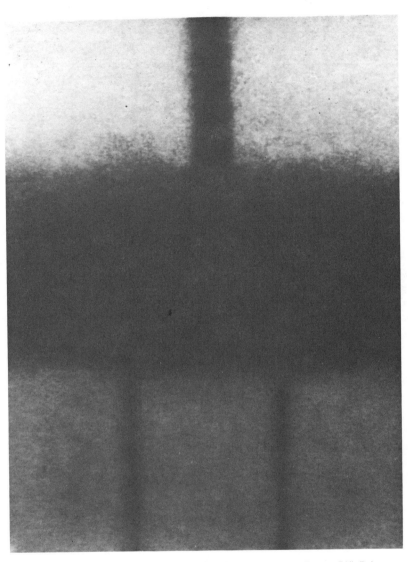

118. Setsuya Kotani. *Untitled*, 1986. Acrylic on paper. 24″ × 17⅞″. Private Collection.

119. Setsuya Kotani. *Untitled*, 1987. Acrylic on paper. 17⅞″ × 17⅞″. Private Collection.

geometry is familiar, the exquisite hush brought over it by the artist's color sensibility is not. The brashness of Constructivism has finally been quietened—without losing the mystique of orderliness and clarity that has always given the style its appeal. As noted earlier, Kotani works within twentieth-century tradition. We would be unable to recognize that nascent tradition, were artists of his stature not here today to demonstrate that the revolutions of earlier generations of artists are the culture of a later generation. Culture need not mean weakening; it can signify a deepening.

The spiritual in art cannot be altogether dissociated from mystery. "Looking beyond" may yield greater and finer knowledge, but it often leads as well to an abiding conviction that the pilgrim does not understand all that much. It leads to the cloud of unknowing where our knowledge ends. Kotani's art participates in the mystery and evokes it with love and subtlety.

"The nature of perception, imagination, and the creative process is very enigmatic," he has written.

> Now and then I visit the home of a colleague, a painter and art historian, where an oriental monochromatic scroll hangs on the wall. It never fails to draw my gaze.
>
> In the scroll, I see two macaques or rhesus-like monkeys. The slightly larger one, sitting in the foreground in a self-contained posture, has half-closed pensive eyes turned inward. The other, with a fully extended body, gazes outward with open eyes. Sometimes its gaze seems directed at a wasp overhead, at other times it seems directed into the void.
>
> Figuratively speaking, those two monkeys live in me. They are myself in the figure of monkeys: observation and imagination cohabiting the worlds of noumena and phenomena, immanence and transcendence.
>
> I need to imagine a whole, a universe beyond what might be called the mundane, though the ordinary delights my senses. As a painter, I live with doubt—which is the problem of abstraction. In my commitment to the craft of painting, full of tension between thought and act, I seek to realize an almost invisible conjunction of form/color and thought/emotion in imagined spaces, in a vision, as hand and eye join in search for equivalences.
>
> I hope that I am moving toward greater articulation and clarity of expression, bound only by the responsibility of sustaining a unified sense of self, although I may not realize my hope of certainty.[23]

Kotani speaks for many artists of our time and so provides an appropriate conclusion to this chapter. I have suggested that the spiritual in art is reaching now for a still more sophisticated and vigorous realization than in the past. I have presented some of the evidence for this view. Kotani, Bailey, Dine, Villet, and the others—as well as many whose names and works have not been mentioned for lack of space— have assured us an art of our own in decades when the art market has been for the most part busy with other things.

22   THE MARKETPLACE AND THE STUDIO

Few things are more joyful than the marketplace. I remember a Bedouin market on an arid hillside near Marrakesh. The merchants' camels and donkeys were tethered on the perimeter, quiet under the intense sun. The wares were displayed on carpets: staple foods, brass, bright skeins of wool, yard goods, village weavings, jewelry, leather, medicines—alongside weary machine parts and other signs of the industrial world. People milled in the heat, bargained intently in Berber and Arabic, rested in tea houses defined by carpets under tents open to the breeze. Tremendous vitality was visible, sensible everywhere; the wealth of things and motion was uplifting.

This was a market: an exotic market, of course—but all markets are at base the same. The most sophisticated businessperson in pin stripe and silk has points in common with the bedouin merchant crosslegged beside his wares. The streets and shops of Soho in New York City, a center of the international art market, are hardly less animated than that Moroccan market. There are no fewer exotic people, no less sense of impromptu community. New Yorkers visit Soho to be intrigued and dismayed, more rarely moved by the art on display; to have opinions over pleasant food; to see and be seen; to experience the inspired clutter.

The deliberately dignified galleries of Madison Avenue and Fifty-seventh Street are not all that different. They are another theater for the vivid transactions of the marketplace. Buyers appear with money, desire; sellers make their stock available with shows of noble indifference to price or suggestions of investment potential. The transactions even of this urbane marketplace are cultural and emotional events—buyers diminished financially but almost physically enlarged by the sheer glory of their purchases; sellers satisfied that they have understood their market. All are changed, confirmed by the transaction.

Hidden from the public places where buyers meet sellers are of course back offices, where the merchant carefully prepares the transactions of the marketplace. The merchant gathers inventory from varied sources—some nearby, others distant (all good merchants have a little of Sindbad in them). The merchant thinks out not only what the market demands at a given time but also what it is likely to demand in the future. He develops a business strategy that may well include priming the market through some form of public relations and advertising.

All of this, whether it occurs in the Moroccan scrub or on Madison Avenue, is blameless: it is the free market at work, providing goods and services, responding to customers' demands, reinforcing the desirability of existing inventory. The marketplace is not a deliberate enemy of serious art, although it typically ignores excellence that runs counter to current trends. But the laws of the marketplace are not the laws of art, and their confusion diminishes the well-being of art and the integrity of artists.[1]

THE LAWS OF THE MARKETPLACE

A feature of any market, including the art market, is the uneasy relation between price and value. All goods and services entering a marketplace are priced—that is, their presumed current value is expressed in terms of a neutral medium, money. But price at any moment in the art market may be an inaccurate reflection of value judged by more enduring and objective standards. The paintings of Jan Vermeer, the seventeenth-century Dutch master, changed hands for centuries at prices that reflected nothing of their inherent value. The stained-glass manufactures of the Tiffany Studio, out of fashion for decades, spent years in attics waiting to be perceived in the marketplace as classic—that is, above fashion.

Disparity between price and value operates in the other direction as well: works of art that almost certainly have little objective value fetch high prices for a time because market forces—public-relations campaigns, friendly critics, fads—justify high prices and confer high presumed value. Once this has occurred, such works cannot be erased from history, and they may eventually acquire the satisfying patina and associations of period pieces. Nineteenth-century French salon painting was eclipsed in the marketplace for decades and could be had for a song, but today its sheer skill in the craft of painting, its upper-class eroticism, and its nostalgic historical and mythical themes have raised its price to new heights.

Another feature of all markets, including the art market, is the strategy of striving to be "market-driven." Providers of goods and services study what the market seems to want and make it their business to satisfy those wants. In an efficient art market where dealers are constantly aware of each other's activities, this perfectly sensible strategy leads to a glut of one type of art in preference to many others. When buyers show a preliminary preference for one type over another, art merchants develop a reliable supply and promote its value in order to increase its price. The galleries soon fill with lookalikes. This trait of markets was never more apparent than in the mid-1980s, when galleries were almost uniformly filled with "strong," "expressive" work.

A third feature of all markets and art markets is the attractiveness of innovation. Innovation has long been dignified in the art world by the French term *avant-garde,* and the idea of the avant-garde retains intrinsic value. From time to time there are innovators well ahead of their peers whose work reaches into new and necessary terrain. But in the market setting, innovation is a commercial strategy. A gallery may promote unfamiliar and commercially untried work in order to find out if it generates a market. Under the controlled conditions of a well-managed market test, there is little to be lost and much to be gained. When an innovation catches fire with the public, it can be exploited commercially through the market-driven strategy.

A fourth feature of some markets, including the market for contemporary art, is that the value of new products can be defined and promoted subjectively without doing harm. In these markets, one cannot really trust words. There may be relatively objective standards by which the quality of art can be judged, but buyers are not so often well-versed in applying them, and in any case one can't always be sure. Fortunately, the products are safe no matter how poorly designed. Works of art are not elevators; if one falls, no harm. A great empty plywood box can be described as austere, vigorously antisublime, starkly beautiful—and so on. The emperor may have no clothes, but what if he has an excellent figure? The merchant's job is to test his market and to sell. He makes no mistake to extol the virtues of his inventory in glowing terms. Objective measurement can be left to posterity.

Another feature of all markets—and for many artists the most anguishing feature of the market they address—is a finite capacity to absorb supply and accommodate demand. When the members of the New York Stock Exchange recognized that trading volume threatened to exceed processing capacity, they expanded by installing new electronic systems and revising procedures on the floor of the Exchange. It was quickly enough done. It is not so easy in the art market. There, supply in most product categories greatly outstrips demand. Far more artists seek niches in the market than there are niches available. More "shares" of art are offered than there are buyers to acquire them, and this remains so until an artist's work becomes a blue-chip investment in short supply subject to high demand. The art market often feels to artists more like a mechanism for exclusion than a high-capacity mechanism for absorption and exchange. The development of sophisticated regional art markets in North America—in Los Angeles, Chicago, Scottsdale, Toronto, and elsewhere—has increased overall capacity, but the New York market remains most prestigious and most abundant in disappointment for artists of merit whose work exceeds the capacity of the marketplace to receive it.

Some art merchants are men and women of taste, thorough education, and courage. I can recall a dealer opening cases that he had just received from the Soviet Union with the excitement of a child and with judicious pleasure: he had succeeded in importing hundreds of Russian avant-garde works on paper which the Soviet authorities regarded as valueless, and he could foresee that their exhibition in London would be a cultural event and a commercial success. I know of dealers who have supported artists morally and financially through long rough patches with total faith in the final vindication of the artists' worth. But the art market is not defined by such individuals, and they too are merchants providing desirable products and services at a profit, abiding by the laws of the marketplace and living within its limited capacity.

The profession is mixed; this is one of the traits that makes it interesting. On the one hand, more than a few merchants know art well and love it; they are at their true stations in life. On the other hand, they are in business to make money, not to make history. Further, many are willing to promote artists of doubtful merit if their work has shock value (the innovation strategy) or obvious appeal (the market-driven strategy). There is no penalty for doing so, and it makes for an attractive marketplace that draws customers. The laws of the marketplace prevail in the marketplace.

THE LAWS OF THE STUDIO

The laws of the studio are different. The studio is a workplace where materials and imagination are fused into one. On the physical side, the artist gathers materials and tools filled with potential (recall Kandinsky's memorable description of raw unused paint). On the imaginative side, the artist seeks again and again to touch the stable core of ideas and images that are his current themes, and he seeks the mobile expressiveness that will allow them to enter into material forms, often in unexpected ways.

Some artists prepare for this effort, others do not—or in any case not visibly. Some simply begin: a sudden swoop from ordinary time to studio time, vagrancy to creative action, is their preparation, as if they have to surprise their gifts. Others ready their tools and workplace with ritual seriousness, considering that to prepare outwardly with precision readies a working attitude as well. I have seen a skilled artist's pastel chalks aligned with the precision of a keyboard. Still others, instinctively or in keeping with deliberate spiritual practice, become quiet for a time to awaken to themselves and to the task at hand. They need to be able to adhere to themes, recognize the expressive potential of materials, sharpen the body's memory of working methods, summon the unexpected but just inspirations of the moment. Without awakening, however modest in scope, there is no valid art.

Ready to work, the artist begins to move among opposing forces, searching for a current of confident intelligence and energy that carries him forward, not just as a doer but as a witness. He has his craft, never sound enough. Still, it has matured over the years and can be counted on. But craft implies habits, and this is the first pair of opposites: craft can serve or rule; old thoughts and manual skills can serve or rule. The issue is decided from moment to moment.

The artist knows, up to a point, what he or she wishes to express but also feels it, senses it—feels and senses it so strongly that something like awakening has occurred. The ordinary self that entered the studio is still there, but someone else is there as well. Toward that other, false respect and formality can be an impediment. Self is a friend and one's own deep resource; a rigid relationship can undo the surprising creativity that might occur. This is the second pair of opposites: Self and self, what one is ordinarily and what one is more fully.

The theme, the task at hand, is clear and unclear. The mind may conceive it precisely or, on the contrary, feelings and the body in motion may have a sense of direction that the mind hardly knows. The forces must come together to serve the theme: the sheer energy and closeness to materials dwelling in the body, the sensitivity to small differences dwelling in the feelings, the organizational clarity and critical capacity of the thought. The opposites here are wholeness and fragmentation, and again the issue is decided from moment to moment.

Entering more deeply into the creative process, the artist begins to receive spontaneous gifts: signs and meanings suggest themselves "from nowhere"—forms previously unimagined, new themes or motifs that seem remarkably fertile. The working faculties and the companion self have come to life, shedding seeds with abandon and generosity. The artist may experience a kind of euphoria; he or she entered the studio to experience a degree of spontaneous ability, and it has made itself known, always a gift however much one reaches for it. The opposites here are judiciousness and unthinking acceptance. Like an oak with countless acorns, the creative nature as it awakens produces more than enough to furnish a work of art. Nature may abhor a vacuum, but art does not; art conveys as much by what is left out as by what is included.

The day's work has been *found,* and it becomes difficult to continue searching. The abundance of suggestion from the name-defying, enigmatic source blends with the good habits of the experienced worker to produce painting or sculpture of quality. But art is fond of testing its creature; there is always something more to be sought out and conveyed into a work. It is not all given, even when much is given. Hence the idea, common among artists of many different periods, that the work of art is never finished, always abandoned. The contraries here are searching and finding: to continue the search even when it becomes obvious that much has been found. This is perhaps the only way to avoid self-imitation, even involuntary self-caricature.

There is a knowledge at work in the studio but also an ignorance, and they can serve each other. The knowledge is everything the artist has verified in thought, feeling, and body—about human nature and Nature itself from the ants to the angels, about practical studio skills, about ideas and images that imperiously demand exploration and expression. The ignorance is of these things precisely. Knowledge permits the artist to work, conferring confidence and direction. But ignorance joined with longing and curiosity draws the artist forward, motivates, authorizes free experimentation and play.

Perhaps enough has been said to evoke the studio as a place of transformation not only of paint or clay but of the human being. For clarity, I have described its working life in terms of opposing categories; experience is always more blended than words imply. Nonetheless, it must be evident that the inner life of the studio has nothing in common with the marketplace.

WALK OF LIFE AND CAREER

The contrast between the nearly obsolete expression *walk of life* and the modern word *career* captures much of what needs to be said about the relation between the studio and the marketplace. *Walk of life* implies a deliberate pace, as if one takes time to enjoy and record the landscape through which one is passing. One can arrive anywhere by walking, although it takes more time than careening. One arrives later, one arrives mature. *Career,* on the other hand, at least today implies a nervous, outwardly directed endeavor that tests one's powers but may also abuse them and leave little time for them to develop into deep coherence. Walk of life can be, although often it is not, the inner aspect of career. Similarly, career can be the outer aspect of walk of life; it assures the worldly progress—the personal connections, material opportunities, and social acceptance—of a professional life. Today, and in any era that thrusts art into a competitive marketplace, the artist must find a delicate balance. There is nothing wrong with a career, but it is empty and sometimes corrupting if it lacks the contemplative pace of a walk of life.

The marketplace encourages careers and at present seems to favor the sudden material success of quite young people. The values and words of the twentieth-century masters whom we have met can appear old-fashioned, idealistic chatter in comparison with the almost sexual intensity of the art market. For the most part, we are losing authentic art in the marketplace, although not in the privacy of many studios around the world.

Each artist must find his or her way to negotiate the distance between the studio and the marketplace. Some will deliberately or unconsciously follow market trends, the studio becoming an annex of the marketplace. In the business world, many firms prosper by allowing competitors to launch new products, thereafter vigorously entering the marketplace with improved or less expensive versions. Some artists deliberately attempt to penetrate the market through originality, supported by aggressive self-marketing, like entrepreneurs in the business world. Some artists find ways to remain independent of the art market for their living, however much they retain the normal aspiration to be accepted sooner or later by a broad public. Educational institutions, as well as businesses that employ artists part-time for routine publications work, play a positive role today by providing niches in society for artists who have deliberately or through force of circumstance separated earning their daily bread from their creative careers.

But the values of the marketplace can reach into the schools and annex them. Artists teaching today fall roughly into two categories: those for whom the manual skills and spiritual calling of the artist remain vital concerns and the real substance of what they attempt to pass on, and those for whom school is a preparation for success in the current marketplace. Teachers in the second category ignore the workshop skills and enduring ideas that the market ignores or convey them without the passionate commitment that makes values real to those experiencing them for the first time. Many art students today are not really able to draw because teachers in the second category know that draftsmanship is not so important in today's marketplace. In any case, photographic projection and other techniques can simulate the skill. Many students have not been genuinely awed by the masterpieces of traditional art. Piero della Francesca's magical solemnity and construction have nothing to do with today's marketplace, nor does the fiercely attentive portraiture of Mughal India, in which artists often executed details with a brush made of one hair. Students may have seen them in passing, but to see is nothing without "eyes of fire" that seize the value of things.

Teachers in the second category have lost whatever insight they once had into the delicate balance between the artist's calling and the appeal of the marketplace. On the other hand, students do not need as their teachers hermits with boundless disdain for the marketplace. They do need teachers who incarnate the values of the studio and maintain a distance between studio and marketplace. They also need teachers who remember, to whom the traditions of art in virtually every time and place are familiar—so many languages of body and spirit, none dispensable. The spiritual in art depends on this memory, although not on memory alone.

After a true schooling in the studio, artists have little to fear from the marketplace. They can tether their camels at the perimeter and enter with confidence. They will have few illusions regarding the ability of the marketplace to value their work justly. It may take years; it may not occur at all. They know why they are artists and what it is to be an artist, and they have secured their livelihoods adequately through resources independent of the market mechanism. They can welcome the vigorous test of the marketplace and absorb with some degree of poise the depletion that follows rejection or the influx of energy that accompanies success.

The market is not always wrong, far from it. A shop in Los Angeles is devoted to two wholly distinct businesses, and to visit the shop is to stumble into a parable. In one room is a display of dreadful bronze sculpture, the iconographic extrusions of what appears to be a sadly troubled mind. In the adjoining room is an exquisite collection of antique stained glass, hanging from the walls and ceiling, spilling into the back room, creating a cluttered, warmly Dickensian atmosphere. The owner—who is the sculptor in question—is an unusually skilled stained-glass restorer who earns his living through his craft while waiting for the market to recognize the virtues of his art. The visitor passes from one room to the other as if from heaven to hell. The owner rarely sells sculpture, but the stained-glass business, serving an international clientele, provides more than enough to do. Curiously, the man's joy is in his glass; the rest is kept by pack-rat instinct. He knows himself but slenderly.

The market is not always correct in its judgments—far from it. A very fine painter, a man of spirit for whom art is a walk of life and a means of knowing, earns a marginal living as a carpenter and seasonal fieldworker. Such biographies abound.

An "arm's-length" relationship between the marketplace and the studio offers the best assurance that art will remain substantial. This phrase from the business world refers to the ethical and often legal requirement to remain free of conflicts of interest when conducting negotiations. Vigorous and to the point, it is an item of market wisdom of use to artists—who should of course approach the marketplace when they are ready, and try to share in its fruits.

23 ENLIGHTENED PATRONAGE: DAG HAMMARSKJÖLD AT THE UN

Dag Hammarskjöld (1905–1961) is not remembered as a patron of art. The enterprise of this chapter is to discover him in that role and to explore the values he brought to patronage as both a man of the spirit and a preeminent man of the world.[1] The cohabitation of spirit and world in him was so rare that it may shed light on the question of what kind of patronage best serves the spiritual in art. There are no rules or customs in this domain today; it is unfamiliar.

Secretary-General of the United Nations from 1953 until his death in an air crash during the Congo crisis, Dag Hammarskjöld was an enormously influential leader in international affairs to whom the United Nations, and the world, owe much. His conception of the Secretary-General's role and of the organization he headed was formative. The nasty ideological dramas played out at the United Nations in recent years are all the more sad to those who have been touched by the genius for justice and the mature idealism that Hammarskjöld brought to his work and articulated so fully. The four volumes of his *Public Papers*[2] document his tireless participation in the great international issues of his day and his sometimes stormy fellowship with political leaders from Khrushchev to Chou En Lai and Dwight Eisenhower.

Here and there among the transcripts of press conferences, interim reports, and statements to the Security Council—the voluminous record of Hammarskjöld's UN service—are signs of another man: close reader and skilled translator, cultivated observer of the arts, member of the Swedish Academy responsible for awarding the Nobel Prize in literature, essayist and lecturer in whom liberal European culture found a compelling voice. Still more sparsely represented in the *Public*

Papers is yet another man whom the general public only came to know through the posthumous edition of his private journal. Published as *Markings* (New York, 1964), the journal begins with a few entries written when Hammarskjöld was twenty, then becomes reasonably continuous from 1950 forward—that is, from the years just prior to his selection as Secretary-General until his death. Like the *Meditations* of Marcus Aurelius, *Markings* records the inwardness of a world leader. Like Pascal's *Pensées*, it is a collection of fragments bearing witness to an examined life. Sometimes painfully introspective in the earlier years, it opens out, reflecting the internal sources from which Hammarskjöld would draw as a patron of art.

The journal was an annex to his conscience. Instinctively committed to self-observation and skilled in the diplomatic practice of observing others, he would record what he noted and corrections he might make at least in his own behavior. In the extroverted world of politics where few possess a dignified and trained awareness of themselves, he was aware.

The journal was also an annex to his consciousness. In part an anthology of texts that recalled him to himself—the Psalms and Gospels spoke not just to him but for him, as if they were a part of his voice—it was his place of self-inquiry. He was a searching disciple of Meister Eckhart and Jan van Ruysbroeck, medieval mystics of bold mind for whom Christian doctrine offered not only a code for communal living but also a path to higher knowledge. To some real degree their writings initiated him religiously, although written records are typically held to be poor transmitters of initiation. *Markings* records his assimilation of their thought and his search to open himself to the order of experience which they had explored. There can be no doubt that Hammarskjöld the private man entered enough into vital silence to confirm the medieval mystics' teachings about consciousness and being.

In later years, his journal was also a catchall for his own poetry. He was a friend and translator (into his native Swedish) of Saint-John Perse, as well as a translator of Djuna Barnes and Martin Buber. Many of his own poems are *haiku,* the seventeen-syllable Japanese form popularized in the West in the 1950s; it is the perfect poetic form for a very busy man. His journal also contains reflections on poetry and the visual arts—like so much else in his journal, spare and powerful.

By permitting publication of his journal after his death, Hammarskjöld abandoned the distinction, fiercely preserved in his lifetime, between the public and private realms. No diplomatic *démarches,* as he liked to say, could be disturbed were he to share his spiritual explorations as he had previously shared his political understanding. That publication was the final act of an altogether extraordinary man. By modern standards, there may be some perceived incoherence between international leadership and the painstaking self-creation recorded in the journal. But Marcus Aurelius would have understood him; the dozens of reprintings of the American edition of *Markings* indicate that many have. People who foresee a "New Age" and typically discover its precursors at the mobile fringe of culture rather than at the rigid center will find in Dag Hammarskjöld an exception.

"The 'mystic experience,'" Hammarskjöld wrote in 1955:

> Always *here* and *now*—in that freedom which is one with distance, in that stillness which is born of silence. But—this is a freedom in the midst of action, a stillness in the midst of other human beings. The mystery is a constant reality to him who, in this world, is free from self-concern, a reality that grows peaceful and mature before the receptive attention of assent.
>
> In our era the road to holiness necessarily passes through the world of action.[3]

He was a unique man, surely prince, perhaps saint and even martyr.

Patrons are key members of the "concerned community" that needs and sponsors a living art. An unusually responsive audience, they link artists to the world at large by providing commissions, and they offer a reality test. As in the past, patronage in the twentieth century has been at least as much an institutional and governmental concern as the concern of individuals. Museums, commercial enterprises, and government agencies have become the leading patrons of our time, although outstanding individuals also come to mind—in the United States, for example, Alfred Stieglitz, Solomon Guggenheim in collaboration with Hilla Rebay, and Dominique De Menil. As it happens, each of these individual patrons acknowledged the links between art and spirituality—Hilla Rebay with a sometimes irritating flamboyance that did not prevent her from recognizing Kandinsky and assembling one of the great collections of his art. But few prominent patrons, individual or institutional, have discriminatingly shared this recognition; the spiritual has been a stowaway. Lodged secretly in works admired for other reasons, sensed but not well understood, it arrived all but unnoticed in public and private collections.

Dag Hammarskjöld was one of the few modern patrons who possessed mature spiritual values, and he was unique in his ability to articulate spiritual and aesthetic concerns with compelling spareness. Stieglitz can seem blustery in comparison. Hammarskjöld was more like Abbot Suger—twelfth-century Regent of France, diplomat, and art patron—than like his twentieth-century peers. Like Suger, he directed an institution that embodied many of the highest ideals of his day, he was a gifted expositor of those ideals, he was interested in materially beautifying his institution, and he was drawn to contemporary art. For Suger, "modern art" was the style emerging under his tutelage, which later generations called Gothic. For Hammarskjöld, modern art was Picasso, Braque, Matisse, Hepworth, and others. Like Suger, Hammarskjöld was drawn into the creative process itself—Suger as a formative influence on Gothic, Hammarskjöld as the unofficial co-designer of the only room at the United Nations dedicated to silence rather than talk. Unlike Suger, Hammarskjöld found it difficult to raise money; his leverage over his constituency was secular, and there were fewer kings' rings to be collected.

Notwithstanding, these were men cut from much the same cloth. Hammarskjöld once described the United Nations as a "secular 'church' of ideals and principles in international affairs,"[5] and he did not altogether demur when Pope Pius described him as "his lay counterpart."[6] As to the role of the Secretary-General:

> In a certain sense he is just a secretary; in another sense he is necessarily much more. . . . The Governments of the United Nations expect the Secretary-General to take the independent responsibility, irrespective of their attitude, to represent the detached element in the international life of the peoples.[7]

Committed leader of a secular "church" and the detached element in international life—these characterizations capture something of the complexity of the institution and the man.

Dag Hammarskjöld's art patronage during the UN years was in point of fact intensive rather than extensive; he was associated with only a modest number of works. It was as much the role of his office to deflect well-intentioned gifts as to encourage or receive them. A letter of 1966 from a UN Under-Secretary reflects this situation. "In view of the numerous offers which we receive from all over the world," wrote the official to a potential art donor,

> it has been necessary for us to establish a policy that we cannot accept gifts directly from private individuals and can only consider offers made by Member States themselves.[8]

Hammarskjöld saw early to the enrichment of his UN offices and dining room—a modest matter involving his request, honored at once, to borrow paintings from the storerooms of the Museum of Modern Art. The prominent curator with whom he dealt, Dorothy Miller, expected him to invite museum staff to make the selection; instead he came to the storerooms himself, made his selection largely from School of Paris works, and so impressed museum officials with his knowledge and concern that he was asked to return in October 1954 to give an address on the occasion of the twenty-fifth anniversary of the museum.

Hammarskjöld was in general interested, and meticulous, regarding his personal environment. The furniture in his apartment near the UN was handmade by Scandinavian craftsmen according to his specifications. He was photographed often beside the paintings that he had selected, as if they were deliberately chosen companions. Adlai Stevenson once remarked on Hammarskjöld's "strong artistic sense, which pervaded all his actions and his statements."[9]

On a larger scale, Hammarskjöld interested himself in gifts from member states that might genuinely beautify the United Nations. The windswept equestrian figure in the garden north of the General Assembly building, offered by the Yugoslav government, does not represent his taste in art, but he did suggest its location and saw to it that all parties were satisfied. The great bronze is in fact an effective ornament for the United Nations, blatantly heroic and as such appropriate—obvious sentiments are by no means always contemptible.

Hammarskjöld forged a friendship with the British sculptor Barbara Hepworth that would lead in time to one of the major transformations of the UN environment. He admired the work of Henry Moore and arranged to meet the artist. Some years later, surely in keeping with his wishes, Brian Urquhart secured a bronze sculpture by Moore for the UN grounds. The overall impression received from Hammarskjöld as art patron is of a man interested, judicious, too busy to dwell at length on the question but always ready to give bursts of time and enthusiasm. Mr. Urquhart has written that "the UN Headquarters in New York gave Hammarskjöld a practical field for his interest in contemporary art, and he never tired of walking around the building and the garden and thinking of new ways to improve them."[10] Hammarskjöld himself measured the distance between his own way of life and that of the artist in a memorable paragraph from a letter to Bo Beskow, friend and painter:

> You have the curse of the artist to be your own master, I that of the slave always forced to solve "given tasks." Tertium datur? [Is there a third?][11]

Like all patrons with pride of place, Hammarskjöld did not lightly delegate. One night in the fall of 1960, there was a curious scene on the grounds of the United Nations: a sizable scaffold beside the east flank of the building near the rose garden; a technician perched on it operating a slide projector; on the facing wall, the projected image of a large abstract sculpture; in the darkness below, Mr. Hammarskjöld and his associates deciding just how large the actual sculpture should be (at the time, it was still a model) and just where it should be secured to the wall for maximum effect. The scaffold was patiently rolled about, the projector raised and lowered until the gentlemen resolved the issue. The metal sculpture, a spiky sunburst by the American sculptor Ezio Martinelli, is there to this day.[12]

Dag Hammarskjöld's ally in this venture was Wallace K. Harrison, partner in the architectural firm of Harrison & Abramowitz and chief architect of the UN complex. Hammarskjöld clearly trusted Harrison and could talk with him not only about bricks and mortar but about form and symbol. Harrison in turn clearly respected Hammarskjöld. While they had larger responsibilities as stewards of the enormous UN complex, their most intensive joint venture was the Meditation Room adjoining the public lobby of the General Assembly building. It is this project in particular that clarifies the meaning of enlightened patronage. Emery Kelen, a colleague of Hammarskjöld's, has commented:

> This room was his creation, and it is today his best memorial. But that he was able to establish such a room at all is a latterday miracle.[13]

The Meditation Room has a curious history, resembling a moral fable. It was initiated not by Hammarskjöld but by a pious American Christian group ("Let's Try Christianity") known as the Laymen's Movement. The driving force of this group was one Weyman C. Huckabee, who prevailed on the UN administration in 1951, when the General Assembly met in Paris, to set aside a room for prayer. That room, as described by Kelen, was a modest affair with neutral curtains, a few chairs, and a UN flag in the corner.[14] However, when the UN moved to temporary quarters at Lake Success (Long Island) in 1952, the curtains, chairs, and flag were duly transported from Paris and a room for prayer established. A young architect tried to focus the room by installing a large African mahogany stump "as a sort of nondenominational altar," writes Kelen—"I must confess that it looked to me more like a chopping block."

Apparently in response to persistent Huckabee, a small space was set aside in the permanent headquarters of the United Nations in New

York as a room for prayer and meditation—an odd wedge of space that seemed more a way to dismiss Huckabee's request than to fulfill it. Huckabee meanwhile had formed a group known as the Friends of the United Nations Meditation Room, and Hammarskjöld succeeded to the post of Secretary-General.

At this point the story changes in character. Hammarskjöld knew how to receive the naive but goodhearted intensity of the Friends and channel it toward a more sophisticated goal which reflected his—and their—values. New to the United Nations and immensely burdened with responsibility, Hammarskjöld might never have considered the possibility of a Meditation Room at the UN without Huckabee; further, his sense of privacy would surely have cautioned him against initiating such a venture, which so closely corresponded to his inner life. In the event, he embraced the project wholeheartedly.

Money was collected from private sources by the Friends to remodel the existing shabby Meditation Room, while Hammarskjöld began to think the project through in dialogue with "the chief architect of this house," as he called Wallace Harrison. Hammarskjöld's intimate allegiance to the spiritual way of Meister Eckhart and his undisguised love of contemporary art prompted him to pass from the narrowly defined patron's role to a more complex role, which included codesigner, creative mind, part-time foreman, defender. Working sincerely, not dismissively, Hammarskjöld and Harrison found themselves exploring large issues. A Meditation Room within the precincts of the twentieth-century institution that bears the burden of man's hope, however fitfully, could hardly be left to casual planning or indifferent hands. They felt impelled to find forms capable of speaking to everyone willing to listen. Recognizing that they could not draw from any specific religious or cultural heritage without offending, they sought a universal language that would be neither a bland composite nor an empty universal. They found themselves turning to the aesthetic and spiritual resources of abstract art and to symbols from Nature about which sectarian dispute was unimaginable. We will look at Hammarskjöld's own account of the resulting design (Fig. 120) after looking first at his material participation in the project.

Work on the room progressed well in the mid-1950s under Harrison's direction, with Hammarskjöld taking exceptional interest. A journalist recorded that when Hammarskjöld returned "from his historic trip to Cairo [mid-November, 1956], he surprised aides by going immediately to the Meditation Room. . . . He was not seeking quiet,

120. *Meditation Room at United Nations Headquarters,* dedicated 1957. Fresco by Bo Beskow, interior design by Wallace K. Harrison with the participation of Dag Hammarskjöld. Photo: United Nations.

but his 'okay' was needed on a few last-minute details. . . ."[15] Kelen remembers that Hammarskjöld found the patterns in the rosewood sheathing of the vestibule somewhat carelessly matched and ordered the work redone. As to the chairs in the Meditation Room, he had the existing ones replaced with backless caned benches. In explanation, he offered a memorably dry comment: "The men who come here will have enough force to support their own backs."[16]

Small as it is, the redesigned room called for an imposing block of iron ore to serve as a nondenominational altar, its dark surfaces polished to watery smoothness; it is illuminated by a thin shaft of light from the ceiling. Mr. Urquhart notes that Hammarskjöld remembered an altar of iron ore in Sweden. The six-and-a-half ton slab, delivered under the patronage of the Swedish royal house, required the addition of a structural support down to bedrock through a series of basement garages.

Another dominant element in the room, the fresco facing the visitor when one looks past the altar to the far wall, was executed in an abstract, generally Cubist language by Bo Beskow. Hammarskjöld had initially solicited the participation of Georges Braque, to whom he wrote that "in a setting of entire simplicity we work mainly with effects of light." "For the home of the United Nations," he added, "only the perfect is good enough."[17] However, the elderly artist proved unable to take the commission. Hammarskjöld was fond enough of the Beskow mural to keep a preliminary drawing for it framed on the wall facing his desk in the New York apartment, in the company of another image related to a small modern chapel—a study by Henri Matisse for his chapel at Vence (see chapter 15).

Formally reopened in November 1957, the Meditation Room remains today as Hammarskjöld knew it, apart from the addition of a stained-glass wall by Marc Chagall in the outer vestibule. It is indeed the room of quiet that Hammarskjöld wished. Entering through large smoked-glass doors, the visitor is impressed at once by a peaceful blue light seeping past the perimeter of a floating ceiling and washing the walls. One takes one's place on one of those deliberate benches and looks out into a room otherwise quite dark. A thin shaft of light from the ceiling dimly illumines the great ore altar, which seems more a coffin or dense stone sarcophagus than a proper altar. Aligned lengthwise in the room rather than across, it conveys a perhaps unintended memorial flavor, not entirely out of keeping since Hammarskjöld dedicated the room to "peace and those who are giving their lives for peace." Contrasting with the Malevich-like intensity and simplicity of the altar and shaft of light, the Cubist mural at the narrow end of the room is a dynamic linear composition of folded planes and interrupted arcs, with a dominant caduceus-like motif and the suggestion of a celestial body, sun or moon. The colors are pale, somewhat Mediterranean, the message unclear but generally optimistic.

There is nothing more, unless one counts a pair of low dark pillars flanking the mural which do not show up in original photographs of the completed room but have found their way in since then.

In the spring of 1957, Hammarskjöld formally accepted a donation from the Friends of the United Nations Meditation Room and spoke extemporaneously about the project, by that time nearly completed:

> The Meditation Room is a kind of stepchild of the architects of this house; it was brought into being . . . as an experiment, but now I am happy to confirm that it is a permanent part of the building. . . . However, because of its origin, a very small space was reserved for the room and the problem was how to arrange that small space in such a dignified way that it would not give people the feeling that it was something that had just happened . . . , but that it was a thing of essential importance. . . .
>
> . . . We had at the back of our minds . . . something which is said, I believe, in an ancient Chinese script, that the significance of the vessel is not in its shell but in the void. . . . That was a help because it meant that we could perhaps virtually do without symbols if on the other hand we achieved purity. Finally we felt that if within the framework we could achieve an absolute purity of line and color we could realize all we wanted, a room of stillness with perhaps one very simple symbol—light, striking on stone. It is for that reason that in the center of the room there is this block of iron ore, shimmering like ice in a shaft of light from above. That is the only symbol in the room—a meeting of the light of the sky and the earth.[18]

Later in 1957, Hammarskjöld formalized the ideas in his talk to the Friends for a leaflet given even today to people visiting the Meditation Room. It has become a "tourist attraction," although in Hammarskjöld's day there were times when he and other UN officials could go there undisturbed. His statement is, to my mind, both an extraordinary public document and, like his address at the Museum of Modern Art, a remarkable apprehension of the spiritual in art.

A Room of Quiet

This is a room devoted to peace
and those who are giving their
lives for peace. It is a room of quiet
where only thoughts should speak.

We all have within us a center of stillness surrounded by silence.

This house, dedicated to work and debate in the service of peace, should have one room dedicated to silence in the outward sense and stillness in the inner sense.

It has been the aim to create in this small room a place where the doors may be open to the infinite lands of thought and prayer.

People of many faiths will meet here, and for that reason none of the symbols to which we are accustomed in our meditation could be used.

However, there are simple things which speak to us all with the same language. We have sought for such things and we believe that we have found them in the shaft of light striking the shimmering surface of solid rock.

So, in the middle of the room we see a symbol of how, daily, the light of the skies gives life to the earth on which we stand, a symbol to many of us of how the light of the spirit gives life to matter.

But the stone in the middle of the room has more to tell us. We may see it as an altar, empty not because there is no God, not because it is an altar to an unknown god, but because it is dedicated to the God whom man worships under many names and in many forms.

The stone in the middle of the room reminds us also of the firm and permanent in the world of movement and change. The block of iron ore has the weight and solidity of the everlasting. It is a reminder of that cornerstone of endurance and faith on which all human endeavour must be based.

The material of the stone leads our thoughts to the necessity for choice between destruction and construction, between war and peace. Of iron man has forged his swords, of iron he has also made his ploughshares. Of iron he has constructed tanks, but of iron he has likewise built homes for man. The block of iron ore is part of the wealth we have inherited on this earth of ours. How are we to use it?

The shaft of light strikes the stone in a room of utter simplicity. There are no other symbols, there is nothing to distract our attention or to break in on the stillness within ourselves. When our eyes travel from those symbols to the front wall, they meet a simple pattern opening up the room to the harmony, freedom, and balance of space.

There is an ancient saying that the sense of a vessel is not in its shell but in the void. So it is with this room. It is for those who come here to fill the void with what they find in their center of stillness.[19]

The spirit of this statement is nurtured on Meister Eckhart and Lao Tze, its political ideals on the Charter of the United Nations and the Declaration of Human Rights. It is surely a remarkable achievement of mind to bring these seemingly unlike realms of value together, and to include an irreproachably simple, persuasive interpretation of the artistic ensemble which, no less than the words, brings them together. Hammarskjöld had transcribed a sentence from Meister Eckhart in a journal entry for 1956: "You must have an exalted mind and a *burning heart* in which, nevertheless, reign silence and stillness."[20]

And yet the Meditation Room isn't all that it could be; the patron's intention reached further than the realization. The mural doesn't quite yield to the wish to "read" its statement. Imposing as it is, the altar is forbidding, and it seems terribly unlikely that Hammarskjöld wished it so, although in his private meditations he was never far from the thought of death and in his last years sensed without regret that martyrdom awaited him. "I have watched the others," he wrote in the journal:

> Now I am the victim,
> Strapped fast to the altar
> For sacrifice.[21]

On balance, the joint symbol of the massive altar and the shaft of light best embodies Hammarskjöld's intention, seconded by the overall setting with its rim of quiet light and deliberate emptiness.

Curiously, Hammarskjöld had all but anticipated this mixed result. His address at the Museum of Modern Art three years earlier, conceived with the advice of Bo Beskow, had specifically questioned the ability of twentieth-century artists to integrate art and spirit in a cultural era that has lost touch with ancient spirituality but not yet matured enough to know its own mind. "The art collected here," he said to that audience, referring to the museum collection,

> is not modern in the sense that it has the vain ambition of expressing the latest of the shifting fashions of a mass civilization which long ago lost its anchorage in a firm scale of values, inspired by a generally accepted faith. . . . It is . . . a museum for the art which reflects the inner problems of our generation and is created in the hope of meeting some of its basic needs.
>
> . . . Andre Malraux has said that modern times have not produced a single work of art comparable to the highest achievements of Occidental art in the past. Is he not right? . . . If we demand of art that it should be the expression of a mature and balanced mastery of the relationship of man and his civilization to life, then modern art, to be sure, does not reach levels that were already achieved in a distant past in our Western civilization. No—then it is not progress.
>
> However that may be, there are two qualities which are shared in common by modern art and the scientific sphere. One is the courage of an unprejudiced search for the basic elements of experience. The other one is perseverance in the fight for mastery of those elements.
>
> The need for the courage of search establishes a decisive differ-

ence between modern art and the art of the past, living in and expressing a world of faith. Agnostic search, based on a re-evaluation of all values, is a quality of modern art that is an essential expression of the spiritual situation of our generation. But this quality, in itself, must prevent modern art from achieving the kind of perfection which we meet in the Cathedral of Chartres or in the paintings of Giotto.

The second quality—perseverance in the fight for mastery—is on the contrary the main great quality that modern art shares with the art of the past. . . .

Modern art teaches us to see by forcing us to use our senses, our intellect, and our sensibility to follow it on its road of exploration. It makes us seers. . . . Seers—and explorers—these we must be if we are to prevail. . . .[22]

Hammarskjöld goes on to explore the analogy between the modern artist's work and that of the diplomat and political leader, in a graceful evocation of the challenge of creativity in any sphere.

And so he did not expect the Meditation Room to be a diminutive Chartres; he expected no more than an honest result owing to "the courage of search for the basic elements of experience." This was achieved.

Dag Hammarskjöld died suddenly on September 17th, 1961, victim with all his party of an air crash at Ndola, in central Africa. The fierce conflict brought about by the emergence of Zaire from colonial rule consumed him, as it had already consumed Patrice Lumumba.

He had not quite finished shaping the United Nations complex. For some years he had kept in his office a refined wood sculpture, *Single Form,* by the English artist Barbara Hepworth. He deeply appreciated it and even wrote a series of linked haiku about it.[23] On one of those famous walks around the UN buildings in the company of Dr. Ralph Bunche and others, he expressed interest in reworking the large plaza in front of the Secretariat building, which throughout the 1950s had only a sad little fountain to dignify it. He foresaw a monumental sculpture there, perhaps a work by Barbara Hepworth set in a larger and more handsome fountain or reflecting pool. He did not live to realize the project, but friends and colleagues quickly conceived of it as a fitting memorial.

Barbara Hepworth was notified, and she rose to the occasion, choosing as her motif a vastly more monumental version of the *Single Form*

121. Barbara Hepworth. *Sculpture in Memory of the Late Dag Hammarskjöld (Single Form)*, 1964. Bronze. Height 21'. Photo: United Nations.

that Hammarskjöld had treasured. A foundation chaired by Jacob Blaustein, retired U.S. delegate to the United Nations and devoted friend of Hammarskjöld's, volunteered funds to realize the project "after a wish of Dag Hammarskjöld," as an inscription would read in touchingly international English. The project included not only Hepworth's bronze but also the enlarged fountain and pool that Hammarskjöld had envisaged.

The ensemble (Fig. 121) was dedicated in 1964 at a ceremony where Brian Urquhart, who knew her to be sparing of words but insightful, convinced Barbara Hepworth to speak. She said in part the following:

Dag Hammarskjöld had a pure and exact perception of aesthetic principle, as exact as it was over ethical and moral principles. I believe they were, to him, one and the same thing.[24]

In the opening toward the top of sculpture, she had incised a brief inscription, invisible to observers on the ground: "To the Glory of God and the memory of Dag Hammarskjöld. Ndola 17-9-61."

Perhaps shy of words, Hepworth was not shy of mind. She had expressed herself on more private occasions quite unmistakably. "Nowadays there is nothing done which conveys the feeling of praise," she once said.

We have no time for praise. And yet, without this feeling of inner wealth that can afford to praise we are injuring ourselves and each other. . . . There have never been so many architects, sculptors, and painters as now and there has never been less to show for it. What we really suffer from is spiritual malnutrition.[25]

About the monumental version of *Single Form*, Hepworth had told Mr. Blaustein that it "symbolizes the idealism and singleness of purpose of Mr. Hammarskjöld's life in his quest for peace." Reporting this to the audience at the dedication ceremony, Blaustein added, "I have no difficulty in accepting that this is so"[26]—implying underneath it all that he may have had some doubts. Hepworth herself may have been allaying his doubts when she provided him with such a narrow, straightforward reading. The general motif of the standing abstract form with a single high circular opening had been in her art for years, reworked in dozens of different ways; it surely collected many meanings for her, the most central probably difficult to translate into words.

When U Thant, Hammarskjöld's successor as Secretary-General, took his turn at the ceremonial podium, he said:

Each one who enters this building, from whatever part of the world he may come, will see this sculpture differently, will put into his view of it some part of his own background and take out from it some of its universal quality and meaning.

He also spoke of its "majesty," and of the impressions of vitality and durability it conveyed to him.

Overall, the United Nations under Dag Hammarskjöld's inspiration was once again speaking the language of abstract art—and a little uncertain as to what precisely was being said. The universality and suitability of the abstract idiom was unquestioned, but an unspoken question lingered in the air as to what meaning this woman and these men had brought into the visible center of the United Nations. Hammarskjöld's poem in *Markings* about the small version of *Single Form* that he owned shows him moving from the sculpted form to a much larger universe. One of its stanzas reads:

> Shall my soul meet
> This curve, as a bend in the road
> On her way to form?[27]

But his lines raise more questions and answer none. We had better look at the monument.

From the distance, *Single Form* rises like a great blade or Stonehenge monolith; it has both the abstract modernity of a propeller blade and the antiquity of a prehistoric temple pillar. Seemingly smoothskinned from the distance, it changes as one approaches, the smoothness resolving into a deliberately mottled surface retaining the handworked quality of the original plaster model from which the bronze was cast. A bow in the direction of Abstract Expressionism, this feature of *Single Form* effectively humanizes what might otherwise seem an all-too-perfect, cool composition.

The viewer may be thrown into questioning observation by the stance of the overall form, its great open "eye," and the incised cruciform pattern (the back surface has a more strongly mottled skin and no incised design). The form *stands* enough—and has foot, torso, and head enough—to be read in part as a human figure. The incised pattern supports this perception by dividing the form vertically into the three dominant zones of the human body and horizontally into familiar bilateral symmetry. Some viewers may sense the cruciform pattern, although not rendered in a traditional Christian form, as the "sign of the cross," in effect a consecration of the figure. This value is submerged and uninsistent, as well it should be in a multicultural setting, yet it is there.

The "eye" is of course not an eye; it is an abstract opening. Yet it asks to be read both as "eye" and as all the higher openings of the human body expressed in one. As the viewer continues to observe and collect these multiple meanings—perhaps with few words but not necessarily without precision—the "eye" also begins to convey openness pure and simple, the human capacity to welcome perceptions and connect. This understood, the form as a whole may reveal itself not only as a noble, upright affirmation of humanness, but as secretly youthful, almost prenatal in character—as if human nature is still coming to birth. This is also a submerged value in *Single Form;* we would caricature the sculpture by stressing this value more than the others. Yet it is there, and extraordinarily appropriate to the United Nations. Much of the magic of abstraction, when it *is* magical, lies in its ability to condense many coherent references and values into a single composition. In this sense it is not so much abstract as compact, a new type of metaphor.

Dag Hammarskjöld as statesman and world leader offered one of the larger performances of our time. His activities as an art patron obviously pale in front of his primary work. To my mind, this is a part of what needs to be understood about art patronage, specifically patronage that touches on the spiritual in art. Art is not all for such lives; it fits into a larger whole that includes not only activities in the world, which may be of the most demanding kind, but also activities in the intimacy of self which may be no less demanding. Under such circumstances, art stands a better chance of being correctly placed: not too high, not too low. It is a necessity, a source of rest and refreshment, even of spiritual renewal, neither an obsession nor a game. Hammarskjöld wrote a few thoughtful lines bearing on this point in his journal:

> During a working day, which is real only in God, the only poetry which can be real to you is the kind which makes you become real under God; only then is the poetry real for *you,* the art true. You no longer have time for—pastimes.[28]

Through his moderate austerity, Hammarskjöld courted endless vitality and the possibility of an artist's consciousness entering time and time again into a statesman's life. "In the point of rest at the center of our being," he once wrote,

> we encounter a world where all things are at rest in the same way. Then a tree becomes a mystery, a cloud a revelation, each man a cosmos of whose riches we can only catch glimpses. The life of simplicity is simple, but it opens to us a book in which we never get beyond the first syllable.[29]

24 BURNING IN THE LIGHT: ART AND TEACHINGS IN OUR TIME

TWO STREAMS

Throughout this book, a deliberately warm light has been directed onto the artists and the art of our time. The search for eloquent signs of the reality of ourselves and our world has deserved admiring, even affectionate treatment, and it has been a fruitful search. We can respect Brancusi's birds, Rothko's clouds of color, Kandinsky's images of the unfolding cosmos, and other works alongside the religious art of many times and places. These works have not expressed formally established theologies or spiritual views shared by large communities; they have no such prestige. They have represented search under conditions of uncertainty rather than confident consensus views. Each artist's search has been largely individual, although aesthetic and spiritual ideas were shared by friends, occasionally found institutional settings, and certainly passed from one generation to the next—Matisse's art, for example, entering richly into Rothko, Brancusi entering into Noguchi. This individuality and informal sharing can be accepted, even celebrated as a vigorous response to modern times. Our diverse and apparently transitional culture could hardly elicit a more uniform response. There is no single picture, no undisputed thought, no paramount philosophy.

Nor will there be. Our world, permanently diverse, offers excellent opportunities for anger to people who believe that they possess the one truth, outside of which is no salvation. The best rule, as always, is to judge a tree by its fruits. Another rule, less often quoted, is not to judge a tree until it has had time to produce its fruits. The search of twentieth-century artists for a wise art—an art both beautiful and true—has taken many detours, lost its way again and again, yet persisted. We haven't infallibly known what wisdom, beauty, and truth mean in an era that has seen so much stupidity, ugliness, and falsehood. To ask a search to show the confidence and finish of an accomplished culture that has had centuries to find its way is to ask too much. On the other hand, to ask nothing is to ask far too little.

And so we come to the topic of teachings, which *inform* but also *demand;* they ask questions, and they ask of us. The word *teachings,* as I use it, refers to a considerable range of doctrines and practical approaches to cultivating human nature. It encompasses the major religions, esoteric sects within them, independent teachings that do not stress their descent from a lineage, and psychological teachings that have emerged from medical science to demonstrate a vigorous life of their own.

For clarity, a few examples may be useful. The major religions hardly need comment, although their familiarity and the harshness of this century have brought about the need for reconsideration and reformulation in order to regain the impact of fresh teaching. Religions begin as teachings, deteriorate into routine, and elicit renewal from exceptional people who recognize the deterioration for what it is and restore the teaching. Thomas Merton's encounter with Christian monasticism and mysticism, for example, has greatly helped to renew them and endow them with an unmistakably modern voice. Judaism has survived the twentieth-century assault on its existence and divided into a number of branches: the secular Judaism of many Americans lacks the intentness of a teaching, but the writings of Martin Buber, Adin Steinsaltz, and Elie Wiesel, among others, have retained for Judaism the potential to awaken the vivid hope and challenge of a teaching.

Among esoteric sects bound into the major religions, many more are now known in the West than in earlier decades. One that remains too little known is the finely intellectual teaching of Frithjof Schuon, rooted in Islamic Sufism but instructive on virtually all traditional religious teachings.[1] The various traditions of Tibetan, Chinese, Southeast Asian, and Japanese Buddhism now taught in the United States and Western Europe represent a diffusion of essentially monastic teachings into secular Western society. We may not habitually think of them as "esoteric," but they differ considerably from popular Western religions in their emphasis on meditational practice and their use of retreats and other monastic forms.

Among independent teachings, one of the most widely respected was conveyed by the late J. Krishnamurti. He was Hindu by birth, Theosophical by adoption and early training, fiercely independent in his maturity, and acutely suspicious of unexamined inheritance from religion or any other source.

For American readers, the psychological teachings require little introduction: the ideas of Freud, Jung, Adler, Abraham Maslow, Fritz Perls, and others have illuminated the limitations and potentialities of human nature.

We can rightly regard all of these ways of thought and practice as teachings, although they are far from identical and in some instances take exception to each other. From the perspective of this book, what they have in common is more important than what distinguishes them. Their common strengths are an unusual knowledge of human nature and a persuasive call to men and women to take themselves in hand as physical and spiritual beings: to live deliberately, in an evolving relation with purposes beyond the attainment of material well-being.

In the course of our century, two streams of culture have developed all but independently of one another. They have sporadically touched on one another, drawn on one another, and joined in the lives of a handful of individuals. But for the most part they have remained independent, the finest achievements of the one unacknowledged or acknowledged only superficially by the other. The first is the stream of art; the second, the stream of spiritual and psychological teachings which are not only philosophies but also practical disciplines.

Among these teachings, the most widely accepted by artists has been the Jungian perspective—and naturally so. Jung's passionate yet learned theory of images confirms the innate interest of artists, dignifies it, and guides it toward the interior depths from which resonant images arise. Further, his inherently patient concept of individuation authorizes men and women to mature over time rather than attempt—and fail—to meet some ideal standard all at once. But even Jungian thought can make artists and critics nervous, as if it represents an alien overlay upon the pristine body of art. The presumption is that artists should somehow be able to get on without well-ordered ideas about human nature and a personal discipline that runs deep.

Suspicion is not entirely misplaced, with regard not only to Jungian thought but to all spiritual or psychological teachings. All of the arts, not only painting and sculpture, have their own cultures and traditions, and they defend themselves against advisors in other fields who may not respect or even apprehend the unchanging essence of each art. Jungian thought, for example, can be heavy-handed, in effect substituting a knowledge of the worldwide recurrence and variations of images for their direct, naive impact. Jungians at work sometimes illuminate, sometimes create a dictionary of images and related explanations that is no more interesting than any other dictionary.[2]

Teachings endowed with ancient theological traditions, complex literatures, and high aesthetic standards established centuries ago tend to belabor the twentieth-century artist for failing to reach the depth of meaning and still beauty achieved in classical epochs long past. In effect, they ask the artist of our time to create furnishings for Romanesque cathedrals, Mamluk mosques, and Kamakura monasteries in an era when many serious people, including artists, are buffeted by powerful changes coursing through our culture and quite legitimately do not know where to turn. Perhaps we are waiting, but I doubt that we are waiting for the past to reassert itself with no acknowledgment whatsoever of the present. There cannot be a complete wisdom today about life or art that disregards the social, cultural, and political experience of this century or denigrates the hard-earned findings of contemporary science. We live in a quite new cosmos, and God lives in it, too.

Still other teachings demand of the artist a precision of intention and action that may well result from long work but often seems threatening to artists who do not function in that way—and don't really wish to. Artists dream, and they progress by trial and error; even Brancusi and Mondrian, artists of exceptional precision in concept and execution, spoke of dreaming. Access to deep imagery, new beauty, and new forms in which to embody the truth one knows depends in part on creative dreaming—and then stumbling forward by experiment until the outward form closely matches the inner vision. In this sense, dreaming is a spontaneous exploration of form and meaning which, with good fortune and hard work, issues out into vision. Dreaming has played a role in every artistic and cultural tradition, however conservative and firm its taste and values. Between the magnificently virile calligraphy of early Islam and the equally magnificent fluency of later script, several generations of calligraphers must have dreamed and experimented.

For some artists, dreaming is spontaneously exact. Mozart seems simply to have focused on an innate musicality to draw forth fully realized music. But this is a rare gift; the painstakingly reworked manuscripts of Beethoven illustrate the more typical trials even of the very great. To the degree that spiritual and psychological teachings demonstrate insensitivity to the workshop or imperiously attempt to rework art into what it *should* be, they will be rejected by artists or given only a subordinate place. Teachings, in turn, will not bother much with an arts community that has blind faith in its "gifts," "inspirations," and experimental attitude. There is, of course, much to be questioned in these gifts and inspirations, but that questioning properly begins with the artist. In the end, teachings enter by invitation. When artists are not much interested and fearful of loss, teachings find a community elsewhere, among people who recognize their ignorance and unrealized potential, wish to be and do more, and make no special claims on their own behalf. Artistic talent is arguably a dangerous thing, a half-gift that its owner may not be moved to complete through his or her own efforts. It is already rich, interesting—why tamper with such splendor?

And so throughout the century there has been a standoff between the arts and teachings. Artists have been attracted by many different teachings from Theosophy to Zen and depth psychology, and scarcely a teaching has failed to address the question of art. But art clearly is not a branch of spiritual discipline, and no teaching has generated a visual art that expresses its substance cohesively. Even Surrealism, long and explicitly associated with the Freudian pespective, only scratches the surface of that troubled but deeply humane view of mankind and in some ways caricatures it. No teaching has earned the trust of large numbers of artists. Few artists have earned the esteem of the more aus tere teachers, for many of whom twentieth-century art is a contradiction in terms because the spirituality they expect in art is often plainly absent.

I have tried to respect the uneasy relation between the arts and teachings, allowing artists to speak from their own spirituality and love of art and not attempting to "read in" a greater dedication to spirituality or more orderly philosophy than the artists themselves acknowledged. On the other hand, if we are to have a genuinely cultured art and more than a handful of artists, designers, and architects who create things of the spirit, the two streams must draw closer.

The twentieth century has established a new, varied, and still fertile artistic language. Some communities in our time, in spite of the obstacles, have rediscovered authentic spirituality and show a sober, non-evangelical willingness to share their knowledge. Privately in some studios around the world, the two streams are already merging into one. But the mainstream of art in the marketplace remains for the most part untouched, well insulated from the demands imposed by a searching spirituality that does not applaud so willingly. Much the same is true of architecture: how few buildings, as they move from earth to sky, tell us anything about the earth and sky. To do so would also tell us about ourselves.

Art is not yet burning in the light. Kandinsky, Klee, Mondrian, Brancusi, Rothko, Bissier, and others showed what it means to be an artist-metaphysician, a seeker honoring both Nature and something more than Nature. Needless to say, they did not live in reliably quiet times that favored contemplation, nor was their art generally accepted and rewarded until much time had passed. The earlier generations of twentieth-century artists had struggle enough to discover the new language of art and to assure their personal survival. They were also obliged to piece together from mixed, often cloudy sources a more or less coherent spirituality that said enough about man and the universe. These challenges disciplined their spirits and kept them honest; the light came to them, bright enough to mark out their time and ours as one in which a new art had begun within a new, still unfinished culture.

But what challenge, perhaps unnoticed, faces present generations of artists? Not confronted at the moment with widespread wars and other social disasters, we cannot count on personal hardship as a relentless teacher, although individual exceptions always exist; people in general feel insecure but comfortable enough for the time being. Supported to some real degree by galleries and schools (and in some countries by government subventions) through which a passable living can be made, many artists have become immersed like their fellow-citizens in a strongly materialistic culture. The marketplace has invaded the studio, and marketers know how to keep things reasonably interesting and attractive so that one hardly misses—what?

The unnoticed challenge, first but not fully met by the pioneer artist-metaphysicians, lies in the terrain between art and teachings. The challenge thrown down by the teachings, often insultingly with little faith in the abilities of contemporary artists, is to reunite art and spirit. It is a challenge that some artists feel intuitively; they do not need to be taunted to know of its existence and to work toward reunion.

It is not a challenge for which all artists are equipped. Many will continue whatever work has already succeeded for them in the marketplace, or whatever they expect in time to bring material success. Many others do not aspire to anything more than a pleasant vocation: the watercolorist who goes out on weekends to paint landscapes and enjoy a quiet relationship with Nature, later perhaps selling through a local gallery, is a friend of art. But apart from artists who are tied to market values and others who are content, there are some mature artists and many, many students for whom art still represents an unfulfilled promise, as if they came to art for something that has not yet been achieved and whose very nature is unclear. For them, the teachings have importance—if not directly as deliberately adopted disciplines, then indirectly as guideposts along a way that they prefer to travel on their own.

This is not such a secular age—not any longer. The sheer threat of the times and the unprecedented levels of communication and study linking Asia and the West, the Third World and the industrial world, bring new urgency and possibilities. Science itself, which provided a harsh challenge to religious belief in the nineteenth and early twentieth centuries, has now reached into matter so deeply that few argue any longer that the instruments of empirical science can expect to record the whole of reality. The successes of science no longer erode the confidence of other modes of inquiry. As we detail the new cosmology and adjust our thinking to include such phenomena as black holes and the possibility of antimatter galaxies, we are not losing a metaphysical perspective but laying some of the groundwork for a new metaphysic, based as always on evidence from empirical *and* contemplative disciplines.

In recent decades, teachings that include contemplative methods have opened ways of questioning and learning in the West that yield new insights into consciousness. Such teachings link our time, if only a little, to times long past, in which contemplation was in all but name a scientific discipline. A brave new world has begun to take shape—in spite of our self-destructiveness, and with incomparably more suffering than anyone could have predicted at the turn of the twentieth century. Aggressively scientific and technological, late twentieth-century culture is nonetheless nurturing sciences of the whole person and pursuing questions that lead beyond laboratory science and technology.

Kandinsky sensed the advent of this well-founded, more spiritual culture within the dying nineteenth century. He touched on it through Theosophy and perhaps through astrology and other ancient studies, but it was rarely more than a tangential contact; he did not always penetrate to the heart of the matter. Brancusi had a most unusual individual insight into spirituality and its inevitable symbols but, as he said, he "neglected the technique." Mondrian understood that "the universal towers above us" and that the calling of art is "to bring the universal downward," but there was a fearfulness in his character that restricted his research beyond a certain point. Rothko had genius enough to uncover an icon uniting light and air in a single transcendental image, but he lacked the genius to transcend his achievement and in the end fell prey to personal weaknesses. None of these biographies from the first generations—and there are others pointing in the same direction—show a final excellence that makes further work irrelevant. These individuals initiated a relation between art and spirituality in our time that has not yet achieved a stable form which many people can share. As Hammarskjöld said in a thoroughly secular press conference: "There are no precedents or experiences that would entitle us not to try again."[3] His words resonate far beyond their diplomatic context.

This is the challenge facing present generations of artists—if not those now well into their careers, then those just beginning or soon to begin for whom *art* is still a magical word, a word that unaccountably makes one leap inside with hope, as if there is something to be seen that has not yet been seen, and as if it must come through artists' hands—not nonsense, not just entertainment or personal invention, but something absolutely serious and beautiful.

THE CRAFT TRADITION

To realize this goal, must artists turn to sources beyond art? Is art self-sufficient as a discipline or must it go to school elsewhere in a culture to complete itself? We have heard a number of artists address this question. Mondrian weighed "the two paths leading to the Spiritual," that of the artist and that of the learned student of meditation and other "direct" practices, as he put it. He seemed finally to trust slow growth toward the spiritual through art more than he trusted the accelerated methods of what he called "the Path of learning"; best of all, he thought, when they coincide. Noguchi, decades later, sharply stated in an interview that D. T. Suzuki was not a priest—implying that Zen priesthood represented a restrictive point of view by which Dr. Suzuki, as a scholar, was happily not bound. Clearly, artists attuned to these issues fear being imposed on, yet the question remains: is art self-sufficient or must it school with the teachings to fulfill its highest ideals?

An interesting light is shed on the question by the handcraft tradition, successfully revived in Victorian England after retreating in the face of the Industrial Revolution. The originator of the modern craft tradition was William Morris (1834–1896), the craftsman, painter, social thinker, and poet who gave practical hands to John Ruskin's noble dreams. The tradition has been periodically renewed throughout our century: intellectually through the writings of Ananda K. Coomaraswamy, practically through the Bauhaus craft studios and their migrant instructors, and in the years before and after World War II through Soetsu Yanagi, Bernard Leach, and Shoji Hamada, who revalued the rich Japanese craft tradition and made it known in the West. Needless to say, the tradition has been distorted, sentimentalized, and diluted time and time again, but it has retained real firmness and demonstrated the ability to perpetuate itself.

The ideals and insights of the craft tradition are not easily summarized. There is an insight into human nature and into the discipline of body and mind that allows the craftsperson to work harmoniously. There is acknowledgment of the distinctiveness of materials, the sacredness of Nature, and the craftsperson's participation in materials and impressive natural law. There is an intuition of the Logos informing both Nature and human nature, accompanied by recognition that the Logos hides and must be perseveringly sought. Craftspeople often grasp, at least in theory, that the stages through which a work must pass to reach completion parallel the maturation of the human being and so shed light on our own needs and possibilities. It follows by analogy that to study a craft is to study one's own nature; hence the firm association between craft work and the search for self-knowledge. The study is instinctively known to be dynamic: human nature is surmised to be subject to change no less total, over time, than the shapeless lump of clay that becomes a trim vase. This is the faith underlying some craft traditions that preserve a key reflexive: not only "I work" but also "I work on myself."

Hence the long, generally uncomplaining apprenticeships that craftspeople often serve. The myth and reality of the apprentice is better preserved in the crafts than in painting and sculpture, which have gradually adopted the antithetical myth of the athlete who reaches peak performance early in life. Craftspeople tend to understand that excellence requires patient application over many years. They do not expect a great deal until the person and the technique have matured together.

In sum, hidden below the superheated world of twentieth-century art is this cooler, more modest world of craft, preserving an alternative view of creativity that is closer to Nature and in general less vain, although no less expressive in the works of its accomplished masters. It has its own marketplace and celebrities, and overall a keener conscience than the world of art—less spoiled, still somewhat frightened of the demanding teachers from whom it derives, although competitive juried exhibitions in major cities have lately acquired the gleam of ambitious art markets.

The craft tradition at its best confirms what must have been evident throughout this book: the arts are teachings in themselves. The effort to master difficult manual techniques, often long and humiliating, is also rewarding in a larger sense; it trains its person. The effort to understand the life of materials requires constant renewal. Brancusi himself, who taught awareness of materials and knew them to be thoroughly alive, fractured marble on occasion when he pushed it too far. Beyond the functional understanding that permits the worker to get on with his work, there is a communion with materials that is never achieved once and for all. This communion points beyond itself: "as above, so below" can be a practical and inspiring truth in the studio. The weaver learns the weave of things; the painter learns the act of attention through which Creation came.

The artist's capacity to recognize worthwhile themes and resonant images disappears and reappears almost unaccountably, changing over time, deepening in some, degrading in others. The volatile character of this central capacity, without which art is nothing, prompts in all artists a struggle for clarity and receptivity—and in some a lifelong investigation of self and ego. *Who* is it that can be clear, and *who* receives? From this, from all of the challenges facing the artist, flows the recognition that art can be a discipline of the whole being, not in the puritanical sense of painful effort but in the sense of learning what and how to pay for a knowing spontaneity. It is a work of the mind alert, body alert, feelings turned again and again both toward the task at hand and toward the artist's own internal resources. This struggle and communion with oneself, with materials, with techniques, with ideas and images—how could this not be a teaching?

It often fails to be. The possibility of a lifelong encounter with oneself exists in the artist's studio, the potter's shed, the weaving shop. But to see and make use of that possibility requires an intensity of purpose and seasoned knowledge now rare, perhaps always rare. Long, continuous workshop traditions certainly create more favorable circumstances (although passive continuity has its dangers—many strong traditions have succumbed to repetition). The traditions of the French Companions of Duty survived well into the nineteenth century and are reputed to be more or less intact today; they may reflect something of the life and training available in Renaissance and medieval guilds. Numerous Asian traditions involve comparably stern apprenticeship and philosophical depth. But we needn't look at cultural exotica or ancient times and distant places to find the pattern: much as he railed against teaching, Brancusi clearly sponsored in Noguchi an intensity of purpose and a quality of consciousness that links the two men and shines in their art. Identically, the Bauhaus classes of Klee, Kandinsky, Schlemmer, and others were occasions of teaching in the larger sense, not only exercises in eye/hand coordination but confrontations with self and world.

To become an authentic teaching, art must be thrown into a crucible and ground quite fiercely, quite diligently. Otherwise it lacks the intensity of a teaching, although it may produce works of wit and elegance. Good taste is easier than good art. Narrowly focused on technical skill by a demanding instructor, it offers perhaps a half-teaching, an illumination of the body and its skills but not of the soul and *its* skills.

Something more can occur when a relatively complete teaching and a complete or growing command of artistic technique come together. Such a circumstance apparently prevailed in the workshops that created many universally acknowledged monuments and enduring traditions: the Hagia Sophia and Chartres Cathedral, the Stupa at Borobudur and the Temple at Ise, and on another scale Sung Dynasty landscape painting and the general milieu that produced in successive generations Giotto, Masaccio, Piero della Francesca, and Leonardo.

Such achievements and artists tell us what art can be. The first generations in our own time pointed the way, but as they themselves sometimes said, they did not fully travel it. "Much, much later, the *pure art*," wrote Kandinsky. "Giotto is the summit of my desires, but . . . ," wrote Matisse, acknowledging the limitation imposed by the spiritual uncertainties of twentieth-century culture. These individuals and others pointed the way toward a new unity of art and spirit which they could not fully realize. In their time, art was strong but teachings not so strong. In our time, art is not so strong but teachings strong. An extraordinary wealth of knowledge is available today, easily enough found although not easily mastered.

THE DUTY TO DEAL IN ESSENTIALS

The plurality of late twentieth-century culture is overwhelming: it is a larger phenomenon than any of us can fully grasp or control, yet our fate is bound up with it. It would make as much sense to attempt to order and narrow that plurality as to prune a forest—an endless task, and needless because one of our strengths at the moment is precisely this multiplicity of ideas and purposes. Metaphysicians may rail at it; it is indeed impure and ignorant. It is nonetheless promising, an immaturity not an end.

Plurality of this kind need not imply patternless chaos. On the contrary, it implies multiple centers, some kindred, others so far from one another that they know nothing of each other. This book embodies the hope that certain elements of the twentieth-century tradition in art can speak to virtually all circles and elicit at least respect, at best a renewed sense of purpose and direction.

The last word belongs to Oskar Schlemmer, that sturdy Bauhaus designer of walls and dances. Late in life, in Germany, where he survived the opening years of World War II more or less as an internal refugee, he kept up his correspondence and diary in entire disregard of the general disaster. To his friend Julius Bissier, he wrote from hospital in October 1942:

> I feel we have the duty = obligation to deal in essentials, or at least to render our conception of the essential as well as we are able. This implies ethical standards rather than aesthetic ones—and yet we cannot escape the aesthetic, . . . considering that we derive our best stimuli from sense impressions.[4]

The thought became larger still in a diary entry for the following month:

> Today I once more envisage a sort of painting with . . . "Breadth of Greatness" . . . , large and sweeping, symbolic and yet glowing so beautifully in its material that no one bothers about interpretation. . . . I was reminded of this by the sight of the rusted kettle against the winter landscape. I immediately recognized its "from somewhere" quality, the East Asian element. Compared to this mode of art I envisage, many past and present paintings would look like the products of a petty mind.[5]

He does not, of course, speak for the whole complex weave of works and ideas that we have encountered; no one can. He nonetheless speaks well, from the spiritual center of twentieth-century art.

He is learned, yet wears his learning lightly. He is entranced by sense impressions, yet he knows that the ethical and the symbolic are not distant—they are the very substance of the art he dreams. He understands the primacy of *the image;* no amount of right thinking or right symbols can substitute for works that glow beautifully. He is keenly aware of the ordinary as such, yet he perceives in it something more, evoked earlier in this book in terms of *tathatā:* the "suchness" of all things shining through them and from them, marking the physical with a metaphysical light for those who care to see it. A mainstream Western artist who helped to create the Bauhaus, he is nonetheless learning from Asia; for him the world is not one but many-in-one and infinitely rich. He is discriminating, unafraid to identify the petty. He is modest; he understands that we have the duty to deal in essentials, but he acknowledges that we may lack the wisdom to make a full account of essentials—we can only do "as well as we are able."

All of this is admirable. It evokes an art of our own.

NOTES

The titles of books and articles, generally noted by author and date of publication, are listed in full in the bibliography. Frequently cited titles are abbreviated for convenience; for example, Kandinsky CW refers to Kandinsky, Wassily, *Complete Writings on Art*, ed. Kenneth C. Lindsay and Peter Vergo, two volumes, Boston, 1982. Bibliographic data on infrequently cited publications are given only in the notes. Wherever an author is clearly indicated in museum and gallery catalogues, such publications appear in the notes and bibliography under the author's name.

1. Introduction

1. *Über das Geistige in der Kunst, insbondere in der Malerei (On the Spiritual in Art, and Painting in Particular)*, 1st edition, Munich, 1912, twice reprinted in that year; read aloud at an artists' conference, St. Petersburg, Dec. 1911, and subsequently published in Russian; first English translation, 1914. See Kandinsky CW and Bowlt/Washton Long (1984) for further background.

2. Herbert (1964), 41. Readers are referred to this convenient edition of Kandinsky's *Reminiscences* throughout the notes; the memoir is also published in Kandinsky CW.

3. Geist (1975), 12

4. Wheelwright (1959), 58

5. See Coomaraswamy (1977)

6. Bush/Shin (1985), 40

7. George F. Hill, *Drawings by Pisanello*, Paris and Brussels, 1929 (reprinted New York, 1965)

8. *Four Sleepers*, by the mid-fourteenth-century Japanese painter-priest Mokuan; see Yasuichi Awakawa, *Zen Painting*, Tokyo, 1970

9. Thomas Merton, *The Hidden Ground of Love: Letters*, ed. William H. Shannon, New York, 1985, 129

10. Henri Corbin, "Eyes of Flesh and Eyes of Fire: Science and Gnosis," in *Material for Thought*, No. 8, 1980, 5-10 (a publication of Far West Institute)

11. Picasso (1969), 32. The illuminating idea of the camouflages of the sacred in twentieth-century art was introduced by Mircea Eliade; see Eliade (1985), 32 ff., 81 ff.

2. Abstraction

1. Mondrian (1969), passage 41
2. Evidence for this point is the ambitious Los Angeles exhibition and catalogue, Tuchman (1986). That publication is hereafter referenced in the notes as LA Catalogue. A review in the widely read *Art in America* raised interesting points but minimized the significance of the venture. "Finally, a little spiritualism, however porous, can't hurt." Peter Plagens, "Los Angeles: Two for the Show," in *Art in America,* May 1987, 157
3. Herbert (1964), 42–43
4. Mondrian (1969), passage 39
5. Coomaraswamy, vol. 1 (1977), 323–49

3. Early Guides

1. Matisse (1972), 84n
2. Cézanne (1976), 327
3. Doran (1978), 28; see also the memoir by Ambroise Vollard, *Paul Cézanne: His Life and Art,* New York, 1937 (reprinted 1984 under the title, *Cézanne*)
4. An early, devoted biography is in Henry Steel Olcott, *Old Diary Leaves: The True Story of the Theosophical Society,* New York 1895 (reprinted 1975 under the title, *Inside the Occult*); a recent assessment is Marion Meade, *Madame Blavatsky: The Woman Behind the Myth,* New York, 1980. A general history of occultism can be found in two studies by James Webb, *The Occult Underground,* La Salle (Ill.), 1974, and *The Occult Establishment,* La Salle (Ill.), 1976. The LA Catalogue also provides excellent background.
5. H. P. Blavatsky, *Isis Unveiled,* New York, 1877, vi–vii
6. Kandinsky CW, 143–45
7. See Ringbom (1970), Washton Long (1980), and the LA Catalogue.
8. Besant and Leadbeater (1901), Leadbeater (1902)
9. See Rudolf Steiner, *An Autobiography,* New York, 1977, and Johannes Hemleben, *Rudolf Steiner: A Documentary Biography,* East Grinsted (Sussex), 1975
10. Edouard Schuré, *The Great Initiates: A Study of the Secret History of Religions,* New York, 1979 (1st edition, Paris, 1889)
11. See Lukach (1983)
12. Kandinsky CW, 219; see Ringbom (1970) for an account of sources for the concept of the "epoch of the great spiritual."

4. Wassily Kandinsky in the Years of *On the Spiritual in Art*

1. Major Kandinsky bibliography includes listings under his name in the bibliography, as well as Bowlt/Washton Long (1984), Guggenheim Museum

(1972), Herbert (1964), LA Catalogue, Poling (1983), Ringbom (1970), Rudenstine (1976), Washton Long (1980), Weiss (1979), and the publications of Hans Konrad Roethel.

2. Herbert (1964), 34

3. Herbert (1964), 38–39. Ringbom (1970) explains that the epoch of the great spiritual was associated in Kandinsky's thought with a new revelation of the Third Person of the Trinity, the Holy Spirit.

4. Kandinsky CW, 131

5. Kandinsky CW, 137

6. Kandinsky/Marc (1974), 164–65, 173 (italics in original)

7. Plato, *Apology* 31D

8. Kandinsky (1974), 74n; cf. Kandinsky CW, 211n. The 1947 translation of *On the Spiritual,* while surely less accurate in places, is often more polished than the version in Kandinsky CW. It is also the voice of Kandinsky heard in English for many decades, given that the 1947 translation was a revision of the original 1914 version. Where I quote the 1947 translation, as here, the note gives the corresponding pages in Kandinsky CW.

9. Kandinsky CW, 175–76

10. Kandinsky CW, 400. Kandinsky's reference to the categorical imperative recalls Kantian ethics, evoked here to shed light on inner necessity, which Kandinsky took to be the heart of the artist's ethic.

11. Bush/Shin (1985), 40; cf. 10–17, 39

12. Kandinsky (1947), 39; cf. Kandinsky CW, 152

13. Kandinsky (1947), 36–39; cf. Kandinsky CW, 151–52

14. Kandinsky (1947), 39; cf. Kandinsky CW, 152

15. Kandinsky (1947), 51; cf. Kandinsky CW, 171

16. Kandinsky (1947), 44; cf. Kandinsky CW, 157

17. Kandinsky (1947), 61; cf. Kandinsky CW, 186

18. Kandinsky (1947), 67; cf. Kandinsky CW, 197

19. Kandinsky/Marc (1974), 64

20. Kandinsky/Marc (1974), 259

21. See Washton Long (1980)

22. Kandinsky CW, 396

23. Kandinsky (1947), 77n; cf. Kandinsky CW, 218

5. Cubism

1. Chipp (1971), 262

2. Kandinsky (1947), 39; cf. Kandinsky CW, 153

3. Picasso (1972), 61

4. Eliade (1969), "Paradise and Utopia: Mythical Geography and Eschatology," 88 ff., and Eliade (1985), indexed references to nostalgia

5. Fry (1966), 53

6. Picasso (1972), 61

7. Fry (1966), 116–17

8. Fry (1966), 59
9. Fry (1966), 99

6. Mondrian

1. Mondrian (1986), 121. Referenced hereafter as Mondrian CW
2. Quoted in Jaffé (1956), 145
3. Cf. Mondrian CW, 64–69 (1917)
4. Quoted in Seuphor (1956), 118
5. Mondrian CW, 42
6. Mondrian CW, 70n
7. Mondrian CW, 169
8. Mondrian CW, 46n
9. Mondrian CW, 42
10. Mondrian CW, 137
11. Mondrian CW, 221
12. Mondrian CW, 325
13. Mondrian CW, 259
14. Mondrian CW, 43
15. Mondrian CW, 28–29
16. Mondrian CW, 24
17. Wallace Stevens, *Letters of Wallace Stevens*, ed. Holly Stevens, New York, 1977, 628
18. Mondrian CW, 151
19. Mondrian CW, 101
20. Mondrian CW, 120
21. Mondrian CW, 35 and 59n
22. Mondrian CW, 80
23. Mondrian CW, 296
24. Mondrian CW, 293
25. Charmion von Wiegand, quoted in Seuphor (1956)
26. Peter Gay (1976), 175 ff.
27. William Blake, *A Descriptive Catalogue*, in *The Portable Blake*, ed. Alfred Kazin, New York, 1946, 530
28. Mondrian CW, 42
29. Mondrian CW, 33
30. Mondrian CW, 71n
31. Mondrian CW, 120
32. Mondrian CW, 32–33
33. Mondrian CW, 41
34. Mondrian CW, 48
35. Mondrian CW, 48
36. Mondrian CW, 94
37. Mondrian CW, 72n
38. Mondrian CW, 192

39. Mondrian CW, 35
40. Mondrian CW, 32
41. Mondrian (1969), 36, 40
42. Mondrian CW, 44
43. Mondrian CW, cf. 254–55
44. Mondrian CW, 254
45. Mondrian CW, 67
46. Mondrian CW, 30
47. Quoted in Seuphor (1956), 58
48. Mondrian CW, 103
49. Mondrian CW, 123
50. Mondrian CW, 136
51. Mondrian CW, 90
52. Mondrian CW, 136
53. Mondrian CW, 54
54. Mondrian CW, 95
55. Mondrian CW, 53n
56. Mondrian CW, 93
57. Mondrian CW, 60
58. Mondrian CW, 232
59. Mondrian CW, 265
60. Mondrian CW, 53
61. Mondrian CW, 310
62. Mondrian CW, 93
63. Mondrian CW, 136
64. Mondrian CW, 115
65. Mondrian CW, 40
66. Mondrian CW, 149
67. Mondrian CW, 52n
68. Mondrian CW, 341
69. Mondrian CW, 229
70. Mondrian CW, 59n
71. Mondrian CW, 229

7. Orphism

1. Apollinaire offered the following definition of his new coinage, Orphism: ". . . the art of painting new structures with elements which have not been borrowed from the visual sphere, but have been created entirely by the artist himself, and been endowed by him with fullness of reality. The works of the orphic artists must simultaneously give a pure aesthetic pleasure; a structure which is self-evident; and a sublime meaning, that is, a subject. This is pure art." Quoted in Fry (1966), 117
2. Kupka (1921), 574
3. Apollinaire, "Les Fiançailles," cited by Spate (1979), 67

4. Quoted from Faber Birren, *Principles of Color: A Review of Past Traditions and Modern Theories of Color Harmony,* New York, 1969, 30

5. Delaunay (1978), 81–82

6. Delaunay (1978), 70

7. Delaunay (1978), 81–82

8. Delaunay (1978), 86

9. Delaunay (1978), 115–16

10. Quoted in Spate (1979), 56

11. Spate (1979), 85

12. Spate (1979), 128

13. Spate (1979), 116

14. Quoted by J. P. Hodin, intro. to Vachtovà (1968), 11

15. I forgo illustrating *Vertical Planes III.* Monochrome photography does nothing for this relatively simple composition—a pair of slender planes (black and white) ascending from the lower edge of the canvas, a single plane (purple) descending from the upper edge, all three contained in an airy green space by gray-green bands that run the full length of the canvas at right and left.

16. Quoted in Mladek/Rowell (1975), 190

17. Vachtovà (1968), 286

18. Quoted in Mladek/Rowell (1975), 171

19. Vachtovà (1968), 285

20. Spate (1979), 104

21. Vachtovà (1968), 285

8. Marcel Duchamp

1. Major sources for Duchamp are Cabanne (1971), D'Harnoncourt/McShine (1973), Duchamp (1960), Duchamp (1975), Golding (1972), Paz (1978), and Schwarz (1970).

2. Schwarz (1970), 20

3. Duchamp (1975), 73

4. Duchamp (1975), 124

5. Duchamp (1975), 74

6. Duchamp (1975), 33

7. Schwarz (1970), 131

8. Schwarz (1970), 39

9. Duchamp (1975), 141

10. Duchamp (1975), 5

11. Golding (1972), 60

12. Duchamp (1975), 73

13. René Daumal, "Le contreciel," in *Poésie noire, poésie blanche,* Paris, 1954, 15

14. D'Harnoncourt/McShine (1973), 38

15. D'Harnoncourt/McShine (1973), 134

16. Duchamp (1975), 125

17. Duchamp (1975), 136

18. Schwarz (1970), Golding (1972), and Paz (1978), can initiate the study.

19. See Eliade (1969), "Initiation and the Modern World," 112 ff., and the remarkable essay by George Steiner, "On Difficulty," in *On Difficulty and Other Essays*, New York and Oxford, 1978, 18ff.

20. Victor Danner, ed. and trans., *Ibn 'Ata'illah's Sufi Aphorisms*, Leiden, 1973

21. Schwarz (1970), 103ff., ventures a Freudian interpretation of elements in *The Large Glass* and other works by Duchamp.

22. Duchamp (1975), 137

23. Mondrian CW, 191

9. Chance

1. See Coomaraswamy (1977), vol. 1., "The Intellectual Operation in Indian Art," 131–46

2. Arp (1972), 232

3. Sources for Dada and Surrealism are Rubin (1968), Ball (1974), Breton (1972), Huelsenbeck (1974), Lippard (1970, 1971), Marcel (1980), Richter (1965), and Waldberg (1965).

4. Translated from Léonard de Vinci, *La Peinture*, ed. André Chastel, Paris, 1964, 196

5. Herbert (1964), 34

6. Arp (1972), 232

7. Arp (1972), 246

8. Arp (1972), 242

9. Arp (1972), 238

10. Tristan Tzara, *Approximate Man and Other Writings*, Detroit, 1973, 154–155

11. Rubin (1968), 73

12. Breton (1972), 26

13. Breton (1972), 37

14. Breton (1972), 30

15. Cage (1973), xi

16. Cage (1973), 10–11

17. Cage (1973), 12. A small masterpiece of graphic art, often overlooked, is the colorful score for John Cage's *Aria*, 1960, written for "Voice (any range)."

18. Noguchi (1986), unpaginated interview in the archive of the Noguchi Garden Museum

10. The Russian Avant-Garde

Malevich's writings, edited by Troels Andersen, are noted as Malevich, *Essays*, Malevich, *The World*, and Malevich, *The Artist*, referring respectively to the 1971, 1976, and 1978 publications. Where possible, I will refer to Herbert (1964), which many readers will more easily find. As this book went to press, the Soviet policy of *glasnost* was beginning to result in exhibitions of Russian avant-garde works of the period discussed in this chapter, long officially ignored.

1. Heller/Nekrich (1986), 655–57, offers a vivid discussion of Soviet ideology from the perspective of émigré Soviet historians.

2. Bowlt (1976), 206

3. Malevich, *The Artist,* 12

4. Zhadova (1982), 327–28; on Lunacharsky, see Fitzpatrick (1970)

5. Malevich, *The Artist,* 148

6. Malevich, *The Artist,* 13

7. Malevich, *The Artist,* 25

8. Malevich, *The Artist,* 14

9. Malevich, *The Artist,* 13

10. I am grateful to Dr. Margaret Betz for pointing out that the familiar title *Black Square* is, strictly speaking, a mistranslation of *Black Quadrilateral.*

11. Herbert (1964), 94–95

12. Doran (1978), 36–37

13. Bowlt (1976), 118–19, 113–34

14. Malevich, *The Artist,* 9

15. Malevich, *The Artist,* 35

16. Malevich, *The Artist,* 152

17. Herbert (1964), 94–95

18. See the informative essays by Douglas, Bowlt, and Henderson in the LA Catalogue, as well as Douglas (1980) and Henderson (1983). The latter provides a wealth of information about Ouspensky's early thought and influence.

19. Malevich, *Essays,* 46

20. See James Webb, *The Harmonious Circle: The Lives and Work of G. I. Gurdjieff, P. D. Ouspensky, and Their Followers* (Boston, 1987), which offers a fine biography of Ouspensky and better documentation than interpretation regarding Gurdjieff. See also Anna Butkovsky-Hewitt, *With Gurdjieff in St. Petersburg and Paris,* London, 1978, which describes the young Ouspensky through a friend's eyes.

21. Merrily E. Taylor, *Remembering Pyotr Demianovich Ouspensky,* New Haven, 1978

22. Ouspensky (1959), 145

23. Ouspensky (1959), 220, 232

24. See Henderson, LA Catalogue, 226, fig. 6, and Marcadé (1979).

25. Doran (1978), 29

26. Doran (1978), 36

27. Malevich, *The Artist,* 151–52

28. Malevich, *Essays,* 190

29. Malevich, *Essays,* 31

30. Herbert (1964), 99
31. Bowlt (1976), 129
32. Herbert (1964), 95
33. See Kandinsky/Marc (1974), 64
34. Malevich, *The Artist,* 144–47
35. Malevich, *Essays,* 45
36. Malevich, *The Artist,* 108–09
37. On Tatlin, see Milner (1983)
38. Gmurzynska (1978), 222
39. Malevich, *Essays,* 51
40. Malevich, *The Artist,* 37
41. Lodder (1983), 47–48
42. Bowlt (1976), 206
43. Zhadova (1982), 84
44. Lodder (1983), 48
45. Zhadova (1982), 322–23
46. Illustrated in Gray (1971), fig. 217
47. Zhadova (1982), 42
48. Gmurzynska (1978), 47
49. See especially Milner (1983)
50. Lodder (1983), 64
51. Milner (1983), 194
52. Lodder (1983), 88
53. Bowlt (1976), 167–170
54. Elliott (1979), 130
55. Bann (1974), 19–20
56. Bowlt (1976), 217–23
57. Malevich, *Essays,* 186–87
58. Bann (1974), 84
59. Malevich, *The Artist*
60. Malevich, *The Artist,* 155
61. Malevich, *The Artist,* 215
62. Bowlt (1976), 271
63. Bowlt (1978), 185
64. Bowlt (1978), 185–86
65. Bowlt (1978), 187
66. Bowlt (1976), 265–67
67. Malevich, *Essays,* 183
68. Bowlt (1976), 291
69. Malevich, *The Artist,* 271
70. See Bowlt, Douglas, and Henderson in the LA Catalogue for other artists active in the period.
71. Bann (1974), 244–45

11. Paul Klee

1. Herbert (1964), 74–91, based on Klee (1945).

2. Joel Porte, ed., *Emerson in His Journals,* Cambridge (Mass.) and London, 1982, 523

3. *Zum Urgrund,* words borrowed from Meister Eckhart or a later participant in Christian mystical tradition

4. Liberman (1960), 142

5. Bloom (1973, 1975)

6. The photograph is published in Paola Watts, *Paul Klee, the private life,* Rome (Palazzo Braschi), 1979, fig. 56. The publication is a fascinating photo-biography of the artist.

7. Klee (1976), 122. The phrase is from a penetrating essay, the "Creative Credo" published in 1920, in which he describes the most sophisticated formal techniques of the artist as "not yet art in the highest circle. In the highest circle, behind the multiplicity of meaning stands a last secret, and the light of the intellect is piteously extinguished." The concept is Dantesque in its hierarchy of circles and its final surrender of intellect: "All'alta fantasia qui mancò possa" (*Paradiso* 33, 142)—Dante too lacked the power to conceive the last secret intellectually. A translation of the "Creative Credo" is in Klee (1961), 76–80.

8. Klee (1968), 297

9. Klee (1973), 461

10. Klee (1968), 342–45

11. Klee (1953, 1961, 1973)

12. Klee (1961), 463. The epigraph for this chapter, "closer to the center," is adapted from Klee's memorial stone—which in turn is adopted from his journal. It reads in part:

> Somewhat closer to the heart
> of creation than usual
> but far from close enough

12. The Bauhaus

1. Wingler (1976), 59

2. Schlemmer (1972), 249

3. Wingler (1976), 76

4. Wingler (1976), 69

5. Wingler (1976), 23

6. Wingler (1976), 31

7. Wingler (1976), 36

8. Schlemmer (1972), 139

9. Itten (1975), the revised edition of his original 1963 publication.

10. Itten (1975), 9

11. Schlemmer (1972), 114–15
12. Wingler (1976), 51
13. Wingler (1976), 52
14. Wingler (1976), 52
15. Schlemmer (1972), 123
16. Wingler (1976), 56
17. Wingler (1976), 60
18. Wingler (1976), 97
19. Wingler (1976), 69
20. Wingler (1976), 104
21. Wingler (1976), 73
22. Wingler (1976), 69
23. Wingler (1976), 125
24. Schlemmer (1972), 193
25. *Philebus* 51C
26. Walter Gropius, *Scope of Total Architecture*, New York, 1962, preface

13. Kandinsky at the Bauhaus

1. Primary bibliography for the period: Kandinsky CW, Kandinsky (1947), Grohmann (1958), Kandinsky (1970), Rudenstine (1976), Nina Kandinsky (1978), Poling (1983, 1986), and Bowlt/Washton Long (1984)
2. Lothar Schreyer, *Erinerungen an Sturm und Bauhaus*, Munich, 1956, 235
3. Kandinsky (1970), 169
4. Grohmann (1958), 180
5. Grohmann (1958), 187–88
6. Kandinsky (1947), 133n; cf. Kandinsky CW, 658n
7. Kandinsky CW, 802. A propaganda poster by Lissitzky, *Beat the Whites with the Red Wedge*, 1920, may be a source of Kandinsky's visual language in *Yellow Center*. Using a strictly geometric rather than organic language, Lissitzky dramatized the fighting spirit of the Red Army as a red triangle, flanked by darts, breaking into a white circle. Lizzitzky's work was most recently reproduced in Yve-Alain Bois, "El Lissitzky: Radical Reversibility," *Art in America*, April 1988, 160–81.
8. Grohmann (1958), 188
9. Rudenstine (1976), 308–11
10. Poling (1983), 51–54
11. Poling (1983), 53
12. Poling (1983), 54
13. Kandinsky CW, 533, 537
14. Kandinsky CW, 539–40
15. Kandinsky CW, 570–71
16. Kandinsky CW, 639 40

17. See Godwin (1979) on Fludd; Grohmann (1958), 296 for a reproduction of *Lyrical Oval*.

18. *Fixed Points* is reproduced in Overy (1969), 127

19. Lothar Schreyer, *Errinerungen*, 272

14. Brancusi

1. Zarnescu (1980), noted hereafter as Z, followed by the author's numerical entry for specific citations. This book is far from ideal: its citations are not always correct in every respect, citations on similar themes are blended and thus difficult to sort out, and in at least one instance a critic's words are attributed to the artist. Zarnescu is nevertheless the only source for some publications unavailable in American libraries. Wherever possible, I have cited original sources; citations from Zarnescu are consistent in substance and tone with those taken from original sources. A scholarly edition of Brancusi's writings and sayings is overdue. The selection here gives a taste of what that book might be like but is not itself a "critical" edition.

2. Liberman (1960), 169

3. Lewis (1957), 9

4. Z 47

5. Z 190

6. Comarnescu (1978), 278

7. Liberman (1960), 170

8. See the second part of this chapter for Brancusi's "laws."

9. Pandrea (1945), 158–59

10. Guilbert (1957), 7

11. Lewis (1957), 11

12. Jianou et al. (1982), 13

13. Z 79

14. Cf. Stella Kramrisch, *The Presence of Siva*, Princeton, 1981, and Ananda K. Coomaraswamy, *The Dance of Shiva*, New York, 1918 (with frequent reprints)

15. Z 7

16. Liberman (1960), 171

17. Spear (1969), 35

18. Geist (1984)

19. Cf. (Brancusi) in the bibliography for full reference to the trial transcript

20. Giedion-Welcker (1958), 220

21. Tabart/Monod-Fontaine (1982), figs. 28, 86

22. Giedion-Welcker (1959), 199n

23. Z 162

24. Reprinted Paris, 1971, with an introduction by Marco Pallis; this edition influenced the recent American translation, *The Life of Milarepa*, trans. Lobsang P. Lhalungpa, New York, 1977.

25. Garma C. C. Chang, trans., *The Hundred Thousand Songs of Milarepa,* two vols., Boulder and London, 1977

26. Pandrea (1945), 170–71

27. *Bṛihad Āraṇyaka Upanishad* 4.4.4, cited from Robert Ernest Hume, *The Thirteen Principal Upanishads,* 2nd edition revised, London, 1931

28. *Aitareya Brāhamaṇa* 11.14, cited from A. B. Keith, *Rigveda Brahmanas: The Aitareya and Kauṣītaki Brāhmaṇas of the Rigveda,* Oxford, 1909

29. Z 147

30. Bacot (1971), 142

31. Giedion-Welcker (1959), 202

32. Sidney Geist, conversation with the author

33. Jianou (1963), 56

34. Brezianu (1976), 134

35. Z 143

36. Eliade (1985), 93–101; cf. Mircea Eliade, *Patterns in Comparative Religion,* London, 1958, indexed references to the axis mundi; and as well his *No Souvenirs: Journal, 1957–1969,* New York, 1977, 291–293.

37. Z 148

38. Brezianu (1976), 147

39. Giedion-Welcker (1958), 220

40. Guilbert (1957), 6

41. Pandrea (1967), 245

42. Pandrea (1967), 247

43. Z 166

44. Z 147

45. Z 26

46. Liberman (1960), 170

47. Spear (1969), 32

48. Albert Dreyfus, "Brancusi," in *Cahiers d'Art,* 2/2, 1927

49. Brancusi (1925), 235

50. Giedion-Welcker (1959), 203

51. Brancusi (1925), 236

52. Deac (1966), 48

53. Jianou (1963), 18

54. Jianou (1963), 17

55. Giedion-Welcker (1959), 17

56. Z 64

57. Brancusi (1965), 117

58. Brezianu (1976), 131 (with slight adjustments in translation)

59. Jianou et al. (1982), 51

60. Z 134

61. Jianou (1963), 67

62. Liberman (1960), 171

63. Deac (1966), 46

64. Giedion-Welcker (1959), 205
65. Giedion-Welcker (1958) 196—97
66. Geist (1975), 12
67. Lewis (1957), 38
68. Z 67
69. Lewis (1957), 161
70. Z 49
71. Lewis (1957), 33
72. Giedion-Welcker (1959), 18
73. Geist (1975), 12
74. Spear (1969), 116
75. Pandrea (1967), 248
76. Z 41
77. Comarnescu (1972), 109
78. Brancusi (1925), 236
79. Pandrea (1967), 249
80. Comarnescu (1972), 109
81. Pandrea (1967), 254
82. Giedion-Welcker (1958), 196
83. Giedion-Welcker (1959), 220
84. Jianou et al. (1982), 71
85. Z 54
86. Giedion-Welcker (1959), 24n
87. J. Alvard, "L'Atelier de Brancusi," *Art d'Aujourd'hui,* Jan. 1951, 8
88. Liberman (1960), 171
89. Z 176
90. Pandrea (1967), 248
91. Z 89
92. Z 242
93. Brancusi (1965), 120
94. Comarnescu (1972), 245
95. Paleolog (1967), 212
96. Paleolog (1967), 242

15. Henri Matisse

1. Matisse (1972), 297 (referenced hereafter as HM Ecrits). Translations in this chapter are my own except where noted.
2. HM Ecrits, 252
3. HM Ecrits, 41n
4. Flam (1973) provides, as intended, a literal English translation of many of the texts. Flam (1986) is a particularly rich study of earlier Matisse.
5. HM Ecrits, 85
6. Trans. Flam (1973), 42—43
7. HM Ecrits, 43—45

8. HM Ecrits, 84n
9. HM Ecrits, 60
10. HM Ecrits, 50
11. HM Ecrits, 50n
12. HM Ecrits, 50n
13. HM Ecrits, 50n
14. HM Ecrits, 51
15. HM Ecrits, 318
16. HM Ecrits, 57n
17. HM Ecrits, 300
18. HM Ecrits, 158
19. HM Ecrits, 178n
20. HM Ecrits, 178n
21. HM Ecrits, 120–21
22. HM Ecrits, 257–58
23. HM Ecrits, 93n
24. See Elderfield (1976).
25. See, for example, HM Ecrits, 257–58.
26. HM Ecrits, 203
27. HM Ecrits, 258; Flam (1973), 128
28. HM Ecrits, 313–14
29. HM Ecrits, 196
30. HM Ecrits, 238
31. HM Ecrits, 268n
32. HM Ecrits, 264–65
33. HM Ecrits, 320
34. HM Ecrits, 49
35. From the Matisse-Bonnard correspondence published by Jean Clair, *La Nouvelle Revue Francaise,* July 1970, August 1970
36. HM Ecrits, 237
37. HM Ecrits, 83
38. Reference mislaid, but see HM Ecrits, 221–23, "One must look at the whole of life with the eyes of a child."
39. HM Ecrits, 51n
40. HM Ecrits, 239
41. Trans. Flam (1973), 140
42. See Elsen (1972).
43. Henri Matisse, *Jazz,* Paris, 1947
44. Trans. Flam (1973), 113

16. The Mediterranean Ethos

1. Moore (1966), 32
2. The history of posture and physique could be a cultural history. For example, the armor-like flesh of ancient Assyrian figures differs aesthetically and

spiritually from the gentle physique of Buddha images from the Gupta Period. Kenneth Clark, *The Nude: A Study in Ideal Form,* New York, 1956, with later editions, is the seminal study. Among many other footnotes to it is my article, "The Human Figure as a Religious Sign," *Macmillan Encyclopedia of Religion,* New York, 1986.

3. Hodin (1961), 10

4. Pool (1965), 123

5. See Brendel (1962)

6. See Reinhard Lullies and Max Hirmer, *Greek Sculpture,* New York, second edition 1960, figs. 136−37. The authenticity of this piece has recently been called into question, but priestesses and flute-girls are familiar dramatis personae in vase painting as well.

7. Pool (1967), 198

8. See Bolliger (1956).

9. Moore (1966), 96

10. Packer (1985), 69

11. Packer (1985), 149

12. Moore (1966), 47−48

17. American Epiphany

1. Cited in Ashton (1983) [1], 107. I want particularly to acknowledge Dore Ashton's *About Rothko,* a clear-sighted and compelling book.

2. See esp. Thomas B. Hess, *Barnett Newman,* London (The Tate Gallery), 1972.

3. Cited in Grace Glueck, "The Mastery of Robert Motherwell," *New York Times Magazine,* Dec. 2, 1984, 86. The remainder of this rather long chapter is dedicated to the art and thought of Pollock, Rothko, Louis, and Reinhardt. I hope at a later date to comment on the work of Robert Motherwell, the early Philip Guston, and others who contributed to the spiritual in mid-century American art.

4. Potter (1985), 154−55

5. Potter (1985), 161

6. Potter (1985), 116

7. Friedman (1972), 168

8. Friedman (1972), 65

9. Potter (1985), 154

10. Potter (1985), 197

11. Friedman (1972), 253

12. Tuchman (1977), 142

13. Ashton (1983) [1], 155

14. Ashton (1983) [1], 45

15. Ashton (1983) [1], 79

16. Ashton (1983) [1], 80

17. Ashton (1983) [1], 112−13

18. Seldes (1978), 321

19. Chipp (1971), 548–49

20. Tuchman (1975), 141

21. Seldes (1978), 111

22. Rodman (1957), 93–94

23. Goddard (1979), 37

24. Exodus 24:15–18

25. Evelyn Underhill, ed., *The Cloud of Unknowing,* London, 1912 (with later editions and translations)

26. Underhill (1912), 73–75, 138–40

27. The following paragraphs give only a summary account of Rothko's art and life in later years. See Ashton (1983) [1] and Seldes (1985).

28. Ashton (1983) [1], 155

29. Ashton (1983) [1], 144–46

30. Peter Schjeldahl, "A Visit to the Salon of Autumn 1986," in *Art in America,* Dec. 1986, 18. However, see this critic's quite different approach to Rothko, "Rothko and Belief," in *Art in America,* April 1979, 79–85.

31. Elderfield (1986)

32. Elderfield (1986), 9

33. Upright (1985), 12

34. Upright (1985), 16

35. Klapper (1976), 1

36. Upright (1978)

37. Morris Louis, Letter to Clement Greenberg, 6 June 1954, Archives of American Art

38. Reinhardt (1975), 111. In this remarkable edition, the introduction by Barbara Rose is one of the best contemporary statements on the spiritual in art.

39. See Lippard (1981).

40. Masheck (1978), 25

41. Reinhardt (1975), 13

42. Lippard (1981), 124

43. Reinhardt (1975), 190

44. Reinhardt (1975), 27

45. See Lippard (1981), for reproductions

46. Reinhardt (1975), 206

47. Lippard (1981), 109

48. Masheck (1978), 24. "Latreutic," pertaining to divine service (OED)

49. Reinhardt (1975), 82–83

50. Reinhardt (1975), 70–71

51. Reinhardt (1975), 14

52. Reinhardt (1975), 70

53. Reinhardt (1975), 13

54. Reinhardt (1975), 207

55. Reinhardt (1975), 72−78
56. Reinhardt (1975), 113

18. Isamu Noguchi

1. See Yasuichi Awakawa, *Zen Painting,* Tokyo and Palo Alto, 1970, figs. 71, 91.
d back covers
2. Coomaraswamy II (1977), 386
3. The early pages of Hunter (1979) include photographs and biography, supplementing Noguchi (1968).
4. Noguchi (1968), 16
5. Noguchi (1968), 16
6. Noguchi (1968), 17
7. Interview with the author, April 1987
8. Noguchi (1968)
9. Noguchi (1976), 28
10. See Harold Bloom (1973, 1975).
11. Hunter (1979), 39
12. Noguchi (1968), 21
13. Illustrated in Hunter (1979), 49
14. Noguchi (1950), 24, 27
15. Noguchi, manuscript of the forthcoming catalogue of the Isamu Noguchi Garden Museum, n.p.
16. Noguchi (1968), 167
17. Kuh (1962), 178
18. Hunter (1979), 151
19. Hunter (1979), 182−85
20. Noguchi (1968), 159
21. Gruen (1968), 30
22. Hunter (1979), 187−92
23. Noguchi (1957), 29
24. Noguchi (1968), 39
25. Kuh (1972), 174
26. Artist's Statement for the 1986 Biennale, archive of the Isamu Noguchi Garden Museum
27. Noguchi, manuscript of the forthcoming catalogue of the Isamu Noguchi Garden Museum, n.p.
28. Gruen (1968), 29
29. Ashton (1983) [2].
30. Interview with the author, April 1987
31. Interview with the author, April 1987; unannotated citations in the following paragraphs are from this source

32. Noguchi (1968), 40
33. Noguchi (1949), 55

19. Modest Masters

1. From Herbert Read, ed., *Unit One,* 1934, 89
2. Nicholson, 1935, cited in Ashton (1985), 74
3. Nicholson, 1941, cited in Ashton (1985), 75
4. Roditi (1970), 47–57
5. (Morandi), 1981, 14
6. Roditi (1970), 59
7. Roditi (1970), 59
8. Vitali (1983), text of a 1957 interview (n.p.), trans. by the author
9. See Schmalenbach (1960), (1964), (1977)
10. Cited in (Bissier), 1980, n.p.
11. Schmalenbach (1964), 129
12. Haftmann (1978), intro.
13. (Bissier), 1980, n.p.
14. (Bissier), 1968, 22
15. Schmalenbach (1964)
16. (Bissier), 1968, 22
17. (Bissier), 1968, 24 (1947)
18. (Bissier), 1968, 12
19. (Bissier), 1968, 23
20. (Bissier), 1980, n.p.
21. As so often, the black-and-white illustrations that help to make this book affordable oblige readers to go to other sources for a fuller impression of some works.
22. Schmalenbach (1964)
23. (Bissier), 1980, n.p.
24. (Bissier), 1980, n.p.
25. Lisle (1981), 311. See also O'Keeffe (1976), Lowe (1983)
26. Lisle (1981), 213
27. This composite passage draws on Kuh (1972), 191; O'Keeffe (1976), n.p.; and Lisle (1981), 82.
28. Lisle (1981), 83
29. Lisle (1981), 243, from a 1939 exhibition catalogue
30. Catalogue of *An American Place,* 1940, Archives of American Art

20. The Photographers

1. Frank et al. (1934, 1979), 131
2. Frank et al. (1934, 1979), 62
3. Lowe (1983), 82

4. Lyons (1966), 119
5. Norman (1960), 29
6. Norman (1960), 9
7. See Green (1973) and Margolis (1978).
8. Norman (1960), Seligmann (1966)
9. Norman (1960), 52
10. Norman (1960), 56
11. Norman (1960), 28
12. Greenough/Hamilton (1983), 209
13. Adams (1985), 137
14. Seligmann (1966), 2
15. Lyons (1966), 111
16. See Brandt (1976), Novak (1980), and Jussim/Lindquist-Cock (1985).
17. Greenough/Hamilton (1983), 209
18. Seligmann (1966), 97
19. Hill/Cooper (1979), 2
20. See Novak (1980)
21. Emerson (1940), 406–07
22. John Muir, *The Yosemite,* New York, 1912, reprinted Madison (Wisconsin), 1986, 8–9
23. Adams (1985), 143
24. Adams (1985), 37
25. Lyons (1966), 30–31
26. Adams (1985), 174
27. Adams (1985), 175–76
28. See Ansel Adams, *Classic Images,* Boston, 1987
29. Lyons (1966), 31–32
30. Adams (1985), 191
31. See Meltzer (1978)
32. See Stryker (1973), Stott (1973)
33. Edward Steichen, *The Family of Man,* New York (The Museum of Modern Art), 1953
34. See Maddow (1985), and Max Kozloff, "Photographers at War," *Art in America,* April 1980.
35. Lyons (1966), 67
36. Enyeart (1982), 19
37. Enyeart (1982), 42, 57
38. Andy Grundberg, in the *New York Times,* Sep. 2, 1984
39. Lyons (1966), 164
40. Lyons (1966), 165, 167

21. Seekers and Brats

1. Smithson (1979), 218; see also Hobbs (1981)
2. Smithson (1979), 11

3. Smithson (1979), 56
4. Smithson (1979), 111
5. Smithson (1979), 113
6. Smithson (1979), 203
7. This passage is the epigraph to Krauss (1986), a book to which I am indebted.
8. Article in *The Sentinel* (Winston-Salem, North Carolina), 30 January 1981, 30
9. Krauss (1986), 102–04
10. See the section on Morandi for a brief discussion of this tradition.
11. André Enard, letter to the author, June 1987
12. Cynthia Villet, letter to the author, May 1987
13. Cited in Shapiro (1981), 26
14. Dine (1977), 35
15. Liebmann (1982)
16. Shapiro (1981), 30
17. Cited in *Art News,* November 1979
18. Cited in *Art News,* November 1979
19. Cited in Navrozov, *Arts and Antiques,* October 1986, 59
20. Cited in Navrozov, *Arts and Antiques,* October 1986, 57–58
21. Coomaraswamy I (1977), 296–97
22. Erik Koch, letter to the author, spring 1987
23. Setsuya Kotani, letter to the author, spring 1987

22. The Marketplace and the Studio

1. As this book is going to press, *Art in America,* July 1988, explored at length and in interesting ways the topic of "Art and Money" in the contemporary art world, and Svetlana Alpers published *Rembrandt's Enterprise: The Studio and the Market,* Chicago, 1988. Both are important publications.

23. Dag Hammarskjöld

1. Among secondary works on DH, readers are especially recommended Brian Urquhart (1972), and Gustaf Aulen (1969).
2. See Bibliography.
3. *Markings,* 122
4. See the classic essay by Erwin Panofsky, "Abbot Suger of St.-Denis," in his *Meaning in the Visual Arts,* Garden City (New York), 1955, 108–145
5. DH *Papers* II, 94
6. Kelen (1966), 110
7. DH *Papers* II, 278
8. UN Archive, General Services File, s.v. Gifts, memo of 18 January 1966 from David B. Vaughan
9. UN Archive, Andrew Cordier Papers, Press Release of 30 October 1961

10. Urquhart (1972), 42
11. Beskow (1969), 32
12. This anecdote is preserved in UN Archive, Press Release of 27 October 1961
13. Kelen (1966), 110
14. Kelen (1966), 111
15. Extract from Mary Hornaday, "Re-modelled Meditation Room," *Christian Science Monitor,* December 1956, UN Archive
16. Kelen (1966), 113
17. Urquhart (1972), 43
18. UN Archive, s.v. Meditation Room, typescript
19. DH *Papers* III, 710–11
20. *Markings,* 143
21. *Markings,* 206
22. DH *Papers* II, 372–75
23. *Markings,* 171
24. UN Archive, Press Release of 11 June 1964
25. Hodin (1961)
26. Press Release of 11 June 1964, as cited
27. *Markings,* 171
28. *Markings,* 105
29. *Markings,* 174

24. Art and Teachings

1. Cf. Frithjof Schuon, *The Essential Writings of Frithjof Schuon,* ed. Seyyed Hossein Nasr, New York, 1986; the writings of René Guénon; and Jacob Needleman, ed., *The Sword of Gnosis: Metaphysics, Cosmology, Tradition, and Symbolism,* London and Boston, second edition, 1986 (anthology of writings by Schuon, Guénon, and other traditionalists)
2. Despite the appeal of his ideas to artists, Dr. Jung was not particularly sympathetic to twentieth-century art. See C. G. Jung, "Picasso," in *The Spirit in Man, Art, and Literature,* Princeton, 1966, 135–41; and "The Hell of Initiation" in *C. G. Jung Speaking: Interviews and Encounters,* Princeton, 1977, 219–24 ("I cannot occupy myself with modern art any more. It is too awful.")
3. DH *Papers* II, 488
4. Schlemmer (1972), 404
5. Schlemmer (1972), 406

ACKNOWLEDGMENTS
TO PUBLISHERS

The author and publisher wish to thank the following for permission to quote from their publications.

Portions of this book were first published in *Parabola, Art Papers, The American Theosophist,* and *The Merton Seasonal.* Chapter 2 first appeared as the introduction to a catalogue for the exhibition *Transpersonal Images,* organized by Herb Jackson under the auspices of the International Transpersonal Association (Davos, Switzerland, 1983). I am grateful to Mr. Jackson and the editors of these publications for their early encouragement.

Arted Editions d'Art and Prof. Ionel Jianou, for citations from *Brancusi: Introduction, Témoignages,* Copyright © 1982 Arted Editions d'Art.

George Braziller, Inc., Publishers, for citations from Carola Giedion-Welcker, *Constantin Brancusi.*

Columbia University Press, for citations from *Public Papers of the Secretaries-General of the United Nations,* Vols. II–V, ed. Andrew W. Cordier and Wilder Foote, Copyright © 1969 Columbia University Press. Used by permission.

G. K. Hall & Co., for citations from *Kandinsky: Complete Writings on Art,* ed. Kenneth C. Lindsay and Peter Vergo, Copyright © 1982 by G. K. Hall & Co. All rights reserved.

Hermann, éditeurs, for citations from *Matisse: Ecrits et propos sur l'art.*

Nancy Holt and New York University Press, for citations from *The Writings of Robert Smithson,* ed. Nancy Holt, Copyright © 1979 by Nancy Holt.

Alfred A. Knopf, Inc., for citations from P. D. Ouspensky, *Tertium Organum: The Third Canon of Thought, A Key to the Enigmas of the World,* Copyright © 1950 by Henry W. Bragdon.

The MIT Press, for citations from Hans M. Wingler, *The Bauhaus: Weimar Dessau Berlin Chicago,* Copyright © 1969 by The Massachusetts Institute of Technology.

The Putnam Publishing Group, for citations from Jeffrey Potter, *To A Violent Grave: An Oral Biography of Jackson Pollock,* Copyright © 1985 by Jeffrey Potter.

Rijksbureau voor Kunsthistorische Documentatie, for citations from *Two Mondrian Sketchbooks 1912–1914,* ed. Robert P. Welsh and J. M. Joosten.

Simon & Schuster, Inc., for citations from Robert L. Herbert, *Modern Artists on Art,* Copyright © 1964 by Robert L. Herbert.

Thames and Hudson Inc., for citations from Edward Fry, *Cubism,* Copyright © 1966 by Thames and Hudson Ltd., London.

The University of California Press, for citations from Herschel B. Chipp, *Theories of Modern Art: A Source Book by Artists and Critics,* Copyright © 1968 by The Regents of the University of California.

Viking Penguin Inc., for citations from *Art As Art: The Selected Writings of Ad Reinhardt,* ed. Barbara Rose, Copyright © 1953, 1954, 1963, 1975 by Rita Reinhardt; *Arp on Arp: Poems, Essays, Memories,* ed. Marcel Jean; *Russian Art of the Avant-Garde: Theory and Criticism 1909–1934,* by John E. Bowlt, Copyright © 1976 by John E. Bowlt; *The New Art of Color: The Writings of Robert and Sonia Delaunay,* ed. Arthur A. Cohen, Copyright © 1978 by Sonia Delaunay, Translation Copyright © 1978 by Arthur A. Cohen. All rights reserved. Reprinted by permission of Viking Penguin Inc.

Wesleyan University Press, for citations from *The Letters and Diaries of Oskar Schlemmer,* ed. Tut Schlemmer, Copyright © 1972 by Wesleyan University; John Cage, *Silence,* Copyright © 1939–1961 by John Cage.

Wittenborn Art Books, Inc., for citations from Wassily Kandinsky, *Concerning the spiritual in art;* Kasimir Malevich, *Essays on Art 1915–1933,* ed. Troels Andersen, 1971; and Kasimir Malevich, *The Artist, Infinity, and Suprematism: Unpublished Writings 1913–1933,* ed. Troels Andersen, 1978.

Yale University Press, for citations from Christina Lodder, *Russian Constructivism,* Copyright © 1983 by Yale University.

Diligent efforts were made in every case to obtain permission to include citations that exceed the "fair use" norm of 250 words. In a few instances, publishers did not reply in time for formal acknowledgment in this place. The author and publisher are grateful for the use of these and all citations from published literature.

BIBLIOGRAPHY

Adams, Ansel, *An Autobiography*, Boston, 1985.

Adcock, Craig E., *Marcel Duchamp's Notes from The Large Glass: An N-Dimensional Analysis*, Ann Arbor, 1983.

Andersen, Troels, *Malevich: Catalogue raisonné of the Berlin exhibition 1927*, Amsterdam (Stedelijk Museum), 1970.

Apollinaire, Guillaume, *Apollinaire on Art: Essays and Reviews 1902–1918*, ed. Leroy C. Breunig, New York, 1972.

Apostolos-Cappadona, Diane, ed., *Art, Creativity, and the Sacred: An Anthology in Religion and Art*, New York, 1984.

Arnason, H. H., *History of Modern Art*, Englewood Cliffs and New York, 1968.

Arp, Jean, *Arp on Arp: Poems, Essays, Memories*, ed. Marcel Jean, New York, 1972.

Ashton, Dore, *The New York School: A Cultural Reckoning*, New York, 1973.

Ashton, Dore, *About Rothko*, New York, 1983 [1].

Ashton, Dore (intro.), *Noguchi*, New York (The Pace Gallery), 1983 [2].

Ashton, Dore, and Flam, Jack, *Robert Motherwell*, New York, 1983 [3].

Ashton, Dore, ed., *Twentieth-Century Artists on Art*, New York, 1985.

Aulén, Gustaf, *Dag Hammarskjöld's White Book: An Analysis of* Markings, Philadelphia, 1969.

Ball, Hugo, *Flight out of Time*, ed. John Elderfield, New York, 1974.

Bann, Stephen, *The Tradition of Constructivism* (anthology), New York, 1974.

Barr, Alfred H., Jr., *Matisse: His Art and his Public*, New York, 1951.

Barr, Alfred H., Jr., *Picasso: Fifty Years of his Art*, New York (Museum of Modern Art), 1946.

Barron, Stephanie, and Tuchman, Maurice, *The Avant-Garde in Russia (1910–1930: New Perspectives*, Los Angeles (Los Angeles County Museum of Art), 1980.

Beal, W. J. Graham, *et al.*, *Jim Dine: Five Themes*, Minneapolis (Walker Art Center) and New York, 1983.

Berthoud, Roger, *The Life of Henry Moore*, New York, 1987.

Besant, Annie, and Leadbeater, C.W., *Thought-Forms*, London, 1901 (paperback reprint, Wheaton [Illinois], 1969).

Beskow, Bo, *Dag Hammarskjöld: Strictly Personal*, Garden City (New York), 1969.

(Bissier, Julius), *Julius Bissier 1893–1965: A Retrospective Exhibition,* San Francisco (San Francisco Museum of Art), 1968.

(Bissier, Julius), Exhibition Catalogues published by Lefebre Gallery, New York, 1970s–1980s.

(Bissier, Julius), *Julius Bissier 1893–1965,* Braunschweig (Kunstverein Braunschweig), 1980, n.p.

Bloom, Harold, *The Anxiety of Influence: A Theory of Poetry,* New York, 1973.

Bloom, Harold, *Kabbalah and Criticism,* New York, 1975.

Bolliger, Hans, *Picasso's Vollard Suite,* London, 1956.

Bowlt, John E., *Russian Art of the Avant-Garde: Theory and Criticism 1902– 1934* (anthology), New York, 1976.

Bowlt, John E., "Russian Sculpture and Lenin's Plan of Monumental Propaganda," in Henry A. Millon and Linda Nochlin, *Art and Architecture in the Service of Politics,* Cambridge and London, 1978.

Bowlt, John E., and Washton Long, Rose-Carol, *The Life of Vasili Kandinsky in Russian Art: A Study of* On the Spiritual in Art, Newtonville (Mass.), 1984.

Brancusi, Constantin, Aphorisms and "Histoire de Brigands" in *This Quarter,* Spring 1925.

Brancusi, Constantin, "Aphorisms," collected in *Rumanian Review* 19/1, 1965, 117–120.

(Brancusi), U.S. Treasury Department, Customs court, 3rd Division, Protest 209109-G, C. *Brancusi* v. *U.S.,* New York, October 21, 1927–March 23, 1928; stenographic minutes in the library of the Museum of Modern Art, New York.

Brandt, Bill, ed., *The Land: Twentieth Century Landscape Photographs,* New York, 1976.

Brendel, Otto J., "The Classical Style in Modern Art" and "Classic and Non-Classic Elements in Picasso's *Guernica,*" in Whitney J. Oates, ed., *From Sophocles to Picasso: The Present-Day Vitality of the Classical Tradition,* Bloomington, 1962, 71 ff., 121 ff.

Breton, André, *Manifestoes of Surrealism,* Ann Arbor, 1972.

Brezianu, Barbu, "Pages inédites de la correspondance de Brancusi," in *Revue roumaine d'histoire de l'art,* I/2, 1964, 385–400.

Brezianu, Barbu, *Brancusi in Romania,* Bucharest, 1976.

Bush, Susan, and Shin, Hsio-yen, *Early Chinese Texts on Painting,* Cambridge and London, 1985.

Bunnell, Peter C., intro., *Jerry N. Uelsmann,* An Aperture Monograph, New York, 1974.

Bunnell, Peter C., intro., *Jerry N. Uelsmann: Silver Meditations,* Dobbs Ferry (NY), 1975.

Cabanne, Pierre, *Conversations with Marcel Duchamp,* New York, 1971.

Cage, John, *Silence,* Middletown (Conn.), 1973.

Cage, John, *M: Writings '67–'72,* Middletown (Conn.), first paperback edition, 1974.

Castro, Jan Garden, *The Art & Life of Georgia O'Keeffe*, New York, 1985.

Centre Georges Pompidou, *Paris-Berlin 1900–1933: rapports et contrastes france-allemagne 1900–1933*, Paris, 1978.

Centre Georges Pompidou, *Paris-Moscou 1900–1930*, Paris, 1979.

Centre Georges Pompidou, *Malévitch: architectones, peintures, dessins,* Paris, 1980.

Centre Georges Pompidou, *Jackson Pollock,* Paris, 1982.

Cézanne, Paul, *Letters,* ed. John Rewald, fourth edition, New York, 1976.

(Chauvelin) Galerie Jean Chauvelin, *Suprematisme,* with contributions by Bowlt, Marcade, Martineau, and others, Paris, 1977.

Chipp, Herschel B., *Theories of Modern Art: A Source Book by Artists and Critics,* Berkeley, 1971.

Comarnescu, Petru, *Brâncuşi: mit şi metamorfoză în sculptura contemporană,* Bucharest, 1972.

Coomaraswamy, Ananda K., *Selected Papers, Vol. 1: Traditional Art and Symbolism; Vol. 2: Metaphysics,* ed. Roger Lipsey, Princeton, 1977.

Cooper, Douglas, *The Cubist Epoch,* New York, 1971.

Cummings, Paul, *Artists in Their own Words: Conversations with 12 American Artists,* New York, 1979.

Daix, Pierre, and Rosselet, Joan, *Le Cubisme de Picasso: catalogue raisonné 1907–1916,* Paris, 1979

De Cock, Liliane, ed., *Ansel Adams,* intro. Minor White, Hastings-on-Hudson (New York), 1972.

Deac, Mircea, *Constantin Brâncuşi,* Bucharest, 1966.

Delaunay, Robert and Sonia, *The New Art of Color: The Writings of Robert and Sonia Delaunay,* ed. Arthur A. Cohen, New York, 1978.

(Delaunay, Robert), *Robert Delaunay,* Paris (Réunion de musées nationaux, Galéries du Jeu de Paume et de l'Orangerie), 1976.

D'Harnoncourt, Anne, and McShine, Kynaston, *Marcel Duchamp,* New York (The Museum of Modern Art) and Philadelphia (The Philadelphia Museum of Art), 1973.

(Dine, Jim), *Jim Dine Prints: 1970–1977,* New York (Williams College Museum of Art), 1977.

D'Oench, Ellen G., and Feinberg, Jean E., *Jim Dine Prints: 1977–1985,* New York, 1986.

Doran, P. M., *Conversations avec Cézanne,* Paris, 1978.

Douglas, Charlotte, *Swans of Other Worlds: Kazimir Malevich and the Origins of Abstraction in Russia,* Ann Arbor, 1980.

Duchamp, Marcel, *The Bride Stripped Bare by Her Bachelors, Even* (a typographic version by Richard Hamilton of MD's Green Box), New York and London, 1960.

Duchamp, Marcel, *The Essential Writings of Marcel Duchamp,* ed. Michel Sanouillet and Elmer Peterson, London, 1975.

Elderfield, John, *The "Wild Beasts": Fauvism and its Affinities,* New York (The Museum of Modern Art), 1976.

Elderfield, John, *Morris Louis,* New York (The Museum of Modern Art), 1986.

Eliade, Mircea, *The Quest: History and Meaning in Religion,* Chicago, 1969 (paperback edition, 1984).

Eliade, Mircea, *Symbolism, the Sacred and the Arts,* ed. Diane Apostolos-Cappadona, New York, 1985.

Elliott, David, *Rodchenko and the Arts of Revolutionary Russia,* New York, 1979.

Elsen, Albert E., *The Sculpture of Matisse,* New York, 1972.

Emerson, Ralph Waldo, *The Selected Writings of Ralph Waldo Emerson,* ed. Brooks Atkinson, New York, 1940.

Enyeart, James L., *Jerry N. Uelsmann, Twenty-five Years: A Retrospective,* Boston, 1982.

Fédit, Denise, *L'Oeuvre de Kupka,* Paris (Musée National d'Art Moderne), 1966.

Fitzpatrick, Sheila, *The Commissariat of Enlightenment: Soviet Organization of Education and the Arts under Lunacharsky, October 1917–1921,* Cambridge, 1970.

Flam, Jack, *Matisse: The Man and his Art 1869–1918,* Ithaca and London, 1986.

Franciscono, Marcel, *Walter Gropius and the Creation of the Bauhaus in Weimar: The Ideals and Artistic Theories of its Founding Fathers,* Urbana (Illinois), 1971.

Frank, Waldo, et al., eds., *America & Alfred Stieglitz: A Collective Portrait,* 1st edition, 1934, New Revised Edition, 1979. Cited in the new edition.

Fried, Michael, *Morris Louis,* New York, 1979.

Friedman, B. H., *Jackson Pollock: Energy Made Visible,* New York, 1972.

Fry, Edward F., *Cubism,* London, 1966.

Gay, Peter, *Art and Act: On Causes in History—Manet, Gropius, Mondrian,* New York, 1976.

Geist, Sidney, *Constantin Brancusi: A Study of the Sculpture,* New York, 1968 (reprinted with a new preface, New York, 1983).

Geist, Sidney, *Brancusi: The Sculpture and Drawings,* New York, 1975.

Geist, Sidney, *Brancusi/ The Kiss,* New York, 1978.

Geist, Sidney, "Brancusi's *Bird in Space:* A Psychological Reading," in *Source: Notes in the History of Art,* Spring 1984, 24–32.

Geist, Sidney, *Délicatesse de Brancusi,* Paris, 1985.

Geldzahler, Henry (intro.), *Isamu Noguchi: What is Sculpture?,* Venice (42nd Venice Biennale), 1986.

Giedion-Welcker, Carola, *Constantin Brancusi, 1876–1957,* Basel, 1958.

Giedion-Welcker, Carola, *Constantin Brancusi,* New York, 1959.

(Gmurzynska) Galerie Gmurzynska, *Kasimir Malewitsch: zum 100. Geburtstag,* Cologne, 1978.

Goddard, Donald, "Rothko's journey into the unknown," *Art News,* Jan. 1979, 37–40.

Godwin, Joscelyn, *Robert Fludd: Hermetic philosopher and surveyor of two worlds*, Boulder, 1979.

Golding, John, *Cubism: A History and an Analysis 1907–1914*, second edition, New York, 1968.

Golding, John, *Marcel Duchamp: The Bride Stripped Bare by her Bachelors, Even*, New York, 1972.

Goldwater, Robert, *Symbolism*, New York, 1979.

Goodrich, Lloyd, and Bry, Doris, *Georgia O'Keeffe*, New York (The Whitney Museum of American Art), 1970.

Gray, Camilla, *The Great Experiment: Russian Art 1863–1922*, London, 1962 (cited in its paperback edition, *The Russian Experiment in Art 1863–1922*, London, 1971).

Green, Jonathan, ed., *Camera Work: A Critical Anthology*, Millerton (New York), 1973.

Greenough, Sarah, and Hamilton, Juan, *Alfred Stieglitz: Photographs and Writings*, Washington D.C. (National Gallery of Art), 1983.

Grohmann, Will, *Paul Klee*, New York, 1955.

Grohmann, Will, *Wassily Kandinsky: Life and Work*, New York, 1958.

Gruen, John, "The Artist Speaks: Isamu Noguchi," *Art in America*, March–April 1968, 28–31.

Guilbert, Claire Gilles, "Propos de Brancusi (1876–1957)," in *Prisme des arts*, 12, 1957, 5–7.

Guggenheim Museum (Solomon R.), *Paul Klee 1879–1940: A Retrospective Exhibition*, New York, 1967.

Guggenheim Museum (Solomon R.), *Vasily Kandinsky 1866–1944 in the Collection of the Solomon R. Guggenheim Museum, New York*, New York, 1972.

Haftmann, Werner, "Julius Bissier," Introduction to a Lefebre Gallery exhibition catalogue, New York, 1978.

Hammarskjöld, Dag, "A New Look at Everest," *National Geographic*, January 1961, 87–93.

Hammarskjöld, Dag, *Markings*, trans. Leif Sjoberg and W. H. Auden, New York, 1964 (cited in notes as *Markings*).

Hammarskjöld, Dag, *Public Papers of the Secretaries-General of the United Nations*, vols. II–V, ed. Andrew W. Cordier and Wilder Foote, New York, 1972–75 (cited in notes as DH, *Papers*).

Hayakawa, Masao, *The Garden Art of Japan*, New York and Tokyo, 1973.

Heller, Mikhail, and Nekrich, Aleksandr M., *Utopia in Power: The History of the Soviet Union from 1917 to the Present*, New York, 1986.

Henderson, Linda Dalrymple, *The Fourth Dimension and Non-Euclidean Geometry in Modern Art*, Princeton, 1983.

Herbert, Robert L., *Modern Artists on Art*, Englewood Cliffs, 1964 (contains Kandinsky's 1913 essay, "Reminiscences," an extract from Malevich's 1927 Bauhaus publication, Klee's lecture "On Modern Art," and other valuable documentary sources; this easily found edition is cited, for readers' convenience, whenever appropriate).

Hill, Paul, and Cooper, Thomas, *Dialogue with Photography* (interviews), New York, 1979.

Hobbs, Robert, et al., *Robert Smithson: Sculpture,* Ithaca and London, 1981.

Hodin, J. P., *Barbara Hepworth: Life and Work,* London, 1961.

Hofmann, Hans, *Search for the Real,* ed. Sara T. Weeks and Bartlett H. Hayes, Jr., Cambridge and London, revised edition 1967.

Huelsenbeck, Richard, *Memoirs of a Dada Drummer,* ed. Hans J. Kleinschmidt, New York, 1974.

Hulten, Pontus; Dumitresco, Natalia; and Istrati, Alexandre, *Brancusi,* Paris, 1986.

Hunter, Sam, *Isamu Noguchi,* London, 1979.

Hunter, Sam (intro.), *Isamu Noguchi, 75th Birthday Exhibition,* New York (André Emmerich Gallery and Pace Gallery), 1980.

Itten, Johannes, *Design and Form: The Basic Course at the Bauhaus,* revised edition, London, 1975.

(Itten, Johannes), *Johannes Itten: Kunstler und Lehrer,* Bern (Kunstmuseum Bern), 1984.

Izerghina, A., *Henri Matisse: Paintings and Sculptures in Soviet Museums,* Leningrad, 1978.

Jaffé, Hans L. C., *De Stijl 1917–1931: The Dutch Contribution to Modern Art,* London, 1956.

Jaffé, Hans L. C., *Mondrian,* New York, 1970.

Jaffé, Hans L. C., ed. *De Stijl,* New York, 1971 (anthology).

Jean, Marcel, ed., *The Autobiography of Surrealism,* New York, 1980 (anthology).

Jianou, Ionel, *Brancusi,* New York, 1963.

Jianou, Ionel *et al., Brancusi: Introduction, Témoignages,* Paris, 1982 (with texts by Jianou, Constantin Noica, Mircea Eliade, and Petru Comarnescu).

Jung, Carl Gustav, "Picasso," in *The Spirit in Man, Art, and Literature,* Princeton, 1966, 135–41.

Jung, Carl Gustav, "The Hell of Initiation," in *C. G. Jung Speaking: Interviews and Encounters,* ed. William McGuire and R. F. C. Hull, Princeton, 1977, 219–24.

Jussim, Estelle, and Lindquist-Cock, Elizabeth, *Landscape as Photograph,* New Haven and London, 1985.

Kandinsky, Nina, *Kandinsky et moi,* Paris, 1978 (trans. from the German edition, Munich, 1976).

Kandinsky, Wassily, *Concerning the Spiritual in Art, and painting in particular,* New York, 1947 (revision of the first English translation by Michael Sadleir, published as *The Art of Spiritual Harmony,* London and Boston, 1914).

Kandinsky, Wassily, *Point and Line to Plane,* trans. Howard Dearstyne and Hilla Rebay, New York, 1947 (reprinted 1979); trans. of the original 1926 Bauhaus edition.

Kandinsky, Wassily and Marc, Franz, eds. and authors, *The Blaue Reiter Almanac;* Documentary Edition, ed. Klaus Lankheit, New York, 1974.

Kandinsky, Wassily, *Ecrits Complets*, ed. Philippe Sers, Paris, 1970.

Kandinsky, Wassily, *Complete Writings on Art*, ed. Kenneth C. Lindsay and Peter Vergo, in two volumes, Boston, 1982 (cited in notes as Kandinsky CW).

Kandinsky, Wassily and Schoenberg, Arnold, *Letters, Pictures and Documents*, ed. Jelena Hahl-Koch, London and Boston, 1984.

Khan-Magomedov, S. O., *Rodchenko: The Complete Work*, Cambridge and London, 1987.

Kelen, Emery, *Hammarskjöld*, New York, 1966.

Klapper, Katherine, *Morris Louis: Major Themes and Variations*, Washington, D.C. (National Gallery of Art), 1976.

Klee, Paul, *Über die moderne Kunst*, Bern-Buempliz, 1945.

Klee, Paul, *Pedagogical Sketchbook*, New York, 1953.

Klee, Paul, *Notebooks, Vol. 1: The thinking eye*, ed. Juerg Spiller, London and New York, 1961.

Klee, Paul, *Notebooks, Vol. 2: The nature of nature*, ed. Juerg Spiller, New York, 1973.

Klee, Paul, *The Diaries of Paul Klee 1898–1918*, Berkeley and Los Angeles, 1968.

Klee, Paul, *Schriften: Rezensionen und Aufsätze*, ed. Christian Geelhaaar, Cologne, 1976.

Krauss, Rosalind E., *Beverly Pepper: Sculpture in Place*, Buffalo (Albright-Knox Art Gallery), 1986.

Kuh, Katharine, *Talks with 17 Artists*, New York, 1962, s.v. interview with Noguchi, 171–87.

Kupka, František, "Créer! Question de principe de la peinture," in *La Vie des lettres et des arts*, July 1921, 569–75.

Landolt, Hanspeter, intro., *Music: Das graphische Werk 1947 bis 1962*, Braunschweig, 1962.

Lash, Joseph P., *Dag Hammarskjöld: Custodian of the brush-fire peace*, Garden City (New York), 1961.

Leadbeater, C. W., *Man Visible and Invisible*, London, 1902 (paperback reprint, Wheaton [Illinois], 1975).

Lehman, Arnold L., and Richardson, Brenda, eds., *Oskar Schlemmer*, Baltimore (The Baltimore Museum of Art), 1986.

Lewis, David, *Constantin Brancusi*, London, 1957.

Liberman, Alexander, *The Artist in his Studio*, New York, 1960.

Lippard, Lucy R., et al., *Pop Art*, New York, 1966.

Lippard, Lucy R., ed., *Surrealists on Art*, Englewood Cliffs, 1970 (anthology).

Lippard, Lucy R., ed., *Dadas on Art*, Englewood Cliffs, 1971 (anthology).

Lippard, Lucy R., *Ad Reinhardt*, New York, 1981.

Lisle, Laurie, *Portrait of an Artist: A Biography of Georgia O'Keeffe*, New York, 1981.

Lissitzky-Kueppers, Sophie, *El Lissitzky: Life Letters Texts*, London, 1980.

Lodder, Christina, *Russian Constructivism*, New Haven, 1983.

Lowe, Sue Davidson, *Stieglitz: A Memoir/Biography*, New York, 1983.

Lukach, Joan M., *Hilla Rebay: In Search of the Spirit in Art*, New York, 1983.

Lyons, Nathan, *Photographers on Photography,* Englewood Cliffs, 1966 (anthology).

Maddow, Ben, *Let Truth Be the Prejudice: W. Eugene Smith, His Life and Photographs,* New York 1985.

Malevich, Kasimir, *The Non-Objective World,* L. Hilbersheimer, intro., Chicago, 1959.

Malevich, K. S., *Essays on Art 1915–1933,* ed. Troels Andersen, New York, 1971.

Malevich, K. S., *The World as Non-Objectivity: Unpublished Writings 1922–25,* ed. Troels Andersen, Copenhagen, 1976.

Malevitch, K., *Le Miroir Suprematiste,* trans. V. and J.-C. Marcadé, Lausanne, 1977.

Malevich, K. S., *The Artist, Infinity, Suprematism: Unpublished Writings 1913–1933,* ed. Troels Andersen, Copenhagen, 1978.

Marcadé, J.-Cl., ed., *Malévitch 1878–1978: Actes du Colloque international . . . ,* Lausanne, 1979.

Margolis, Marianne Fulton, ed., *Camera Work: A Pictorial Guide,* New York, 1978.

Martineau, Emmanuel, *Malévitch et la philosophie: La question de la peinture abstraite,* Lausanne, 1977.

Macheck, Joseph, "Five Unpublished Letters from Ad Reinhardt to Thomas Merton and Two in Return," in *Artforum,* Dec. 1978, 23–27.

Matisse, Henri, *Ecrits et propos sur l'art,* ed. Dominique Fourcade, Paris, 1972 (cited in notes as HM Ecrits).

Matisse, Henri, *Matisse on Art,* ed. Jack D. Flam, New York, 1973.

McCully, Marilyn, ed., *A Picasso Anthology: Documents, Criticism, Reminiscences,* Princeton, 1982.

Meltzer, Milton, *Dorothea Lange: A Photographer's Life,* New York, 1978.

Melville, Robert, *Henry Moore: Sculpture and Drawings 1921–1969,* New York, 1968.

Messer, Thomas M., *Julius Bissier,* San Francisco (San Francisco Museum of Art), 1968.

Miller, Dorothy C., *14 Americans,* New York (Museum of Modern Art), 1946.

Milner, John, *Vladimir Tatlin and the Russian Avant-Garde,* New Haven, 1983.

Mladek, Meda, and Rowell, Margit, *František Kupka 1871–1957: A Retrospective,* New York (Solomon R. Guggenheim Museum), 1975.

Moffett, Kenworth, *Morris Louis in the Museum of Fine Arts, Boston,* Boston (Museum of Fine Arts), n.d.

Moholy-Nagy, Sibyl, *Moholy-Nagy: experiment in totality,* Cambridge and London, second edition, 1969.

Mondrian, Piet, *Two Mondrian Sketchbooks, 1912–14,* ed. Robert P. Welsh and J. M. Joosten, Amsterdam, 1969. Facsimile with English translation.

Mondrian, Piet, *The New Art—The New Life: The Collected Writings of Piet Mondrian,* ed. and trans. Harry Holtzman and Martin S. James, Boston, 1986 (cited in notes as Mondrian CW).

Monod-Fontaine, Isabelle, *Matisse,* Paris (Centre George Pompidou), 1979.

Moore, Henry, *Henry Moore on Sculpture,* ed. Philip James, London, 1966.

Moore, Henry, and Hedgecoe, John, *Henry Moore: My Ideas, Inspiration, and Life as an Artist,* San Francisco, 1986.

(Morandi, Giorgio), *Giorgio Morandi (1890–1964),* Rome (Galleria Nazionale d'Arte Moderna, Villa Giulia), 1973.

(Morandi, Giorgio), *Giorgio Morandi,* Des Moines (Des Moines Art Center), 1981.

Neumann, Erich, *The Archetypal World of Henry Moore,* Princeton, 1959.

Noguchi, Isamu, "Meanings in Modern Sculpture," *Art News,* March 1949.

Noguchi, Isamu, "Toward a Reintegration of the Arts," *College Art Journal,* Autumn 1949, 59–60.

Noguchi, Isamu, "The 'arts' called 'primitive,'" *Art News,* March 1957, 24–32, 65.

Noguchi, Isamu, "New Stone Gardens," *Art in America,* June 1964, 84, 89.

Noguchi, Isamu, *A Sculptor's World,* New York, 1968.

Noguchi, Isamu, article in *Art Now: New York,* March 1971, n.p.

Noguchi, Isamu, "A reminiscence of four decades," *Architectural Forum,* Jan./Feb. 1972 (esp. rich account of his friendship with Buckminster Fuller).

Noguchi, Isamu, "Noguchi on Brancusi," *Craft Horizons,* August 1976, 26–29 [1].

Noguchi, Isamu, "Isamu Noguchi, Sculptor," in Yamada, Chisaburoh F., ed., *Dialogue in Art: Japan and the West,* Tokyo, New York, and San Francisco, 1976, 289–93 [2].

Noguchi, Isamu, Interview at the 42nd Biennale, Venice, 1986; unpublished (Archive of the Isamu Noguchi Garden Museum).

Norman, Dorothy, *Alfred Stieglitz: Introduction to an American Seer,* New York, 1960.

Norman, Dorothy, *Alfred Stieglitz: An American Seer,* New York, 1972.

Novak, Barbara, *Nature and Culture: American Landscape Painting 1825–1875,* New York, 1980.

O'Connor, Francis V., *Jackson Pollock,* New York (The Museum of Modern Art), 1967.

O'Keeffe, Georgia, *Georgia O'Keeffe,* New York, 1976.

Ouspensky, P. D., *Tertium Organum: The Third Canon of Thought, A Key to the Enigmas of the World,* New York, 1959 (revised translation, New York, 1982).

Packer, William, *Henry Moore: An Illustrated Biography,* London, 1985.

Pacquement, Alfred, and McConathy, Dale, *Ad Reinhardt,* Paris (Galeries nationales du Grand Palais), 1973.

Paleolog, V. G., *Tinereţea lui Brâncuşi,* Bucharest, 1967.

Pandrea, Petre, *Portrete şi controverse, I,* Bucharest, 1945.

Pandrea, Petre, *Brâncuşi Amintiri şi exegeze,* Bucharest, 1967.

Passuth, Krisztina, *Moholy-Nagy,* New York, 1985.

Paz, Octavio, *Marcel Duchamp: Appearance Stripped Bare,* New York, 1978.

Penrose, Roland, *Picasso: His Life and Work,* revised edition, New York, 1973.

Picasso, Pablo, *Picasso Says* . . . , ed. Hélène Parmelin, London, 1969.

Picasso, Pablo, *Picasso on Art: A Selection of Views*, ed. and intro. by Dore Ashton, New York, 1972.

Pilgrim, Richard, "Intervals (Ma) in Space and Time: Foundations for a Religio-Aesthetic Paradigm in Japan," in *History of Religions*, Feb. 1986, 255–277.

Poling, Clark V., Kandinsky: *Russian and Bauhaus Years, 1915–1933*, New York (The Solomon R. Guggenheim Museum), 1983.

Poling, Clark V., *Kandinsky's Teaching at the Bauhaus*, New York, 1986.

Pool, Phoebe, "Picasso's Neo-Classicism: First Period, 1906–6," and "Picasso's Neo-Classicism: Second Period, 1917–25," in *Apollo*, Feb. 1965, 122–27, and March 1967, 198–207.

Potter, Jeffrey, *To a Violent Grave: An Oral Biography of Jackson Pollock*, New York, 1985.

Reinhardt, Ad, *Art as Art: The Selected Writings of Ad Reinhardt*, ed. Barbara Rose, New York, 1975.

Rewald, John, *Morandi*, New York, 1967 (*Taurus No. 4*, a publication of the Albert Loeb & Krugier Gallery).

Richter, Hans, *Dada: Art and Anti-Art*, London, 1965.

Ringbom, Sixten, *The Sounding Cosmos: A Study of the Spiritualism of Kandinsky and the Genesis of Abstract Painting*, Acta Academiae Aboensis, ser. A, XXXVIII, Abo (Finland), 1970.

Robertson, Jack, *Twentieth-Century Artists on Art: An Index to Artists' Writings, Statements, and Interviews*, Boston, 1985.

Roditi, Edouard, *Dialogues on Art*, Santa Barbara, 1980 (interviews with artists).

Rodman, Selden, *Conversations with Artists*, New York, 1957.

Rosenblum, Robert, *Cubism and Twentieth-Century Art*, New York, second edition, 1966.

Rosenblum, Robert, *Modern Painting and the Northern Romantic Tradition: Friedrich to Rothko*, New York, 1975.

Rubin, William S., *Dada and Surrealist Art*, New York, 1968.

Rubin, William S., "Pollock as Jungian Illustrator: The Limits of Psychological Criticism," in *Art in America*, Nov./Dec. 1979, 70ff. and 104 ff.

Rubin, William S., *Pablo Picasso: A Retrospective*, New York (The Museum of Modern Art), 1980.

Rudenstine, Angelica Zander, *The Guggenheim Museum Collection*, in two volumes, New York (The Solomon R. Guggenheim Museum), 1976.

Russell, John, *Ben Nicholson: drawings paintings and reliefs 1911–1968*, New York, 1969.

(Russian avant-garde), *Art Journal*, Fall 1981 (special issue).

San Lazzaro, Gualtieri di, *Klee: A Study of His Life and Work*, New York, 1957.

Sandler, Irving, *The Triumph of American Painting: A History of Abstract Expressionism*, New York, 1971.

Sandler, Irving, *The New York School: The Painters and Sculptors of the Fifties,* New York, 1978.

Schapiro, Meyer, *Modern Art: Nineteenth & Twentieth Centuries,* New York, 1978.

Schiff, Gert, ed., *Picasso in Perspective,* Englewood Cliffs (New Jersey), 1976 (anthology).

Schlemmer, Oskar, *The Letters and Diaries of Oskar Schlemmer,* ed. Tut Schlemmer, Middletown (Connecticut), 1972.

Schmalenbach, Werner, *Julius Bissier: Farbige Miniaturen,* Munich, 1960.

Schmalenbach, Werner, *Bissier,* New York, 1964.

Schmalenbach, Werner, and Cannon-Brookes, Peter, *Julius Bissier 1893– 1965,* The Arts Council of Great Britain, 1977.

Schwarz, Arturo, *The Complete Works of Marcel Duchamp,* New York, 1978.

Seldes, Lee, *The Legacy of Mark Rothko,* New York, 1978.

Seligmann, Herbert J., *Alfred Stieglitz Talking,* New Haven, 1966.

Selz, Jean, *Henri Matisse,* New York, n.d.

Seuphor, Michel, *Piet Mondrian: Life and Work,* New York, 1956.

Smithson, Robert, *The Writings of Robert Smithson,* ed. Nancy Holt, New York, 1979.

Sonfist, Alan, *Art in the Land: A Critical Anthology of Environmental Art,* New York, 1983.

Sontag, Susan, *On Photography,* New York, 1977.

Spate, Virginia, *Orphism: The evolution of non-figurative painting in Paris 1910–1914,* Oxford, 1979.

Spear, Athena T., *Brancusi's Birds,* New York, 1969.

Steichen, Edward, *A Life in Photography,* Garden City (New York), 1963.

Stott, William, *Documentary Expression and Thirties America,* New York, 1973.

Stryker, Roy Emerson, and Wood, Nancy, *In This Proud Land: America 1935–1943 as Seen in the FSA Photographs,* Boston, 1973.

Szarkowski, John, *Looking at Photographs: 100 Pictures from the Collection of the Museum of Modern Art,* New York (The Museum of Modern Art), 1973.

Tabart, Marielle, and Monod-Fontaine, Isabelle, *Brancusi photographe,* Paris (Centre Georges Pompidou), 1982.

Tate Gallery, *Towards a New Art: essays on the background to abstract art 1910–1920,* London (Tate Gallery), 1980.

Tuchman, Maurice, ed., *New York School: The First Generation, Paintings of the 1940s and 1950s,* Greenwich, 1977.

Tuchman, Maurice, ed., *The Spiritual in Art: Abstract Painting 1890–1985,* Los Angeles (Los Angeles County Museum of Art), 1986 (cited in notes as LA Catalogue).

Uelsmann, Jerry N., *Process and Perception: Photographs and Commentary,* Gainesville (Florida), 1985.

Upright, Diane (Diane Upright Headley), "In Addition to the Veils," *Art in America,* Jan./Feb. 1978, 84–94.

Upright, Diane, *Morris Louis, The Complete Paintings: A Catalogue Raisonné,* New York, 1985.

Urquhart, Brian, *Hammarskjöld,* New York, 1972.

Urquhart, Brian, *A Life in Peace and War,* New York, 1987.

Vachtovà, Ludmilla, *Frank Kupka: Pioneer of Abstract Art,* New York and Toronto, 1968 (intro. by J. P. Hodin).

Vitali, Lamberto, *Morandi: Catalogo Generale,* 2 vols., Milan, 1983 (2nd edition).

Vollard, Ambroise, *Paul Cézanne: His Life and Art,* New York, 1937 (reprinted as *Cézanne,* New York, 1984).

Waldberg, Patrick, *Surrealism,* New York and Toronto, 1965.

Waldman, Diane, *Mark Rothko, 1903–1970: A Retrospective,* New York (Solomon R. Guggenheim Museum), 1978.

Warhol, Andy, *The Philosophy of Andy Warhol (From A to B and Back Again),* New York, 1975.

Washton Long, Rose-Carol, *Kandinsky: The Development of an Abstract Style,* Oxford, 1980.

Watts, Harriett, *Chance: A Perspective on Dada,* Ann Arbor, 1975.

Watts, Paolo, *Paul Klee e il privato: Paul Klee, the private life,* Rome (Centro Di), 1979.

Weiss, Peg, *Kandinsky in Munich: The Formative Jugendstil Years,* Princeton, 1979.

Welsh, Robert P., "Mondrian and Theosophy," in *Piet Mondrian Centennial Exhibition,* New York (Solomon R. Guggenheim Museum), 1971, 35–52; reprinted in Kaplan, Patrick E., and Manso, Susan, *Major European Art Movements 1900–1945: A Critical Anthology,* New York, 1977, 250–74.

Wheelwright, Philip, *Heraclitus,* Princeton, 1959.

Whelan, Richard, *Robert Capa: A Biography,* New York, 1985 (paperback edition, 1986).

White, Minor, *Mirrors, Messages, Manifestations,* New York, 1969.

White, Minor, ed., *Octave of Prayer,* New York, 1972.

White, Minor, *Rites & Passages,* with an essay by James Baker Hall, New York, 1978.

(White, Minor), *Minor White: A Living Remembrance, Aperture,* Summer 1984.

Willett, John, *Art and Politics in the Weimar Period: The New Sobriety, 1917–1933,* New York, 1978.

Wingler, Hans M., *The Bauhaus: Weimar Dessau Berlin Chicago,* Cambridge (Mass.) and London, second edition, 1976.

Zarnescu, Constantin, *Aforismele şi textele lui Brancusi,* Craiova, 1980.

Zhadova, Larissa A., *Malevich: Suprematism and Revolution in Russian Art 1910–1930,* New York, 1982.

INDEX